Peasants in Arms

This series of publications on Africa, Latin America, and Southeast Asia is designed to present significant research, translation, and opinion to area specialists and to a wide community of persons interested in world affairs. The editor seeks manuscripts of quality on any subject and can generally make a decision regarding publication within three months of receipt of the original work. Production methods generally permit a work to appear within one year of acceptance. The editor works closely with authors to produce a high quality book. The series appears in a paperback format and is distributed worldwide. For more information, contact the executive editor at Ohio University Press, Scott Quadrangle, University Terrace, Athens, Ohio 45701.

Executive editor: Gillian Berchowitz
AREA CONSULTANTS
Africa: Diane Ciekawy
Latin America: Thomas Walker
Southeast Asia: William H. Frederick

The Monographs in International Studies series is published for the Center for International Studies by the Ohio University Press. The views expressed in individual monographs are those of the authors and should not be considered to represent the policies or beliefs of the Center for International Studies, the Ohio University Press, or Ohio University.

Peasants in Arms

War and Peace in the Mountains of
Nicaragua, 1979–1994

Lynn Horton

Ohio University Center For International Studies
Monographs in International Studies
Latin America Series Number 30
Athens • *1998*

The books in the Center for International Studies Monograph Series
are printed on acid-free paper ∞

Library of Congress Cataloging-in-Publication

Horton, Lynn, 1964–
     Peasants in arms : war and peace in the mountains of Nicaragua, 1979–1994 /
Lynn Horton.
     p.   cm. — (Monographs in international studies. Latin America series :
no. 30)
     Includes bibliographical references and index.
     ISBN 0-89680-204-3 (pbk. : alk. paper)
     1. Nicaragua—History—1979–1990.   2. Nicaragua—History—1990–   .
3. Milicia Popular Anti-Sandinista (Nicaragua) 4. Counterrevolutions—
Nicaragua—Quilalí (Municipio)—History.   5. Frente Sandinista de Liberación
Nacional.   6. Peasants—Nicaragua—Quilalí (Municipio)—Social conditions. I.
Title. II. Series.
F1528.H655   1998
972.8505'3—cd21   98-22065

Contents

Illustrations

Maps

Photographs
(following page 172)

Boy leading an oxcart (in the early morning mist)

Quilalí's ambulance, spray-painted by the recontras with their initials, "F.N.3.80" ("Frente Norte 3-80")

Holy Week procession down Quilalí's main street

Army soldier standing guard in the rain on a street corner of Quilalí

Quilalí's pool hall in the center of town

Contras waiting to demobilize in 1990

Contra soldier during the 1990 demobilization process

Boys fishing in the Coco River

Girls collecting water from a communal faucet

Tables

Preface and Acknowledgments

This study explores the role of peasants in the north-central region in the war between the revolutionary Sandinista government and U.S.-supported antigovernment *contra* rebels in Nicaragua from the early 1980s to 1990. While *Peasants in Arms* focuses on a rural interior zone, Quilalí, which experienced intense conflict in the 1980s, my own initial contact with Nicaragua's war came about more indirectly.[1] In 1987 I lived for six months on an agricultural cooperative near the town of Tonalá in the Pacific zone department (an administrative unit equivalent to a province or state) of Chinandega. Following the cotton boom of the 1950s in northwestern Nicaragua, the majority of these *campesinos,* as rural Nicaraguans refer to themselves, led a precarious existence as landless day laborers on large haciendas picking cotton several months of the year.[2]

In the 1960s and 1970s the Tonalá zone became an epicenter of peasant resistance, and several cooperative members participated in land invasions of haciendas that were violently repressed by the National Guard (see Gould 1990b). Some also later fought in the urban insurrections that the Sandinista National Liberation Front (Frente Sandinista de Liberación Nacional, FSLN) led against the forty-year dictatorship of the Somoza family. After the FSLN took power in 1979, these peasants occupied an abandoned cotton estate and in 1983 received formal collective title to the property. While critical of certain specific Sandinista policies, cooperative members as a whole strongly supported the FSLN and the revolutionary process.

Although the cooperative was not located in a zone of conflict, Nicaragua's war still cast a constant shadow over daily life in 1987. Every family in the cooperative had at least one close male relative "in

Nicaragua's Interior War Zones in the 1980s

the mountains" on active military duty with the Sandinista Army. Geographically, the war was confined to Nicaragua's mountainous northern and central interior departments, where the main contra forces, known as the Nicaraguan Democratic Force (Fuerza Democrática Nicaragüense, FDN) operated. In addition, a southern front was active in the Río San Juan department along the Costa Rican border and indigenous anti-Sandinista forces operated in the Atlantic coast region. Overall, the contras carried out military actions in a largely rural territory of over 41,945 square kilometers (CIERA 1989, 6:281). In 1987 members of the cooperative where I was staying were generally sent to fight in the southeastern departments of Boaco and Chontales, the contras' region of greatest military activity in the late

1980s. Although they were of rural origin themselves, cooperative members reported that in the interior war zone they often felt themselves to be in enemy territory, in which it was difficult know if the local peasant population were potential allies or spies for the contras. The reality of the war came even closer when the oldest son of the family I lived with, Miguel, was drafted into the Sandinista Army. As the months passed the family spent a great deal of time in the city of Chinandega trying to collect Miguel's minimal pay and passing messages back and forth to their son through an informal support network. Several months before he was due to be discharged, Miguel stepped on a mine and lay for hours in the underbrush until a helicopter was able to evacuate him to a regional hospital. A Cuban physician was able to save Miguel's badly injured leg from being amputated, but he did not regain sufficient mobility or strength in his leg to work as an agricultural extension agent as he had once planned. When I returned to the cooperative in 1989 Miguel was no longer the vibrant, carefree young man I had known just a year earlier. Rather, as his mother told me, her son returned from the war with "the face of an old man."

By any measure, Nicaragua's armed conflict of the 1980s took a devastating human and economic toll. Out of a population of approximately 3.5 million, 30,865 Nicaraguans were killed during the war, which caused over $9 billion worth of direct material and economic damage (cited in Walker 1991b, 52). Over 350,000 Nicaraguans, mainly from rural areas, were displaced by the war, and an estimated 170,000 men and women served in the Sandinista armed forces over the course of the decade (Barry and Serra 1989, 42; Walker 1991a, 89). The war officially came to an end in 1990, following elections in February in which the FSLN was defeated by a coalition of opposition parties known as the UNO (Unión Nacional Opositora; National Opposition Union). One of the first acts of UNO president-elect Violeta Chamorro was to initiate disarmament negotiations with the contras. In late May contra troops began to lay down their arms in large numbers in exchange for promises of "development poles"—control over large tracts of land on the agricultural frontier, infrastructure, and services. Over the following weeks, a total of 22,341 contras demobilized.[3] Nicaragua's decade-long war formally ended on 27 June 1990, when top contra leaders and several thousand of their remaining troops gathered in the town of San Pedro de Lóvago to hand their weapons over to President Chamorro.

The 1990 peace process provided further information about the origins and makeup of the contra forces. Although throughout the decade ex-National Guardsmen continued to dominate the contras' Honduran-based administrative leadership, the great majority of contra field commanders and combatants were peasants from Nicaragua's mountainous interior. Of 18,225 contra combatants who gave their place of origin in an Organization of American States demobilization survey, over 15,000 listed Nicaragua's eight northern and central mountain departments as their home (CIAV-OEA 1990b). Only 3 percent (627) of former contras for whom data is available gave their home as the Pacific coastal plain, where two-thirds of Nicaragua's population is concentrated. The greatest absolute number of contra combatants came from the relatively more populated northern departments of Jinotega and Matagalpa, while a greater proportion of the rural population in the southeastern departments of Boaco and Chontales joined the contras. If the number of contras estimated to have been killed during the war is added to the total number of contras who demobilized in 1990, it is possible that 30,000 or more Nicaraguans fought at some point with antigovernment forces, making the contras one of the largest armed mobilizations of peasants in contemporary Latin American history. In addition, thousands more peasants participated in civilian collaborator networks that provided contra troops with food, shelter, and vital military information.

Evidence of more general anti-Sandinista political sentiments among a portion of Nicaragua's rural population, if not specifically support for the contras, comes from the 1990 election results in which only 31.4 percent of rural interior residents voted for the FSLN, as compared to 44.1 percent of the national urban population (CIPRES 1990b, 26, 28, 30; Castro 1992, 131). This poor rural electoral performance led Sandinista leader Daniel Ortega to conclude in 1991, "We didn't lose the peasantry because we never had it" (quoted in IHCA 1991, 11). Such an assessment may be overly pessimistic, however. Although it is true that the Sandinistas' strongest base of support was in urban areas, as the present study of Quilalí suggests, even in zones of strong contra support a significant minority of peasants actively supported the FSLN throughout the 1980s and their efforts were crucial in preventing anti-Sandinista forces from consolidating political and military hegemony in conflictive zones.

During the months following the contra disarmament process, I traveled extensively throughout Nicaragua's mountainous interior. My first encounter with the contras came in late March 1990, while I was traveling in an old cattle truck down a dirt road in the department of Chontales toward a UN-controlled demobilization camp. As the truck slowly pulled to the top of a hill we were surrounded by several hundred or so armed young men wearing mismatched olive-green and camouflage military uniforms. Talking to these contras, who were also headed toward the UN camp, it became clear that they did not consider themselves a defeated military force, but rather members of the "Army of the Resistance," which they believed had played a key role in removing the FSLN from power and bringing democracy to Nicaragua.[4] From the doorways of their small wooden farmhouses along the road, peasant families gathered to watch the group of contras move down the road; some showed no emotion on their faces, others waved happily and shouted greetings. The driver of the truck, a local rancher clearly sympathetic to the anti-Sandinista cause, explained, "Those boys are our sons, our neighbors. They are coming home."

Inside the nearby El Ayote security zone, in the department of Chontales, the atmosphere was tense over the following weeks.

Thousands of restless and often poorly disciplined contra troops passed their time visiting with family members, drinking, firing off their weapons at night, and at times harassing suspected Sandinista supporters, before finally laying down their weapons in June. Political tensions and violence, however, did not diminish in the months following the official conclusion of the disarmament process. In many interior rural zones of Nicaragua that I visited in 1990 and 1991, anti-Sandinista groups, composed of both former contras and rural civilians, mobilized to carry out land invasions, highway blockades, and violent occupations of government offices and towns. Peasants from the interior I met during this time shared with me a very different history than that of the rural population of the Pacific zone. They spoke of their earlier struggles to open up virgin lands on the agricultural frontier and to establish their farms in the perceived tranquility of rural life before the revolution arrived, and in the case of anti-Sandinistas, they listed a series of complaints against the FSLN.

Listening to these often emotional postwar outpourings of criticism against the former Sandinista government, I was struck by the deeply contrasting perceptions and experiences of Nicaraguan peasants I had come to know. To cooperative members in Chinandega the revolution had provided land, credit, material benefits, and a tangible sense of political and social empowerment. In contrast, many peasants in Nicaragua's mountainous interior remembered the years of FSLN rule as a time of violent turmoil and repression. My interest grew during this period in further exploring these conflicting and seemingly irreconcilable rural narratives of a decade of revolutionary transformation and war. What factors—structural, historical, cultural—contributed to such different peasant experiences of revolution and war?

A number of studies have analyzed U.S. policy toward the Sandinista government in the 1980s and the critical role the United States played in the development of the contra forces.[5] As these works amply document, from 1981 through 1989 the United States provided over $400 million in funding for the contra forces, as well as vital support in organization, training, intelligence gathering, and logistics. In contrast, relatively little information about Nicaragua's conflict has been available from the bottom-up perspective of the peasants themselves, who made up the bulk of contra combatants and collaborators.[6]

To help to address this relative silence of peasant voices on Nicaragua's conflict and to explore in greater depth the complex issues of rural political and military mobilization, I carried out a series of interviews from 1992 to 1994 in the interior municipality *(municipio)* of Quilalí, an administrative unit roughly equivalent to a county. Quilalí was in the heart of the war zone in the 1980s and has been the site of continuing rural violence in the 1990s. The study that follows draws upon interviews with over 100 ex-contras, pro- and anti-Sandinista peasant civilians, former army officers, and community leaders.[7] It attempts to weave together from varied and at times contradictory testimonies the contemporary history of Quilalí and explore the complex internal dynamics of revolution and counterrevolution from the perspective of peasants who participated in the conflict, shaped its outcome, and most directly suffered its consequences. This study seeks to address two fundamental questions: What factors influenced Quilalí peasants to collectively mobilize both for and against revolutionary change in the 1980s and why does conflict persist in the postwar period?

Many individuals contributed to the preparation of the this book. I would like to express special gratitude to the Ortiz family for their friendship and very generous hospitality during my stay in Quilalí. I also owe a great debt to many individuals in Quilalí, who shall remain anonymous, for patiently taking the time to answer my many questions and sharing with me their fascinating and at times difficult life experiences. While researching this study my admiration and respect steadily grew for the resilience and courage demonstrated by Quilalí residents, and this work is dedicated to them in the hope of peace and reconciliation. I have tried to convey their story as fairly and accurately as possible, although of course, all errors and misrepresentations remain my responsibility. In Managua I greatly appreciated the moral and logistical support provided by WFP volunteers and staff. I am indebted as well to several anonymous reviewers whose insightful comments helped improve this book substantially. Finally, I would like to give special thanks to Rigoberto for his unfailing support over this long process.

Abbreviations

AMNLAE	Asociación de Mujeres Nicaragüenses Luisa Amanda Espinosa (Luisa Amanda Espinosa Association of Nicaraguan Women)
ARDE	Alianza Revolucionaria Democrática (Democratic Revolutionary Alliance)
ATC	Asociación de Trabajadores del Campo (Association of Rural Workers)
BLC	Batallón Ligero Cazador (Light Hunter Battalion)
BLI	Batallón de Lucha Irregular (Irregular Combat Battalion)
CAS	Cooperativa Agrícola Sandinista (Sandinista Agricultural Cooperative)
CCS	Cooperativa de Credito y Servicios (Credit and Service Cooperative)
CDS	Comité de Defensa Sandinista (Sandinista Defense Committee)
CEPA	Comité Evangélica de Promoción Agraria (Evangelical Committee for Agricultural Promotion)
CIAV-OEA	Comisión Internacional de Apoyo y Verificación—Organización de Estados Americanos (International Support and Verification Commission—Organization of American States)
COPETE	Compañía Permanente Territorial (Permanent Territorial Company)

COSEP	Consejo Superior de la Empresa Privada (Private Enterprise Coucil)
CSM	Cooperativa de Surco Muerto ("dead-furrow" cooperative)
CT	Colectivo de Trabajo (work collective)
ENABAS	Empresa Nacional de Alimentos Básicos (National Enterprise for Basic Foodstuffs)
EPS	Ejército Popular Sandinista (Sandinista Popular Army)
FDN	Fuerza Democrática Nicaragüense (Nicaraguan Democractic Force)
FSLN	Frente Sandinista de Liberación Nacional (Sandinista National Liberation Front)
IAN	Instituto Agraria Nicaragüense (Nicaraguan Agrarian Institute)
INRA	Instituto Nicaragüense de Reforma Agraria (Nicaraguan Institute for Agrarian Reform)
LCBS	Lucha contra Bandas Somocistas (anti-Somocista military patrols)
LIW	low-intensity warfare
MICOIN	Ministerio de Comercio Interior (Ministry of Internal Commerce)
MIDINRA	Ministerio de Desarrollo Agropecuario y Reforma Agraria (Ministry of Agricultural Development and Agrarian Reform)
MILPA	Milicia Popular Anti-Sandinista (Anti-Sandinista Popular Militia)

MINT	Ministerio del Interior (Ministry of the Interior)
MZ	manzana (a unit of land measure equal to 1.7 acres)
ONUCA	Organización de las Naciones Unidas para Centroamérica (United Nations Organization for Central America)
PRODERE	Programa de Desarrollo para Desplazados, Refugiados, y Repatriados (Development Program for the Displaced, Refugees, and the Repatriated)
SMP	Servicio Militar Patriótico (Patriotic Military Service)
TPA	Tribunal Popular Antisomocista (Anti-Somocista People's Tribunal)
UNAG	Unión Nacional de Agricultores y Ganaderos (National Union of Farmers and Ranchers)
UNO	Unión Nacional Opositora (National Opposition Union)

Peasants in Arms

Chapter 1

Introduction

THIS STUDY of armed peasant mobilization explores a series of interrelated political, military, and economic transformations that took place in the rural municipality of Quilalí from 1979 to 1994. Quilalí was selected as the subject of this book on the belief that important insights into Nicaraguan peasant response to revolutionary change can be gained by locating rural mobilization within a specific historical and community context. *Peasants in Arms* examines the ways in which policies and dislocations generated largely at the national and international level were concretely manifested, mediated, and perceived in a local setting.

Several key questions will be addressed in this study. What are the structural, historical, and cultural roots of the deep polarization of the municipality? Why did a majority of Quilalí peasants turn politically against the revolution in the early 1980s? What factors influenced anti-Sandinista peasants to channel their discontent into armed rebellion? How has over a decade of revolutionary and counterrevolutionary struggle transformed Quilalí peasant consciousness and fostered a continuation of violence in the 1990s?

Quilalí shares a number of characteristics with dozens of other rural municipalities in Nicaragua's mountainous interior that were at the heart of the war zone in the 1980s. Like other interior zones, Quilalí formed part of Nicaragua's agricultural frontier after World War II and received an influx of thousands of peasant migrants. A strong culture of rebellion also emerged in Quilalí and other zones of the Segovias dating from Augusto Sandino's guerrilla war against U.S. Marines in the 1920s. Several decades later, on the eve of the revolution, Quilalí had developed into a relatively prosperous and economically heterogeneous municipality. The land in the mountains to the north and west of the town was the stronghold of wealthy and middle peasants—a pattern of landholding typical of many other interior zones—while in the river valley large cattle haciendas dominated. In the early 1980s conflict erupted in Quilalí, and like other north-central municipalities, Quilalí was the site of ongoing combat for most of the decade.

Yet while Quilalí shares these features with other interior zones, the municipality also presents several unique characteristics that make it a particularly interesting zone to study. First, as will be seen, Quilalí and several neighboring municipalities were an important internal "cradle of the counterrevolution" and entered into conflict with the new revolutionary regime at an unusually early stage. Well-off ranchers and coffee farmers from Quilalí and surrounding areas who had earlier collaborated or fought with FSLN guerrillas organized one of the first armed antigovernment movements and attacked the town of Quilalí on the first anniversary of the revolution in July 1980. These same sons of local elites later joined with ex-National Guardsmen and played an important field leadership role in the contra forces.

Quilalí is also unusual for the high number of peasants from the municipality who took up arms with the contras. As many as 800 Quilalí peasants fought with the contras in the 1980s, while thousands more civilians participated in contra collaborator networks. In the postwar period of the early 1990s as well, the mountains of Quilalí served as a base for one of Nicaragua's most politically focused re-contra bands (groups of rearmed ex-contras), the *Frente Norte 3–80*. A final important characteristic of Quilalí is that although, as the above facts suggest, the municipality was an unusually strong center of rural resistance to the revolution, a significant minority of peasants from Quilalí and recent migrants from other zones actively supported the revolution. Unlike other interior areas of contra influence, such as the south-central departments of Boaco and Chontales, where the presence of pro-Sandinista peasants was very limited, the FSLN was able to consolidate an important pro-revolutionary cooperative sector in Quilalí's river valley and to maintain an economic and military foothold there throughout the war. The existence within the boundaries of the municipality of both a strong pro-Sandinista cooperative sector and extensive anti-Sandinista networks provides a unique opportunity to explore the factors that influenced the polarized mobilization of peasants who share a common local history.

Among scholars of peasant rebellion there is an ongoing debate as to whether peasants are fundamentally rational and individualistic actors (Popkin 1979; Bates 1984; Lichbach 1994) or whether peasants' common orientation toward subsistence production, shared history and culture, and subordinate status are the fundamental basis of collective action (Wolf 1969; Shanin 1972; Scott 1976). The most well known proponent of rational peasant theory, Popkin asserts that peasants strive continuously to improve their individual well-being and that of their immediate family and that peasant culture and social structures often serve not to unify peasants, but rather to divide them. According to this perspective, peasants choose to participate in rural uprisings not to defend shared values or broader ideological causes or to achieve collective rewards, but rather to obtain selective incentives and to avoid sanctions targeted at individuals who do not participate.

In contrast, Scott (1976) argues that, under what he terms moral economy, peasants are deeply attached to communal village structures.

They share a common subsistence ethic, which places a premium on reciprocity and mutual assistance, and a system of norms in which a "just" overlord limits the expropriation of surplus to a tolerable level. Under moral economy, peasant rebellion draws its strength, cohesion, and ideological content from relatively homogenous, closed communities bound together by common social values and norms.

In her 1994 study of three Nicaraguan villages, Anderson (1994b) attempts to bridge the gap between Popkin and Scott, arguing that peasants recognize it is in their long-term "rational" interests to actively participate in community support networks, which she terms political ecology. Anderson asserts that community-based political ecology is critical in understanding why certain villages chose to actively aid the FSLN in the late 1970s while others remained quiescent during the insurrection against the Somoza dictatorship.

Gould (1993; 1990b) also stresses the importance of community in the struggles of Matagalpan indigenous groups to resist forced labor, taxes, and loss of land in the late 1800s, as well as in more contemporary invasions of cotton haciendas in the department of Chinandega. The dynamics of peasant mobilization in Chinandega in the 1950s and 1960s documented by Gould also highlight some of the complexities and variations in the ways in which "community" and peasant identity are constructed. On the one hand, a shared peasant identity may be the product of long tradition passed on from one generation to the next in communities that are relatively autonomous and still sheltered from the full impact of market forces (Scott 1976; Wolf 1969).

In contrast, Gould (1990b) emphasizes that the Chinandegan communities that initiated land invasions were not long-established villages, but rather the more recent product of ongoing land conflicts and engagement with Somocista discourse by peasants who were the "precipitates of capitalism." In the course of several decades of political struggle, these peasants moved from dependent to autonomous political consciousness and constructed a common peasant identity in relational terms, coming to define their interests as distinct from those of local large landowners. Kincaid (1987) also links stronger localized solidarity in El Salvador in the 1980s with a greater likelihood of peasant support for the leftist guerrillas. He emphasizes as well that these Salvadoran communities were not traditional villages, but rather deliberately re-created by activist Catholic church members and reinforced by the indiscriminate repression unleashed against peasants by the government.

In addition to distinguishing whether communities that may serve as the basis for peasant mobilization draw on precapitalist traditions or are re-created in some manner, it is also important to consider the class makeup of the communities that anchor rural identity. Scott suggests that members of peasant communities share not only a common culture, but also relative equality as subsistence smallholders. In this case the dynamics of community and class are mutually reinforcing, and peasants' similar economic and social position of subordination enables them to respond in a unified manner to threats from predatory outside elites or the state. Additional subordinate rural sectors that scholars have identified as likely to rebel are middle peasants (Wolf 1969), sharecroppers and migrants (Paige 1975), and squatters (Wickham-Crowley 1992). The autonomous collective mobilization of poor peasants also implies the breakdown of any previous patron-client ties. Peasants must come to articulate political interests distinct from those of rural elites, who remain outside both the geographical and ideological boundaries of peasant community.

In contrast, other scholars have criticized Scott in particular for failing to recognize the degree of stratification and conflict within many peasant villages (Brass 1991; Akram-Lodhi 1992; Haggis et al. 1986). Brass (1991) contends that many acts of collective rural mobilization are carried out not by relatively equal, subordinate peasants, but rather by economically and socially stratified rural coalitions, generally under the leadership of rich peasants. The class composition of rural rebellions in turn influences their choice of strategies, ideological content, and the outcomes of struggle. According to Brass (1991, 181) unifying appeals to precapitalist traditions, or religious, ethnic, or nationalist discourses are akin to false consciousness and may serve "to disguise and simultaneously advance the class-specific objectives of rich peasants." Moore (1966) also distinguishes between egalitarian groupings of poor peasants, which may lead to radical solidarity, and communities in which the poor are dominated by the wealthy, which may manifest conservative solidarity.

The present study argues that while Quilalí peasants were 'rational' and concerned with their individual and family safety and well-being, they did not mobilize as individual, atomized actors. Rather Quilalí peasants' collective efforts both in favor of and against the revolution were strongly influenced by participation in kinship and social networks that were utilized by both the FSLN guerrillas and later the contras to mobilize peasant support to their cause. It is also important to note that peasant community in Quilalí was not of the closed, traditional subsistence type, but rather was open, re-created, and by the mid-1970s relatively stratified.

As will be seen, the nature and boundaries of peasant community and identity in Quilalí were deeply contested in the 1980s. On the one hand, the FSLN attempted to mobilize peasants politically and militarily through a nationalist and broad class-based discourse, which emphasized the common interests of poor peasants in alliance with the urban poor and middle sectors. The contras, on the other hand, built a multiclass coalition of supporters, reinforcing and re-shaping a common "peasant" identity in relational opposition to "outside" Sandinista ideology and programs. It will be shown that in this intense competition for peasant support, Quilalí peasants responded both to selective incentives—land, material benefits, and protection from violence—as well as to ideological appeals.

Scholars generally agree that the dislocations associated with the penetration of capitalism into rural communities are a key causal factor in contemporary peasant rebellion (Moore 1966; Wolf 1969;

Migdal 1974; Paige 1975; Scott 1976; Walton 1984). Wolf (1969) argues that the expansion of capitalism increases exploitation and insecurity of peasants by replacing personalistic ties with more distant, uncertain market relations, and by transforming land from an object of customary rights and obligations into a commodity. Most of these scholars suggest that peasant reaction will be strongest in the early phases of market encroachment, particularly if capitalist dislocation proceeds rapidly and there are few mitigating factors or subsistence alternatives.[1]

In his study of contemporary Central America, Williams (1986) links the post–World War II growth of export products such as cotton and cattle to increased insecurity of land tenure, loss of traditional access to land, and worsening standards of living for the rural poor. Such discontent, Williams argues, laid the groundwork for peasant rebellion in Central America in the 1970s and 1980s. Wheelock (1978), Gould (1990b), and Wickham-Crowley (1992) have also posited a direct link between the growth of export products in Nicaragua and prerevolutionary rural conflict and peasant support for the FSLN in the 1970s.[2]

Other scholars expand upon the structuralist approach to Central American peasant rebellion and argue that political contingencies and human agency, particularly the political strategies of national governments and guerrilla forces, also played an important role in the formation of revolutionary movements (Selbin 1993; Booth 1990; Brockett 1991). Booth (1990), for example, identifies regime response—the failure of the Nicaraguan state to address worsening rural conditions—as an important element in pre-1979 peasant mobilization in favor of the FSLN.

The present study will argue that in interior zones such as Quilalí the potentially negative impact of capitalist penetration was mitigated by several factors: the relative availability of good land; opportunities for upward economic mobility; the presence of the agricultural frontier nearby, which served as a political safety valve; and the continuation of paternalistic ties, which partially buffered poor peasants from the erosion of subsistence security. As will be seen, Quilalí's rural population remained relatively quiescent in the 1960s and 1970s as the municipality became more deeply integrated into national and international markets. Only later, in the 1980s, did Quilalí peasants mobilize on a large scale. They reacted both in favor of and against a series of dramatic transformations and dislocations, brought not by capitalism, but by a revolutionary government and war. It will also be argued that this peasant mobilization in Quilalí can best be viewed as a complex interaction of structural preconditions and local political strategies employed by both pro- and anti-Sandinista forces, set in a larger geopolitical context of U.S. low-intensity warfare against the Sandinista regime.

It is also important to distinguish analytically the reasons why peasants rebel, the factors that influence the manner in which peasant discontent will be expressed, and the often unintended outcomes of peasant rebellion. In later works, Scott (1985; 1989; 1990) suggests that too much attention has been paid to more overt and dramatic forms of peasant resistance. He argues that peasants as a subordinate class are generally unable to express complaints openly because of the "dull compulsion of economic relations" and the "realities of power" and instead opt to carry out everyday resistance, which may take such forms as pilfering, lying, gossip, and work slowdowns. Along similar lines, Colburn (1986; 1989a) argues that Nicaraguan peasants, who were "nearly defenseless" under the revolutionary government and essentially rational actors concerned with their individual well-being, not abstract ideologies, expressed their discontent with Sandinista policies by employing the weapons of the weak described above. In so doing, Colburn asserts, they undermined the overall economic goals of the FSLN.

This study suggests that Quilalí anti-Sandinista poor peasants in particular recognized their own vulnerability and many preferred everyday resistance as their first option. As will be seen, anti-Sandinista women and older men were partly successful in maintaining an outward appearance of neutrality, often while secretly collaborating with the contras. However, the dynamics of militarization in war zones like Quilalí made it extremely difficult for young men to avoid taking up arms with either the Sandinista Army or the contras.

It is also important to note that much of the literature on contemporary peasant mobilization has focused on actual and potential peasant support for progressive social movements and leftist guerrillas, while less attention has been paid to systematically addressing the question of why peasants in Latin America may resist leftist guerrillas or revolutionary governments and support counterrevolutionary movements. Studies from Peru suggest that the Shining Path (Sendero Luminoso) guerrillas were most successful in zones where there was a political vacuum, while communities that retained traditional authority structures were the least receptive to Sendero's revolutionary appeals (Coronel 1996). In addition, peasants opposed Sendero authoritarian efforts to impose controls and increased demands upon the rural population, as well as specific guerrilla measures such as limiting access to markets, the prohibition of fiestas and drinking, and the targeting of Pentecostal churches (Del Pino 1996; Palmer 1992; Isbell 1992).

It also appears that in Peru and Guatemala a shift by the national armed forces from indiscriminate terror against rural communities to more selective repression combined with civic action campaigns was successful in weakening peasant support for leftist guerrillas and facilitated the development of counterinsurgency *rondas campesinas* (peasant patrols) and civil patrols (Degregori 1996; Starn 1995; Stoll 1993).[3] While Wilson (1991) argues that Guatemalan peasant participation in government counterinsurgency efforts was primarily a product of deep fear, Stoll asserts that in addition to repression, military forces were also able on an ideological level to convince some peasants that the guerrillas were to blame for "provoking" army violence that destroyed numerous indigenous communities in the early 1980s.

In Quilalí, as will be seen, contras used selective repression as a means of military recruitment and to control the civilian population, while at the same time convincing many of their supporters that the FSLN was to blame for bringing war to the municipality. The Sandinista government employed more moderate coercive measures against civilian contra collaborators, which were partly successful from a military standpoint, but appear to have often increased anti-Sandinista moral outrage against the FSLN.

Turning specifically to studies of the Nicaraguan contras, a number of excellent works explore in detail revolutionary transformation in rural Nicaragua in the 1980s, including the process of agrarian reform, FSLN policy debates and shifts over the decade, and the development of rural organizations.[4] A number of these authors also briefly address the issue of peasant support for the contras. Additional studies focus on U.S. government funding and organizational support for the contra forces (Kornbluh 1987; Robinson and Norsworthy 1987; Gutman 1988; Kagan 1996), and examine in detail the origins, internal organization, and military and political activities of the contra forces during this period (Morales Carazo 1989; Bendaña 1991; Dillon 1991; Garvin 1992).

In this literature on contemporary Nicaraguan rural history, analysts have identified a series of factors that may account for both relatively low peasant support for the FSLN as well as the participation of interior peasants in the contra forces. These explanatory factors of peasant opposition to the revolution, which are not necessarily mutually exclusive, may be grouped into three broad categories: (1) larger geopolitical struggles and external agents, specifically U.S. government policies in support of the contras; (2) the unique structural and cultural features of Nicaragua's interior peasantry that made this rural population particularly receptive to contra appeals; (3) a series of FSLN biases and policy errors toward the rural sector.

Some analysts and policy makers in Nicaragua and abroad have characterized the contra forces as primarily a product of external aggression by the United States, and in fact until the late 1980s many FSLN leaders did not recognize the conflict as even partially a civil war (CIPRES 1991, 21). According to this perspective, the origins of Nicaragua's conflict were less internal than a reflection of the greater geopolitical interests of the United States and its attempt to "roll back the advance of communism" in a region considered vital to U.S. national interests. This argument, while generally recognizing that other factors are involved, asserts that without the funding, large amounts of weaponry, and the technical, intelligence, and logistical support provided by the U.S. government, the contras would have remained a local, easily-defeated rural uprising. In the postwar period, several analysts have also suggested that the war can best be understood as a convergence of interests between the U.S. government, the Nicaraguan rural bourgeoisie, and Nicaragua's mountain peasantry (CIPRES 1991; Bendaña 1991).

Underlying this argument is often an implicit assumption that the true interests of peasants lie in revolutionary change. Peasants who supported the counterrevolution are seen less as historical subjects than as victims unwillingly caught up in larger global and national political struggles they did not necessarily even comprehend. Bendaña (1991) and CIPRES (1991) argue, for example, that peasants were little more than an instrument of the contra leadership and of their U.S. sponsors, whose objectives had little to offer poor and middle peasants, who made up the bulk of the combatants. Along similar lines, many pro-Sandinista peasants in Quilalí tend to stress the importance of contra repression, propaganda, and manipulation in recruiting peasant support for their cause.

Another approach to peasant opposition to the revolutionary process argues that the unique historical, cultural, and economic structures of Nicaragua's agricultural frontier forged a peasantry that resisted modernizing change, be it capitalist or socialist, and that was susceptible to counterrevolutionary appeals (Bendaña 1991). According to this perspective, the expansion of cotton and other export crops on Nicaragua's Pacific zone largely replaced paternalistic ties with impersonal market relations and created a substantial displaced rural population that in the 1970s provided important support for the FSLN.

In contrast, land was relatively abundant in much of Nicaragua's mountainous interior, particularly along the agricultural frontier, which received a steady flow of peasant migrants after World War II. In these interior zones extensive cattle ranches, a strong middle-peasant sector, patron-client ties, and a traditional campesino culture continued to predominate into the late 1970s (CIPRES 1990a, 1991; Castro 1990b; CIERA 1989). This view point argues that interior peasants' conservative values—precapitalist relations of production, intense religiosity, family loyalties, respect for private property—led them to oppose revolutionary change in the 1980s. Several studies also highlight the role of local rural elites, who served as ideological intermediaries between poorer peasants and the outside world in forging the anti-Sandinista alliance (CIERA 1989, 6; Castro 1990; Bendaña 1991; Serra 1993).

In most of these studies, interior middle peasants are identified as the core rural sector that supported the contras. Enriquez (1997) also links varied degrees of rural support for the FSLN to peasant class origins as well as to the organizational form of their agricultural production. She identifies poor peasants as potentially the most revolutionary subjects and indicates that peasants most closely tied to the land as individual farmers were the least likely to support the FSLN. Although Enriquez's study focuses on political opposition in Nicaragua's Pacific zone, it lends weight to the argument that the pre-1979 consolidation of a relatively strong small- and medium-landholding peasant sector in Nicaragua's interior was an important factor in low levels of support for the revolution in those zones.

A number of studies, from contrasting political perspectives, have also asserted that a series of FSLN biases and errors were an important element in interior peasant opposition to the FSLN and support for the contras.[5] It is argued that Sandinista urban and technocratic biases against a peasantry considered to be socially and technologically backward, led FSLN policy makers to implement policies that at best neglected, and in many cases harmed, the interests of the rural population, and in particular middle peasants.

One specific Sandinista policy that has been criticized from several different angles is land reform. On the one hand, some analysts as well as FSLN party leaders in the postwar period have identified "arbitrary" and politically motivated expropriations of farms of all sizes by the FSLN as a source of resentment and fear among the rural population (Bendaña 1991; IHCA 1991). At the same time it is also generally recognized that the FSLN's land reform policies, which first turned expropriated land into state farms and later required peasants to join production cooperatives to gain access to land, failed to satisfy poor peasants' demands for land in the early 1980s (Martinez 1993; Kaimowitz 1988; Ortega 1990). In addition, scholars suggest that the FSLN directed a disproportionate share of economic resources, credit, and technical assistance toward state farms and later collective cooperatives, and neglected individual peasant producers (Baumeister 1991; Zalkin 1990; Martinez 1993).

Scholars have cited FSLN market interventions as another key source of tension with the peasantry. Middle and wealthy peasants in particular, it is argued, resented Sandinista government controls over the buying and selling of basic grains and export crops, epitomized by the roadblocks *(tranques)* on the edge of rural towns to control the black market sale of crops. Other economic difficulties faced by Nicaragua's rural population in the 1980s include declining terms of urban-rural trade, rationing measures, and shortages of consumer goods, agricultural inputs, transportation, and labor. Scholars also suggest that the Sandinista draft was particularly burdensome to peasant families, who depended on family labor. In addition, in interior zones where the contras were active, abuses by the Sandinista Army and State Security contributed to peasant opposition to the FSLN.

While the present study focuses primarily on exploring the internal dynamics of peasant resistance to the FSLN and armed mobilization in the municipality of Quilalí, it should be emphasized that this local study is located within a larger geopolitical context in which the U.S. government served as a powerful external agent in Nicaragua's war. That is, although in their narratives of the origins of conflict anti-Sandinista peasants in particular tend to downplay the role of the United States, at several key junctures U.S. material and organizational resources were critical in transforming localized rural rebellion into large-scale war. Specifically, U.S. government policies of low-intensity warfare and support for the contras served to reinforce internal contradictions of the revolution, promote the use of violence as a means to express peasant grievances, and rapidly expand the scope and intensity of the conflict.

Overall, this study supports four additional main points. First, resistance to the revolution in the municipality of Quilalí was community-based, multiclass, and built upon a discourse of common "peasant" identity. Second, this resistance was not only a reaction to the FSLN policy "errors" discussed above, but also an expression of more intractable tensions between the revolutionary program and ideology and preexisting interior structures and values. In addition, the dynamics of militarization in the municipality, which pushed anti-Sandinistas into direct armed confrontation with the government, made it all but impossible for the FSLN to reverse this process of polarization by the mid-1980s. Finally, this study emphasizes that Quilalí peasant consciousness is complex, contested, and dynamic, and in the course of the 1980s shifted from prerevolutionary quiescence to a high degree of mobilization.

Peasants in Arms asserts that the support of a majority of Quilalí peasants for the contras in the 1980s was not the act of individual, isolated peasants. Rather, resistance to revolutionary change in the municipality was linked to a perception of a common interior peasant identity and drew upon family, community, and clientelistic networks. As was suggested earlier, Quilalí, which formed part of the agricultural frontier and attracted hundreds of peasant migrants in the 1950s and 1960s, was not a traditional community of subsistence farmers. On the eve of the revolution, the municipality was an economically dynamic zone linked to national and international markets by the production of cattle, coffee, tobacco, and corn. The partial penetration of capitalism into the municipality left key interior values and structures—patron-client ties, respect for private property, autonomy, a strong work ethic, and family loyalties—at least partially intact, but also promoted greater economic stratification in the municipality and the consolidation of a sector of locally powerful rich peasants, or *finqueros*. In 1980 a dozen such finqueros, many of whom had gained military skills and confidence as FSLN guerrillas, organized with friends and workers one of the first rural uprisings against the FSLN. Soon afterward these men joined ex-National Guardsmen in Honduras and with access to U.S. aid assumed the role of field commanders in an integrated contra force. There they played a key intermediary role in recruiting middle and poor peasants to the anti-Sandinista cause. While the FSLN attempted to mobilize peasants through a nationalist and class-based discourse, which emphasized the shared interests of poor peasants, finquero contra leaders worked to forge a multiclass base of peasant support by drawing on clientelistic ties and in their discourse highlighting common elements of interior rural history, culture, and forms of production.

A second important finding of this study is that while, as will be seen, a significant minority of Quilalí peasants supported the FSLN, a majority of municipality residents began to distance themselves from revolutionary programs and ideology that, as suggested above, challenged prerevolutionary values and structures and in the words of Quilalí peasants, "turned everything upside down." Essentially, hastened by a contra campaign of selective repression, the municipality began to polarize politically and militarily in the early 1980s around competing Sandinista and anti-Sandinista worldviews. The basic ideological dichotomies of these worldviews include: exploitation versus cross-class solidarity; equality versus hierarchy; land reform versus respect for private property; state economic intervention versus free markets; nationalism versus local family and communities loyalties; urban versus rural interests; and militarization versus prerevolutionary tranquillity.

As a general rule, Quilalí's finqueros and middle peasants tended to covertly and openly oppose the Sandinista model, while the position of poor peasants toward the revolution was more complex and contested. Poor peasants were attracted to certain aspects of the revolutionary programs, particularly land reform, and a substantial number of them supported the FSLN. Other poor peasants, however, became resentful when in their minds the Sandinista government failed to live up their expectations for land and other benefits or were drawn into the counterrevolutionary struggle by continued economic and ideological dependence on local elites.

In addition to these underlying ideological tensions, a series of what I term secondary or reinforcing factors served both to push anti-Sandinista young men into active armed opposition to the revolution and to reinforce the dynamics of military conflict in the municipality. Most important among these factors were the Sandinista draft, intimidation by Sandinista State Security, and repression and forced recruitment by the contras, as well as family and community pressures and loyalties. As will be seen, in the mid-1980s the FSLN undertook a series of pragmatic policy reforms to attempt to win back peasant support in Quilalí, but in part because of the reinforcing factors mentioned above these policies had only limited success.

A final important point that emerges from the Quilalí experience of revolution and counterrevolution is the complex and dynamic nature of peasant consciousness. While it is true that many Quilalí peasants actively or passively supported the contras, the FSLN was able to win and maintain the support of an important minority of mainly poor Quilalí peasants and through land reform to consolidate a substantial pro-Sandinista cooperative sector. In addition, among peasants who fought with the contras in defense of prerevolutionary values and relationships, the struggle itself and the example of the FSLN transformed their attitudes and expectations. Anti-Sandinista Quilalí peasants of the postwar period were no longer the quiescent peasantry of a decade earlier. In the 1990s they demanded for themselves and their families selective rewards and were willing to employ violence to bring about government response. This highly mobilized peasantry, combined with a weak central government, national political conflicts, and economic recession, was a key element in continued postwar rural instability and violence in the municipality.

Chapter 2

The Agricultural Frontier

As RESIDENTS proudly inform visitors, the municipality of Quilalí lies in the heart of the Segovia mountains at the meeting place of the region's most important body of water, the Río Coco, and the smaller Río Jícaro. Centuries ago indigenous peoples named the fertile valley where the rivers converge Quilalí, "the place of waters." As will be seen, Quilalí is also known as a rebellious zone with a strong culture of resistance dating from the 1920s, when Augusto Sandino based his guerrilla struggle against U.S. Marines in the zone. After World War II, Quilalí formed part of Nicaragua's agricultural frontier and thousands of peasants were drawn to the zone. These migrants developed their own unique *modo de vivir* ("way of life"), which emphasized self-sufficiency, clientelistic ties, patriarchy, respect for private property, and a strong work ethic. From the 1960s onward, however, the municipality entered a new phase of development characterized by the growth of exports, increased stratification, continued patron-client ties, and a relatively quiescent poor peasant population.

Winding dirt roads link the municipality of Quilalí to both the departmental capital of Ocotal, fifty-five kilometers northwest, and the northern city of Estelí, seventy-five kilometers southwest of Quilalí, where several times a day old trucks that have been transformed into passenger vehicles depart to make the arduous six- to eight-hour journey "into the mountains" *(montaña adentro)* to Quilalí. Passengers seat themselves on rough wooden planks in the back of the truck and a ragged piece of canvas tarpaulin is stretched over the metal frame of the truck to provide protection from the sun, dust, or rain, depending on the season. Once loaded with passengers, sacks of rice, beans, and corn, boxes of consumer goods, and small livestock, the truck pulls out of the city of Estelí and travels north along the Pan-American Highway toward the Honduran border. After reaching the town of Palacaguina the vehicle heads east onto a dirt road that leads through the rural heart of the western sector of the Segovia mountains. The western Segovias, often referred to as the dry zone, encompass a portion of three northern departments—Estelí, Madriz, and Nueva Segovia—and sixteen municipalities.[1]

Rainfall in the western Segovias averages 1,000 mm (forty inches) per year or less and in the dry season the zone appears barren and desolate (CIERA 1984, 33). Brown deforested hills and wilted, dust-covered vegetation dominate the landscape. Along the roadside, bony cows graze on the withered remnants of the prior year's corn crop. This western section of the Segovias was the birthplace of many present-day Quilalí residents. In the decades following World War II, the expansion of large cattle ranches and deteriorating ecological conditions here pushed hundreds of peasants to migrate eastward toward Quilalí and the agricultural frontier.

After the passenger truck passes the town of Telpaneca the landscape is gradually transformed. The mountains are steeper, more rugged, and there is now a lingering aroma of moisture in the air. Small waterfalls spill down the mountainsides and coffee bushes cover many of the slopes along the road. In the distance across the gullies, pastures, groves of pine trees, and an occasional farmhouse, smoke pouring from the rooftop, are visible. This zone, the municipality of

The Segovias

San Juan del Río Coco, marks the end of the dry western portion of the Segovia mountains and the beginning of the more humid eastern Segovias, of which Quilalí is a part. The road from San Juan del Río Coco to Quilalí is particularly slow and at times dangerous. In the rainy season vehicles often lose traction completely on steep muddy inclines or become stuck in quagmires several feet deep and must be pulled out with chains. Even in the best of weather flat tires and breakdowns are common. Passengers, who risked contra mines and ambushes to travel to Quilalí during the war years of the 1980s, in the 1990s faced the threat of assault by armed groups—recontras and bandits—active in the northern mountains in the postwar period.

The truck moves slowly up one final steep slope and as it rounds the bend, the town of Quilalí appears suddenly below: a collection of houses and one-story cement buildings nestled among green hills. The most visible landmarks are the bright yellow Catholic church steeple on the eastern edge of the central park and the newly painted hospital perched on a hillside above the town. The shimmering Río Jícaro wraps around the edges of the town past the baseball field several kilometers southeast to where it meets the Río Coco.

From this overlook, one can clearly distinguish the municipality's three main geographic zones. The first is the town of Quilalí itself, home to 7,870 people, a little more than one-third of the municipality's total population of 20,741 (INEC 1996, 9). Local government offices, a bank branch, larger general stores, the hospital, and the municipality's only high school are located within the town limits. For entertainment, the town of Quilalí also boasts a cinema, pool hall, discotheque, and numerous cantinas. At the height of the war in the 1980s, hundreds of Sandinista Army soldiers were stationed in the town of Quilalí and as a result the town itself always remained firmly under FSLN control and provided refuge to those families fleeing the violence in the surrounding countryside. Years after the end of the war, in the early 1990s, dozens of soldiers remained in makeshift camps overlooking the central park to protect the town from attack by recontra groups.

Quilalí's second important geographic zone covers the southeastern section of the municipality, where the Río Coco passes through the broad valley that is Quilalí's agricultural heartland. For many years five large cattle haciendas controlled over half the land of this fertile 23,800 MZ valley.[2] These haciendas were expropriated by the Sandinista government in 1979 and three years later Quilalí's river valley became the site of three large cooperative settlements and the

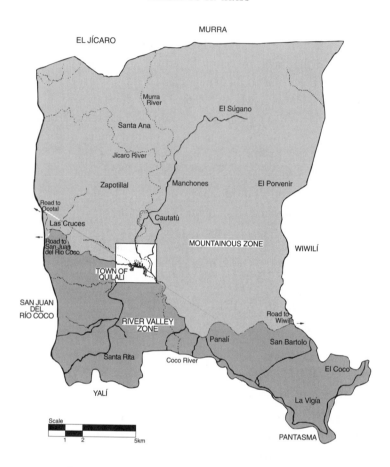

The Municipality of Quilalí's Three Geographic Zones

FSLN's strongest rural base of support in the municipality, outside the town limits. Where cattle and pastures once dominated, small peasant farmers now grow corn, beans, vegetables, and tobacco year round.

Quilalí's third geographic zone covers the more remote northern and western sections of the municipality, whose rugged terrain is dominated by hills and mountains 350 to 1,150 meters high. Only a few dirt access roads enter this area and the majority of its twenty-seven *comunidades* (communities) or rural hamlets are accessible only on foot or horseback. Wealthy and middle peasants own much of the 45,300 MZ of land in this zone, which includes over 39,000 MZ of pasture and more than 1,000 MZ of coffee fields. They coexist with hundreds of poor peasants who grow food crops on several manzanas of marginal land and pick coffee from November to February. The northern mountains of the municipality, in particular the zone of El Súngano, have also traditionally served as a refuge for guerrilla bands, including those of Augusto Sandino in the 1920s, and FSLN guerrillas in the 1970s. In the early 1980s, many residents of these same northern communities collaborated and fought with the contra forces before they were evacuated in 1985. In the early 1990s, armed recontra groups proliferated in this zone.

The municipality's commercial and administrative functions are centered in the town, where some 15 percent of the zone's economically active population is employed in artisanry, commerce, and service positions such as teachers, health workers, local government employees, and domestic workers (PRODERE 1991). The remaining 85 percent of the municipality's economically active population work in agriculture. The zone's thirty-three rural valley and mountain communities and their fields and pastures remain the productive core of the municipality, where planting and harvesting cycles set the rhythm of daily life and sustain the population. The rains begin in May in Quilalí. In the afternoon thunderclouds gather to the north and suddenly dump sheets of rain on the land; at other times it drizzles weakly and intermittently for days on end. Peasants descending from the mountains toward town must guide their horses through thick mud, and the Río Jícaro, little more than a sluggish stream in the dry season, fills and deepens into a swiftly flowing river that often must be crossed by boat.

The rains also signify the beginning of the year's planting cycle of the municipality's most important crop, almost 7,000 MZ of corn. Using traditional technology, a digging stick *(espeque)*—or in the river valley, oxen-pulled plows or tractors—peasants plant their first corn crop in May. In August, when the corn has matured, men, women, and children work from dawn to dusk in the fields to pick the corn and load it into 100-pound sacks. Food is abundant in the harvest period as women prepare sweet corn pancakes *(guirila)*, tamales, roasted corn on the cob, and *atol* and *pinol* (drinks made from corn). Most Quilalí peasants sell three-fourths or more of their crop to pay back loans and to buy basic family necessities. There is sufficient rainfall in the municipality to allow peasants to plant a second smaller corn crop in September and sometimes a third crop later in November. Peasants also plant two bean crops, one in September and another in November or December. November is also the beginning of the coffee harvest in half a dozen northern and western communities in the municipality.

Quilalí's rainy season is critical as well to the municipality's cattle sector. Quilalí's cattle ranchers, most of whom are middle peasants and finqueros, have traditionally concentrated on the raising of young calves up to one year of age which they then often sell to larger cattlemen in the western Segovias for further weight gain and eventual sale to slaughterhouses. Quilalí cattlemen generally employ rudimentary technology and rarely provide their animals with dry-season feed or supplements, relying instead on Quilalí's natural pastures during the rainy season to put weight on their cattle for sale.

Among Quilalí farmers there is concern that the amount of annual rainfall, key to the zone's agricultural productivity, is gradually diminishing. Older Quilalí residents remember that twenty or thirty years ago the Río Jícaro regularly flooded during the rainy season and left the town isolated from the rest of Nicaragua for days at a time. The river rarely floods now, and many residents fear that Quilalí is on its way to becoming as arid as the western Segovias they left behind a generation ago. Deforestation is one of the main causes of the looming ecological crisis faced by Quilalí and other zones that once formed part of the agricultural frontier. Since the 1950s thousands of manzanas of Quilalí's forests have been destroyed to create pasture and farmland and on many mountain slopes close to the town of Quilalí only a few scattered trees remain. Agricultural practices, such as planting corn and beans on steep or fragile land unsuited for annual crops and overgrazing by cattle, have also contributed to the degradation and erosion of Quilalí's soils.

Early History of Quilalí

Quilalí farmers share a deep affection for the mountains and river valley that sustain them, and the image of the municipality as a fertile, bountiful land remains strong in peasant consciousness even as ecological conditions deteriorate. It is only older Quilalí residents, however, who remember firsthand the days when thick forests still covered the mountains and unclaimed land and wildlife were abundant. The municipality's almost legendary natural riches have in fact attracted immigrants to the zone for over 400 years. In the early 1500s, Spanish explorers came to Quilalí drawn by the precious woods found in Quilalí's dense forests and gold deposits in the river valley. In 1543 the Spanish built Ciudad Segovia along the Río Coco only a few kilometers from the present-day site of the town of Quilalí. Spanish colonization did not advance further beyond the Quilalí zone, perhaps because this area represented the easternmost limit of sedentary indigenous groups who were more easily dominated by the colonizers and the beginning of the territory of more difficult to control Miskito and Sumu groups (Keller 1986, 40).

At the time of the Spanish arrival, indigenous people the Spanish referred to as Chondales grew corn as their principal crop in Quilalí's valleys. While the exact origins and nature of the Indians who inhabited Quilalí are still under investigation (Werner 1996, 88), it is clear that the impact of the arrival of the Spanish was devastating. Some indigenous people were forced to work as slaves extracting gold for the Spanish crown, while others fled deeper into the mountains to escape the brutal conditions in Spanish mines. Overall, it is probable that disease, warfare, the slave trade, and forced labor reduced the Segovias' sedentary indigenous population by 90 percent or more (Schroeder 1996, 392). Throughout the 1500s, however, Miskito Indians allied with local Indians, the British, and filibusters organized a number of attacks on the settlement of Ciudad Segovia. Most likely because of these constant attacks and a lack of labor, the Spanish eventually ceased mining and the town of Ciudad Segovia was abandoned altogether in 1611 (Werner 1996, 33).

From the 1600s until the late 1800s, the zone of Quilalí and the eastern Segovias remained inaccessible and sparsely inhabited. Not until the beginning of the twentieth century did the lure of gold draw hundreds of prospectors to the zone. According to older residents, from 1910 onward individual prospectors began to make the difficult journey on foot and by mule to Quilalí to seek their fortune. Gold was relatively plentiful, and prospectors and several small U.S. companies collected up to 4,000 ounces of gold per month from Quilalí and surrounding areas (Guerrero and Soriano de Guerrero 1969, 43). U.S. interests also established half a dozen mines to the north of Quilalí near El Jícaro and Murra.

Although the zone of Quilalí, which until the 1970s included the area of Wiwilí, had 2,431 residents by 1920, the town of Quilalí itself was little more than a collection of grass and palm leaf huts (DGEC 1964a, xiii). Older residents remember that Quilalí's four leading merchant families, themselves recent migrants to the zone, owned the town's only brick houses. Staple foods like corn, rice, and beans, as well as luxury items such as imported liquors were carried from the departmental capital, Ocotal, and from Jinotega by mule train along mountain trails to Quilalí. Quilalí in this era had a prosperous, if rough, frontier atmosphere. Personal feuds were common, and bars and prostitution flourished with the gold boom. According to merchants of the time, prospectors often spent their money as quickly as they earned it, and it was store owners who benefited most from gold mining.

Quilalí's advantageous location on the Río Coco, on which it was still possible to travel by small boat to the Atlantic port of Cabo Gracias a Dios, and the zone's natural resources brought it into contact with international commercial interests in the first half of twentieth century. In the 1920s North American lumber companies contracted Quilalí residents to enter the virgin forests and locate valuable trees such as cedar and mahogany. These men, equipped with little more than axes, would spend up to three days chopping down a tree, which they would then haul by rope to the nearest river port. In later years, American rubber companies, operating through Nicaraguan contractors, purchased rubber sap on a piece basis from individual collectors. The equipment costs as well as all the risks of venturing into the forest to seek out rubber trees were assumed by the collectors.

Longtime resident Pedro Zamora traveled as a young boy to the Quilalí zone, where his father worked for a number of years as a rubber collector.[3] He remembers:

> My father would tell me how he entered the mountain forests prepared with provisions, a hunting rifle, tools. He received no cash advance to purchase these things. It all came out of his own pocket. . . . He would climb the tree making cuts with his machete. . . . Two weeks after cutting the tree he would gather the sap . . . [and] put it on his back and carry it to the collection station on the Río Coco, where it would be taken to the port of Gracias a Dios.

Some of these foreign companies, such as the Nicaraguan Pine Company, continued to operate in Quilalí as late as the 1950s, while others pulled out of the zone because of political violence in the 1920s and 1930s, or when resources became scarce and operations were no longer profitable. These companies appear to have reinvested few of their profits in the Quilalí zone, leaving behind little more than diminished forests, a few primitive roads, and warehouses along the Río Coco. Quilalí residents remember that the wood cutters and rubber collectors generally dispersed once there was no paid work available, with only a small number choosing to settle in Quilalí and take up farming.

Sandino

While the Quilalí zone provided a series of primary products directly to international markets, its integration into the larger national economy and national politics was still weak at the beginning of the twentieth century. Politics in postindependence Nicaragua was dominated by at times violent conflicts between the Liberals based in León and the Conservatives of Granada, which generally were less disputes over ideological differences than they were struggles between Nicaragua's elite families for control of the central government's limited finances and oligarchic control over each region's territory (Walter 1993, 6).

The Segovias fell largely under the political and economic influence of León, but not until the late 1920s was the more remote Quilalí zone affected on a large scale by political violence when Augusto Sandino launched a guerrilla struggle against the U.S. Marines who had occupied Nicaragua almost continuously since 1912. In 1926 General José María Moncada launched a Liberal revolt and Sandino was among those who joined this struggle against Conservatives and their U.S. backers. After achieving a series of military successes, Liberal leaders reached a peace accord with Conservatives in May 1927 and agreed to lay down their arms in exchange for the opportunity to participate in U.S.-supervised elections in 1928.

Sandino, however, declared that he would not disarm until all U.S. Marines had left Nicaragua and began his five-year armed rebellion in the Segovia mountains, where he had earlier worked in the San Albino mine near El Jícaro. After an unsuccessful conventional assault on the city of Ocotal, Sandino made a strategic retreat to El Chipote, an 1,110-meter mountain twelve kilometers north of the town of Quilalí. Assisted by local peasants who carried supplies by mule along a series of secret trails, Sandino's followers constructed a guerrilla base on this inaccessible peak, where in September 1927, Sandino officially constituted his Army for the Defense of Nicaraguan National Sovereignty (Ejército Defensor de la Soberanía Nacional de Nicaragua).

In the following months and years, Sandino successfully built a strong base of peasant support throughout the Segovia mountains with appeals that focused primarily on the nationalist struggle against the U.S. Marines and subordinated issues of social justice to the primary goal of expelling the Yankees from Nicaragua (Schroeder 1993, 513; Paige 1997, 171). Beyond calls for fair wages and improved working conditions in mines, Sandino and his followers made few explicit references to labor or class issues in their discourse. With the exception of certain coffee and mining zones, land was also not an issue of contention in the Segovias in the 1920s and likely not an important factor in Quilalí peasant support for Sandino. Rather, in Quilalí and the rest of the Segovias, a tradition of support for the Liberal party and, even more important, persecution and abuses by Conservatives and U.S. Marines were critical elements that motivated peasants to collaborate with Sandino's nationalist struggle (Schroeder 1993, 225). In Quilalí, U.S. Marines burned houses in half a dozen communities and at times fired on fleeing unarmed peasants suspected of collaborating with Sandino.[4] A Quilalí resident who fought with Sandino stated, "We could not surrender to those invaders [the U.S. Marines] who wanted to usurp our rights and make our families their slaves" (quoted in Schroeder 1993, 233).

One of Sandino's earliest recruits in Quilalí was sixteen-year-old Victoriano Rodríguez, a member of a relatively well-off family that had moved to Quilalí from León in the early 1920s and opened a general store. According to Rodríguez, he joined Sandino's guerrillas in 1927 because he opposed the U.S. Marine occupation of Nicaragua, just as he later opposed U.S. intervention in favor of the contras in the 1980s. "Every invasion is destructive," he states. Rodríguez recalls that Sandino's guerrillas often lacked ammunition and weapons, had no uniforms, and wore only flimsy sandals on their feet. Rodríguez and other guerrillas would wait along a forest path and when a U.S. Marine patrol passed by, "We would shoot four times and run like hell, just like the contras did in this latest war."

By late 1927, the U.S. Marines had located the mythical El Chipote and began a series of bombing raids on Sandino's guerrilla base, and in early January 1928 they bombed the town of Quilalí itself, whose residents strongly supported Sandino. Rodríguez remembers, "The planes flew so low you could almost hit them with a stick. Everyone fled with the bombardment." An undetermined number of Quilalí residents were killed in the bombing and when U.S. Marines entered the virtually deserted town soon after the raid they burned down all the houses in its center except for several that they converted into a military post (IES 1986, 77). The Marines, who were still under siege by Sandino's troops, also built an airstrip along what is presently the main street of Quilalí to allow supply flights to land. Several weeks later they launched a search-and-destroy mission that took six days to reach the summit of El Chipote. Sandino had already received word of the expedition, however, and when the Marines reached the guerrilla stronghold on 26 January they found only abandoned camps and straw dummies Sandino's men had left behind to fool the aerial reconnaissance teams (Macaulay 1967, 98–104). Sandino and his men had retreated south across the Río Coco into the zone of Jinotega to continue their guerrilla struggle.

From 1928 onward an average of about forty-five U.S. Marines along with their recently trained Nicaraguan counterparts, the National Guard, maintained a permanent presence in the town of Quilalí and during that period were able to build a base of civilian support in the municipality (Schroeder 1993, 312). The Marines' social base did not equal the strength of Sandino's, but it did play an important role in sustaining a critical anti-Sandino counternarrative in Quilalí. In the words of one such informant: "To some people Sandino was a good person, but those who were with him were bandits [*bandoleros*]. . . . When Pedro Altamirano came everyone had to hide because he carried a knife to kill all the people, even children."[5]

Overall, the strongest support for the Marines and National Guard came from rural elites, including town residents, finqueros, merchants, and local government officials, who were often able to profit economically from the Marine presence and who were increasingly fearful and resentful of Sandino's attacks on private property and extortionist tactics (Schroeder 1993, 474). In Quilalí several family members of merchants from that era were among those who remember the Marines as "good men" who always paid well and in dollars. In contrast, Sandino's supporters were largely poor peasants.

By the 1930s the Quilalí zone was no longer a focal point of Sandino's struggle as his guerrilla actions instead expanded into central Nicaragua and the Pacific coast departments. During this period, as the number of U.S. Marines in Nicaragua was reduced, the National Guard, whose numbers had reached over 2,300 by 1931, assumed an increasingly important role in the campaign against Sandino and his guerrillas (Macaulay 1967, 180). In January 1933 the U.S. government abandoned its attempt to defeat Sandino militarily and withdrew the last contingent of Marines from Nicaragua. With the Marines gone, Sandino negotiated a peace settlement with Liberal president Juan B. Sacasa, and as part of the peace accord, Sandino was given control of 36,800 square kilometers of territory in the zone of Wiwilí (248). Over the next year Sandino and some one hundred of his soldiers dedicated themselves to organizing farming and gold-washing cooperatives along the banks of the Río Coco approximately twenty kilometers east of the town of Quilalí. In February 1934, Sandino traveled to Managua for further peace negotiations and was assassinated under the orders of General Anastacio Somoza García, head of the National Guard. In the days following Sandino's death, National Guardsmen attacked and destroyed Sandino's cooperatives along the Río Coco. Some accounts put the death toll as high as 300 men, women, and children (Millett 1979, 215).

Once his opponent Sandino was eliminated, General Somoza proceeded to consolidate his personal control over the National Guard and Nicaragua as a whole, formally assuming the presidency in January 1937. In Quilalí and the surrounding areas, Somoza's National Guard carried out counterinsurgency campaigns to exterminate Sandino's guerrillas and supporters throughout the 1930s. According to Quilalí informants, members of some of the municipality's most well-off families, who had initially supported Sandino, later switched sides. Some also denounced their neighbors as Sandino supporters to the National Guard. Pedro Zamora explains: "The National Guard displaced them [Sandino's followers] and put in their own people. In [the rural community] La Luz, for example, they settled justices of the peace [*jueces de mesta*] to spy and tell the National Guard who was there. The *jueces de mesta* might say, 'This man is a Sandinista' so that the [National] Guard would kill him and they would get his land." An unknown number of peasants were killed during this period, while others fled the zone or sought to save their lives by lying low, deep in Quilalí's more remote mountains. Victoriano Rodríguez was forced to leave Quilalí and live on the Atlantic coast under an assumed name for a number of years. Overall it appears that National Guard repression was partially successful in dispersing Sandino's network of peasant supporters in the northern mountains of Nicaragua, even in former strongholds such as Quilalí.

When they took power almost fifty years later, some FSLN supporters report that because of Sandino's struggle, they assumed that they would find in the northern mountains a peasant majority inculcated with nationalist ideals of an earlier era and eager to support the revolutionary cause.[6] But in fact in Quilalí, the legacy of Sandino's Army for the Defense of National Sovereignty was more complex and contested. On the one hand, some pro-Sandino families did escape National Guard persecution in the 1930s and shared their ideals and experiences with the next generation. In the mid-1970s, as will be seen, such families served as collaborators to the FSLN guerrillas and after 1979 often became Sandinista activists in their communities. On the other hand, Quilalí families who had supported the U.S. Marines, some of whom later collaborated with the Somoza government, perpetuated in the municipality an anti-Sandino narrative of a bandit who abused the civilian population. Still other peasant families—the majority of residents on the eve of the revolution—came to the Quilalí zone long after Sandino's death and often had little direct family experience, either positive or negative, of Sandino.

After Sandino's death, Quilalí's strategic location near the Honduran border as well as its rugged terrain continued to make the municipality attractive to guerrilla movements. Quilalí informants remember that up to half a dozen small anti-Somoza and revolutionary guerrilla groups crossed from Honduras into the municipality from the 1940s to the early 1960s. As a boy, Pedro Zamora traveled throughout northern Nicaragua with his father, a rubber collector and a construction worker on the Pan-American Highway, as well as an anti-Somoza union leader. Inspired by his father's example, Zamora traveled to Honduras, where he met Nicaraguan students and professionals who were organizing against Somoza. In 1960 he joined an internationalist and Nicaraguan revolutionary guerrilla band remembered as the bearded ones *(los barbudos):*

> We carried out an incursion on 28 October 1960. . . . We were sixty men. We took the town of Quilalí, entering in civilian vehicles we had found along the road. . . . One guardsman was killed, three wounded, and three put up no resistance and surrendered. We spent two hours in town. We held meetings. Our objective was to take the

high areas [of the municipality] like El Chipote and from there carry out warfare in the style of Sandino. But we didn't have a timetable of activities, a structure; all we had was ideas.

At the time of the barbudo raid only half a dozen National Guardsmen were posted permanently to the Quilalí area. After the attack, however, the National Guard launched a full scale counterinsurgency campaign in the Quilalí mountains. Zamora explains: "A ton of guardsmen arrived in a plane. There was a tremendous uproar that year. The counterinsurgency units of the [National] guard patrolled here. Peasants who had given the guerrillas food, who had assisted them were hunted down and jailed. The [National Guard] would grab any guerrilla or active collaborator they found and shoot him. They would kill him." The barbudos were unfamiliar with Quilalí's mountainous terrain and had not taken the time to develop a solid network of peasant collaborators. Unprepared for the scope of the National Guard repression launched against them, they soon retreated back to Honduras.

Several points should be made about the series of guerrilla incursions into Quilalí carried out by groups like the barbudos. First, these post-Sandino guerrilla groups generally passed rapidly through Quilalí and rarely took the time to build strong networks of peasant collaborators. Nor did they carry out the long-term political work of "consciousness raising" with peasants about their nationalist and revolutionary programs. The result, as will be seen, was that in the 1950s and 1960s paternalistic relationships and quiescence on the part of the poor came to dominate peasant consciousness in Quilalí, with limited challenge from more radical alternative ideologies. Yet although these ephemeral guerrilla movements did not lay a clear political groundwork for revolutionary change in the 1980s, the presence of such guerrillas, along with Sandino's earlier struggle, did help shape the municipality's culture of resistance. It also likely served to legitimize the use of violence within Quilalí peasants' repertoire of instruments of collective action and political change.

The Agricultural Frontier

Along with passing guerrilla bands, in the 1950s and 1960s the municipality of Quilalí received an influx of peasant migrants from the western Segovias who came to the zone in search of unoccupied government-owned land on which to settle. Such population movements toward agricultural frontier zones like Quilalí in turn had their roots in Nicaragua's rapid postwar expansion of exports. A cotton boom took hold of Nicaragua's northern Pacific zone in the early 1950s and the amount of land on which cotton was grown increased almost five times from 1950 to 1955 (Biderman 1982, 179). While in some zones cotton opened up new economic opportunities for small and middle peasants, the overall impact of the cotton boom was to undermine traditional peasant access to land, increase the insecurity of the rural poor, and promote the development of a landless migratory seasonal rural workforce (Williams 1986, 71–72). Likewise, the expansion of coffee, first introduced to Nicaragua in the mid-1800s, intensified land pressures in certain zones of the northern and central mountains, such as the eastern Matagalpa and Jinotega highlands.

It was the postwar expansion of cattle ranching, however, that most deeply transformed northern Nicaragua in the 1950s and 1960s. From the early 1900s onward, cattle ranches, mining operations, and coffee had linked the Segovian economy in a partial and uneven manner to national economic markets (Schroeder 1996, 393). By the early 1960s, the construction of the Pan-American Highway (which linked Estelí to Managua and Honduras), the opening of bank branches in the north and a slaughterhouse in Condega, as well as high demand for beef in the United States laid the groundwork for Nicaragua's cattle boom in the north. Nationwide, the value of Nicaragua's total cattle exports rose from $1.3 million in 1960 to $44.5 million in 1973 (Biderman 1982, 177). In the western Segovias cattle production expanded particularly rapidly in the municipalities of Las Sabanas, Somoto, San Lucas, Pueblo Nuevo, Cusmapa, and San Juan de Limay and in general increased land inequalities in the western Segovias (CIERA 1984, 216). On the eve of the revolution in the department of Nueva Segovia the largest one-fifth of farms held 76 percent of the land (DEA-UNAN 1985, 9). Quilalí informants remember that a number of poor peasants in their native communities lost their land altogether, due to expanding cattle haciendas during this period, while others were limited to farming the more marginal lands of the western Segovias.

In addition to the expansion of cattle ranches, northern peasants experienced other important demographic and ecological pressures (CIPRES 1990a, 22; CIERA 1984, 282, 321–25). Rural Nicaraguan families typically divide their landholdings among all their male children and sometimes daughters as well. Family parcels were divided and subdivided, in some cases to the point that sons no longer had sufficient land to support their families. Ecological deterioration, as a result of deforestation and inappropriate agricultural and ranching practices, has also been particularly severe in the western Segovias. Quilalí residents who grew up in this region remember that in the time of their grandparents in the 1920s and 1930s rainfall was plentiful from June until October and it was rare that they did not harvest enough corn to feed the family for the year. Since the Second World War, however, the western Segovias have suffered droughts and drying rivers. Peasants report that by the 1960s their corn yields had fallen substantially and the poorest families suffered chronic hunger. In contrast, as late as the 1970s average corn yields in the municipality of Quilalí, (16.5 *quintales* per MZ)[7] were double those of many zones of the western Segovias (CIERA 1980, 145).

Poor peasants of the western Segovias in such precarious circumstances were forced to choose between several survival strategies. Some peasants entered into sharecropping *(medería, aparcería)* or tenant *(colonato)* relationships with wealthy cattle ranchers to obtain access to land, or they migrated to urban centers.[8] In several areas of the western Segovias, such as San Lucas in the department of Madriz and Pueblo Nuevo in the department of Estelí, peasants actively resisted encroachment by cattle haciendas in the 1960s and were repressed by the National Guard (DEA-UNAN 1985, 16). However, such organized peasant resistance appears to have been the exception, not the rule, in the western Segovias.

Hundreds of other peasants decided on their own initiative to migrate east to Nicaragua's agricultural frontier, the thousands of square kilometers of unsettled, government-owned land *(tierras baldías)* that stretched from the central mountains to the Atlantic coast. In the 1950s towns such as Nueva Guinea, Matiguás, Rancho Grande, El Cuá, and Quilalí lay on the edge of this agricultural frontier and attracted hundreds of new settlers a year. In the case of Quilalí, the

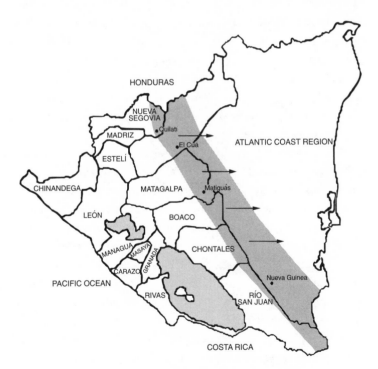

Nicaragua's Agricultural Frontier in the 1950s

majority of migrants came from the western Segovian municipalities of Somoto, Las Sabanas, San Lucas, Santa María, and Condega (MIDINRA 1987, 16).

A number of studies have highlighted the negative factors discussed above, expanding cotton, coffee, and cattle production which pushed poor peasants to abandon their native communities, and the involuntary nature of peasant migration to Nicaragua's agricultural frontier (Wickham-Crowley 1992, 241–42; Wheelock 1978). The experience of Quilalí suggests, however, that migration to the agricultural frontier was also viewed by peasants in some cases as a positive alternative to conditions in their native communities. Many of these peasant migrants were young, ambitious, and committed to creating a better life for themselves. The risks were high and years of isolation, hard work, and sacrifice lay ahead. Yet for some the agricultural frontier represented an opportunity to gain possession of fertile land and advance economically beyond subsistence farming. Even in later years, as the amount of unoccupied land and opportunities for poor peasants in the municipality shrank, this image of the agricultural frontier as the bountiful hope for the future remained deeply etched in Quilalí peasant consciousness.

When peasant migrants from the western Segovias came to Quilalí in the 1950s, much of the municipality's land, particularly in the northern and eastern mountains, was either unsettled or could be purchased cheaply. Even in Quilalí's river valley, where several haciendas had been established in the early 1900s, there were still substantial tracts of forested land waiting to be claimed. When a peasant family decided to build a farm in the mountains, the men usually entered the mountains first, by themselves. Sixty-five-year-old Manuel Valdéz, originally from the western Segovias, decided as a young man to leave his home town of Condega and head into the mountains in search of land to farm. Valdéz describes the work involved in clearing a path *(carril)* through the virgin forest: "There I would leave everything behind and enter the [virgin forest] with great difficulty, cutting away the underbrush, pulling my mule along, because the ground that animals have never passed over is soft. The mule sinks into the ground, and people too. It was hard work, suffering the cold, climbing trees with my ax to chop them down. I would make a shelter out of branches and leaves and sleep there underneath the trees." Once Valdéz had cleared away trees and vegetation to create a mule path through the forest, he selected a good spot with a water source nearby on which to settle. Later, with his family, Valdéz constructed a small house and cleared several parcels of land to farm using traditional slash-and-burn *(roza y quema)* techniques.

Earlier Nicaraguan laws that allowed squatters to obtain permanent title to land after five years of use were eliminated in 1939, and in the 1950s only the executive, President Somoza, had the legal authority to distribute private titles to public land, although in practice regional authorities continued to issue provisional titles (Taylor 1969, 74–75). The law also allowed peasants to use the resources of public land. According to Valdéz and other Quilalí informants, peasant squatters rarely made any effort to legalize the parcel of mountain land on which they squatted because in this era, custom on the agricultural frontier held that the peasant who opened the first path into the virgin forest acquired "rights" *(derechos)* over this land. Valdéz explains this rural code: "On the national lands all you had to do was make a carril. No one would kick you off. People respected the carril. Later you couldn't do that. The land was in private hands." Once a peasant had acquired derechos he could choose either to settle the land himself or sell his rights to someone else for a small amount of money. If the peasant had worked the land for several years, the buyer would also have to compensate the seller for any improvements *(mejoras)* to the land, such as fences or sections cleared of trees. These land transactions were generally outside formal Nicaraguan law, and rarely involved lawyers or were noted in the public registry.[9]

In the municipality of Quilalí, the Somoza government seems to have made little attempt to regulate, legalize, or evict peasants squatting on national lands. The government did, however, initiate a series of colonization projects along the agricultural frontier in the 1960s.[10] These land grants from the Nicaraguan Agrarian Institute (Instituto Agraria Nicaragüense, IAN) were designed both to ease land conflicts on the Pacific coast and to build a base of support for the Somoza regime in the interior. According to the departmental public registry in Ocotal, in the late 1960s in the Quilalí, Murra, and Wiwilí zones the government distributed at least 2,500 MZ to twenty-eight or more families in tracts of 10 to 200 MZ. Another seventeen families received legal title to the land they occupied. Somoza's land grants in Quilalí, however, included no bank credit, technical assistance, or development of infrastructure. Like the families who spontaneously settled in the mountains, the IAN land beneficiaries were largely left to their own devices to succeed or fail on the agricultural frontier.

As will be seen, in the following years the conditions under which migrants established and developed their farms on the agriculture frontier reinforced their peasant identity and distinct way of life, in particular their ties to their land and values of hard work, autonomy, patriarchy, paternalistic ties, and extended family and communities loyalties. It should be noted that while this peasant identity appears to have been particularly strong on the agricultural frontier, several studies suggest that elements of this culture were more generalized throughout Nicaragua's mountainous interior (CIPRES 1990a; Castro 1992; CIERA 1989, 6: 284–87).

Quilalí peasants remember that the first years they planted crops on newly cleared land, the soil was generally very fertile. Using a system of crop rotation, families harvested large amounts of corn, beans, plantains, bananas, sugar cane, cassava, *quesquisque,* and *malanga* (tubers). Peasants supplemented their diets with wild fruits; hunted deer, iguana, and wild pigs; and fished in nearby rivers. Older peasant migrants to Quilalí like Manuel Valdéz still speak with wonder of the natural abundance of Quilalí three decades ago: "Before, the Río Coco was deep, to the top of your head and filled with fish. There were many mountain cats *(tigres)*, wild boars, howler monkeys. Before you didn't need fertilizer. The soil was better and there weren't as many pests. You could produce 150 *arrobas* of corn, 200 *arrobas* in a good year."[11]

For these peasants, the natural world around them offered all they needed for their survival. In the words of one peasant migrant: "The campesino is a friend of a mountain. We like the freedom to walk through the forest with our .22 [rifle] for hunting, our dogs, our ax. People make fun of the mountains, but there you find everything." Yet if the forests and mountains of Quilalí represented natural wealth, a great deal of hard work and sacrifice was required to tap this richness. Many of the municipality's early migrants still remember with a sense of pride and achievement the hardships they endured to obtain a piece of land. Families faced a difficult journey by mule or on foot through underbrush and mud to reach their farms. In Quilalí's low-lying areas clouds of mosquitoes swarmed around peasant families day and night. Older Quilalí residents also remember the numerous poisonous snakes that were a constant danger and the wild cats that howled and played along the banks of the Río Coco and killed their pigs. FSLN guerrilla leader Francisco Rivera, who was based in the northern mountains, describes peasant living conditions:

> Those were regions of silence, lost and forgotten, where a shout echoed from hill to hill. . . . [poor peasants] lived in huts [*chozas*] held up by forked branches; walls made of sticks; roofs of palm, banana or *bijao* leaves. [These were] refuges that served more as a defense against the eternal rains than as a place to live in. The children naked and barefoot, played on the dirt floor with the pigs, the dogs, and the chickens and turkeys; the kitchen fire burned next to the wooden boards where they slept, exhausted from their day's work. (Rivera Quintero 1989, 87)

For drinking and washing, women and girls hauled buckets of water from nearby springs and creeks. To light their homes at night peasants burned pine boughs and made lamps out of discarded jars filled with kerosene.

According to older informants, in the first few years they farmed a cleared piece of land; they were often able to produce a surplus of corn beyond their food needs for the year, even without fertilizer. There were no roads out of the mountains, however, and some peasants raised pigs as a way of "walking" their corn out of the mountains. Once or twice a year peasants herded their pigs several days to northern towns to be sold. Peasants report that they received approximately 70 *cordobas* ($10) per pig from merchants who would then sell the animal in the city for upward of 200 cordobas ($28.50). Some families also grew sugar cane and with small wooden mills *(trapiches)* produced raw sugar, which they also sold in northern towns.

While men and boys worked in the fields, women and girls were responsible for all work in the house. Peasant women typically rose before dawn to carry out the time consuming task of preparing tortillas, the family's staple food, and other chores such as hauling water, cleaning the house, feeding the family's animals, caring for children, and washing clothes in nearby streams and rivers. Girls often formed common-law marriages at an early age, and families were large, with as many as nine or ten living children. Patriarchal authority was the norm within these peasant families. As a study of peasants who settled the agricultural frontier of Nueva Guinea found, the male authority figure in the family "gives orders, directs the tasks to be done, works outside of the home to support the family. . . . above all else he makes the most important economic decisions and manages the money" (Aznar et al. 1989, 128). With women and children subordinated to adult male authority, peasant families worked together as a largely self-sufficient unit. Peasants report that they consumed little they did not grow or make themselves in this era. Adolfo Hernández remembers: "We had two pairs of pants, one for work and the other for going into town. Our visiting pants would last ten years because we only went to Ocotal once a year. . . . We used water jugs made out of clay, griddles made in the communities to cook tortillas, rope made out of vines." Peasants regularly purchased only basic provisions such as salt, cooking oil, and sugar, and perhaps once or twice a year items such as machetes, blade sharpeners, barbed wire, medicines, clothing, and shoes.

Quilalí peasants were also isolated from the rest of Nicaragua. Most had no radio or regular access to news from the rest of the country, and rarely traveled even to nearby northern cities. Older informants remember that the Somoza government offered them little assistance or services and generally did not interfere with their lives. Schooling was only available to those Quilalí residents who lived in town, and 80 percent or more of Quilalí rural residents over age ten were illiterate (CIERA 1980, 178). Access to health care was also limited. In the case of illness or accident, peasants often used medicinal plants and herbs to treat themselves, and women gave birth in their homes with the assistance of family members and neighbors who acted as midwives. While no accurate statistics are available, it is likely that infant and child mortality was high among Quilalí peasants. In interviews, women typically count their children in terms of those living and those who died as babies or young children, and even in the 1990s many mountain families report having lost at least one child.

End of the Agricultural Frontier

By the mid-1960s, unclaimed land in the municipality of Quilalí had grown increasingly scarce. The boundary of the agricultural frontier had shifted eastward and peasant migrants who sought uninhabited land to settle now passed through Quilalí, leading their mules toward settlements such as Wiwilí and Wamblán in the department of Jinotega. The decade of the 1960s in Quilalí was characterized by the growth of infrastructure and services, new links to national and international markets, and deepening inequalities among peasants. Large cattle haciendas, owned by regional elites, came to control more than half of Quilalí's river valley land, and by the late 1970s Quilalí's landless population reached some 250.[12] A powerful group of finqueros who profited from new export opportunities in cattle, coffee, and tobacco also emerged in this period, along with a strong middle-peasant sector. Yet even as the municipality of Quilalí modernized and further integrated into national and international markets, many of the earlier values of the agricultural frontier remained intact. Increased rural stratification did not necessarily rupture cross-class community ties, but rather led to the adaptation of a complex web of clientelistic relationships between the well-off and poor peasants in Quilalí and prerevolutionary peasant quiescence.

One of the first concrete signs of Quilalí's modernization was the new dirt highway, completed in the mid-1960s, that linked Quilalí to the departmental capital, Ocotal. A dry-season road was also built parallel to the Río Coco, which for the first time connected the town of Quilalí to its river valley. The zone's population had almost doubled, from 4,899 residents in 1950 to 8,753 in 1965 (DGEC 1954, 80; Banco Central de Nicaragua 1975, 83). By 1965 the town of Quilalí was no longer simply a grassy airstrip and a collection of grass-and-palm houses, but a bustling commercial center that boasted fifteen concrete or brick houses, a gas station, and a telegraph office (Guerrero and Soriano de Guerrero 1969, 224). A constant flow of families, including Miskito Indians who traveled by boat on the Río Coco, passed up and down Quilalí's main street, shopping in the town's twelve stores. The government opened a health clinic in town and a new local bank branch offered credit to the municipality's wealthiest farmers. Quilalí's streets were still unpaved and the town's residents still had to haul their water from the Río Jícaro, but a generator now provided Quilalí's well-off citizens with electricity in the evenings. These improvements and services did not extend beyond the town of Quilalí, however. The municipality's population continued to grow

44

at least 3 to 4 percent a year, and three-fourths of these new residents lived in the countryside in the same primitive conditions as a decade earlier, without electricity, potable water, roads, or access to schools and health care (MIDINRA 1987, 13). Where there was once a single isolated farm, dozens of scattered houses, often owned by members of the same extended family, now formed rural communities.

The municipality's growing links to regional, national, and international markets had a mixed impact on its peasant population and overall served to increase the complexity of Quilalí's economic and social structures. To a minority of rural families, generally those who initially possessed good land and some type of family capital, greater market links brought new opportunities to accumulate wealth in Quilalí's expansive prerevolutionary economy. For many of Quilalí's poor peasants, however, the growing importance of cattle, coffee, and to a lesser degree tobacco production, appears to have begun to worsen their overall position in the municipality as access to land became more difficult and life more insecure. This negative impact was at least partially mitigated by several factors including the continuance of paternalistic relations between the poor and elites and the presence of the agricultural frontier nearby as a safety valve.

Large Landowners

By the mid-1970s, among the more than 80 percent of the municipality's population who were engaged in agricultural activities, four broad rural sectors had emerged in the municipality of Quilalí: large landowners, wealthy peasants or finqueros, middle peasants, and poor peasants.[13] Table 2.1 details the number of producers in each sector, the amount of land they held, and other characteristics of each sector. The first sector, the large landowners, or *terratenientes,* were members of regionally powerful, wealthy families who saw in the Quilalí zone new economic opportunities and, particularly from the 1950s

Table 2.1
Rural Sectors in Quilalí, 1979

Rural Sector	Size of Farm (MZ)	# of Producers	% of Producers	Area (MZ)	% of Area	Buy or Sell Labor	Geographical Zone & Type of Production	Other Characteristics
Large Landowners, or Terratenientes	1,000+ MZ	5	0.5%	13,200 MZ	19.1%	Employ from 20 to 45 colonos and/or workers	River valley; cattle production; commerce	Reside in departmental capitals; outside economic interests; largely Somocista
Fingueros (Wealthy Peasants, or Chapiollos)	200 to 999	68*	6.8*	25,000	36.1	Employ a small group of colonos	Northern and western mountains; cattle, coffee, and tobacco; commerce	Considered self-made; locally influential; generally anti-Somoza
Middle Peasants	10 to 199	347*	34.7*	28,000*	40.5*	Limited buying and selling of labor	Northern and western mountains; basic grains, coffee, small cattle herds	Limited information available on this sector
Poor Peasants	0 to 9	580	58.0	3,000*	4.3*	Sell labor on a temporary or permanent basis	Large number of landless peasants in the river valley; 2/3 of peasants in western mountains are poor; basic grains	250 of these poor peasants are landless; patron-client ties to fingueros and large landowners
TOTAL		1,000*	100.0%	69,200 MZ	100.0%			

*Estimates.
Source: Calculated from MIDINRA (1987).

onward, purchased and fenced in large tracts of land in Quilalí's river valley to raise cattle.[14] By the mid-1970s, Quilalí's five large landowners held close to 13,200 MZ of land, or 20 percent of farmland in the municipality, and more than half of Quilalí's fertile river valley land. Quilalí's largest landowner, Asunción "Chon" Molina, owned a total of 5,000 MZ of land, including the cattle ranch, Guaná, which extended from just beyond the Quilalí town limits across the valley to the community of San Bartolo. Quilalí's other large landowners included Maurico "Wicho" Portillo, who owned 3,000 MZ of valley land; René Paguaga, a member of a wealthy Ocotal family; and Alejandro Chang. In addition, the Somoza family owned 2,000 MZ of Quilalí's most fertile land along the Río Coco (MIDINRA 1987, 18).

These large landowners shared many characteristics.[15] All lived outside of the municipality primarily in regional capitals, held important agricultural and commercial interests in other zones, and with the exception of Molina, were Somoza supporters. Portillo was a deputy in Somoza's Liberal Nationalist Party, the mayor of the town of Telpaneca, and the owner of several cattle ranches in the western Segovias. Portillo used his Quilalí hacienda, Santa Rosa de Ventilla, to raise young calves that were later shipped to his other haciendas for fattening before slaughter. The Paguaga family in turn, was part of a prominent group of families known as the Ocotal oligarchy, while Molina, a Conservative, lived in Jinotega, where he owned other haciendas and factories. All of these men had purchased their land relatively cheaply, either from other wealthy landowners in debt to the bank or from the government. Some of them, like Molina and Portillo, also seem to have simply fenced in forested, uncultivated land in the river valley to expand their haciendas. According to the Ocotal public registry, Portillo only legally registered ownership of 600 MZ of his 3,000 MZ cattle ranch in the 1970s. As their main economic interests were outside Quilalí, these large landowners invested little time or money in modernizing their farms and left day-to-day administration of their farms in the hands of foremen.[16]

For La Vigía, the Somoza family purchased the land in the 1940s.[17] The almost 2,000 MZ of forested land along the Río Coco, approximately sixteen kilometers from the town of Quilalí, was both of good quality and located on a geographically strategic crossing point between the Segovias and the department of Jinotega. The Somozas repaired La Vigía's airstrip built by the U.S. Marines and converted an old rubber warehouse into a small National Guard command post. Beyond this military outpost, the Somoza family seems to have invested little capital or attention in La Vigía and day-to-day administration of the farm was left in the hands of a foreman.

Although after 1965 there was little unoccupied national land available on which a family might settle, the municipality of Quilalí continued to attract poor peasant migrants well into the 1970s. These later migrants either purchased land, which could still be acquired relatively cheaply in outlying zones of the municipality, or entered into dependent relationships with elites to gain access to land to farm. Around forty-five landless peasant families, for example, worked as *colonos* (tenant farmers) for Chon Molina in the 1970s. Like other Quilalí cattlemen, Molina made profits not through increasing productivity, but by keeping costs, particularly labor costs, to a minimum. As much of his land was still forest, Molina allowed poor peasants to clear a plot of land in exchange for a year's use of the land.

Quilalí resident Noris Pardo, who grew up in a small hut on the edge of the Guaná hacienda, remembers that both his grandfather and father worked on the Molina hacienda clearing land for a number of years. As neither Pardo nor his family had their own land to farm, he worked as a colono:

> Molina would give us a piece of land. We would cut down all the trees and grow corn and beans mixed in with the grass planted for the cattle. All he provided was the barbed wire and the grass seed. Everything else we had to provide. And he said he wasn't responsible for damage his cattle did to our crops. Once we picked our first harvest, we would

plant the year's second crop. After that we weren't allowed any more crops. We cleaned out the plot and left a pasture ready for the cattle.

The next year the cycle would be repeated on a new plot of land. As can be seen, with a minimal investment in barbed wire and grass seed, Molina was able to have up to 100 MZ of land cleared and turned into pasture each year. In addition, he was guaranteed a pool of peasant workers available to take care of his cattle and repair fences year round. Workers were paid the going wage, equivalent to about a dollar a day, and long-term and trusted colonos were often given use of a plot of land *(solar)* on which to build their houses. On the La Vigía hacienda, the Somozas also allowed colonos to sharecrop land, for which they paid about ten quintales of corn per manzana as rent in kind.

Finqueros

In addition to these large landowners from outside the municipality, another locally powerful sector of wealthy producers or finqueros emerged in Quilalí by the late 1960s.[18] Unlike the terratenientes, these finqueros were long-term Quilalí residents who owned from 200 to 1,000 MZ of land and had up to several dozen colonos working for them.[19] They had prospered raising cattle, coffee, and to a lesser degree tobacco, the profits from which they often combined with earnings from local commerce. By the mid-1970s, sixty-eight finqueros, who represented less than 10 percent of Quilalí's farmers, owned approximately 25,000 MZ of land, or more than one-third of Quilalí's farmland and pasture (MIDINRA 1987, 18). While some of them held farms wedged between the large haciendas of Quilalí's river valley, the majority of finqueros owned cattle ranches and coffee farms to the north and west of town in the mountains. They directly oversaw their farms, often putting their sons to work for them, and had relatively little formal education. Although the combined landholdings of some of the wealthiest finquero families were comparable to those of the terratenientes, finqueros were distinguished by their strong roots in the municipality and the pivotal role they played in the social and political life of Quilalí.

In contrast to the poor, landless migrants who came to Quilalí from the western Segovias with little more than the belongings they could carry with them, many finquero families originally migrated to Quilalí with some family savings.[20] One of Quilalí's most influential finquero families, the Hernández brothers and their father, moved to Quilalí in the late 1940s from the zone of La Concordia, where they had sold the family farm. With the profits, the Hernández brothers purchased the rights to over 1,000 MZ of forested land in Quilalí's river valley. They grew sugar cane for several years and then with their earnings began to buy cattle. Roberto Hernández, son of one of the original brothers, remembers that although they employed only rudimentary technology, their cattle flourished: "When I was sixteen years old I milked forty-five cows. We also had 200 beef cattle we raised and fattened in other pastures. It was very traditional. In later years we began to use some chemicals, vaccinations for parasites, disinfectant baths, but back then there was no such thing as a mechanized stable. We did everything by hand." By the mid-1960s the Hernándezes were able to obtain bank loans of over 50,000 cordobas ($7,143) to expand their farms and herds. They began to hire workers, and like other finqueros bought houses in the town of Quilalí. In the 1970s the Hernándezes also took advantage of government assistance to diversify into tobacco, and several of them became leading grain and cattle merchants in the Quilalí area.

In other cases, Quilalí town families who were successful in commerce invested their earnings in land, cattle, and coffee, particularly in Quilalí's river valley. One of the municipality's wealthiest families, the Corderos, came to Quilalí in the early 1960s and, drawing on political connections and family capital, opened a general store and pharmacy. They used their profits to buy land for cattle and by the time of the revolution, Humberto Cordero had become one of the municipality's leading ranchers. Generally, there was a fluid inter-twining of interests between agriculture and commerce and Quilalí's wealthiest families combined both activities when the opportunity presented itself.[21] These wealthy producers, who unlike less well-off peasants had access to cash year around, typically offered credit to middle and poor peasants, charging interest rates of from 2 to 5 per-cent a month. They also served as middlemen in the sale of cattle and bought coffee crops eight to ten months in advance of the harvest, generally only paying the grower about half the going price for coffee (Keller 1986, 188). If the grower had a bad harvest and could not pro-vide all of the coffee he owed, he had to provide double the amount the next year or hand over title to his farm (188).

Nationwide, Zalkin's (1989) reinterpretation of the 1980 Rural Workers Survey presented in table 2.2 indicates that the rich-peasant *(campesino rico)* sector, roughly equivalent to what is classified here as Quilalí's finquero sector and the municipality's most well-off mid-dle peasants, was larger in Nicaragua's interior (19.0%) than on the Pacific coast (13.3%). Rich peasants, defined by Zalkin as those who hire labor on a regular basis, were particularly numerous in the inte-rior departments of Jinotega, Chontales, and Nueva Segovia.

Middle Peasants

On the eve of the revolution, roughly one-third of Quilalí families (about 350), most of whom lived to the north and west of the town of Quilalí, could be very broadly classified as middle peasants.[22] They owned from ten to 199 MZ of land and combined production of basic grains with export crops. Middle peasants generally relied on immediate and extended family members and reciprocal labor ex-changes *(mano vuelta)* to meet their needs for labor and may also

Table 2.2
Agrarian Class Structure in Nicaragua by Department, 1980

Departments	Poor Peasants	Middle Peasants	Rich Peasants	CAS	Marginal	Worker Workers
PACIFIC COAST						
Chinandega	27.4%	20.7%	12.5%	1.4%	6.2%	32.0%
León	30.9	27.6	13.0	1.4	4.8	22.4
Managua	40.4	22.9	9.8	1.0	7.9	18.0
Masaya	39.0	17.1	15.3	1.3	3.6	23.8
Carazo	38.6	20.8	15.3	1.0	7.4	17.1
Granada	37.1	16.0	11.0	0.6	2.3	33.1
Rivas	37.6	23.3	16.5	1.2	7.1	14.5
Average Pacific Coast	**35.9%**	**21.2%**	**13.3%**	**1.1%**	**5.6%**	**23.0%**
INTERIOR						
Nueva Segovia	31.8%	27.7%	22.8%	1.8%	5.6%	10.3%
Madriz	39.8	30.1	15.7	1.2	7.6	5.7
Estelí	36.9	30.7	19.0	2.0	5.2	6.0
Jinotega	29.3	30.5	23.5	1.3	6.3	9.2
Matagalpa	32.3	30.3	15.5	1.5	5.7	14.9
Boaco	37.8	28.0	15.9	1.0	8.3	9.2
Chontales	32.0	28.3	20.8	0.5	6.4	12.2
Río San Juan	28.1	44.7	18.1	1.2	4.7	3.1
Zelaya	29.8	42.8	19.4	0.9	4.5	2.8
Average Interior	**33.1%**	**32.6%**	**19.0%**	**1.3%**	**6.0%**	**8.2%**
NATIONAL TOTAL	**33.9%**	**27.2%**	**16.8%**	**1.3%**	**5.8%**	**15.2%**

Source: Zalkin (1989).

have hired several temporary workers during peak planting and harvesting periods.

Although relatively little information is available about the middle peasant sector, it appears that many of these families originally squatted national land or purchased it relatively cheaply. In subsequent years some families were able to accumulate savings by keeping their consumption and expenses to minimum, as well as by working several months a year picking coffee, and by selling pigs and raw sugar. Other peasants were also able to obtain informal loans from local elites and although the interest rates they paid were often much higher than official rates, peasants who invested the money well were able to consolidate and even expand their farms.[23]

As a rule, middle peasants possessed agricultural tools and animals, but did not own heavy machinery or vehicles. Although middle peasants achieved a greater degree of self-sufficiency than poor peasants, they still often depended on finqueros and terratenientes for such services as loans, advance purchase of crops, initial processing of their coffee crop, and transportation and marketing of crops and cattle. It seems likely that middle peasants had an ambivalent attitude toward Quilalí's wealthiest farmers, who represented both a model to be emulated and a potential threat to the security of their landholdings. At the same time, middle peasants who were subordinate to wealthier producers often fulfilled the role of patron to poor peasants from their community, serving as intermediary buyers and suppliers, or loaning money that they themselves may have borrowed from others. Nationwide in 1980, the middle peasant sector averaged only 21.2 percent of the population on the Pacific coast, but comprised 32.6 percent of all rural residents in Nicaragua's interior, and was particularly strong in the agricultural frontier zones of Río San Juan and Zelaya (see table 2.2).

Poor Peasants

The municipality's fourth major rural sector consisted of 580 poor peasants who owned less than 10 MZ of land. In Quilalí's isolated twenty-seven northern and western mountainous zone communities approximately two-thirds of families were poor peasants. Often far from roads and any type of services, these peasants typically grew corn and beans on a few manzanas of land they had managed to squat or purchase. Poor peasants who did not possess land of their own obtained access to land by paying rent in kind, medería or aparcería, or in exchange for labor on cattle ranches. In the northern zone of the municipality informants report that it was unusual for a poor peasant to have no access to land at all. According to the 1980 Rural Workers Survey, in the municipality as whole, 13 percent of Quilalí residents surveyed participated in sharecropping arrangements (CIERA 1984, 64).

Quilalí's greatest absolute concentration of poor peasants was found in the river valley where on the eve of the revolution there were approximately 250 poor landless peasants. Among these poor peasants, colonos who established close ties to large landowners or finqueros in their communities were generally in a relatively advantageous position. These peasants had fairly secure access to land on which to farm and build their houses, as well as a variety of services such as transportation of crops and loans of oxen, oxcarts, farm equipment, and money. In contrast, residents remember that recently arrived or less well-connected peasants in Quilalí's river valley led a more precarious existence. They often worked as day laborers on the cattle haciendas when work was available and joined hundreds of peasants who picked coffee in Quilalí and San Juan del Río Coco from November to January. Roberto Hernández explains: "They [their houses] were calamities you passed by. Those campesinos lived very precariously on the narrow strip between the barbed wire fence and the side of the road. They had to go to the hacienda to gather firewood, to collect water, and to find work to survive. Among the colonos there were some who managed to buy a cow and 20 MZ of land, but those families on the roadside never had any possibilities at all for the future." For Nicaragua as a whole, while the average percentage of rural poor in 1980 in interior departments like Quilalí (33.1%) was only slightly less than on Nicaragua's Pacific coast (35.9%), the average percentage of rural workers dependent largely on wage labor in the interior (8.2%) was significantly lower than the Pacific coast, where 23 percent of the population were rural workers (see table 2.2).

Patron-Client Ties

On Nicaragua's Pacific coastal plain and in certain coffee growing regions of Jinotega and Matagalpa the expansion of export haciendas and the formation of a large seasonal rural proletariat led to the general breakdown of paternalistic bonds between patrons and their workers. Personal ties and reciprocal duties and obligations were largely replaced by impersonal market relations in which land and labor became strictly commodities (Williams 1986, 71–72). In the municipality of Quilalí, however, as the above discussion suggests, increased market integration did not signify the complete rupture of paternalistic or precapitalist relations of production, but rather the adaptation of such relationships to the new realities of the municipality. In other words, both patron-client ties and mutual aid between peasants of relatively equal status in Quilalí in the 1970s were not simply backward ideological remnants from an earlier era, but instead continued to serve the perceived economic and social needs of the population, even as capitalism penetrated the municipality more deeply. To poor peasants such relationships had both an affective aspect and also represented a means to mitigate the growing economic insecurity they faced. As Kaimowitz states, "The exchanges involved were typically unequal but were the only available source of land, support in times of crisis, and scarce commodities, and were cemented by an elaborate ideological foundation based on kinship, dependence, and shared value systems."[24]

In his study of the neighboring municipality of Wiwilí, Keller (1986, 189) also identifies a complex chain of clientelistic ties in which, for example, a middle peasant might be the client of a finquero and at the same time serve as a patron for poorer peasants in his community. According to Quilalí residents, clientelistic ties were particularly strong between colonos who often lived on the same farm for a number of years, and the finquero patrons with whom they worked closely. In the words of poor river valley peasant Noris Pardo: "People respected their patrones. They were like your family, your father. We were the same, all on the same level. And no one spoke out or complained. He [the patron] told you, 'I'll give you this much,' and no one ever complained."

As this comment suggests, many poor peasants depended on elites not only in a concrete material sense for access to land, loans, and services, but also as transmitters of ideas and values.[25] Even in the 1970s many Quilalí peasants had limited access to outside sources of information and finqueros served as their key intermediaries to and interpreters of the outside world. In Quilalí, such ideological dependence served to conceal unequal and even exploitative relationships. At the very least, these relationships served the interests of elites by guaranteeing them a generally loyal and quiescent labor force at critical moments in the agricultural cycle in a relatively isolated zone with no systematic offer of labor (CIPRES 1990a, 74). If a colono did question the authority of his patron or fall out of favor, the patron could employ a number of coercive tactics to reinforce his authority, including denying a colono work opportunities and services, forcing him off the "borrowed" piece of land where he had built his house, or even calling on the National Guard. The fact that elites at times relied on economic and even physical coercion to maintain their authority in the municipality also suggests that their control over the "symbolic means of production" in prerevolutionary Quilalí was by no means absolute or all-pervasive. It is likely, particularly given the expansion of haciendas and finquero landholdings, that at least some poor and middle peasants maintained "hidden transcripts" of resistance (Scott 1990). Poor and middle peasants may well have questioned in private the low prices they received for crops and cattle, the interest rates they were charged for loans, or why large haciendas held hundreds of manzanas of land without cultivating them. However, with the exception of one incident on Somoza's hacienda, La Vigía, described below, none of the pro- or anti-Sandinista informants interviewed could recall any cases when such resistance to local elites was expressed in an open or organized form.[26]

In the words of Pardo: "Here the campesino knew nothing about strikes. He came [to Quilalí] to work however he could. There were no organizations or unions. Those things didn't exist. The campesino didn't have anywhere to look for support and didn't protest. He was submissive. It wasn't like the campesinos on the Pacific coast. There were no land takeovers in Quilalí. Here things were bottled up. Campesinos still didn't have any greater ambitions." In contrast in certain rural zones on Nicaragua's Pacific coast, where thousands of peasants participated in rural protests and organized land invasions against expanding cotton haciendas, a climate of quiescence and a worldview of community solidarity and class harmony continued to prevail in the municipality of Quilalí.[27] As one peasant explained her family's lack of prerevolutionary political activism: "It's true we were very poor, but all we'd ever known was poverty."

When conflicts over land did occur in the municipality of Quilalí, they were usually limited to individual families whom large landowners or finqueros wished to remove from their property. Isolated and with no outside support, most of these families decided to leave the farm and even the municipality rather than to resist the landowner. After an argument with Molina, for example, Noris Pardo's parents were forced to leave the hacienda where they had lived for years. They made their way east toward Wiwilí and managed to buy a small farm with their savings. Pardo explains why his parents decided to leave Guaná without a struggle: "It's not that the campesino doesn't feel things. He's just timid and thinks it's better to leave and avoid problems. Maybe he will live isolated, but at least he will live peacefully [*tranquilo*]." As this testimony suggests, those families who were unable to consolidate their farms in Quilalí, or at least ensure their subsistence, had the exit option of moving deeper into the mountains. In social terms, the availability of land on the nearby agriculture frontier likely served as a safety valve that prevented land pressures from reaching an explosive point in Quilalí. A study of Wiwilí to the east of Quilalí found, for example, that recent migrants from Quilalí made up more than half the population of some rural communities (Keller 1986, 80).

As will be discussed in the following chapter, church leaders promoting liberation theology and FSLN guerrillas did make limited contact with Quilalí peasants later, in the mid-1970s. Before that time, however, no unions, rural organizations, or political groups were active in the municipality that might have offered poor Quilalí peasants material or organizational resources to challenge elites in a collective manner. More generally, in certain zones of Matagalpa peasants carried out organized resistance to expanding cattle ranches with assistance from the Nicaraguan Socialist Party.[28] It appears, however, that such open struggle was more the exception than the rule in Nicaragua's interior and that the prerevolutionary quiescence of Quilalí was more typical.

The growing scarcity of land in Quilalí in the 1970s, however, did lead to several spontaneous cases of peasant resistance in Quilalí's river valley on the eve of the revolution. The municipality's most important incident of prerevolutionary peasant resistance was carried out by Somoza's colonos on his hacienda, La Vigía. Mario Aguero, originally from Mozonte in the western Segovias, explains why he migrated to La Vigía in the early 1970s: "Our life was very difficult. We didn't have any work. We didn't have a house. We didn't have land.

One day news came that on the farm of the general [Somoza] there was work. A guardsman there gave us land to farm."

Many families who migrated to La Vigía from the western Segovias came from poor rural communities known as cradles of the National Guard because of the large number of National Guardsmen recruited from these zones. Aguero, for example, had a brother who joined the National Guard apparently for economic reasons. It seems likely that politically trustworthy peasants who were members of Somoza's Liberal Nationalist Party or family members of National Guardsmen were encouraged to settle on La Vigía.

For a number of years La Vigía's colonos worked with few complaints. In a good year peasants remember that they would harvest thirty quintales of corn per manzana of land, ten to fifteen quintales of which they paid to the National Guardsmen as rent in kind. In the mid-1970s, however, a new foreman from Jinotega tried to force the peasant colonos off the land they had been farming. Aguero, who had rented a small plot of land for approximately five years, remembers: "This came from the managers, not from the general [Somoza]. They decided that they were going to take our land from us, just because it would be good pasture. They wanted the land to feed their cattle. They were very wealthy cattlemen." Mario Aguero and other colonos from La Vigía believe that the foreman and National Guardsmen acted on their own, and that President Somoza knew nothing of the eviction plans. Their image of Somoza as a friend and protector of poor peasants remained intact, although it is likely that the foremen were acting directly on the Somoza family's orders. Pressured to leave, these peasants felt that their very survival was at stake and struggled to keep their land:

We carried out opposition, not with force or with arms. What we did was resist and refuse to leave because we had nowhere to go. We had our houses, our chickens, our corn there. . . . The foremen let loose 500 cows onto our fields to trample our crops. We lost forty MZ of our second crop of corn, but we didn't care about our losses. We said we weren't going to go, that the land was ours and not the general's [Somoza's]; that they should leave us alone and let us farm.

Letting cattle loose on fields to destroy a peasant's crops was a method by which landowners in Quilalí tried to force peasants to abandon a rented or borrowed piece of land. In the case of La Vigía, where as many as 100 peasant families resisted leaving the land, the National Guard took more drastic measures: "The foreman began burning the houses of men, elderly people, humble women. We went to confront him, to speak with him very seriously and to explain to him the harm he was doing to us campesinos . . . that we are poor people who depend on the land to survive." Eventually the foreman abandoned his attempt to force the peasants off the land and a new National Guard commander was sent to La Vigía who established a better relationship with the colonos. Soon afterward, the FSLN overthrew the Somoza dictatorship and La Vigía residents would begin a new phase of resistance.

There are several important points to note about this struggle over access to land, the only one of its kind that informants interviewed could remember in prerevolutionary Quilalí. First, La Vigía's colonos carried out their nonviolent resistance without the help of any outside agents. They did not seek political allies from the town of Quilalí or make contact with FSLN guerrilla forces that were passing through the municipality at that time. In the latter case, the peasants' ties to Somoza and the presence of National Guardsmen on La Vigía made this an unlikely option. The struggle remained very local—a single ranch—and never spread to other haciendas in the river valley. Nor were any formal organizational structures ever created. Once the peasants' goal of preserving their access to land was achieved, the informal organization dissipated. Also, while La Vigía colonos have very negative opinions of certain foremen and National Guardsmen, they never reached the point of questioning the Somocista or landowning system in itself. Instead, it was felt that once the "bad" foreman was replaced with a "good" foreman, although the system of land ownership remained intact, the problem was resolved. It is interesting to speculate that perhaps if these peasants had come into contact with progressive church groups or FSLN guerrillas their struggle would have taken on broader ideological and political dimensions. As it was, in the prerevolutionary period class-based consciousness remained incipient in Quilalí and did not emerge to openly challenge the prevailing ideology of cross-class harmony of interests.

Chapter 3

The Sandinista Revolution

Prerevolutionary Politics

As THE previous chapter suggests, despite its geographical remoteness Quilalí's history has been shaped in important ways by larger international and national political conflicts and economic dislocations. After 1950 the growth of the cattle industry in northern Nicaragua was an important element in promoting the settlement of the agricultural frontier. The subsequent partial incorporation of Quilalí into wider markets led to growing stratification and increasingly complex social and economic networks in which patron-client ties persisted. In turn, Quilalí residents have not only been subject to the impact of external forces, but have also at certain points played an active role in influencing the outcome of larger conflicts, as in the late 1920s when residents lent support to Sandino's nationalist guerrilla struggle against the U.S. Marine occupation of Nicaragua.

This chapter covers the period from the mid-1970s through the first year of the Sandinista government (1980) and examines the impact of national political struggles on the municipality in the prerevolutionary period, with particular focus on liberation theology and the FSLN guerrillas as key external agents of change. Later, when the urban-based Sandinista government took power, it initiated a rapid series of transformations in the municipality, most importantly land expropriations that disarticulated Quilalí's terrateniente class but failed to satisfy peasant demands for land. At the same time, it will be shown that a small group of Quilalí peasants, many with earlier ties to liberation theology or Sandino's struggle, became committed supporters of the FSLN, which they believed to be the first government in Nicaragua's history to address the needs of the poor peasantry.

Overall, the relationship between the Somoza government and the population of Quilalí was characterized by relative neglect and non-interference, limited use of repressive force, and a series of loose, clientelistic ties that linked some Quilalí elites to the Somoza regime. Quilalí informants report that the Somoza government provided the municipality with minimal services and material resources, but generally intervened little in political and economic activities of the zone. In the 1960s and 1970s the Somoza government funded education and health services in the town of Quilalí and, with donations of private capital and labor, assisted in the development of a basic road system. In terms of agricultural production, government aid was largely limited to the granting of titles to national lands and, in the 1970s, technical assistance to tobacco growers in the river valley. Quilalí residents interviewed could recall no Somoza government programs targeted at the poor. As a rule during this period poor Quilalí peasants looked not to the government to assure their basic subsistence, but rather to extended family networks and the well-off as their primary safety net.

In the prerevolutionary period the most important civilian authority in the municipality was the mayor, whose principal duty was to oversee basic administrative tasks such as preparing deeds of sale for land, houses, vehicles and animals, as well as the registration of births, deaths, marriages, and cattle brands. The coercive arm of government authority in Quilalí was represented by half a dozen National Guardsmen who, until the mid-1970s when FSLN guerrillas became active in the municipality, focused primarily on law enforcement. The guardsmen dealt with routine problems such as drunkenness, bootlegging, and fights in town, and were also involved in petty corruption augment their income. The mayor also appointed justices of the peace *(jueces de mesta)*, usually wealthy or middle peasants who served in each of Quilalí's several dozen rural communities. Roberto Hernández describes the role of the juez de mesta:

> If two guys were fighting over a piece of land, he tried to resolve the problem and then charged a commission. The juez de mesta helped to clear roads and to capture someone who had stolen a sack of coffee, a cow. . . . Later when the guerrilla movements began, every time a small group of guerrillas would pass by they [the justices of the peace] would run to tell the [National Guard] commander.

As discussed earlier, the National Guard also led campaigns against small guerrilla groups that passed through the area. The scope of such counterinsurgency efforts was fairly limited in the municipality of Quilalí, however, and does not appear to have involved ongoing, wide-scale persecution of civilian peasants. Few of the informants interviewed for this study who were living in Quilalí in the 1970s directly experienced any serious National Guard abuses.

In Quilalí as elsewhere in Nicaragua the Somoza regime combined the threat of repression with a strategy of co-optation of local elites to maintain political control. The continuing stigma of being associated with the Somoza regime makes it difficult to judge the extent of Somoza's clientelistic network of supporters in Quilalí.[1] It is known, however, that several of Quilalí's large landowners were representatives of Somoza's Liberal Nationalist Party in the National Assembly in Managua, although their local political influence in Quilalí appears to have been limited by their other outside interests and commitments. Also, some merchants and finqueros actively supported the

Somoza government less for ideological reasons than for expediency. Under the Somoza regime power was not governed by formal rules, but rather was discretionary and highly personalistic, and Nicaraguan elites commonly used relationships with powerful figures to secure special privileges for themselves (Spalding 1994, 47). In Quilalí, supporters of Somoza's Liberal Party in the 1970s had access to both influential contacts on a local and departmental level and a series of informal favors, such as access to government land, loans, and scholarships for their children.

Such support for the Somoza government, however, was by no means universal among Quilalí's well-off citizens. A number of Quilalí's finqueros came from Conservative families that traditionally opposed the Liberal regime, which had failed to incorporate them into the political system, and felt their economic and political advancement stifled by the dictatorship (Baumeister 1991, 231–32; CIERA 1989, 6:286). Until the appearance of FSLN guerrillas in the mid-1970s, however, these finqueros did not carry out active or organized opposition to the government. Political differences among Quilalí elites were tacitly recognized in the prerevolutionary period, but according to informants were not a source of open conflict. In the words of Roberto Hernández, member of a traditionally Conservative family: "Everyone knew who was a Liberal and who was a Conservative, but there was harmony. There were no ideological confrontations."

In Quilalí, as in other parts of Nicaragua, the majority of peasants lacked a prior tradition of representative democracy or experiences with effective political participation, and civil society remained weak and fragmented (Ortega 1990, 123). Poor peasants in particular report little knowledge of or involvement in traditional party politics in the 1970s. A typical comment is: "We were from the mountains. We didn't know about politics." Many of these poor peasants identify political parties and issues as something alien, outside their everyday experience, that could be understood only by Nicaraguans living in towns and cities. In the words of a colono from Quilalí's river valley, "Before, politics confused us." During the largely fraudulent elections called by Somoza, paternalistic relationships played an important role, and poor peasants remember that they often voted for the party their patron told them to support, with little understanding of the issues involved.

Liberation Theology

An important exception to Quilalí's prerevolutionary pattern of limited political and social mobilization was a small group of several dozen Quilalí peasants who became active government opponents in the 1970s, largely through their participation in two movements whose origins and leadership lay beyond the boundaries of the municipality, liberation theology, and the FSLN's Northern Front. In broad terms, the liberation theology movement, which originated from Vatican II and the 1968 Medellín Conference, broke with the Catholic church's traditional support for the temporal order, and instead endorsed social and political activism and the transformation of unjust political, economic, and social structures. Liberation theology called upon the poor to move from passive acceptance of the world as it was to become active agents in history.

In Nicaragua in the 1970s church groups became active in urban areas such as Managua and Estelí as well as in Pacific rural zones such as Carazo and Masaya, where Jesuit-organized Evangelical Committee for Agricultural Promotion (Comité Evangélica de Promoción Agraria, CEPA) groups were key in the later formation of the pro-Sandinista Association of Rural Workers (Asociación de Trabajadores del Campo, ATC). In Nueva Segovia as well, several Capuchin priests organized progressive youth groups in Jalapa and other nearby zones. These groups and other Christian Base Communities established in Yalí were later severely repressed by the National Guard, and one of the most active priests in liberation theology, Father Evaristo Bertrand, was arrested and expelled from the country in 1976 (Foroohar 1989, 150).

In Quilalí, Catholic church activity was kept largely within traditional bounds by the North American priest who served the parish from the 1950s until the early 1990s. A small number of Quilalí residents, however, were drawn into liberation theology activities through contacts with progressive church leaders such as Father Evaristo. Roberto Hernández, who joined a progressive Christian study group in the mid-1970s, explains:

> It was there that the idea began to awaken in me of the liberation of the people and I came to understand that Nicaragua wasn't only where I lived, but something bigger; that in all of Nicaragua there were problems. . . . We were almost blind. . . . We couldn't see the reality around us and then we began to wake up, to see our reality, and we began to struggle. First by means of the church, and then we saw that the best path was the FSLN, which was the only force that identified Nicaragua's real problems.

Other Quilalí peasants use similar language to contrast an earlier ignorant and confused state of consciousness to their subsequent "awakening" with liberation theology that opened their eyes to the unjust reality around them. Many of these peasants also abandoned the traditional belief that the spiritual world of the church and the secular world of politics were separate and distinct and came to see political struggle as a natural continuation of their Christian beliefs. Roberto Hernández explains this convergence:

> It's not enough only to pray and sing and preach the word of God. We have to go and search out the reality of the community and work in the community. This is true Christianity. . . . We had meetings in Managua where they [the Sandinistas] talked about popular power and they explained that they were struggling so that the poor would have land, so that the merchant would have loans to be able to work. They wanted to create the kingdom of God on earth.

Where liberation theology groups were active in northern Nicaragua they served to lay a groundwork of rural support for revolution and undermine the existing sociopolitical order by legitimizing rebellion and providing organization and resources to the Sandinistas (Booth 1991). In many cases, northern peasants involved in liberation theology later collaborated directly with the FSLN and by the late 1970s open association with such groups was quite dangerous. As will be seen, in the long term liberation theology activists from Quilalí and those from other zones who later moved to the municipality formed an important core group of peasants who supported the FSLN politically and militarily in the 1980s.

FSLN Guerrillas

A second external movement that led dozens of Quilalí peasants into confrontation with the Somoza regime was the arrival of FSLN guerrillas in the mid-1970s. The Sandinista National Liberation Front, founded in 1961, sought to overthrow the Somoza family dictatorship and implement an anti-oligarchic, nationalist liberation revolution that would favor Nicaragua's poor majority. In the 1960s and early 1970s, the FSLN's largely urban middle- and upper-class student leadership established a series of base camps in Nicaragua's mountainous interior. In remote zones such as Pancasán and Zinica, the FSLN was able to build networks of peasant support, although such networks were somewhat limited geographically and vulnerable to National Guard repression.

In the mid-1970s, FSLN guerrillas also began passing through Quilalí, the neighboring municipality of Yalí, and the communities of Cerro Blanco and Quibuto in San Juan del Río Coco (CIERA 1989, 6:44). They did not linger in the Quilalí area or attempt to establish a more permanent presence, but they did convince a dozen or so Quilalí peasants to aid their guerrilla struggle. Over time, the FSLN developed a small but solid clandestine network of supporters in Quilalí who offered the guerrillas food, shelter, and information when they crossed through the zone. The most well-known FSLN guerrilla leader to recruit support in the municipality of Quilalí was a peasant from the Chinandega Department, Germán Pomares Ordóñez, known as El Danto. Pomares was associated with what became recognized by 1976 as the *tercerista*, or third-way, tendency of the FSLN. This tendency, led by the Ortega brothers Daniel and Humberto, came to promote a strategy of national unity through the formation of a broad anti-Sandinista alliance that included all social and economic sectors except that small portion of the bourgeoisie that was directly linked to Somoza or the nation's key financial institutions. In contrast, the other two FSLN factions, the "proletarian tendency" and the "prolonged popular war" tendency, focused on the urban working class and rural guerrilla warfare respectively.

Germán Pomares and other FSLN guerrilla leaders who passed through the Quilalí area had a deliberate strategy to focus their recruiting efforts on merchants, finqueros, and foremen who possessed the material resources and community influence to most aid the guerrillas (CIERA 1989, 6:46). In other words, rather than challenge the authority of local elites, FSLN tercerista guerrillas like Pomares attempted to use Quilalí's multiclass networks of kinship, friendship, and patron-client ties to their own ends.[2] The FSLN, pragmatically recognizing that "a finquero can recruit a colono, a poor peasant, but a poor peasant can never recruit a finquero," would first win over a finquero and then give that producer the autonomy to build his own network of collaborators, which generally included his extended family and his workers and colonos (46).

Such was the case with the traditionally Conservative and anti-Somoza Hernández family from Quilalí's river valley community. Once FSLN guerrillas won over several of the brothers to their cause, the Hernández's leadership converted their community into the municipality's clandestine guerrilla center. Several of the younger

Hernándezes joined the guerrillas as combatants, while older family members were pursued by the National Guard and forced into exile. The FSLN received similar support from finqueros in the department of Jinotega who "hid an entire column [of guerrillas] in their coffee fields; talked to one of the commanders like Germán Pomares; offered them [the FSLN] food and transportation and logistical support to move their men" (CIERA 1981a, 18). It is important to note, however, that families were not always united like the Hernándezes in their support for the FSLN guerrillas. In several cases the FSLN was able to recruit the sons and daughters of some of Quilalí's wealthiest families, some of whom had been sent to study in high schools in Estelí or Ocotal. In these urban centers Quilalí young people came into contact with the Sandinistas' clandestine student networks and a few began to collaborate with the FSLN without the knowledge or support of their families.

An important question remains to be addressed: what factors influenced finqueros in Quilalí and other zones to risk National Guard repression by assisting the FSLN guerrillas? The answer lies partly in that fact that Quilalí finqueros, like elites in the rest of Nicaragua, came to oppose the Somoza government on largely political grounds. The regime traditionally coopted sectors of the bourgeoisie without fully incorporating them and the deterioration of Somocista quasi-corporatist and clientelistic mechanisms and elites' desire for a developmentally competent state apparatus led to a deepening crisis in the 1970s.[3] Particularly after the 1972 earthquake, elites perceived the Somoza regime as increasingly corrupt and greedy and by 1978 joined a broad cross-class opposition coalition that also included a portion of the church hierarchy and the FSLN.

In Quilalí, the finqueros and their sons who collaborated with the FSLN in the 1970s were independent, self-sufficient families who resented the imposition of forty years of dictatorship and the fact that political appointments in the municipality were based to a great degree on support for the Somoza regime. These finqueros state in interviews that they collaborated and fought with the FSLN to bring to Nicaragua democracy like that found in Costa Rica, which would leave existing economic and social structures largely intact.[4] In the words of one finquero who fought with the FSLN: "The idea was only to defeat Somoza and eliminate the army he had. Then they [the FSLN] would establish a national and social democracy in Nicaragua." Another important point to consider is that in prerevolutionary Quilalí the FSLN guerrillas were the only organized alternative of struggle available to residents who opposed the Somoza regime. Given no alternative, a number of the finqueros "did not support the FSLN out of true conviction, but out of the necessity of the moment" (CIERA 1981a, 18). In other words, Quilalí finqueros may not have necessarily been committed to the more profound transformations such as agrarian reform, government interventions in the economy, and nationalist policies supported by the FSLN.

Many of them who later supported the counterrevolution claim in fact that the FSLN "deceived" *(engañó)* them, misrepresenting its true intentions. It is possible that some tercerista guerrillas, with their strategy of national unity, emphasized to finqueros the immediate and common struggle against the Somoza dictatorship and downplayed the divisive questions of social and economic transformations. Other Quilalí residents who continued to support the FSLN in the 1980s, however, argue that FSLN guerrillas were explicit about their revolutionary ideology and goals. They suggest that finqueros who later turned against the revolution made a tactical decision to overlook those aspects of the FSLN program they did not agree with, in hopes that such revolutionary programs would never actually be implemented after the defeat of Somoza.

Also, as we have seen, this emerging class of finqueros was Quilalí's most dynamic sector that benefited from the development of infrastructure and access to new markets. Their further economic advancement was hindered, however, by Somoza supporters, who monopolized Quilalí's best valley land and held important commercial interests. Although ex-FSLN collaborators and combatants deny it, there may have been a measure of calculated opportunism in their decision to join the Sandinista guerrillas. In other words, if Somoza's allies were removed from the scene, new economic opportunities and a "quota of power" would be available for finqueros (CIERA 1989, 6:51). A final factor that also may have influenced the sons of Quilalí's finquero families to join the guerrillas was the municipality's culture of resistance dating from the Sandino era. Joining the FSLN offered not only an opportunity to gain status in communities where guerrilla combatants have historically been admired, but also adventure and physical challenge. As will be seen, this tactical alliance between Sandinista guerrillas and finqueros in Quilalí and neighboring zones effectively provided the nascent guerrilla force with material and logistical support. Only a few years later, however, when the internal tensions and contradictions of the FSLN's alliance with finqueros erupted into open conflict, it was this same wealthy sector that would help lead the counterrevolution against the Sandinistas.

In the case of interior poor peasants who supported FSLN guerrillas in the late 1970s some analysts have noted that this sector came to oppose the Somoza government as the result of National Guard repression and fears of expanding cattle haciendas that threatened the security of their landholdings.[5] As we have seen, however, the evidence suggests that the process of mobilization in Quilalí was more complex than this. In many cases poor peasants did not mobilize independently against the wealthy, but rather alongside local elites whose authority was tacitly reinforced by FSLN guerrillas themselves. In other words, the relative success of the FSLN in gaining support in Quilalí can be attributed in part to the close community ties and leadership role of finqueros whose long-term interests did not necessarily coincide with the revolutionary program. At the same time, unlike the finqueros, who saw formal democracy as their principle goal, several poor peasants interviewed who collaborated and fought with the FSLN guerrillas report that they were attracted to

FSLN class-related discourse. In the words of one landless Quilalí peasant: "On 8 July 1979 I joined the FSLN guerrillas because I was convinced by their promises that we poor weren't going to be as poor as we are now. . . . They said that we were going to own things in common—the land, houses, animals; that we were going to have equality, which they always called communism."

In addition to peasants mobilized through cross-class and extended family networks, FSLN guerrillas also received support from peasants active in liberation theology, as discussed earlier, and families with historical ties to Sandino or anti-Somoza movements. One Quilalí resident who belonged to the latter category was Pedro Zamora, who was introduced to the anti-Somoza struggle by his father, a leader in a construction workers' union in northern Nicaragua in the 1950s. In 1960, Zamora participated in the failed barbudo guerrilla raid on Quilalí. Later, in Honduras he met early leaders of the FSLN:

> I saw that those men [the Sandinistas] were forging something better for the people. They didn't want to defeat a dictatorship to put another dictatorship in its place. They wanted a real change, a change that would be completely democratic; that we would all participate in democracy; that we would all give our opinions; that everyone would be taken into account; . . . that we are all one social class. That's what it was like in the environment where I grew up. I liked their ideas.

Zamora eventually moved to Quilalí to work as a foreman on a cattle ranch and served as an FSLN collaborator along with his wife. His sister in turn fought as an FSLN combatant in the city of Estelí and was killed by the National Guard.

In addition to historical collaborators, dozens more peasants joined the Sandinista insurrection in its final days as the balance of power shifted against Somoza and the diminished threat of the National Guard gave them the courage to openly mobilize against the regime for the first time, or because they saw in the local and national power vacuum opportunities to gain material benefits for themselves. Finally, it is also important to keep in mind that even on the eve of the revolution only a minority of Quilalí residents, perhaps one hundred or less, actively supported the FSLN guerrillas and the great majority of Quilalí peasants remained largely quiescent, as they had in earlier years.

The Insurrection

As the FSLN developed a small guerrilla presence in Quilalí and other zones of the northern and central mountains in the late 1970s, opposition to the Somoza regime was growing across Nicaragua. A portion of the Nicaraguan business sector, the Catholic church hierarchy, other Central American governments, and finally even the Carter administration distanced themselves or actively opposed the Somoza government. In early 1978 the assassination of popular anti-Somoza newspaper editor Pedro Joaquín Chamorro was followed by a national strike led by the business sector and the first urban uprising in Monimbó, an indigenous neighborhood in the town of Masaya. While the National Guard was able to soon crush the Masaya uprising, another series of spontaneous urban uprisings, guided and channeled by the FSLN, occurred in late August and early September in Estelí and other key cities. The National Guard response was again fierce. In Estelí, Somoza's airplanes dropped 500-pound bombs to quell the street fighting, and hundreds of civilians were killed in the aerial bombing and artillery shelling, or were summarily executed in National Guard cleanup operations following the pacification of the city (Booth 1985, 166).

More distant interior areas like Quilalí, however, were spared the brunt of combat and National Guard repression in late 1978 and early 1979. FSLN Northern Front guerrillas under Germán Pomares launched attacks and ambushes in the northern mountains, drawing

National Guard attention away from urban areas that strongly needed a respite. Compared to the intense fighting in the cities, Pomares's troops faced relatively light combat. They clashed with the National Guard in the town of El Jícaro, to the north of Quilalí, and later in the community of El Súngano which was bombed by National Guard. Despite the proximity of the National Guard, FSLN members from Estelí were also able to organize several clandestine cells of collaborators in the town of Quilalí who distributed pamphlets, operated safe houses, and relayed information to FSLN guerrillas. Later they organized small protests against the dictatorship and set tires on fire on Quilalí's main street.

In the final days of the Somoza regime, the barricades rose again in Estelí and many of Nicaragua's major cities and finally Managua itself. Quilalí peasants heard distant bombing, saw the military planes and helicopters pass overhead, and listened to news of the combat on their radios. On 17 July 1979 the announcement came over the radio that President Somoza had fled into exile and that his National Guard forces had collapsed. Two days later, as thousands of FSLN guerrillas marched triumphantly into Managua, the town of Quilalí was liberated in a somewhat less dramatic fashion. A small patrol of FSLN guerrillas entered the town and exchanged gunfire with a dozen or so National Guardsmen who were holed up in their headquarters, a fortified brick building a block from the central park. Later that night the National Guardsmen fled and when the Sandinistas found the building empty the next morning, they burned it down. Most of Quilalí's Somocista collaborators had already fled town in the days and months preceding the FSLN final offensive, but at least one National Guard informant was captured by the Sandinista guerrillas and killed on Quilalí's main street. The killing of this informer appears to be one of the few cases of "revolutionary justice" in Quilalí. Several Somoza supporters, such as the mayor, were also captured and jailed, but in the mayor's case, he was released after a few months and emigrated to the United States.

In assessing the defeat of the Somoza regime, there is debate as to how important a role Nicaragua's peasantry played in the insurrection. Gould (1990a) and Wickham-Crowley (1992) stress the key role the FSLN's five rural-based guerrilla fronts played in dispersing and weakening the National Guard, while in the Pacific coastal region, displaced cotton workers and other rural residents participated in the urban insurrections. Yet ultimately in northern and central Nicaragua it was urban residents who experienced the worst of the street fighting, bombardments, and National Guard repression. In all, probably not more than twenty-five Quilalí residents were killed on both sides during the insurrection. In contrast, in the city of Estelí entire neighborhoods rose up on three separate occasions to confront the National Guard, and thousands of people were killed during the insurrection. For Nicaragua as a whole, it is estimated that at least 35,000 people were killed in the insurrection, largely in urban areas (CEPAL 1981, 87).

The fact that violence and casualties were limited in Quilalí and other interior rural zones had several important consequences. First, it meant that many peasants did not identify the struggle and triumph against Somoza as directly their own. The great majority of Quilalí residents interviewed describe the events of 1979 as a rebellion carried out by largely by city dwellers, of which they have only second-hand knowledge. Also, because peasants in remote zones did not experience the same degree of repression that urban residents did, most did not share the sense of deep moral outrage against the National Guard and the Somoza regime found among many urban Nicaraguans. Very few peasants who lived in Quilalí in 1979 mention any National Guard abuses. In urban areas in contrast, anger at civilian deaths as well as the bonds formed during fierce street combat helped forge a commitment to the revolutionary process, among young people in particular, that was largely absent in Quilalí and other remote rural zones.

The First Months of FSLN Rule

In broad terms, the Sandinista government, which can be characterized as more anti-oligarchic than anticapitalist, promoted a mixed
economy in which ownership of industry and agriculture was to be
shared between the state, small producers, and the capitalist sector;
and sought nonalignment in the international arena. In its first
months in power, the FSLN expropriated factories and farms owned
by Somoza and his close associates, nationalized the banking system,
and established a government monopoly over foreign trade. Along
with expanding the role of the state, the FSLN was also obligated to
spend many of its limited material and human resources on simply re-
building Nicaragua's infrastructure as well as economic, governmental, and military structures. Portions of Nicaragua's major cities were
in ruins and many factories had been bombed and destroyed, bringing industrial production to a virtual standstill. National Guard bombardment and the insurrection against Somoza caused approximately
$480 million worth of property damage (CEPAL 1981, 35). Produc-
tive activities in Nicaragua's rural zones also had been disrupted during the insurrection and there were widespread food shortages and
unemployment. In Quilalí, many fields had lain fallow the first half of
the year because farmers were unwilling to plant in the tense, uncertain situation. Quilalí's large Somocista landowners smuggled thousands of head of cattle to Honduras to be sold and finally fled in the
weeks before the Somoza regime collapsed.

While in Quilalí, as in most of Nicaragua, there was widespread euphoria and celebration of the defeat of the forty-year Somoza dictatorship, the many demands on the new revolutionary government limited
the material and human resources available to the municipality. The
power vacuum created by the collapse of Somocista political and economic structures in Quilalí was largely filled by inexperienced personnel, many of whom were outsiders to the zone. Soon after taking

power, FSLN departmental authorities appointed Plutarco Olivares, an artisan originally from Estelí, to head Quilalí's new three-member municipal governing board that carried out many functions of the former mayor. Olivares, who had secretly collaborated with the FSLN before the revolution, was a relative newcomer to Quilalí and had little political or administrative experience.

In the first years of the revolution, departmental FSLN authorities also appointed a series of political secretaries to head the party in the Quilalí zone, few of whom were residents of the municipality. Most were young people from Estelí or Pacific coast cities who were committed to the revolution, but unfamiliar with the culture of Nicaragua's rural interior. Keller (1986, 228, 232) describes, for example, an urban ATC official who arrived in the municipality of Wiwilí in 1980 and gave long speeches full of jargon and slogans that put peasants to sleep and who alienated the population with his domineering attitude. In Quilalí, Gilberto Santana, originally from León, served as FSLN political secretary in the early 1980s. He came to the northern mountains for the first time as part of the 1980 literacy campaign and was assigned to Quilalí a year later. Santana describes his duties: "The [FSLN] political secretary was understood to be [Quilalí's] highest authority. This was not formally stated, but implicitly people recognized this. It was understood that the job of the political secretary was to coordinate the government, to offer people social support."

Santana recalls that resources from the national government were scarce in the early 1980s and that it was difficult to find local personnel with sufficient education and skills to fill administrative government posts. Out of necessity, some people who served under Somoza continued their functions under the FSLN, although they were not entirely sympathetic to the revolution. Keller (1986, 216) notes that in Wiwilí as well, rich merchants took control of Sandinista Defense Committees (Comités de Defensa Sandinista; CDSs) and at times manipulated them for personal financial gain.[6] As will be seen, in the following years this situation left the Sandinistas in a weak position to compete with the contra forces for the support and loyalty of the municipality's peasant population.

In the months following the defeat of Somoza, as the FSLN struggled to consolidate political and administrative control in Quilalí, the new Sandinista authorities were also forced to contend with and contain a series of raised expectations and demands on the part of the population. As we have seen, the Somoza regime provided few benefits to Quilalí peasants and peasants in turn expected little from the government, relying instead on extended family and community networks as well as a strong work ethic to ensure family survival. The violent overthrow of the Somoza dictatorship in 1979, however, and the sudden collapse of previous political, economic, and coercive structures meant that for the first time submerged aspirations and demands on the part of the poor were openly expressed.[7]

Many Quilalí peasants interviewed indicate that with the arrival of the revolution they expected that everything would be better. Some peasants explain that to them *better* meant little more than the normalization of their lives in Quilalí, an end to the tension, uncertainty, and violence of the final months of the Somoza regime. For other Quilalí poor peasants, the phrase "everything would be better" encompassed hopes that the revolution would provide banks loans, schools, roads, health services, and most importantly land. Such expectations on the part of Quilalí poor peasants were reinforced by Sandinista mobilizing rhetoric and the FSLN's presentation of itself as the vanguard of a popular nationalist revolution that was committed to bettering the lives of the poor. Some peasants appear to have taken such promises quite literally, with little awareness of the constraints that the FSLN would have to confront in carrying out such projects. Some peasants who joined the anti-Somoza insurrection, particularly in its final days, seem to have understood the revolution to mean an immediate redistribution of wealth in their favor. Ada Hernández, wife of Pedro Zamora, remembers: "The first guerrilla fighters came to break into our store. The stores were full of merchandise that they wanted to carry away. These were people who had been with the guerrillas two or three days. I stopped them. I said this would not continue. Some stores were looted, but we put a stop to it here." Where looting occurred in Quilalí, the new Sandinista authorities acted to halt these spontaneous actions by their supporters and impose discipline in support of broader revolutionary goals and social stability. Such looting was a relatively minor matter, however, in comparison to the conflicts over control of land that emerged in the weeks following the defeat of Somoza.

Land Invasions

Shortly after taking power, the FSLN passed decrees 3 and 38, which expropriated some 1.2 million MZ of land held by the Somoza family and its close associates—approximately 20 percent of Nicaragua's agricultural land (Deere and Marchetti 1981, 51). The average size of the farms expropriated was 1,083 MZ (Baumeister 1991, 238). In Quilalí roughly half the municipality's valley land, 13,200 MZ, was subject to expropriation under the decrees. Before Sandinista officials could act to establish state control over these haciendas, however, local peasants moved to claim part of the land for themselves.

In the final days of the Somoza regime, Quilalí's five large landowners abandoned their farms, and in Mauricio Portillo's case, smuggled out as many cattle as possible to Honduras. With the owners gone and the National Guard in disarray, peasants saw an opportunity to obtain land for themselves and acted quickly. The first group of peasants to seize land in Quilalí's river valley were the dozens of colonos who had rented land from the Somoza family in La Vigía. Shortly before the FSLN took power, the last National Guardsman stationed at La Vigía fled on his motorcycle with his girlfriend. With no visible authority in control of the hacienda, La Vigía's colonos held a meeting and gave each family a five-to-twenty MZ parcel of land. Some of the former colonos claim that before Somoza went into exile, he sent word that they were to be given the land. Although this cannot be verified, the colonos feel that Somoza's alleged final instructions added legitimacy to their occupation of his hacienda.

Soon after the La Vigía land takeover, a second series of land invasions occurred. Hundreds of peasants, many of them FSLN collaborators from Quilalí's river valley and neighboring areas, occupied a portion of Chon Molina's 5,000-MZ hacienda, Guaná. In this case, the invaders were a mixture of poor landless peasants and more opportunistic peasants who already owned farms. When officials from the newly created National Institute of Agrarian Reform (Instituto Nicaragüense de Reforma Agraria, INRA) discovered two of Quilalí's most important haciendas occupied by peasants, their response was to attempt to convince squatters to leave the land so that the farms could be converted into state cattle farms.[8]

This Sandinista policy decision to turn expropriated land into state farms was in turn shaped by the FSLN's commitment to national unity, external political and economic constraints, and internal policy debates (Deere et al. 1985, 75). Sandinista internal policy debates, which were never fully resolved during the FSLN's ten years in power, centered on two broad groups, the developmentalists *(desarrollistas)* and the pro-peasant group *(campesinistas)* (Kaimowitz 1986; Deere et al. 1985). The developmentalists, whose most well known proponent was Jaime Wheelock, the head of the Ministerio de Desarrollo Agropecuario y Reforma Agraria (Ministry of Agricultural Development and Agrarian Reform; MIDINRA), viewed Nicaragua's prerevolutionary rural structure as increasingly polarized between the capitalist agro-export sector and an impoverished semiproletariat and saw the proletarianization of the peasantry as inevitable and even preferable (Kaimowitz 1986, 102; Enriquez 1997, 32). The developmentalists, drawing upon the agricultural models of advanced socialist countries, sought to convert expropriated haciendas into state farms and concentrate resources on capital-intensive, high-technology agricultural projects. In contrast, policy makers sympathetic to the pro-peasant approach challenged the model of two antagonistic rural classes as an erroneous simplification of Nicaragua's complex rural structure and argued that developmentalists overlooked an economically important peasant capitalist sector that was particularly strong in the mountainous interior of Nicaragua (Baumeister and Neira Cuadra 1986; Kaimowitz 1986; Zalkin 1989). Campesinistas argued that the FSLN should meet peasant demands for land and provide greater technical assistance, resources, and credit to Nicaragua's middle and semiproletariat peasantry.

From 1979 until 1982, the viewpoint of the developmentalist policy makers predominated and influenced the FSLN to prioritize the development of state farms over the demands of the peasant sector. Sandinista policy makers were reluctant to turn expropriated land over to individual peasants because they felt that such a policy would be a step backward in terms of promoting greater cooperative development in agriculture and would set off further invasions and demands for land that would threaten the government's policy of national unity, a continuation of the FSLN's tactical wartime alliance with the bourgeoisie (Deere et al. 1985, 80). Policy makers were also influenced by economic concerns. FSLN authorities considered the continued production of agro-export crops and the hard currency they provided to be vital to national economic development. They feared that if large haciendas were handed over to poor peasants, peasants would divide the land into parcels to grow food crops and would no longer be available to meet the seasonal labor needs of export crops (Enriquez 1997, 32). Ideally, state farms were to become model farms that would generate economic surpluses for the government and stimulate the surrounding rural areas. State farmworkers would actively participate in running the farms and receive fair wages, as well as a number of social benefits they had been denied under the Somoza regime.

Confronted with land invasions in Quilalí in 1979, local and regional Sandinista officials followed national policy guidelines and employed their political and moral authority to convince squatters to abandon the land. Carlos Sánchez, a landless peasant from the river valley community of Jiquelite, fought for several months with Germán Pomares in the insurrection. Soon afterward he participated in the takeover at Guaná. He remembers: "After the owner and the National Guard left, we arrived [at Guaná]. We were a group of twenty [FSLN] combatants. We expected to receive twenty MZ of land. Instead the land was taken over by INRA, the government. They wanted to register us, give us worker cards. We could build our *ranchitos* by the old hacienda house, but they wouldn't lend us land to work." Sandinista authorities allowed the squatters to plant a corn and bean crop in the second half of 1979, but were firm in their decision to assume direct ownership of the hacienda. After the harvest, the invaders peacefully gave up their claims to the land. INRA took control of Guaná and the neighboring ranch Santa Rosa de Ventilla and began to administer them as part of the larger Laura Sofía Olívas Paz state farm complex.

On the La Vigía hacienda the outcome was quite different, however. It appears that the experience of La Vigía colonos in successfully resisting National Guard attempts to dislodge them gave them the confidence and determination to also withstand FSLN pressure to take the land under state control. Faced with the refusal of La Vigía peasants to relinquish the land, the FSLN never attempted to forcibly remove peasants, as the Somozas had done. Instead the FSLN reluctantly came to respect the colonos' de facto control of the hacienda, while continuing to pressure residents in the following years to work collectively and to share their land with poor peasants from other zones.

The First Phase of Agrarian Reform

In 1979, a total of 14,200 MZ, roughly 20 percent of the municipality's land, was expropriated and turned into state farms, approximately the same percentage of land that was confiscated in Nicaragua as a whole. Of the total land expropriated in 1979, 13,200 MZ (93%) belonged to the five large landowners whose haciendas dominated Quilalí's river valley, where the pattern of landholding resembled that of Nicaragua's Pacific coast, with its large haciendas and concentration of landless peasants. An additional 1,000 MZ were expropriated from eight or so finquero-merchants, most of whom had previously held the position of mayor or juez de mesta and were associated with the Somoza regime. Several of these individuals had also left the country in 1979. Except for these latter expropriations, the twenty-seven mountain communities to the north and west of Quilalí, where more than half of the municipality's poor peasants lived, were relatively untouched by land reform. They remained the stronghold of finqueros and middle peasants, a structure typical of other zones near or along the agricultural frontier.

One of the most important results of this initial phase of land reform in Quilalí was the collapse of the once dominant terrateniente class.[9] As might be expected, these large landowners were deeply resentful of the actions of the FSLN. In the words of a member of a wealthy Ocotal family who had a number of farms expropriated in Quilalí and the rest of the Segovias: "I was a good man, a decent hardworking man. Those communists [the Sandinistas] stole my land without justification." Most of these landowners went into exile abroad, their economic and political power diminished for at least the time being. Some of them later lent their financial and moral support to the counterrevolution, but few participated directly in the creation or administration of the contras, and terratenientes were largely absent from the violent conflict that ensued. But while the first phase of Sandinista land reform effectively dismantled Quilalí's sector of large landowners, the locally powerful finquero sector was left mainly intact. After the initial phase of expropriations in Quilalí, these wealthy farmers and merchants still controlled roughly 25,000 MZ (36%) of Quilalí's farmland and pasture and would continue to assert economic and social influence in the municipality throughout the 1980s.

A third important result of the initial phase of land reform is that with its decision not to respond to peasant demands for land in 1979 the FSLN lost an important opportunity to build political support for the revolution among poor peasants in the critically short period before the counterrevolution became active. In the following years, as will be seen, the performance of state farms was disappointing, and by 1983 the FSLN had shifted policy and began to dismember state farms to distribute land to peasants organized in agricultural cooperatives. By that time, however, the climate of deepening political and military polarization and the requirement that peasants farm collectively meant that receiving land from the FSLN was not an attractive option to many Quilalí peasants. As will be shown, frustrations over the nature of Sandinista land reform were one grievance that made some landless peasants receptive to contra recruitment efforts.

Other FSLN Rural Policies

In addition to land reform, another important component of Sandinista rural policy was an outpouring of rural credit, which led to a 600 percent increase in the credit available to small producers the first year of the revolution (cited in Martinez 1993, 477). Under Somoza only Quilalí's wealthiest producers had access to formal credit. Poor and middle peasants could usually only obtain informal loans from merchants and finqueros by selling their harvest in advance at below market prices and by paying interest rates of 2 to 5 percent a month. For the spring planting of 1980, however, bank officials report that the FSLN gave credit to over 500 poor, middle, and wealthy peasants in

Quilalí. Well-off producers generally applied for credit individually, while middle and poor peasants joined Credit and Service Cooperatives, (Cooperativas de Credito y Servicios, CCSs). In CCSs, members applied for credit as a group, farmed individually, and then repaid the loan jointly. Membership in a CCS was not obligatory, but in Quilalí seems to have been an informal criterion for poor peasants to receive credit. By 1981 almost 400 Quilalí peasants belonged to nine CCSs (MIDINRA 1984d, 50). In rural Nicaragua as a whole, 43,265 peasants were organized in CCSs by 1983 (Deere et al. 1985, 97).

Quilalí's nine CCSs were only one part of an explosion of grassroots organizations in the first years of the revolution that reached even remote zones like Quilalí. In the months following the defeat of Somoza, FSLN supporters in Quilalí initiated half a dozen new organizations modeled after national structures.[10] These organizations included Sandinista Defense Committees, militias, the Luisa Amanda Espinosa Association of Nicaraguan Women (Asociación de Mujeres Nicaragüenses Luisa Amanda Espinosa, AMNLAE), the Sandinista Youth Organization (Juventud Sandinista–19 de Julio), the Association of Rural Workers, and later the National Union of Farmers and Ranchers (Unión Nacional de Agricultores y Ganaderos, UNAG).

In accordance with national Sandinista directives, Quilalí residents formed CDSs, which had first emerged in urban areas during the insurrection to provide support for FSLN combatants and wounded civilians, by neighborhood in the town of Quilalí and in rural communities. According to the original organizers, the role of the CDSs was to coordinate the rationing of food supplies, a variety of community projects, and the 1980 literacy campaign, as well as to maintain "revolutionary vigilance"—that, is to detect counterrevolutionary activities. Volunteer militias were also created in the town of Quilalí and in a number of outlying rural communities, although participants remember that training was minimal and weapons were often in short supply.

To reactivate agricultural production, in 1979 local Sandinista activists organized peasants into several loosely structured work collectives, although such spontaneous grassroots organizing was not always encouraged by the FSLN (Ortega 1989, 206). Ada Hernández and her husband, Pedro Zamora, formed such a collective to plant beans on the land of Ada's father, who was in exile in Costa Rica. According to Zamora: "It wasn't really an organized cooperative. It was the need to face the crisis and improve things. We organized a collective in San Bartolo with 110 people. It was beautiful to see, a huge group of people working together." As it turned out, however, Hernández's father returned from exile in Costa Rica no longer in favor of the revolution. According to Ada, when her father found neighboring peasants farming his land, he cried, "this is communism!" and angrily demanded that the collective disband. While some work collectives dissolved once the immediate need for food had been met, in other cases such as the San Bartolo group, collectives formed the basis for more formal agricultural cooperatives established after 1982.

While participation in all these organizations was voluntary, in the first years of the revolution residents remember that there was a degree of social and political pressure to join militias and mass organizations. As it turned out, many of these organizations weakened or disintegrated all together after the first year of the revolution because of a combination of factors. First, these organizations were generally imposed from the outside and structured according to national guidelines and did not necessarily respond to the felt needs of the community. In addition, as will be seen, popular organizations were weakened because of lack of sustained support from the FSLN and the growing military pressures in the municipality.

One important exception to this was UNAG, which maintained a strong base of peasant support in the municipality throughout the 1980s. UNAG was created in 1981 as a breakaway organization from the ATC, the Sandinista rural union that originally included both rural wage workers and peasants. After 1981, ATC membership was limited to rural workers, largely those on state farms, while UNAG's membership included small, middle, and by 1984, large producers. Within several years of its creation, UNAG had 42,000 members nationwide (Luciak 1995, 80). In Quilalí, local UNAG representatives estimate that at its height in the mid-1980s roughly 700 Quilalí peasants, or almost one half of all producers, were members of UNAG. UNAG leaders attribute the organization's success in Quilalí to its relative autonomy from the FSLN, which allowed it to better represent peasant demands in national policy debates, and its practical focus on the problems of peasants through technical assistance and concrete development projects (79).

In addition to these new organizations, in the first two years of the revolution the FSLN also launched a series of educational and health projects in Quilalí. In 1980 the national literacy campaign brought some eighty volunteer teachers to the most remote areas of the municipality. Quilalí Sandinista representatives estimate that in this single campaign they were able to substantially reduce illiteracy in Quilalí, perhaps by as much as 30 or 40 percent. The FSLN also constructed several new schools in town, and nine schools in rural communities. By 1984 the municipality had over 1,800 children enrolled in twenty-five schools (MIDINRA 1984d, 27). In addition, over 700 adults attended evening classes to learn to read and write and completed first through third grade in 101 rural Centers for Popular Education (28). The new revolutionary government also began a program to train community health promoters, who were sent out into the communities to give vaccinations. Two new rural health centers were established in El Súngano, in the northern mountains, and near La Vigía, in Quilalí's river valley. In the town of Quilalí, a health center was built on the remains of the National Guard headquarters, which had been burnt to the ground by Sandinista guerrillas. Other Sandinista projects included the construction of a high school and a baseball field on the edge of town, as well as the extension of water services in town and street repairs.

Such FSLN programs in the first years of the revolution had wide support among Quilalí's population. To the present day, many Quilalí peasants, including some who later supported the contras, have positive memories of the literacy campaign in particular and comment that "it was beautiful." Peasants from more remote mountain communities report that the visits by literacy volunteers and health promoters were often the first access to education and government services they ever had, and such contacts offered peasants a glimpse of the larger world beyond their isolated communities. For families who lived outside of Quilalí's town limits and the river valley, however, these positive contacts with the revolution were extremely brief and the new opportunities and benefits they brought were soon wiped out by political violence.

FSLN Supporters

As we have seen, Quilalí residents who collaborated and fought with the FSLN in the 1970s were a heterogeneous group. They included a small group of finqueros deliberately recruited by FSLN guerrillas; peasants acting out of religious commitment; families with historical ties to Sandino and the anti-Somoza struggle; and young people in contact with urban student movements. While key aspects of the FSLN's rural revolutionary program—land reform and rural credit—primarily benefited poor peasants, who formed the core of the Sandinistas' social base in the municipality, a small number of well-off individuals also supported the revolution and assumed leadership roles in the new mass organizations and community projects. Members of one well-off San Bartolo family, for example, helped found the Quilalí branch of UNAG, and the women's organization AMNLAE.

Sandinista informants estimate that in the municipality of Quilalí some 450 residents were affiliated with the FSLN, 150 of whom were full members *(militantes)*. In addition to the sectors described above, Sandinista community leaders report that other important bases of support for the party were artisans and small merchants based in the town of Quilalí, as well as teachers, health workers, and local government employees. Also, as will be discussed in chapter 5, through the development of an extensive cooperative sector the FSLN was able to consolidate support among many of those landless poor in Quilalí's river valley who were relatively unconnected to local elites. In addition, peasants from zones of the western Segovias such as Telpaneca and Cusmapa, who independently migrated to Quilalí after 1979 or were encouraged to do so by the FSLN, provided a strong base of support for the party. One government report suggests that with the conflicts they experienced with large landowners in their native communities still fresh in their minds, these migrants were more receptive to revolutionary discourse (MIDINRA 1986).

Quilalí residents who had no earlier ties to either the FSLN or liberation theology report that personal relationships, a process of education and "consciousness raising," and their belief in the FSLN's commitment to the poor majority influenced them to become Sandinista supporters in the first several years of the revolution. Daniel López is a poor peasant whose family owned a small piece of land in Quilalí's river valley and who was only able to attend school for a year. He later felt frustrated by his lack of education and came to believe that Quilalí's wealthy sector had taken advantage of the ignorance of poor peasants like himself: "They [the rich] didn't want us to learn, so that we wouldn't demand our rights."

In 1980, friend and Sandinista activist Pedro Zamora convinced López to participate in the San Bartolo agricultural collective and in the organization of the literacy campaign in his community. As we have seen, most Quilalí peasants viewed the 1980 literacy campaign as a positive experience, yet in many cases their desire for education did not extend beyond basic literacy skills. Other peasants like Daniel López, however, had a more profound yearning for knowledge and a curiosity to learn about the world beyond their immediate experience. The revolution offered such individuals the opportunity to attend accelerated adult education classes in order to complete their elementary school degree, as well as the opportunity to travel and attend seminars and training courses outside Quilalí. López remembers: "I more or less knew how to read, but I wanted to learn more. I felt happy to learn about new things. They [FSLN representatives] took me to visit various parts of Nicaragua, to a training school in Ocotal. I was hoping to receive my sixth grade diploma when the attack on El Coco came."

A number of these peasants in fact used their newfound knowledge to become teachers themselves. According to these Sandinista supporters, the FSLN offered them not simply a formal education, but also the means by which to understand and analyze the world around them, a new vision of the political, economic, and social realities of Quilalí and Nicaragua as whole. In language similar to that used by peasants active in liberation theology groups, these pro-Sandinista peasants describe themselves as "submissive" and "asleep" before the revolution. They report that they blindly accepted the views of their patrons before the FSLN, through a process of consciousness raising, "awakened" them to historical and structural injustices and the need to defend their rights. They came to believe that that the wealth of a few and the poverty of the majority was not inevitable or willed by God, but the product of unjust economic, political, and social structures. They also came to employ an explicitly class-based discourse and identify themselves as members of a larger popular class of campesinos and urban workers with whom they shared a series of common interests.

Specific aspects of the new revolutionary ideology that resonated with pro-revolutionary Quilalí peasants were the Sandinista condemnation of exploitation of the poor and its emphasis on equality; its nationalist stance and promotion of democracy; and most important, the FSLN's policies and concrete projects aimed at bettering the lives of Nicaragua's poor majority.[11] As we have seen, in prerevolutionary Quilalí large landowners and finqueros were generally viewed in their communities as good men who provided work and assistance to poor and middle peasants and served as a model to emulate. Sandinista representatives in Quilalí, however, suggested that the wealthy were motivated by self-interest, not generosity, in their treatment of poor peasants. They challenged the construct of class harmony that prevailed in Quilalí and argued that many of Nicaragua's elites accumulated their wealth by unethical and illegal means at the expense of the poor. This message resonated in particular with the minority of pro-Sandinista informants, some 15 percent of those interviewed, whose families had lost all or part of their land through debt before the revolution. Other Sandinista supporters believe that such predatory practices, while relatively uncommon in the municipality of Quilalí, were widespread in other regions of Nicaragua. Under this discourse of class conflict, which many FSLN supporters in Quilalí came to share, practices such as buying a poor peasant's crop in advance at a low price and charging high interest rates for loans were now denounced as exploitation. In the words of former colono Noris Pardo: "At that time we [poor peasants] were ignorant of so many things. I didn't know what exploitation was. Before the revolution, I was so naive that I thought that we the campesinos were exploiting the terrateniente, that he was doing us a favor when he lent us land. Then we came to realize that we poor were the ones who were being exploited."

The new revolutionary ideology also explicitly and implicitly questioned the social and economic hierarchy on which Quilalí's power structures rested. Sandinista representatives challenged class distinctions by referring to all Quilalí residents as *compañeros* and set the example that no longer were the wealthy to be automatically treated with deference and respect. Peasants were encouraged for the first time to organize through the ATC and UNAG and under certain circumstances to confront their patrons about wages and working conditions. Many pro-revolutionary peasants came to hold the ideal that "we would all be one social class" and believe that injustice was rooted not simply in the behavior of local elites, but in broader national and international economic structures. In the words of Daniel López: "To speak frankly, in capitalist countries the poor every day become poorer and the rich richer. Every day the poor are more and more suffocated."

In addition, a number of pro-Sandinista informants credit the FSLN with bringing, for the first time in history, democracy and opportunities for democratic participation to Nicaragua. They point with approval to the FSLN's role in defeating the Somoza regime, popular organizations such as the UNAG and AMNLAE, and the 1984 and 1990 elections. More than half of pro-Sandinistas interviewed also list the FSLN's nationalism as a positive aspect of the revolutionary program. While it appears that local concerns over the distribution of land, resources, services, and power were of the greatest importance to peasants, after 1979 many pro-Sandinista peasants also began identify with national and international issues. A former Sandinista mayor states: "We liked it when they [the FSLN] talked about liberty, about political independence [for Nicaragua]. We knew that Nicaragua was a dominated country."

Finally, at the heart of these peasants' support for the revolutionary process was the belief that the FSLN was the first government in the history of Nicaragua to support and defend the rights of Nicaragua's rural and urban poor majority. Every pro-Sandinista Quilalí resident interviewed listed at least three specific FSLN policies or projects—including land reform, education, credit, health, housing, women's projects, children's kitchens, and so forth—which they themselves or other municipality residents had benefited from as concrete evidence of the FSLN's commitment to the poor. As a poor peasant FSLN supporter explains: "We liked various points of the historical program; that it would be a government of workers. They [the Sandinistas] explained that they fought so that the campesinos would have land; so that the workers would participate in running the factories; so that we would have a better life, more schools, more medical care."

In analyzing peasant support for the Sandinista revolution, proponents of the rational peasant school of thought might well argue that Quilalí peasants who supported the FSLN did so largely in return for selective material incentives such as land, housing, and credit listed above, and not for abstract, moral reasons of social justice. As will be shown in chapter 5, it certainly is true that pro-Sandinista peasants, like all Quilalí peasants, were deeply concerned with ensuring their own survival and the well-being of their families. Likewise, a majority of FSLN supporters in the municipality received some type of direct benefits and subsidies from the revolution. A number of these benefits, however—such as access to bank credit, improved health care, and basic educational opportunities—were collective and widely available in the municipality to peasants of varying ideological sympathies. Neither do other more selective benefits provided by the FSLN fully explain the Quilalí pro-Sandinista commitment to the revolution, particularly the sacrifices many FSLN supporters made during the 1980s—working on community projects under difficult and dangerous conditions for little or no remuneration and extensive voluntary participation in military service. Rather this study argues that a majority of pro-Sandinista peasants supported the FSLN both because of its material benefits and services that favored the poor and because on an ideological level they shared to some degree the revolutionary vision of a more egalitarian society in which the needs of the poor majority would have priority. A transformation of identity took place in which peasants came to see themselves not simply as members of a particular family or rural community, but also as participants in a larger struggle in defense of collective class and national interests.

Chapter 4

Rise of the MILPAs

As WE have seen, even in remote areas of Nicaragua's interior such as Quilalí, the first year of the revolution brought rapid changes to many peasants' lives. In the space of a few weeks, Somoza's government collapsed and many of his wealthy supporters abandoned Quilalí for exile abroad. In the following months, Quilalí's large haciendas were occupied by peasant squatters or converted into state farms. For the first time in their lives, hundreds of peasants received bank loans to plant crops and participated in community organizations, health and education projects, and armed militias. Many Quilalí peasants celebrated the end of the forty-year dictatorship and describe this period as a "beautiful" time full of energy, excitement, and new possibilities. To other Quilalí residents, however, these changes were abrupt, imposed by urban outsiders, and appeared to challenge established economic and social power structures. A counterreaction arose among those well-off sectors who felt their interests threatened by the revolution, and in Quilalí it was unusually swift and violent.

On 23 July 1980, just over a year after the FSLN took power, an armed group led by the sons of local finqueros launched an attack on the town of Quilalí. They called themselves an Anti-Sandinista Popular Militia (Milicia Popular Anti-Sandinista, MILPA ["cornfield"]).[1] Although the MILPA was unable to take the town and quickly retreated, this 1980 raid on Quilalí was the opening salvo of a bitter ten-year war in Nicaragua's rural interior. In Quilalí the leaders of the first counterrevolutionary MILPAs, also known as *chilotes* (young ears of corn), were many of the same finqueros who had fought in the FSLN's Northern Front during the insurrection against Somoza, but who had not necessarily supported the Sandinista revolutionary program. These ex-combatants were unwilling to accept the central authority of the FSLN and resentful because they did not receive the power or material rewards they expected. Above all else, they felt that their economic aspirations and local status were threatened by Sandinista land expropriations and market interventions, the FSLN's promotion of mass organizations, and a revolutionary ideology that sought to mobilize the poor. These ex-guerrillas chose to take up arms, the method of struggle they were most familiar with, to halt revolutionary transformation in the mountains and promote procedural democracy and a free market economy. Although their actions were militarily insignificant, in the long run MILPA leaders, who by 1982 had formally joined the U.S.-sponsored contra forces organizing along the Honduran border, served as important intermediaries between ex–National Guardsmen and Nicaragua's rural population and helped legitimize the contra forces as protagonists of a "peasant struggle."

Finquero Discontent

As table 4.1 suggests, the group of finqueros from Quilalí and neighboring areas who first organized the MILPAs shared very similar family histories, life experiences, and ideological beliefs. In the municipality of Quilalí, where approximately seventy finqueros represented less than 10 percent of rural producers, the MILPA leaders were sons of the most well off families in this sector. In spite of their relatively privileged background, these finqueros stress the common background and interests they share with Quilalí's poor campesino majority.[2] Many refer to their families' impoverished roots and attribute what their families have achieved to hard work and sacrifice. A study of the rural department of Jinotega summarizes this finquero perspective, "he [the finquero] went into the mountains with a faith that has accompanied him in all of life's difficulties, without trucks, without neighbors, without a house, without a business those first years. For this, he [believes that he] deserves all he has" (CIERA 1981a, 23).

Antonio Mendoza, a MILPA leader and later contra commander from Quilalí, remembers that his grandfather regularly walked for days through the mountains of northern Nicaragua selling pigs and raw sugar. According to Mendoza, through hard work and personal sacrifice his family was able to gradually expand their landholdings. By the time Mendoza was born, the family was well established economically, but continued to live relatively frugally and even young children like Mendoza were expected to work to earn their keep: "I carried water from the river with my burro and sold the jugs at a peso each. I would get up at three in the morning and by six in the morning I had made four trips and had four pesos. I handed the money over to my mother for the expenses of the day. That's how I managed to complete elementary school."

Other Quilalí MILPA leaders were unable to complete their elementary school education because their fathers placed little importance on education and preferred to have their sons work full-time on the farm. The majority of these young men, however, did complete enough school to learn to basic reading and math skills. Like many Quilalí residents in the 1970s, these finqueros saw the municipality as a rich and fertile zone. Mendoza remembers: "[Quilalí] was a very productive zone. . . . It was a pleasure in those times to see the

Table 4.1
Key MILPA-Contra Leaders

Name	Place of Origin	Status and Family Background	Contra Regional Command Led (1987)*
Encarnación BALDIVIA Chavarría, "Tigrillo"	Carmen del Pita (Jinotega)	Sharecropper(?); ex-FSLN soldier (brother was also head of a regional command)	Rafaela Herrera Regional Command
Luis FLEY González, "Jhonson"	Matagalpa	Merchant; well-off rural family	15th of September Regional Command
Freddy GADEA, "Coral"	Quilalí (Nueva Segovia)	Well-off coffee grower and merchant; ex-FSLN combatant	Quilalí Regional Command
Israel GALEANO Cornejo, "Franklyn"	Jinotega	Well-off cattle rancher and coffee grower; family owned 6,000 MZ; recruited by Tigrillo in 1982; 8 brothers were contra commanders	Jorge Salazar Regional Command #2
Pedro Joaquín GONZÁLEZ, "Dimas"	Matagalpa	Well-off rural family; ex-FSLN combatant	Killed in 1980
Diógenes MEMBREÑO Hernández, "Fernando"	Matiguás (Matagalpa)	Well-off cattle rancher and merchant; pentecostal pastor	Jorge Salazar Regional Command #3

Name	Location	Description	Regional Command
Justo Pastor MEZA Aguilar, "Denis"	Yalí (Jinotega)	Well-off coffee grower; ex-FSLN collaborator; at least 5 close relatives were also MILPA/contra leaders	Santiago Meza Regional Command
Tirzo Ramón MORENO Aguilar, "Rigoberto"	Yalí/Wiwilí (Jinotega)	Cattle rancher and merchant; ex-FSLN collaborator; friend of Dimas; at least 23 relatives fought with the contras	Jorge Salazar Regional Command #1
Oscar SOBALVARRO García, "Rubén"	Jinotega	Well-off rural family	Salvador Pérez Regional Command
Marvin ZELAYA Zeledón, "Douglas"	Quilalí (Nueva Segovia)	Well-off coffee grower and merchant; ex-FSLN combatant	Pedro Joaquín González Regional Command

* Each regional command had from 800 to 1,000 troops.

Sources: U.S. Department of State (1988), Morales (1989), Dillon (1991), and Mendoza (1990).

campesinos at three o'clock, four o'clock in the morning entering Quilalí with buckets of milk; campesinos coming and going in ox-carts; ten or twelve mules loaded down with coffee." Many of these young men were eager to take advantage of the opportunities the municipality offered. In the words of Mendoza: "Like my father I wanted to be a good merchant and to farm the land. To be a good farmer you have to know about everything. I wanted to learn about carpentry, bricklaying, how to make harnesses and oxcarts. . . . I was envious. I liked money."

In the years immediately before the revolution, sons of finqueros in Quilalí perceived themselves to be in an upward spiral of accumulation. They report that with access to family money or bank loans and land it was relatively easy to make a profit during the Somoza era. Mendoza explains: "I bought a coffee farm. . . . The price of coffee rose to a little over 100 cordobas per quintal. I earned 300,000 cordobas [$42,857] that year. . . . I lived a comfortable life with everything my own. In 1976 I had two trucks, a Toyota pickup and a Toyota diesel jeep. I had my farm and a warehouse in town." As was suggested earlier, in Quilalí and other interior zones of Nicaragua it appears that coffee and cattle enabled at least a minority of producers to advance economically and that such zones were characterized by "expansive economies" and "a high level of upward economic mobility" (Escuela de Sociología–UCA 1987, 8).

Most of these young men, who were in their early to mid-twenties, had also fought at least a few months as FSLN guerrillas and were charismatic and ambitious natural leaders. As we have seen, when FSLN guerrillas began recruiting in Quilalí in the mid-1970s, finqueros opposed the Somoza regime primarily on political, not economic grounds. According to Mendoza, in 1976 FSLN guerrillas Germán Pomares, Francisco Rivera ("El Zorro"), and Jaime Meza convinced him to join the FSLN. Like other ex-FSLN combatants who turned against the revolution, Mendoza is adamant that at the time he understood the goal of the FSLN to be only formal democracy and not the "communist" policies that followed. Mendoza states that his FSLN commander, Germán Pomares, was "a personal enemy of Somoza's National Guard. He was no brilliant politician. . . . He didn't have any communist or Marxist ideals. . . . We dreamed of having a democracy, not the same as, but better than Costa Rica." As discussed earlier, in joining the FSLN, finqueros like Mendoza may also have been motivated by a calculation of their own personal and economic interests and the lack of alternative organized opposition to the Somoza regime.

MILPA leaders from Quilalí report that after taking power the FSLN commonly sent ex-guerrillas of rural origin to marginal military and police posts in interior zones. Some of these ex-FSLN rural guerrillas, who believed that they played a vital part in the defeat of the Somoza government, were not happy to be relegated to the role of poorly paid local officials. In contrast, they complain, better educated middle- and upper-class FSLN combatants and collaborators from the cities were given the most attractive political and administrative positions, and they argue that such policies were typical of generalized class and antirural bias on the part of FSLN officials whose origins and perspectives were predominantly urban.

FSLN representatives from Quilalí who knew these ex-combatants offer a different interpretation of events. According to these sources, many of these rural ex-FSLN combatants were unable to adjust to the postinsurrection discipline and centralized authority of the FSLN (CIERA 1989, 6:247–48). Alcohol abuse was common and many ex-combatants missed the autonomy and authority that they had enjoyed as guerrillas. Quilalí Sandinistas also suggest that these ex-guerrillas expected special material rewards and privileges for their role in the insurrection. According to Quilalí's former FSLN mayor, Plutarco Olivares: "Some [former FSLN combatants] thought that because they fought with the FSLN they were going to receive privileges, farms, land. . . . They asked for farms and other things. The government said no, and they got angry and left [for the counterrevolution]." It should be noted that MILPA leaders themselves strongly deny that they sought personal gain when they joined the FSLN guerrillas or that this was a factor in their subsequent decision to organize the MILPAs.

An excellent illustration of these issues lies in the story of the man many northern peasants consider to be the founder of the MILPA bands, Pedro Joaquín González. González, whose pseudonym was Dimas, came from a well-off Matagalpa coffee-growing and ranching family. As a teenager he joined the Sandinista guerrillas operating in the northern mountains of Nicaragua and fought under Germán Pomares for several years. After the FSLN victory, González was given command of Quilalí's Sandinista military forces. To anti-Sandinista Quilalí peasants, González is an almost mythical figure, remembered as a striking man with a long, thick beard and as a skilled fighter, and it is not always easy to separate fact from fiction. According to the U.S. State Department (1988, 35) biography of González, he broke with the FSLN because "the makeup of the new Sandinista Army General Staff favored men of upper class or aristocratic background and not the sons of the 'authentic people,'" as González considered himself. As suggested earlier, González may well have expected a more important posting than Quilalí after his years with the FSLN guerrillas.

Other observers such as former Sandinista mayor Plutarco Olivares, who worked with González, believe, however, that his difficulties were rooted in discipline problems and a lack of ideological commitment to the revolution:

> He [González] got drunk and fired off his .45 when some school children were passing by. The Ocotal police took his pistol away and threw him in jail. . . . From then on he had continuous arguments with [a Sandinista official] until he finally went to the mountains [as a MILPA guerrilla]. . . . He had no reason to go to the mountains. He would have been promoted, maybe even to colonel, but he lacked political clarity.

Although specific details on González's lack of "political clarity" are not available, it is likely that González, like other ex-FSLN guerrillas from the interior, joined the FSLN in a tactical alliance to defeat Somoza and was not necessarily in agreement with key aspects of the Sandinista revolutionary program. It is difficult to determine after the fact whether MILPA leaders were truly "deceived" by the FSLN before 1979. However, what is clear and of great importance in the struggle that followed is that in their later discourse MILPA leaders portrayed Sandinista policies as betrayal, and this interpretation of events came to be widely accepted among anti-Sandinistas in Quilalí.

Conflicts over Land Reform

The Sandinista program that finqueros most strongly objected to was land reform, which even some FSLN policy makers themselves have criticized as "arbitrary" and "bureaucratic," and as such, a key source of tension in the countryside.[3] In Quilalí and neighboring zones, however, land reform in the first year of the revolution clearly targeted Somoza supporters. In the initial phase of land reform in Quilalí, from 1979 to 1980, approximately 14,200 MZ of land were expropriated. Roughly 93 percent of this land, almost 13,200 MZ, was taken from just five terratenientes, each of whom owned from 1,000 to 5,000 MZ of land in Quilalí's river valley. The remaining 1,000 MZ of land were expropriated from eight well-off merchant-finquero families, all of whom Quilalí informants identify as having had some formal link to the Somoza regime, although in at least three cases the families were politically divided. Some older members supported the Somoza government, while one or more younger male family members had collaborated or fought with the FSLN guerrillas.

The most well-known expropriation in this latter category was that of Ernesto Reyes, who owned several medium-sized cattle ranches and a modern 375-MZ coffee farm in the western sector of the municipality. Several of his sons fought with Germán Pomares in the FSLN's Northern Front, but according to Sandinista informants, Reyes himself was a Substitute Deputy for Somoza's Liberal Nationalist Party in the National Assembly. FSLN authorities took possession of his coffee farm in late 1979, apparently without ever formally registering the expropriation, and turned it into a state farm administered from the nearby town of San Juan del Río Coco. Quilalí residents offer differing explanations as to why the decision to confiscate the farm was taken. Sandinistas emphasize that the elder Reyes was a Somoza supporter and that workers on the farm pressured the government to expropriate the land. Other Quilalí informants suggest that the action was the result of "envy" on the part of FSLN officials, or a desire to punish Reyes for his sons' active participation in antigovernment activities by late 1979.

Just over a year after this initial wave of confiscations in Quilalí, in July 1981 the FSLN passed decree no. 782, which gave the government legal authorization to expropriate idle, underutilized, or rented land of estates over 500 MZ on the Pacific coast, and over 1,000 MZ in the interior.[4] In the case of the municipality of Quilalí, after 1980 there remained no more privately owned farms 1,000 MZ or larger. In theory all Quilalí landholders were excluded from legal expropriation until a new agrarian reform law was passed in 1986 that eliminated the lower size limit on farms that could be expropriated.

Despite the 1981 law, however, from 1983 to 1985 in Quilalí Sandinista officials appear to have taken de facto control of at least a dozen farms ranging in size from 100 to 500 MZ without legally registering the expropriations. In interviews, informants suggest two possible explanations for these apparently extralegal expropriations by the FSLN of land and in some cases animals and vehicles as well. First, Sandinista officials may have used expropriations as a political instrument to attempt to control or punish rural support for the contras.[5] In at least four of these expropriations the owner and most immediate male family members had joined the contras as foot soldiers or mid-level commanders. A second reason that the land may have been taken over by the government was that with most of the men of these families off fighting with the contras, the farms appear to have been partly or completely abandoned by the women and children left behind. In another well-known case in 1985, the FSLN, in need of land in San Bartolo on which to settle evacuated peasants, attempted to purchase a farm owned by a member of a well-known finquero family who was an opponent of the FSLN. The man refused to negotiate a sale price for his farm, and it was finally taken from him by the government without compensation. That same year several additional farms were seized for reasons of public utility and the FSLN negotiated compensation with owners, or in at least one case, offered the owner another farm in exchange.

It is important to emphasize that while the FSLN's "unjust" expropriations became a rallying cry in Quilalí for the fledgling MILPA bands, less than a dozen merchant-finqueros lost their land during the critical period from 1979 to 1981 when the MILPA bands formed. The later, possibly politically motivated expropriations, did not occur until 1983 to 1985, when the war was already in full swing in the municipality of Quilalí.[6] That is to say, the timing strongly suggests that while these expropriations may have further intensified elite resentment against the FSLN, they were essentially a reaction to the MILPA (and later contra) activities and not a root cause of them.[7] The relatively limited direct impact of Sandinista land expropriations on the finquero sector is reflected in national trends as well. From 1978 to 1988 the percentage of agricultural land held in farms from 200 to 500 MZ dropped only slightly (from 16.2% to 13.5%), and land held by farms from 50 to 200 MZ fell less than 2 percent (from 30.1% to 28.4%) (Wheelock 1990, 115, table 7).

Keeping in mind that expropriations directed at finqueros were limited in scope, those MILPA leaders whose immediate family members did lose property and goods considered it a deep injustice. More than a decade later many are still able to recite from memory the possessions they lost. MILPA leader Mendoza describes the moment in which he discovered that his grandparents' coffee farm near San Juan del Río Coco had been expropriated:

> I went to my mother's house to visit her. I asked her about our truck. I asked about the oxen I had left there. I asked her about all our possessions. With tears in her eyes she responded, "I told you it was communism and you said it wasn't. Today can't you see what they've done with our property. Eighty families have occupied our land, taking two MZ each." . . . And I was filled with anger, a personal grudge against the Sandinistas. I made my final decision to go [and join the MILPA guerrillas].

Ernesto Reyes, whose coffee farm was confiscated, believes that the FSLN was not simply targeting him as an individual, but rather was attempting to destroy Quilalí's well-off citizens as a class:

> When they [the Sandinistas] saw that we had money, they became our enemies. They kicked us off our farm, out of our house by force. They manhandled us with weapons. . . . Everyone who had a little bit of money to live more or less comfortably, they robbed. It wasn't only us that they robbed; because if they had only stolen from us maybe we would have asked why. But it wasn't only us, it was everyone, and we had to fight back.

In reality, large landowners and the finqueros who lost their land in Quilalí were only a small fraction of the municipality's landowning population. Yet, in the inwardly focused zone of Quilalí, many of those affected, such as the Reyes, were prominent and respected members of family and community networks. As fears deepened among some elites that their class interests were under attack, these expropriations stood as examples of what the FSLN might do, in spite of all reassurances and legislation to the contrary.[8] Even those finqueros who did not directly fear that they would lose their farms still identified with those friends and family whose land had been expropriated. For ex-Sandinista guerrillas in particular, when abstract concepts like "revolution," "anti-imperialism," and "people's power" competed with concrete, deeply held family and community loyalties, the latter often prevailed.

Other State Interventions

In addition to concerns about land reform, many of these rebellious finqueros also saw Sandinista economic interventions as a threat to their economic well-being. As Mendoza explains: "In 1975 I wanted to have thirty different outfits and thirty pairs of shoes and I worked for that. The Sandinistas wanted everyone to have only one set of clothes, one pair of shoes, rich and poor." Specifically, medium-sized producers of coffee and cattle in the interior "felt threatened by government attempts to limit social differentiation, curtail private rural commerce and centralize investment and other planning decisions" (Kaimowitz 1988, 125). A number of analysts argue that FSLN economic policies, which at best neglected and at worst harmed wealthy and middle peasants, were the most important factor that led this sector to oppose the revolution (CIPRES 1991; Kaimowitz 1988; Bendaña 1991). In other words, finqueros were disgruntled with a government that paid them low prices for their export crops, displaced them in commerce, and was unable to ensure the adequate and timely supply of agricultural inputs.

In terms of the first MILPA groups, however, several circumstances suggest that their initial opposition to the FSLN economic model was based more on general principle than on harm they suffered personally. First, in 1980, when many finqueros and their sons began to organize the MILPAs, agricultural production in the municipality was still in a relatively dynamic phase of recovery fueled in part by a very generous FSLN credit policy. While the municipality suffered shortages of agricultural inputs in 1980, the full impact of rationing measures and labor scarcity had yet to be felt, and it was not until after 1983 that coffee and cattle production began to decline sharply in Quilalí. In addition, as will be seen, a number of Quilalí finqueros who maintained a degree of political neutrality received concessions and subsidies from the FSLN and prospered economically during the 1980s.

As we have seen, during the Somoza era, finqueros were powerful figures in their communities who provided access to land, work opportunities, and services to trusted colonos and the surrounding community. Some finqueros, however, felt that their economic and ideological influence was being undermined by the transformations taking place in Quilalí after 1979. Overall, throughout the 1980s, the attitude of the FSLN toward wealthy rural producers was ambiguous and not entirely consistent. On the one hand, the FSLN promoted a policy of national unity, a broad-based multiclass alliance that included what later came to be known as patriotic producers, who were encouraged to continue to produce export crops and earn a reasonable, if not excessive, profit (Luciak 1995). On the other hand, the Sandinista government was also ideologically committed to blunting the economic and social power of elites (Spalding 1994, 65). The FSLN's promotion of "popular hegemony"—its efforts to improve the situation of the rural poor through expanded credit, technical assistance, and access to land after 1982, and to organize peasants in the ATC and the UNAG—implicitly and explicitly challenged prerevolutionary structures of inequality and exploitation from which finqueros benefited.

On a local level, attitudes toward rural elites seem to have varied according to the FSLN authorities in control of the zone. Just across the river from Quilalí in the Pantasma zone, for example, a militant group of FSLN officials alienated wealthy and middle peasants in the early 1980s. In Quilalí, on the other hand, most informants report that the first FSLN leaders were not unusually radical either in their speech or actions. By most accounts, rather than openly challenging the authority of Quilalí elites, FSLN officials instead often attempted to persuade the well-off into putting their influence behind the revolution. Despite the relatively moderate political stance of many local political Sandinista officials in Quilalí, in a broader sense revolutionary discourse offered an alternative source of information and worldview to poor and middle peasants.

The testimony of Quilalí MILPA leaders and participants suggests that calculated economic interests were not sufficient in themselves to explain their break with the revolution. Rather these finqueros also felt a sense of "moral outrage" against the FSLN, which challenged not simply their material advancement, but also their status and authority in the municipality (Spalding 1994, 113). A relative of Ernesto Reyes, who later joined the MILPAs along with his four brothers, explains why he believes FSLN criticism of his family was unfair: "Everyone knew that we were honest people who never hurt anyone. My father was even a dentist. He pulled people's teeth, practiced medicine, and served as a lawyer for the community. If anyone was jailed they came to my father for help. We were well-loved by the people." MILPA leader Mendoza gives another example of perceived FSLN hostility: "Then came a ton of organizations that the people had never seen before, and even the [Sandinista] combatants had never seen. . . . When they organized in this way, there was always that word, *bourgeoisie*."

The break between former FSLN guerrillas and the new revolutionary government may also have been hastened by the shrinking of neutral political ground in Nicaragua after 1979. Finqueros who later joined or supported the MILPAs report that because of their earlier ties to the FSLN and their local influence Sandinista officials pressured them to actively support revolutionary programs. Some believed that in this early atmosphere of revolutionary fervor, political withdrawal or criticism of the new government would label them in the eyes of the FSLN authorities as counterrevolutionaries. In Quilalí armed conflict was preceded by a rapid breakdown of communication and trust between the supporters and emerging opponents of the revolution.

Armed Struggle

As the above discussion suggests, there appears to have been nothing unusually radical about Sandinista policies and land reform as implemented in the municipality of Quilalí. It also seems logical to surmise that rural elites in other parts of Nicaragua shared some of the same disagreements with the FSLN's land reform, government interventions, and attempts to organize the rural poor. Yet why did only finqueros from Quilalí and neighboring zones decide so quickly that there were no peaceful channels to express their growing opposition to revolution and take up arms not as a final resort, but as virtually a first option? One factor that may have discouraged ex-guerrillas from attempting to organize civic opposition to the FSLN was the widespread support Sandinistas enjoyed, even in Quilalí, during the first year of the revolution, as well as the lack of organized viable political opposition to the FSLN to which the ex-guerrilla combatants might have turned for support or guidance. Nicaragua's private sector lacked an oligarchic center and a tradition of independent political organization. Even after opposition representatives Violeta de Chamorro and Alfonso Robelo broke with the FSLN and resigned from the Governing Junta of National Reconstruction in April 1980, private sector civic opposition to the Sandinista government had little outreach to rural areas (Spalding 1994, 30). As will be seen, the first MILPA leaders did attempt to form an alliance with several well-known opposition politicians, but when these efforts fizzled out political struggle was rapidly abandoned for the battlefield.

Another factor that likely influenced MILPA leaders to take up arms is the municipality's history of organized violence and resistance dating from the Sandino era. In fact, in Nicaragua as a whole peaceful transitions of power were the exception, not the rule, and the FSLN-led insurrection against Somoza likely served to further legitimize the use of violence as a means of political change in the eyes of some ex-combatants.

In addition, it should be kept in mind that the Quilalí, Yalí, and Wiwilí zones had an unusually strong and coherent finquero sector. In contrast, well-off producers from other regions of Nicaragua may have shared some of their same grievances, but lacked the combination of military and leadership skills and appropriate terrain to make guerrilla struggle a viable option. The time Quilalí finqueros had spent fighting with the FSLN gave them not only a sense of their own importance, but also the confidence to launch their own rebellion.[9] Whereas these men were inexperienced and unfamiliar with formal political organizing, they were effective guerrilla fighters and were intimately familiar with the paths, hills, and valleys of the northern mountains, a terrain ideal for guerrilla struggle. While with the FSLN guerrillas, many ex-combatants had also developed a range of rural contacts who might potentially support their new struggle. As will be seen, ex-Sandinista combatants were also encouraged to take up arms by the presence of groups of armed ex-National Guardsmen along the northern border with Honduras and the possibility of military aid from the U.S. government.[10] From the outset MILPA leaders viewed both the ex-National Guardsmen and the U. S. government as powerful potential allies in their guerrilla struggle, and this was a critical factor in channeling rural discontent with the FSLN into armed opposition.

Finally, not all of Quilalí's approximately seventy finqueros and their families actively supported the MILPA cause. Quilalí observers suggest that only about half of Quilalí's finquero families collaborated or fought with the contras. Other finqueros were not necessarily Sandinista supporters, but were careful not to openly associate themselves with the MILPAs and later contras and to maintain at least the appearance of neutrality. As will be seen, many of these "neutral" finqueros in fact, made good use of FSLN assistance and the low price of land during the war to buy up farms and consolidate their economic position. It should be emphasized that although the finqueros who did organize the MILPAs were only a small fraction of the municipality's population, their combined economic and social influence still made them a serious challenge to the FSLN.

Attack on Quilalí

While he still officially worked for the FSLN, ex-Sandinista guerrilla Pedro Joaquín González met with about thirty of his former comrades-in-arms to form the first anti-Sandinista MILPA. According to Mendoza who participated in these first meetings, it was relatively easy to recruit this core group to their cause: "I'm a native of Quilalí, born and raised in Quilalí. I'm not a great political speechmaker, but I have a good reputation. . . . I easily gathered these people together. They were born in Quilalí of well-off parents. . . . All these people spoke the same language and followed the same line of thinking."

The original MILPA leaders included "Douglas" (Anroyce "Rudy" Zelaya Zeledón), a member of a wealthy Quilalí family; "Coral" (Freddy Gadea Rivera), whose family owned several coffee farms; the eldest son of Ernesto Reyes; and "Chepito" (Jose Valladares), a finquero from Wiwilí. One of the first actions the Quilalí MILPA leaders took was to seek outside support for their small group. In December 1979 the guerrilla group held meetings in Managua with national opposition leaders Jorge Salazar, Alfonso Robelo, and then Sandinista comandante Edén Pastora, who later deserted the FSLN to organize an antigovernment force along the Costa Rican border. Within the newly formed opposition group, González was given the responsibility of organizing an armed group in the mountains of northern Nicaragua. Concrete support from Edén Pastora and other politicians for the Quilalí MILPA failed to materialize, however. Mendoza explains: "We lost all those contacts because they were afraid to come to the mountains to talk with us. We couldn't go to the city. . . . We lost our political leadership arm."

After this failure to find allies within Nicaragua, MILPA leaders decided to seek out assistance to the north in Honduras, where ex-National Guardsmen had fled in 1979. González and several other MILPA leaders went to Honduras in February 1980 to seek military and political aid from ex-National Guardsmen in exile. González carried with him a list of MILPA demands to be negotiated with National Guard officers, and he returned apparently having reached at least a partial agreement with the guardsmen.[11] MILPA leaders report, however, that they received no aid from the groups in Honduras or other outside sources until late 1981, when they began to formally integrate themselves into the ex-National Guard groups in Honduras.[12]

MILPA leaders next decided to launch simultaneous attacks on the towns of Quilalí and Yalí, across the Río Coco, to establish their credibility as a guerrilla group.[13] When MILPA leaders began to recruit men for their planned assaults they looked no further than the workers on their parents' farms and members of their immediate network of friends and acquaintances. Mendoza states that he was able to bring twenty or so of the peasants who worked for him into the MILPA movement. The Reyes family was also able to convince several dozen of their workers to participate in the attack on Quilalí. Across the Río Coco in the coffee-growing community of La Rica, the contacts of the locally influential and well-off Meza family were key in the formation of the Yalí MILPA band.

The fact that these finqueros were able to convince their workers and colonos to take up arms in the defense of elite property and economic interests is an indication of the strength of patron-client ties in this zone of Nicaragua. In some cases, colonos may have been attempting to preserve their relatively privileged position with their patron (CIERA 1989, 6:254–55). In addition, MILPA leaders were able to take advantage of the frustration that poor peasants who had fought or collaborated with the FSLN guerrillas earlier felt over not receiving land. According to poor peasant participants in the uprising later captured and questioned by the FSLN, MILPA leaders promised that they would take state farms from the government and distribute the land to MILPA members.[14]

In early 1980 a clandestine guerrilla training camp was established in the plantain groves of a farm, El Caracol, on the banks of the Río Coco southwest of Quilalí. As a general rule, the sons of finqueros participated directly in military training and combat, while their fathers provided the MILPAs with food, shelter, funds to purchase weapons, and transportation (CIERA 1981a, 19). MILPA leaders also obtained weapons by convincing the leaders of several Sandinista militias to turn over their arms. In late July the plan to attack Yalí was uncovered by Sandinista authorities and many of its instigators arrested. The assault on Quilalí went forward as scheduled, however, on 23 July, when some eighty men attacked the town of Quilalí. The MILPA briefly occupied Quilalí's main military headquarters, the police station, and the office of the Association of Rural Workers (ATC). While witnesses report that a number of the MILPA combatants fled in fear at the beginning of the attack, MILPA leaders claim that they killed five Sandinista soldiers and seized twenty-two weapons, including three M-16s. The armed band quickly fled the town and the next day ambushed a Sandinista military vehicle on the road outside Quilalí.

The MILPAs succeeded in drawing national attention to their cause, but they also brought down upon themselves a swift response on the part of the Sandinista military, which poured troops into Quilalí and surrounding areas. Because of their familiarity with the terrain, however, Mendoza and other MILPA members were largely able evade the Sandinista soldiers. In view of the large-scale counterinsurgency campaign the Sandinistas launched against them, González decided to go to Honduras to try again to contact ex-National Guardsmen.

These plans were cut short, however, when González was killed in September 1980. The circumstances of González's death are a legend in Quilalí, and the story has become part of González's mystique among many contra troops. Mendoza relates one version:

> Dimas's [González's] best friend was Mamerto Herrera. Through Mamerto Herrera he made some contacts and was trying to win over some friends who had fought with him. It seems that Mamerto sent [González] a letter through a messenger. . . . The letter said that Dimas should wait for Mamerto in the tobacco sheds of San Bartolo, and that he would arrive there with 250 new recruits. The new recruits were on their way, tired and well-armed. . . . [González] dressed in civilian clothing and left for the place mentioned in the letter. When he arrived at the shed, Mamerto was there with food and rum.

What González did not realize was that his friend Mamerto Herrera was a double agent who worked for the FSLN. The story continues:

> Dimas waited all night long and the men never arrived. At two or three in the morning . . . he was very sleepy and a little drunk . . . Mamerto said to him, "What a beautiful pistol you have. Let me see it." Dimas took off the gun and handed it to Mamerto. Then one of Mamerto's bodyguards sent a bullet into Dimas's back, below his left rib, and it pierced his heart.

The widely known story of González's death contains several symbolic elements of the anti-Sandinista peasant narrative of the revolution. Mamerto Herrera, the secret Sandinista, at first offers González friendship, food, and drink to lure him to the tobacco shed, only to betray and kill him. In much the same way, in anti-Sandinista discourse, the FSLN originally promised Nicaraguans a series of benefits that in the end were only a trick to lure peasants into supporting the revolution that soon betrayed those who had once been its strongest supporters. Also, Sandinismo in this story is an outside force that ultimately destroys the friendship between Herrera and González, just as anti-Sandinistas portrayed the revolution as responsible for turning family member against family member and neighbor against neighbor and so "piercing the heart" of rural Nicaragua.

With the death of González the Quilalí MILPA band lost a great deal of coherence. Some MILPA guerrillas sought refuge in Honduras, while others continued as ragtag bands in the mountains armed only with rifles and pistols. Quilalí peasants remember meeting the MILPA groups in the mountains and thinking they didn't have much future. The Nicaraguan government estimated that there were sixteen small armed bands including the MILPAs operating in northern Nicaragua in 1980 who engaged Sandinista soldiers and militias in small skirmishes (Bendaña 1991, 30).

While in the longterm the military significance of the MILPA bands was minimal, the rural origins and perceived initial sacrifices of the first MILPAs were crucial in several ways.[15] First, as will be seen, from 1982 onward MILPA leaders served as key intermediaries between the ex-National Guardsmen who dominated leadership positions of the contra forces in Honduras and Nicaragua's interior peasant population. In addition, long after the MILPA bands had merged with the ex-National Guardsmen as part of the U.S.-funded FDN contra forces, the myth of the MILPAs was an important tool employed by anti-Sandinistas to legitimize the contra struggle in rural areas.[16] When asked who were the first people to take up arms against the FSLN, peasants in the mountains almost invariably name the MILPA leaders from their area. Quilalí peasants who joined the contras remember that their commanders told them stories about González and the first MILPA leaders. Contra leaders' emphasis on the early internal uprising of the MILPAs served to draw attention away from the more contentious role of ex-National Guardsmen and the U.S. government in funding and organizing the contra forces. Highlighting the internal rural origins and leadership of the MILPA uprising enabled contra leaders to downplay their dependence on U.S. funding and to counter Sandinista charges that theirs was a mercenary army. In contrast to Sandinista discourse, which made both broad class-based and nationalist appeals to peasants, the myth of the MILPAs allowed contra leaders to frame their cause as a peasant struggle for liberty and democracy against the "outside" revolutionary ideology of the FSLN.

Organization of the Contras

In 1981, as the MILPA groups struggled along in northern Nicaragua, relations between the FSLN and the newly inaugurated Reagan administration began to deteriorate rapidly. The Reagan administration viewed the FSLN as an aggressive exporter of revolution and a threat to U.S. national security. It saw in Nicaragua an opportunity to advance its policy of "rolling back communist advancement" within the U.S. sphere of influence and initiated a decade-long campaign of low-intensity warfare against Nicaragua. Low-intensity warfare (LIW) avoids politically costly direct conventional military engagement and relies instead on "maintaining a multiplicity of pressures—political, economic, diplomatic, psychological, and ideological—against the enemy, and synchronizing those pressures with permanent but low-key military aggression. At its heart is the political invalidation, rather than the military defeat of the enemy" (Robinson and Norsworthy 1987, 16). While this strategy may be of "low intensity" and represent a relatively small political and economic cost for the implementing country, to the receiving nation LIW is "total war at the grassroots level" (quoted in Robinson and Norsworthy 1987, 27). During the 1980s the Reagan administration employed such tactics as economic sabotage, a financial blockade, and disinformation campaigns against the FSLN. But by far the most powerful weapon the Reagan administration turned against the Sandinista regime was the over $400 million dollars of military aid, as well as organizational, technical, and logistical support it provided to the contra forces, who would inexorably drain away the FSLN's economic, political, and human resources over the next decade.

In August 1981, under U.S. guidance, several small groups of exiled ex-National Guardsmen were united to form the Nicaraguan

Democratic Force (Fuerza Democrática Nicaragüense, FDN) headed by former National Guard Colonel Enrique Bermúdez, known as "Comandante 3–80." The FDN forces received a vital boost in November 1981 when the Reagan administration approved $19.5 million in military funds for the contras. With these funds the contras purchased new weapons, such as FAL rifles, M-79 grenade launches, 60 mm mortars, and machine guns (Dillon 1991, 72). The contras established five base camps in Honduras and began a series of raids into northern Nueva Segovia led by lower-ranking ex-National Guard officers such as "Suicida," well-known both for his aggressiveness in combat and the serious human rights abuses he and his men committed against civilians that were documented by journalists. The limited evidence available suggests that these ex-National Guardsmen were motivated by a deep personal animosity toward the Sandinistas and a profound sense of anticommunism.[17] When a former National Guardsman from Quilalí was asked if he had ever considered remaining in Nicaragua after the FSLN took power, he replied: "Never! I never thought about it because everything in Nicaragua was death. The FSLN was nothing more than death. . . . If the FSLN came back to power tonight, I would have to leave the country again at four in the morning." This ex-Guardsman also repeatedly frames his struggle in terms of a global battle against Marxism: "The FSLN is communist, governed by Fidel Castro, Moscow, Russia. They depend on those sources." Such strong anticommunism, which as will be seen is more weakly echoed among Quilalí peasants who joined the contras, may well be a product of the intense indoctrination these men received in National Guard training schools.

MILPA and National Guard Integration

As was mentioned earlier, in 1981 MILPA leaders pursued by the Sandinista military often sought refuge in Honduras, where they came into contact with ex-National Guardsmen and Somoza sup-porters. By late 1981, Mendoza, like most of the early MILPA leaders and their recruits, had joined the Honduran base camp of Pino 1, under the command of Suicida at the time. Despite their status as guerrilla leaders in Nicaragua, once in Honduras the MILPA leaders chose to subordinate themselves to the formal authority of ex-National Guardsmen. They entered the contras as foot soldiers, al-though most would rise rapidly to positions of operational leadership in the field. As we have seen, finquero MILPA leaders turned against the Sandinistas because of personal conflicts and opposition to revo-lutionary policies and ideology. They were not, however, Somoza supporters and few shared the National Guard's anticommunist fer-vor. In addition, many MILPA leaders who fought as Sandinista guer-rillas had experienced firsthand the repression of the National Guard. The question must be addressed then, why were these ex-Sandinistas so quick to seek an alliance with National Guardsmen they had fought against less than two years earlier?

According to MILPA leaders like Mendoza, it was their common enmity against the FSLN that united the two groups: "There was a time when we were enemies, but when we took up arms for the sec-ond time we realized that we were part of the same struggle. The [Na-tional Guard's] fundamental objective was to liberate Nicaragua." Just as some MILPA leaders had made a tactical alliance with the FSLN guerrillas to fight the common foe, the Somoza dictatorship, in the early 1980s they made a "bargain of necessity" with ex-National Guardsmen to struggle against what they now perceived to be an even greater threat, the Sandinistas.[18] Another factor that strongly in-fluenced the MILPA leaders to integrate with the National Guard were the abundant material and political resources to which the Na-tional Guard–led organizations had access. After their failed contacts with Nicaragua's internal opposition, the MILPAs depended princi-pally on limited local sources for weapons and funds. MILPA leaders possessed neither the connections to U.S. government officials nor the education and experience in managing formal administrative and military structures that would have allowed them to operate independently. Therefore, Enrique Bermúdez, with his close ties to U.S. funders, was able to offer MILPA leaders a strong enticement: MILPA leaders could have access to modern weapons, equipment, uniforms, and funds in exchange for integration into the ex-National Guard organization, the FDN. As part of this complete package of military aid, however, came the National Guard leadership. MILPA leaders understood that if they rejected the role of the National Guard, they would also lose access to U.S. assistance and therefore accepted an often tension-filled subordinate relationship with the ex-National Guard (CIERA 1989, 6:246).

In addition to the main FDN forces along the Honduran border, on Nicaragua's Atlantic coast tensions between the FSLN's nationalist, revolutionary program and growing ethnic militancy led to the massive flight of Miskito Indians to Honduras and the formation in 1981 of indigenous antigovernment armed bands (Vilas 1989; Hale 1994). Along Nicaragua's southern border with Costa Rica as well, former FSLN guerrilla leader Edén Pastora organized the counterrevolutionary Democratic Revolutionary Alliance (Alianza Revolucionaria Democrática, ARDE).

As the newly integrated ex-National Guard and MILPA forces organized in the early 1980s, the FSLN for its part moved quickly to rebuild Nicaragua's armed forces. With the collapse of the National Guard July in 1979, the FSLN faced the enormous task and unique opportunity of creating armed forces from scratch and established the Sandinista Popular Army (Ejército Popular Sandinista, EPS) under the control of the Ministry of Defense. In its early years, the Sandinista Army was voluntary and its first recruits were many of the thousands of young people who joined in the fierce street fighting of the last months of the insurrection against Somoza. Some of these initial recruits formed a core group of mid-level army officers who in a few years would lead counterinsurgency campaigns in Nicaragua's mountainous interior and Atlantic coast.

Rodrigo Sosa, who fought for seven years with the EPS in Quilalí, is typical of these first volunteers. Sosa grew up in a poor family in Managua and completed only the third grade in school. In 1978 an older brother of Sosa who collaborated with the FSLN was killed by the National Guard. His brother's death convinced Sosa to join the FSLN. He explains: "The war against Somoza was a persecution against all young people by the National Guard. I was barely thirteen years old when I joined [the FSLN]. I was carried away by the passions of people older than me. We young people saw it almost like a movie, to go into the mountains with the guerrillas." Over a decade later Sosa still vividly remembers the "euphoria" and "passion" of the final months of the insurrection against Somoza. His experiences fighting behind the barricades in Managua and the deaths of his brother and friends forged in him a deep commitment to the revolution and after the FSLN took power Sosa eagerly joined the new armed forces the Sandinistas were organizing.

Like other volunteers who had fought in the insurrection but lacked formal education and military training, Sosa attended training courses where he received not only military instruction but also literacy and political classes. Sandinista leaders did not want to create a traditional "apolitical" Latin American army, but rather a revolutionary and nationalist armed force. Political training for EPS soldiers emphasized the legitimacy of the FSLN's role as vanguard of the revolutionary process, the need to defend the well-being of the poor masses and the nation, as well as the responsibility of soldiers to set a moral example for the population (Gorman and Walker 1985, 99). Sosa recalls that during his first year, the armed forces were high on morale and enthusiasm. Recruits, however, were also at times desperately short of weapons, supplies, and money as the new Sandinista Army expanded rapidly from 5,000 to as many as 18,000 soldiers and officers by mid-1980 (100). Sosa remembers: "We didn't have boots. We didn't have equipment. For six months they didn't pay us anything. It was pure romanticism."

The Sandinistas turned to the Soviet Union, Eastern Europe, and

Cuba for military assistance, although substantial aid did not begin arriving until 1982.[19] Despite the growing number of contra forces, top FSLN commanders in the early 1980s tended to view the contras as little more than ex-National Guardsmen and mercenaries who would serve as the spearhead for a large-scale U.S. invasion. As a result, the EPS was organized and equipped largely to defend against a direct invasion, not to track down guerrillas in the mountains, and most of the EPS's most sophisticated equipment and best-trained personnel were concentrated around Managua and other major cities on the Pacific coast. Months passed and the feared U.S. invasion did not occur. Instead, the contras began to launch large-scale attacks on northern border towns, particularly Jalapa, in an attempt to capture and "liberate" a piece of Nicaraguan territory and potentially bring about direct U.S. military intervention. The Sandinista Army, which had grown to 24,000 by 1983 (Walker 1991a, 86), and militias were successful in halting contra attempts to hold territory in this more conventional warfare of fixed positions between two armies. The contras in 1983, however, were by no means a defeated force, and continued to grow in size and strength.

During this period of rapid expansion of the contras, quarrels among the expanding contra field leadership were commonplace. These conflicts appear to have had less to do with ideological differences than personal rivalries and power struggles, as well as human rights abuses and corruption on the part of certain guardsmen. An example of this was the bitter quarrel between MILPA leader Mendoza and ex-National Guard lieutenant Luis Moreno Payán, known as Mike Lima (see Dillon 1991, 75–76). In the early 1980s, Mike Lima led the Diriangén band of some 400 men. Mendoza, then Mike Lima's second-in-command, describes Mike Lima: "To some troops and *comandos* the man [Mike Lima] was an eminence because he had some schooling and had attended the [National Guard military] academy. He was also a man of action. To some he was good. To me no, because he was also hard and on some occasions committed errors [sic] like attempted rape, killings." Tensions between Mike Lima and Mendoza grew when, while on patrol in the mountains, Mike Lima executed some contra combatants suspected of being Sandinista double agents. Mendoza decided to leave: "I handed over my troops, handed over the money, everything I had. . . . I left as a civilian." Back in Honduras, Mendoza sought out Enrique Bermúdez and remembers telling him: " 'I'm going to return to Nicaragua, but I don't want any National Guardsman to lead my troops. I'll go alone as a commander or as a soldier, but I don't want any guardsmen in the group. If you want to support me in this, here I am at your service. If not I'll retire.' So, he [Bermúdez] accepted and gave me his support."

Mendoza then gathered together a small of group of personal friends and ex-MILPA members from the Quilalí area and entered Nicaragua again with fewer than a dozen troops. In Quilalí and neighboring zones, Mendoza reports that he was able to quickly recruit over 200 new combatants. Several other former MILPA leaders, who served under abusive ex-National Guardsmen such as Suicida, also chose to strike out on their own and create new rebel bands under their direct command. Over the next five years many of these men would rise rapidly in authority and by the mid-1980s, men such as "Douglas," "Coral," and Justo Pastor Meza ("Denis") from Yalí, were directing battalions of up to 1,000 men in the mountains of Nicaragua.

Finally, while this study focuses primarily on the internal tensions between Nicaragua's interior peasantry and the FSLN, and on the dynamics of conflict from a local perspective, it is important to emphasize that the large amounts of external assistance provided by the United States were critical in several ways. U.S. organizational and material support for the contras served to reinforce and intensify peasant grievances against the FSLN, channel that discontent into armed struggle, and broaden the scope and intensity of the military conflict.

Initially, U.S. government contact with the ex-National Guardsmen and MILPA combatants was limited, with the CIA relying on

Argentinean military officers to train contra recruits. When the Argentineans withdrew from contra training by 1983, the CIA assumed a more active role in the organization and training of the contras, although, with the exception of certain airborne operations and specialized sabotage actions, such as the 1984 mining of the port of Corinto, CIA agents generally did not participate directly in contra military actions. The agency was, however, deeply involved in contra funding; purchase and delivery of weapons and supplies; establishing logistical infrastructure; intelligence gathering; and coordination of training programs and overall contra strategic planning (Dillon 1991, 87). The CIA also maintained close contact with the contras' military commander, Enrique Bermúdez, and the contras' political wing, a constantly shifting group of prominent Nicaraguan politicians and business people promoted by the Reagan administration as the true leaders of the contra movement in order to counter criticism in Congress and among the U.S. public that the contra forces were dominated by ex-National Guardsmen.

It seems likely that without access to the over $400 million in military aid from the United States, the Quilalí area MILPA groups would have remained uncoordinated, poorly-supplied local rebel groups that the FSLN could have contained, if not completely eliminated. Instead, in 1981 there was a "convergence of interests" in which ex-National Guardsmen, resentful finqueros from the northern mountains, wealthy Nicaraguans, and U.S. government officials came together to create a large counterrevolutionary army (CIPRES 1991, 18).

Chapter 5

Retreat of the Revolution

THIS CHAPTER will explore the factors that led a majority of poor and middle peasants in Quilalí, particularly those in more remote zones, to oppose revolutionary change outright or withdraw their support for revolutionary projects, and that made this sector receptive to contra proselytizing and recruitment efforts. Yet, while the peasant grievances discussed in this chapter provide clues to understanding why a majority of Quilalí peasants opposed the FSLN, they do not provide a complete answer to the analytically distinct question: Why did anti-Sandinista Quilalí peasants choose armed struggle as the principle means to express their discontent? Those additional factors that transformed peasant grievances into active collaboration and armed rebellion with the contras will be explored separately in the following chapter.

The present chapter first examines repression carried out by bands of contras to force the FSLN and its peasant supporters to withdraw from outlying communities in the municipality. During this same period, as will be seen, a shift in land reform policy enabled the FSLN to consolidate a strong pro-Sandinista base of support in

Quilalí's river valley. The following section details conflicts between Sandinista programs and ideology and the worldview of the emerging anti-Sandinista peasant majority in the municipality. Key tensions centered on revolutionary challenges to rural hierarchy, the nature of FSLN land reform, and Sandinista economic interventions. As will be seen, although a majority of finqueros and middle peasants identified with the anti-Sandinista model, the position of poor peasants was more complex and contradictory. Poor peasants were both drawn to certain aspects of the FSLN program such as land reform, and distanced from Sandinismo by economic and ideological dependence on elites, doubts about the model's viability, and frustrated expectations of the revolution.

In 1982 and 1983 much of Nicaragua's and the world's attention was focused on the intense battles between contras and the Sandinista Army along the Honduran border and the seemingly imminent possibility of a direct U.S. invasion of Nicaragua. Beyond the public gaze, however, small groups of contras, now integrated to include both ex-National Guardsmen and former MILPA leaders and combatants, were infiltrating deeper and deeper into Nicaraguan territory, laying the groundwork for the large-scale recruitment of mountain peasants. Contra groups headed south through the mountains of Nueva Segovia passed regularly through the Quilalí area and by early 1983 had penetrated as far into Nicaragua as the department of Matagalpa. These groups maintained a relatively low profile, occasionally launching small-scale attacks and ambushes, but in general trying to avoid attracting the attention of the Sandinista Army. Their immediate mission was as much political as military: to make contact with local peasants in more isolated interior zones, establish collaborator networks, and recruit new contra combatants.

The mission of the contras during this period in Quilalí was made easier by the weak military and political presence of the FSLN in the municipality, particularly in more remote communities. After the Sandinista military campaign against the MILPA band that attacked Quilalí in 1980, the number of Sandinista soldiers in the zone was greatly reduced. The task of hunting down armed counter-revolutionary bands was left in the hands of specially created anti-Somocista military patrols (unidades de Lucha Contra Bandas Somocistas [LCBS]), small groups of soldiers led by experienced Sandinista guerrillas who patrolled the northern mountains (CIPRES 1991, 272).

Despite the efforts of the LCBSs, and later the EPS, however, small mobile groups of guerrillas continued to multiply and spread throughout large areas of the Segovias and the departments of Jinotega and Matagalpa to the south. Local militias in Quilalí were also often unable to effectively deal with the contra groups. Many militia members received only minimal political orientation and military training and were poorly armed, carrying little more than old rifles. In some cases, militia leaders who had little commitment to the revolution even turned their weapons over to contra bands operating nearby. EPS soldier Rodrigo Sosa, who was promoted to lieutenant and transferred to Quilalí at age sixteen, remembers: "At that time Quilalí was a no man's land. . . . The MILPAs had full authority and control over the outlying zones. . . . The Sandinista Army wasn't able to contain those armed groups."

As Sosa suggests, its weak military control over the municipality made it difficult for the FSLN to offer either adequate physical protection or even sustained moral support to its civilian supporters living on isolated farms in the mountains. In addition, to further weaken the FSLN's influence the contras attempted to eliminate any actual or potential benefits the revolution could bring to the civilian population in those zones. From 1981 onward they carried out a campaign of intimidation and violence against peasants who participated in revolutionary projects or activities. Contra repression was "selective" in the sense that the targets were generally "pro-Sandinista" peasants. At the same time, the contra definition of *Sandinista* was very broad. Essentially, any peasant who participated in a mass organization or government-sponsored program could be the subject of intimidation, harassment, or violence by passing bands of contras. A rural school teacher or health worker, for example, would often be identified by contras as a Sandinista supporter, regardless of whether she or he was formally active in the FSLN. For many mountain residents the objectives of the contras were clear. In the words of one pro-Sandinista woman from the mountains: "The problems began when the *brigadistas* [Sandinista volunteers] came to teach people to read and write. We began receiving threats. The MILPAs would leave us slips of paper in our yard that said, 'Long live the MILPAs. Death to the CDSs.' They threatened to kill my family if they didn't find my husband."

Another incident of violent intimidation occurred in the community of El Súngano, twenty kilometers north of the town of Quilalí. Soon after taking power the FSLN built a health clinic in the community to provide residents with access to health services, some for the first time in their lives. In 1983, however, the contras frightened the health staff into abandoning the post and then burned it down. After that experience, the FSLN decided not to construct any more schools or health posts in Quilalí's northern mountain communities as they could not adequately protect these installations and their personnel. After 1983 a total of twelve primary schools out of thirty-four in the municipality were abandoned (MIDINRA 1987, 64). Four, including a school in El Súngano, were burned down by contras. The other eight schools were closed because the physical safety of teachers was threatened and because of the growing climate of insecurity in the mountains. Likewise, by 1982 FSLN informants report that government land reform, education, and health officials could only visit the municipality's more distant rural zones with great caution and carrying arms. In some communities in fact, Sandinista supporters concede that the contras had virtual free rein to come and go as they pleased, spread their message, forge support networks, and recruit peasants as combatants.

When bands of contras began to harass revolutionary project leaders in the municipality's outlying communities, some peasants decided to distance themselves from the revolution in general, and Sandinista organizations and projects in particular, so as to avoid "problems" with the contras. Such a process occurred in the river valley community of Jiquelite, where several dozen poor peasants joined the FSLN guerrillas in the final months of the insurrection. One of these prerevolutionary Sandinista supporters and son of a poor colono, Carlos Sánchez, remembers: "In all the valleys [rural communities] the Sandinistas organized people. But the war came quickly and everything fell apart. When things got hard, ugly, everyone went his own way to work individually." Most of the new revolutionary organizations, which had not developed strong roots outside the town limits of Quilalí, collapsed under the pressure of contra repression. By 1983, CDSs had disappeared from Quilalí's northern mountains. Some Credit and Service Cooperatives continued to function in rural communities, even those where bands of contras were present, but they were little more than a formal vehicle for collecting bank credit. The UNAG also remained active in the municipality, but as will be seen, its organizing efforts were focused largely on the river valley cooperatives.

Committed Sandinista Supporters

In contrast to those peasants who distanced themselves from the FSLN, a small group of peasants were unwilling to abandon their commitment to the revolution. As discussed earlier, some had prerevolutionary family histories, contacts with liberation theology, or experiences of consciousness raising that forged in them a more profound support for the FSLN even in the face of contra intimidation. The proliferation of contra bands meant, however, that by the end of 1982 virtually all such pro-Sandinista families living in outlying communities were forced to abandon their farms and seek refuge in the town of Quilalí. The Solís family, who were relatives of a general of Sandino and lived in the northern community of Las Palancas, for example, received word one day that a group of contras planned to kill them. Along with half a dozen other pro-Sandinista families, they quickly gathered what clothing and possessions they could carry on their backs and fled on foot to the town of Quilalí. Other peasants also left the mountains in 1982 and 1983, not out of direct fear of persecution, but to escape the climate of growing insecurity and violence in the countryside. The number of families living inside Quilalí's town limits increased by 6 percent in 1985, in part because of this exodus of peasants from the surrounding countryside (MIDINRA 1987, 13). This process of concentration of pro-Sandinista peasants in urban centers and later cooperative settlements also occurred in a number of other zones of Nicaragua's interior.[1]

As a result, Quilalí FSLN authorities were obligated to focus their limited resources not on expanding the Sandinista base of support in the countryside, but simply on ensuring the physical and economic survival of their displaced peasant supporters. Many of these families needed housing and land to work, yet the FSLN could not guarantee their safety if they were given individual parcels of land, even in communities close to the town of Quilalí. In addition to these internally displaced peasants, the municipality received an influx of almost 1,000 poor peasants from the dry zones of the western Segovias, Murra, and Wiwilí (MIDINRA 1987, 15). Some of these peasants migrated to Quilalí of their own initiative in search of better land to farm or were brought to Quilalí by FSLN officials, who saw little possibility that they could ever live more than a precarious existence in their native communities. Still others were displaced by the war from neighboring municipalities. In fact, in spite of the burgeoning conflict, the municipality of Quilalí, with its productive land, continued to be a zone of attraction for peasants until the mid-1980s, and between 1980 and 1986 the population tripled, from 6,016 people to 18,366 (MIDINRA 1987, 14).

Faced with a large group of displaced and migrant peasants in need of land, FSLN officials decided in late 1982 to take land from state cattle ranches to create three farming cooperatives in Quilalí's fertile river valley. These actions in Quilalí reflected a shift in policy at the national level taken by the Sandinista government to move away from state-centered models of agrarian reform and promote a range of tenure patterns and productive relations (Deere et al. 1985, 91). In addition to the immediate need for land, two other considerations that influenced FSLN rural policy reform were poor state farm performance and a desire to build peasant political support for the revolution (Zalkin 1987, 967).

While specific financial data about Quilalí state farms are not available, it seems likely that, as with two-thirds of state farms nationwide, they were run at a loss in the first half of the 1980s.[2] Problems faced by Nicaragua's state farms included inefficient administration, lack of capital investment, under-utilization of land and resources, and poor labor discipline, as well as supply and distribution problems. Also, in theory Quilalí peasants would willingly seek employment on state farms in exchange for fair wages, a guarantee of year-round employment, and social benefits. By 1981, however, state farms in Quilalí and other northern zones were a favorite target of the contras. A 1983 study of state coffee farms in the Quilalí and San Juan del Río Coco zone concluded that it was increasingly difficult maintain adequate personnel on state farms because technical staff who lived in town feared ambushes on the drive out to the farms and unskilled workers often deserted in the face of contra threats (MIDINRA 1983, appendix).

During the Somoza era, large cattle haciendas were the center of economic activity and services in Quilalí's river valley (MIDINRA 1987, 38). Patrons gave peasants access to land, loaned money in emergencies, provided transportation and storage services, and in general offered a flexible, personal response to poor peasants' problems. In 1979 the FSLN eliminated the large landowners, but left a void the state farms were unable to fill.[3] Quilalí residents report that under government control the municipality's state cattle farms, formerly Santa Rosa de Ventilla and Guaná, fell into neglect and disrepair. Cattle herds were small and the number of workers minimal. As in other parts of Nicaragua, Quilalí's state farms became virtual enclaves with little outreach or interaction with the surrounding communities. As a result, the revolution lost prestige in the eyes of some Quilalí peasants and their belief that haciendas functioned better under the old patrons was confirmed (MIDINRA 1987, 38).

In addition to disappointing state farm performance, by 1982 Sandinista officials had become aware that the MILPAs and later contras received support from the civilian population, although it was not until several years later that Sandinista officials began to recognize the true extent of peasant involvement in the counterrevolution. An FSLN shift in policy to distribute land directly to peasants, therefore, was also seen as a means to respond to peasant demands for land and build support for the FSLN in rural areas that were emerging as a weak flank of the revolution. Although by 1982 FSLN officials had decided to reduce the state farm sector and to distribute land to peasants, policy makers were still reluctant to provide parcels of land to individual peasants. They argued that the parcelization of large farms represented a step backward both in terms of agricultural production and the FSLN's long-range goal of socialist development (Enriquez 1997, 32). In addition, in conflictive zones such as Quilalí it was felt that only self-defense cooperative settlements would offer peasants sufficient security against contra attacks. Sandinista policy makers therefore made membership in a Sandinista Agricultural Cooperative (Cooperativa Agrícola Sandinista, CAS) a requirement for peasants wishing to benefit from land reform.

Table 5.1 provides a summary of land reform in Quilalí from 1979 to 1988. From 1979, when Quilalí's five largest haciendas and eight smaller farms were confiscated, until 1983 no further land was officially expropriated in the municipality. To provide land to cooperatives in 1983, Sandinista authorities, who were apparently reluctant to

Table 5.1

Land Reform in Quilalí, 1979–1988

Year	Amount of Land Transformed	Means by Which Land Obtained	New Use of Land[1]
1979	14,200 MZ	The farms of 5 terratenientes and 8 finqueros were formally expropriated largely under decrees 3 and 38	11,000 MZ converted into state farms; 2,000 MZ occupied by La Vigía colonos
1983–1984	6,500 MZ (1,500 new, 5,000 state)	5,000 MZ taken from state farms; 1,000 MZ purchased largely from finqueros;[2] 500 MZ expropriated from finqueros	Majority of the 6,500 MZ given to river valley agricultural cooperatives
1985–1986	7,900 MZ (1,900 new, 6,000 state)	6,000 MZ taken from state farms; 1,900 MZ expropriated or purchased largely from finqueros;[3] 1,033 MZ exchanged[4]	6,500 MZ given to cooperatives; 600 MZ given to individuals
SUMMARY: 1979–1988	17,600 MZ	17,600 MZ expropriated or purchased	13,000+ MZ given to cooperatives; 2,000 MZ occupied by colonos; 600 MZ given to individuals

[1]The data are not clear on the final use of all the land transformed.

[2]Such buyouts were both voluntary and involuntary.

[3]It is not clear if these MIDINRA totals include informal expropriations.

[4]Owners agreed to turn their farms over to the government in exchange for another property.

Source: MIDINRA (1987). Land amounts are rounded estimates.

expropriate large amounts of privately owned valley land, took the politically less costly decision to hand over 5,000 MZ of state farmland to the new cooperatives, reducing the amount of land owned by the government from almost 16 percent to 9 percent of all the land in the municipality. During this same period, MIDINRA also purchased 1,000 MZ of land and expropriated 500 MZ of river valley land (MIDINRA 1987, 20).

Nationwide, the amount of land held by state farms peaked in 1983 at 21 percent and then was gradually reduced in subsequent years to 12 percent by 1988 (cited in Spoor 1995, 55). In addition, by 1984, 8.6 percent of land in Nicaragua had been turned over to CASs, an amount that increased to 11.4 percent by 1988.

With the 5,000 MZ of land taken from the Sofía Olívas state farms, three cooperatives—the Santos López, the Edward Barahona, and the Augusto César Sandino—were formally established in late 1982 (MIDINRA 1984d, 14). Approximately sixteen families joined the Santos López cooperative, named after a general who fought with Sandino, and cultivated 135 MZ of land that had originally been part of Chon Molina's hacienda, Guaná. Ten kilometers further east, in the community of San Bartolo, the sixty-member Edwin Barahona cooperative received almost 2,000 MZ of valley land that had also formed part of the Gauná hacienda. Quilalí's third and most isolated cooperative was the Augusto César Sandino CAS, known as El Coco. In El Coco, sixteen families occupied 1,334 MZ of land that was formerly part of Maurico Portillo's hacienda. A fourth cooperative was also established approximately a year later in the western sector of the municipality on what had been the La Reforma state coffee farm.

Founding cooperative members interviewed generally report that while they would not necessarily have chosen this option of their own initiative, they were willing to attempt collective farming. Many of these pro-Sandinista peasants had had some previous positive collective experiences through the Catholic church or FSLN organizations in Quilalí or their native communities that may have made them more

Table 5.2
Distribution of Land in Nicaragua by Size and Tenancy, 1978–1988
(in thousands of manzanas)

Sector	1978 Area (MZ)	%	1984 Area (MZ)	%	1988 Area (MZ)	%
Private Farms	**8,073**	**100.0%**	**5,021**	**62.2%**	**3,708**	**45.9%**
500+ MZ	2,922	36.2	928	11.5	515	6.4
50–500 MZ	3,738	46.3	3,407	42.2	2,127	26.3
0–50 MZ	1,413	17.5	686	8.5	1,066	13.2
Reformed Sector			**3,052**	**37.8%**	**3,905**	**48.4%**
State Farms			1,550	19.2	948	11.7
Cooperatives						
Production			695	8.6	921	11.4
Credit & Service			807	10.0	134	1.7
Work Collectives					24	0.3
Dead Furrow					37	0.5
Individual Assignations					210	2.6
Special Titling of Land					1,460	18.1
Titling of Indigenous Communities					171	2.1
Abandoned Area					460	5.7
TOTAL	**8,073**	**100.0%**	**8,073**	**100.0%**	**8,073**	**100.0%**

Sources: Figures for 1978 and 1988 from CIERA (1989, 9:39); 1984 calculated from Deere et al. (1985, 79).

disposed to join a cooperative. With the growing strength of contra bands in the municipality, Quilalí's small group of pro-Sandinistas also felt an increasing need to join together for protection. In the words of Daniel López, who was forced to flee his small farm: "Alone in the mountains we never slept well. In the cooperative we had more support. We could rest easy. Here we had shelter. The [Sandinista] army was in charge."

Quilalí's first three CASs followed national organizational guidelines. Official members *(socios)*—generally male heads of households—elected a board of directors to administer the cooperative. Members worked collectively in the fields to raise corn, beans, rice, and plantains as food crops, and tobacco, coffee, and cattle for export. After the harvest, families received a portion of the crop for their own consumption, as well as a share of any profits, calculated according to the number of days they had worked. The cooperatives also received bank loans and aid from the FSLN in the form of housing, tractors, and irrigation equipment. In addition to their work in the fields, all the men and a number of women participated in self-defense militias that were on alert twenty-four hours a day.

While there were no formal political criteria for joining a cooperative, in practice through self-selection, the peasants who joined Quilalí's first cooperatives were largely FSLN supporters. In fact, the decision to provide these peasants with river valley land and substantial material and technical assistance was a critical factor that enabled the Sandinistas to consolidate a military and political base of support outside of Quilalí's town limits. Like peasants elsewhere, pro-Sandinista peasants put safety first and only if their basic survival was assured could they maintain an open political stance in favor of the revolution.[4]

Also, in the opinion of many founding cooperative members, the FSLN's distribution of land to them was tangible evidence of the Sandinistas' commitment to poor peasants like themselves. Land distribution and cooperative members' subsequent collective organizational experience and struggle to defend their land served to reinforce the revolutionary commitment of those peasants who remained in the cooperatives (Enriquez 1997). This was demonstrated in the 1990 elections, in which members of the Edwin Barahona, El Coco, and La

Reforma cooperatives voted strongly in favor of the FSLN, although the Sandinistas lost in the municipality as a whole. Furthermore, a survey after 1990 found that in Nicaragua as a whole 50.6 percent of "collectivized peasants" supported the FSLN in the 1990 elections as compared to 36 percent of the rural population as a whole.[5] As will be seen, however, anti-Sandinistas soon came to criticize the new cooperatives on several grounds, including their perceived partisan nature and military functions. In the following years tensions grew between the cooperatives and surrounding rural communities where the contras were building networks of peasant supporters, until the cooperatives became virtual islands of Sandinista support in a countryside under the hegemonic influence of the counterrevolution.

Retreat of the Revolution

Outside of the three river valley cooperatives and the La Reforma coffee cooperative, what little revolutionary activity that existed in the mountains generally collapsed with the departure of Sandinista community leaders and the FSLN lost its shaky foothold in isolated communities to the north and west of the town of Quilalí. From 1983 onward virtually the only Sandinista presence in the mountains would be a military one, and peasants' contact with the revolution would be limited to Sandinista Army patrols and State Security. In competing for peasant support in ideological terms, the FSLN was now at a serious disadvantage. FSLN projects and programs that might benefit in particular the poor peasant smallholders in these zones were no longer viable, and virtually all information residents of these communities received about the revolution would be second-hand, in many cases filtered and distorted through contra networks. It appears that this dynamic of political and military polarization was not unique to Quilalí and occurred even in some interior zones such as Bocana de Paiwás where the FSLN initially had a strong social base.[6] In the departments of Jinotega and Matagalpa as well, the contras extended their influence over the countryside, while the towns and cooperatives remained under Sandinista control.[7]

Because very limited empirical data are available on the political views of Nicaragua's interior peasantry in the 1980s, it is useful to examine the results of the 1984 elections summarized in table 5.3. These results may provide a rough measure of peasant political support and opposition to the FSLN, although they should not be taken as a direct indicator of peasant support for the contras. In 1984 the FSLN won 65 percent of the rural vote as compared to 68 percent of the urban vote. The rural abstention rate, however—what Castro (1992) considers to represent "potential opposition"—to the FSLN, was particularly high in Nicaragua's conflictive interior departments, ranging from 35 percent in the department of Matagalpa to 46 percent in Jinotega (IHCA 1985b, 6b).

In the municipality of Quilalí the FSLN won 52.3 percent of the valid votes, with 38.6 percent of registered voters abstaining (IHCA 1985b, 20b). "Potential opposition" to the FSLN in the municipality, as expressed through a combination of abstention, null votes, and support for the opposition parties, may have been as high as 68.1 percent of registered voters (20b). Nationwide, in 70 percent of interior municipalities with a "traditional" peasantry such as Quilalí, the abstention rate was higher than the national average. In contrast, in only 29 percent of municipalities with a "proletarian" peasantry, did voters abstain in greater numbers than the national average (21b). Overall, as will be discussed in the following chapter, the zones in which the contras were able to recruit a high number of combatants also tended to rate highly in terms of "potential opposition" in the 1984 elections. The 1984 vote suggests that despite the FSLN's success in consolidating a base of peasant support in the river valley and town of Quilalí, a significant number of peasants may have already come to oppose the FSLN by the mid-1980s. It is worthwhile then to take a closer look at underlying cultural, structural, and ideological tensions

Table 5.3
Election Results by Department, 1984

Department	Abstention Rate (% of registered voters)	FSLN (% of valid votes)	Other Parties
PACIFIC COAST			
Chinandega	20.5%	74.5%	25.6%
León	20.2	71.2	28.9
Managua	18.2	67.1	32.8
Masaya	24.0	57.3	42.7
Carazo	22.3	67.6	32.4
Granada	22.2	54.5	45.4
Rivas	21.7	68.4	31.5
Average Pacific Coast	**21.3%**	**65.8%**	**34.2%**
INTERIOR			
Nueva Segovia	28.7%	72.0%	28.1
Madriz	18.1	69.2	30.9
Estelí	14.0	74.7	25.1
Jinotega	45.5	65.8	34.3
Matagalpa	34.7	61.0	39.2
Boaco	36.8	53.6	46.4
Chontales	39.8	64.5	35.5
Zelaya Central	39.7	64.5	35.5
Río San Juan	25.2	78.6	21.5
Average Interior	**31.4%**	**67.1%**	**32.9%**
NATIONAL TOTAL	**24.6%**	**67.0%**	**33.2%**

Source: IHCA (1985b, 6b).

between the Sandinista program and Quilalí's peasantry, and the important role peasant perceptions of the conflict played in shaping support or opposition to the revolution.

Some scholars argue that in the 1980s the FSLN dominated ideological discourse and successfully established the legitimacy of its hegemonic revolutionary project (Luciak 1995; Selbin 1993). The present study suggests, however, that at least in Quilalí, revolutionary political and ideological discourse was, and remains, deeply contested. As earlier chapters have suggested, although most of Quilalí's peasantry had only minimal involvement in traditional party politics before the revolution, they were by no means simply blank slates, open and willing to be molded by the revolution. Instead, the new Sandinista ideology and mass organizations had to challenge and compete with established prerevolutionary forms of consciousness, values, and beliefs. In other words, while the FSLN ideology and programs applied in Quilalí were not appreciably different than in other parts of Nicaragua, the historical, economic, social, and cultural characteristics of the municipality's population meant that the Sandinistas would have a much more difficult time establishing the hegemony of its class-based discourse.

Some FSLN policy makers and analysts characterize Nicaragua's mountain peasantry as a traditional, backward, conservative sector resistant to revolutionary change often implicitly assumed to be in their best interests. This view of Nicaragua's peasantry, however, seems ahistorical and overly static. As earlier chapters have suggested, the cultural and social values of Quilalí's peasantry—patron-client ties, respect for private property, independence, intense religiosity, and family and community solidarity—were closely linked to the municipality's history of migration and the material and economic conditions of life on the agricultural frontier. As will be seen, even into the 1980s, given the economic and military dynamics in the municipality, these earlier values and relations continued to make sense to some peasants and they resisted the new revolutionary ideology and programs that challenged their way of life *(modo de vivir)*. In other cases, the rapid nature of change in post-1979 Quilalí appears to have led to a divided or dual consciousness among some poor peasants, who were both attracted to and even incorporated certain aspects of revolutionary discourse into their worldview, while at the same time still bound to earlier forms of consciousness.

Table 5.4 presents a summary of the two polarized and competing pro-Sandinista and anti-Sandinista worldviews. While this table is meant only to synthesize pro- and anti-Sandinista ideal types, in fact many peasants interviewed for this study did fall fairly consistently within one of the two positions. A minority of peasants, however, particularly the poor and women, did not express clearly defined opinions on all these topics, or held mixed or even seemingly contradictory views from both perspectives.

One peasant whose story illustrates some of these issues is Mario Aguero from La Vigía, who expresses satisfaction with campesino life, the hard work of farming and caring for cattle and pigs, hunting deer in the mountains, and searching for honey in the forest with his children. Aguero took part in the resistance movement against the National Guard and the 1979 land invasion of La Vigía. He explains:

> We didn't know about the war [against Somoza] until the moment of liberation. It was an urban war. We belonged to a political party. I was a Liberal. . . . But we didn't really know much about politics. Sometimes because so and so is from the government we would mark their name on the ballot, not really understanding anything. . . . Later no one took the initiative to say, "I'm going to be a Sandinista or a contra." No one. We all waited for something good.

In the early 1980s Mario Aguero helped organize adult literacy classes in his community. But while he supported FSLN efforts to expand educational opportunities, Aguero disagreed with the political messages presented in the new government textbooks, which urged Nicaraguans to take up arms to defend the revolution. Mario Aguero and other community members eventually dropped out of the adult education program, and mistrust between La Vigía residents and town FSLN representatives grew: "We also realized that it [the revolution] wasn't what we had hoped for because we saw that they [the Sandinistas] had ideas different from our ideology. We didn't understand their ideas. . . . We campesinos are sometimes backward.

Table 5.4

Sandinista and Anti-Sandinista Worldviews in Quilalí

Issue	Pro-Sandinistas	Anti-Sandinistas
Patron-Client Ties	The wealthy exploit the poor; Sandinistas support horizontal class solidarity between poor peasants; poor peasants and workers share common interests	Continued ideological and economic dependence on patrons; in competition with pro-Sandinista peasants for limited resources and benefits
Equality	Support greater rural equality; FSLN is first government in Nicaraguan history to be truly concerned with the poor	"Rich need poor and poor need rich"; a degree of rural hierarchy is necessary and acceptable
Land Reform	Land reform justified when land acquired illegally or unethically, and as response to needs of landless peasants; agrarian reform is key to consolidation of pro-Sandinista peasant support	Fingueros and middle peasants generally oppose land reform; the poor are more divided; FSLN land reform is criticized for its political nature as well as for defense and collective work requirements
Collective Agriculture	Collective farming is not first choice, but peasants are willing to try it; seen as necessity in wartime as means of self-defense	Prefer to work individually and within informal family and social networks
FSLN and Contra Leadership	Contra leadership are resentful members of well-off sectors who deceive poor peasants into fighting against their own interests; ex-National Guardsmen play key role in contras	Contras led by northern peasants; FSLN leaders are opportunistic urban outsiders
State Economic Interventions	Generally positive view of role of state in economy to ensure greater equality and promote national economic goals	Oppose FSLN rationing measures, controls over buying and selling of crops, and shortages

Militarization	War is largely result of U.S. and National Guard aggression; war has inhibited FSLN from benefiting population as much as it would have liked	FSLN generates conflict in once harmonious communities; Sandinistas responsible for bringing war to Quilalí and for subsequent deaths and destruction
Nationalism	View role of U.S. government toward Nicaragua in negative terms; willing to fight to defend Nicaragua's national sovereignty	Consider U.S. government to be "great friend" of Nicaragua; seek accommodation not confrontation; struggle for dignity and freedom of peasantry
Religion	Participation in liberation theology groups leads to political activism in favor of FSLN	Largely evangelical; religious faith offers emotional solace, neutral space, and means to resist FSLN
Human Rights	Critical of contras for extensive human rights abuses against civilians	Critical of FSLN repression, particularly military recruitment, imprisonment by State Security, and use of artillery

We don't have much education and maybe because we lack education we couldn't understand the FSLN."

Part of the new Sandinista ideology that resonated deeply—in both a positive and negative sense—with Quilalí peasants were the concepts of "exploitation" and "equality."[8] Specifically, as Quilalí peasants perceived it, FSLN national discourse criticized large landowners and finqueros as "exploiters" who had accumulated their wealth at the expense of the poor, and promoted as an alternative greater rural economic and social equality.[9] As we saw earlier, Quilalí's MILPA leaders rejected this perceived challenge to their moral authority and economic interests. Some middle and poor peasants were also reluctant to apply this type of analysis and criticism to the municipality of Quilalí. One middle peasant and former contra comments: "I didn't like it that the Sandinistas were always asking us to meet to criticize the *patrones* who have been my friends. I don't believe we should criticize them just because they have more money or a better standard of living or because they have more education." Instead, these peasants continued to view their municipality as a harmonious zone of agricultural richness, where there was ample room for all, wealthy and poor. Successful landowners and finqueros were not necessarily a threat, but rather a potential source of assistance and employment, as well as a model to be emulated.

Even after 1979 some poor and middle peasants remained bound to paternalistic relationships by both affective ties to patrons and a recognition of their continued economic dependence of the wealthy. One example of the emotional element of paternalistic ties felt by some poor Quilalí peasants is found in the story of Juana Gómez from the northern mountains of Quilalí. After her first husband left her, Gómez struggled to support her three children alone. A finquero allowed her to rent a small plot of land on which to build a house and grow corn and beans. Gómez also washed clothes, cooked for wealthy members of the community, and baked bread to sell. When her oldest son turned twelve, their patron occasionally paid the boy the equivalent of a dollar for a day's work on the farm. In the mid-1980s, land reform officials apparently considered expropriating the finquero's farm. They tried to convince Gómez to support this move, suggesting that she might eventually receive land for herself. Gómez reacted with indignation at the idea: "We always lived very close to the people who were well-off. It would be unjust for us to allow the Sandinistas to confiscate [the property] of the man who out of generosity gave us our land and our house. We could never pay our patron back in that manner. We would never accept that." Juana Gómez chose instead to remain without land and distance herself from the revolution. Shortly afterward, two of her sons took up arms with the contras, and Gómez herself actively collaborated with the contras.

While feelings of affection some Quilalí poor and middle peasants had for local elites should not be underestimated, underlying this were the "realties of power" of the municipality—that is, the continued economic dependence of some poor and middle peasants on the wealthy.[10] Although the revolutionary ideology and mass organizations may have encouraged peasants to loosen or break their prerevolutionary clientelistic relationships, the FSLN did not always provide peasants the necessary economic support and material resources that would have allowed greater autonomy. It was not until late 1982 that the FSLN began to distribute land to peasants. And even then, as will be discussed below, the climate of political polarization and conditions the FSLN attached to land reform made this an unattractive option to many poor peasants. Throughout the 1980s some landless peasants remained dependent on the goodwill of finqueros, who continued to control over one-third of the municipality's land, to gain access to a parcel to farm. Likewise, the failure of state farms to provide adequate services to the surrounding community, as well as the growing shortages of transportation, agricultural inputs, and consumer goods, at times served to actually increase the influence of finqueros in Quilalí and other interior zones.[11]

Under the revolution, poor and middle peasants did gain access to bank credit and a farmers' union, the UNAG, to represent their interests. But for some peasants these new benefits were insufficient to convince them to risk antagonizing powerful figures in their community, particularly when it was uncertain that the FSLN offered a viable alternative. To peasants living in extreme poverty in particular, elites represented security and protection, and it was difficult to imagine who or what would fill the void left by their absence. Poor peasants were skeptical that they would reach a level of economic self-sufficiency so as not to need the wealthy. Poor peasant and ex-contra Miguel Abrego explains:

> I was talking with an EPS [Sandinista Army] lieutenant who told me that I was someone who could understand these things. He told me, "The rich man exploits the labor of the poor." But I told him, "The rich need the poor and the poor need the rich." Now if we're all on the same level, what can we do? If I have someone sick, who is going to lend me 100 pesos? No one, because we're all in the same situation. But if I go to the rich man, he'll lend me the money, although sooner or later I'll have to work with a machete for him. The rich sustain the poor. We poor need the rich, unless we are all well-off, which is never going to happen.

In the eyes of this peasant the rich and poor are mutually dependent and the best option for the poor is to accept their place at the bottom of a hierarchy where life may be hard, but at least survival is assured.[12] In contrast to the FSLN's call for greater rural equality, several anti-Sandinista peasants comment: "There are rich and poor. That's how things should be arranged."[13]

In addition to challenging existing rural inequalities, another key component of the revolutionary ideology was its nationalistic call to Nicaraguans to prioritize and defend the *patria*. While Quilalí's pro-Sandinista peasants were most attracted to the FSLN's land reform and programs in favor of the poor, many of them also came to share Sandinista nationalist ideals. These peasants drew inspiration from

Sandino's struggle half a century earlier and suggest that their experiences in the Sandinista military and mass organizations in particular broadened their outlook beyond the limits of the municipality of Quilalí. When pro-Sandinista peasants took up arms with militias to defend the town or their cooperatives, or served in the Sandinista Army Reserve, they report that they fought both for their interests as the rural poor and to defend Nicaragua's national sovereignty against National Guard and North American aggression.

To other Quilalí peasants who had not shared these experiences, however, the nation of Nicaragua, which the FSLN called on them to defend, was a distant, abstract concept that competed with their loyalties to their local community, markets, extended family, and networks of friends (CIPRES 1991, 170). Such a conflict of loyalties occurred when Quilalí resident and later contra collaborator Virginia Moreno took a job as a cook on a Sandinista Army base. Moreno remembers that one day she asked the commanding officer for a leave of absence from her job to visit her son. When the army officer denied her permission to leave, she decided to quit her job with the army: "I left because they wouldn't let me see my children. They said that military personnel had to sign an agreement to forget their children and parents. They told me that I must put the revolution, the patria first, before anything else."

As part of their nationalist views, Quilalí pro-Sandinista peasants are generally critical of the U.S. government's historical relationship with Nicaragua, in particular its more recent funding of the contra forces. Many anti-Sandinista peasants, on the other hand, who did not believe that Quilalí elites exploited their workers, also rejected the premise that the U.S. government exploited Nicaragua or was their enemy. In general, these peasants had little direct knowledge of either Sandino's struggle or U.S. companies, and those who remember the North American lumber and mining companies that operated in the Segovias into the 1950s consider them to have been a good source of employment. These peasants do not view the United States

as a hostile government, but rather, as several anti-Sandinista peasants comment, "a great friend." In the words of a former contra upset
about Congressional funding cutoffs to his organization: "We're
never going to be enemies of the United States. We've always been allies. But it was a bad deal, because [the U.S.] is the greatest power in
the world and didn't have any reason to abandon us, leave us to be
killed; because a friend cares for you, a friend defends you."

Just as within their rural communities, vulnerable peasants sought
to link themselves with a powerful patron, in the international arena
their strategy was to seek accommodation, not confrontation, with
their powerful neighbor the United States. To many of these Quilalí
peasants, such as Ricardo Pérez, the FSLN's hostile rhetoric toward
the United States simply did not make sense. Pérez, a middle peasant
who over the past decade has been able to accumulate some forty MZ
of land through a combination of hard work and shrewd business
deals, states: "In his heart, the Sandinista hated the Yankís. They
even convinced people to take up arms against the United States if it
invaded. It's ridiculous to think that a small country like Nicaragua
could defeat the United States, which has technology, a powerful
army." As the conflict deepened in Quilalí peasants like Pérez, experts
in the art of survival and accommodation, would decide to go with
the "winner," the U.S.-supported contras.

Another source of tension between the revolution and some interior peasants was the FSLN's often strained relationship with the
Catholic church hierarchy and certain evangelical churches, as well
its perceived challenge to traditional religious values.[14] Somewhat
surprisingly, however, none of the anti-Sandinista peasants interviewed in Quilalí mentioned conflicts between the FSLN and local
churches as a complaint against the revolution. In fact, throughout the
1980s Quilalí's Catholic church and local Sandinista officials maintained relatively cordial relations. Evangelical Quilalí peasants also report that the FSLN generally respected their religious activities.

In other zones of Nicaragua, however, religious clashes were an important peasant grievance. In a rural community in Yalí, Jinotega, for example, State Security agents searched and damaged a local evangelical church suspected of antigovernment activities. According to a church member interviewed by the author, he and supporters of the sect were so outraged at this perceived desecration that as a group they made the decision to begin actively supporting the contras. Several studies also suggest that the contras more effectively employed— some would say manipulated—traditional religious symbols in favor of their political and military struggle than did the FSLN (Castro 1990b, 28; CIPRES 1991, 401).

Land Reform

Perhaps the most important component of the revolutionary program in Quilalí and other rural zones was Sandinista agrarian reform. In the peasant culture of Nicaragua's mountains, land is much more than a means of production for a campesino or indigenous person, "It is his security, the material cement that joins him to his family, to the market, to the community" (CIPRES 1991, 170). On the agricultural frontier, a man's farm—in Quilalí land titles were overwhelmingly held by men—was generally viewed as his just reward for the personal sacrifice and hard work he invested in obtaining it.

While land pressures in Quilalí were not as intense as other areas of Nicaragua, the municipality did have a substantial landless population (approximately 250 families) on the eve of the revolution. In addition, hundreds of displaced families arrived to Quilalí from the western Segovias in the early 1980s. As stated earlier, in 1979 the FSLN expropriated 14,200 MZ of valley land, 93 percent of which came from the large cattle haciendas of Somoza and his supporters, and converted it into state farms. In 1983 the Sandinista government shifted policy and took 5,000 MZ of state farmland and bought and expropriated a further 1,500 MZ of land to hand over to three peasant agricultural cooperatives. Pro-Sandinista Quilalí peasants strongly supported Sandinista agrarian reform in the municipality under which the right to private property could be challenged when land and houses were acquired by means judged to be illegal or unethical, or were not being adequately utilized. According to pro-Sandinista peasant leader Daniel López: "Before all of Nicaragua was owned by one man called Somoza. He owned La Vigía [hacienda], farms all over Nicaragua, and his associates, the parasite Liberal deputies, were the large landowners here." Under these circumstances, López believes that land reform in Quilalí's river valley was an act of social and economic justice in favor of the poor: "In Quilalí they [anti-Sandinistas] just don't understand that it's just to take land away from one man to give it to fifty families who don't have any land." In addition, the distribution of land to peasant cooperatives beginning in late 1982 enabled the FSLN to provide a relative degree of physical and economic security to its followers and consolidate a political base of support outside Quilalí's town limits.

In contrast, as we have seen, Sandinista land reform was strongly opposed by most finqueros, even those who were not directly affected by the process. A smaller number of middle and poor peasants share the opinion of well-off MILPA leaders and collaborators that Sandinista expropriations were in principle a violation of the property rights of family and friends. More commonly, however, middle and poor peasants opposed specific aspects of the agrarian reform— the requirement to join cooperatives and participate in militias and its perceived political biases—or were unwilling to risk involvement in the project in the municipality's increasingly polarized political and military climate. Poor peasants in particular tend to have more complex and sometimes contradictory attitudes toward land reform in comparison to the firm opposition of many finqueros and some middle peasants.

Former contra Ramón Moreno and his four siblings traveled from hacienda to hacienda in northern Nicaragua with their mother, Virginia, who worked as a cook and coffee picker. In 1979, seventeen-year-old Ramón joined the FSLN guerrillas and after the insurrection served for a year as an army platoon leader before deserting in 1981. Paradoxically, although he was initially attracted to Sandinista promises of redistribution of land and goods, Moreno disagreed with the expropriations the FSLN carried out in Quilalí: "The Sandinistas began to call anyone who owned large properties—anyone who had cattle, pastures, and fruit trees—"bourgeoisie," "traitors," a lot of things. Everyone who had something through his own efforts or through inheritance, everyone who had a good farm, had his land confiscated by the FSLN."

Other poor peasants interviewed did not condemn land reform as a whole, but opposed specific expropriations of families they knew personally. One landless peasant and ex-contra from the northern mountains recalls the FSLN's forced buyout of a wealthy friend's father as one reason why he came to oppose the revolution: "[His] son fought with them [the Sandinistas], and still they took his pickup truck, his land, and the cattle he had." Likewise, when the FSLN expropriated the property of a well-known finquero from San Juan del Río Coco who was allegedly aiding the contras, the move was widely opposed by the population and peasants organized a large demonstration, asking the FSLN to return the man's farm (MIDINRA 1983, 6). On the other hand, some anti-Sandinista poor peasants express support in principle for a moderate redistribution of land if it could be carried out in a way that would not harm friends and neighbors. The ex-contra who felt the forced buyout of his finquero friend was unjust also argues that poor peasants like himself have a right to land to work: "The poor survive on what they harvest. I would say that if a terrateniente has 1,000 MZ of land and you take away 300 MZ to give to the poor, that would be good, because it's not only the rich who have a right to life. The poor also have rights." In another case, Juana Gómez, the woman who opposed the confiscation of her patron's farm, would prefer a voluntary land reform on the part of landowners: "It would be better if it came from their hearts to give a little land to someone who doesn't have any, because there are a lot of poor people who don't have anywhere to plant their corn. But it's wrong to take something away from someone who has worked for it. Still, there are rich people who have a lot of land and don't even use it." In these statements, poor peasants attempt to balance two conflicting values: respect for private property closely linked to the municipality's work ethic and the "right to life" of Quilalí's poorest peasants. They search for a compromise solution that would leave intact the right to private property, yet would also meet the basic needs of landless peasants like themselves.

Some anti-Sandinista poor peasants interviewed also express resentment against the FSLN land reform because they believe they were excluded from its benefits. It is generally recognized that during the first three years of the revolution, FSLN policy concentrated land and resources in the state sector and did not satisfy the demands of the rural poor for land, even in zones like Quilalí where land pressures were less intense.[15] In late 1982 the FSLN, in part out of recognition of such peasant frustrations, began to formally distribute land to peasants who agreed to join agricultural cooperatives. This requirement of collective land ownership, however, effectively "locked out the majority of the peasantry from any land distribution" (Martinez 1993, 479).

During the Somoza era peasants had little or no experience with formal organizations or collective activities. Rather, families farmed individually and relied on a series of informal extended family and community networks—which varied from mutual aid to exploitation disguised as paternalism—as a source of labor and economic security. Such networks were flexible, self-defined, and responded to specific needs among peasants. In contrast, Sandinista cooperative models were largely developed and imposed from outside. Ex-contra Mario Aguero expresses the concerns of many anti-Sandinistas: "At least in terms of collective farming, we don't believe in working that way. We have to farm the land, to work as farmers, but we want to work freely with no one controlling us. We wanted them to hand over the land with individual titles."

In the case of Aguero's community of La Vigía, those peasants who seized Somoza's land in 1979 for many years resisted pressure from Sandinista officials to organize agricultural cooperatives. These peasants were willing to join Credit and Service Cooperatives to obtain loans, but refused to farm collectively or move from their scattered farmhouses into a single settlement community or even to allow the settlement of displaced families from Wiwilí and other zones on their land.

Previous negative experiences also discouraged some peasants from joining agricultural cooperatives. As we have seen, some peasants briefly joined revolutionary organizations in the first months of the revolution and then withdrew because some hastily organized rural organizations lacked experienced leadership and resources and functioned poorly. These peasants were accustomed to setting their own work pace and hours, and coming and going as they pleased.[16] They report that they felt bored and frustrated with long, often disorganized meetings and the disputes that inevitably arose among peasants not accustomed to working together. Ex-contra Carlos Sánchez explains: "Why should I spend two weeks arguing about how to carry out one little job? You can't work in your own way. I saw that in the agricultural collectives some worked and others didn't. With so many people on the land, how was there going to be a profit? I didn't see much future in that, working in masses."

In addition to their reluctance to farm collectively, a number of poor anti-Sandinistas believe that the FSLN used the expropriated river valley land not to benefit the poor as a whole as Sandinista rhetoric proclaimed, but as a reward for political loyalty.[17] In the words of former contra Ramón Moreno: "The Sandinistas said that land was going to be for the poor, but they confiscated the land and gave it to their people. The best farms, located in the best places, were given to the Sandinista followers, their sympathizers." As we have seen, although there were no formal political requirements to benefit from land reform, in practice through a process of self-selection it was largely pro-revolutionary peasants who chose to join cooperatives. These peasants were willing to work closely with Sandinista government agencies such as MIDINRA, and even more important, they were willing to participate in self-defense militias.

As soon as they were established the new cooperatives were targeted by bands of contras for intimidation and violence. In this polarized military and political climate, a Quilalí peasant who joined a cooperative was taking an open stance against the contras and committing himself and his family to militarily defending the cooperative against potential attack. For many poor peasants this loss of neutrality was too high a price to pay to gain access to land. It is also noteworthy that anti-Sandinista peasants interviewed largely blame the FSLN and not the contras for, in their minds, making the taking up of arms a requirement to obtain land. Ex-contra Moreno explains: "I was very young, but I said to myself that it was unfair. . . . How was it possible that the land was for the campesino, yet to obtain the land I had to arm myself? . . . I have a big family, my mother, and her other children. Why couldn't I have a piece of land to farm?" From 1982 onward, anti-Sandinista envy and resentment grew in some communities surrounding the cooperatives toward those peasants who received land. To the present day, peasants like Moreno speak disparagingly of those in Quilalí who received land under the Sandinista agrarian reform as "bums" (*vagos*) who accepted "stolen" land and are living off FSLN handouts.

To summarize, the political impact of the first two phases of Sandinista agrarian reform, from 1979 to 1984, was mixed in the municipality of Quilalí. On the one hand, the distribution of land to cooperatives enabled the FSLN to consolidate the support of a significant minority of Quilalí peasants. On the other hand, despite the limited number of finquero landholdings confiscated and FSLN reassurances that efficient producers would not lose their land, agrarian reform was a source of tension between the FSLN and Quilali elites and an important factor in the MILPA uprising. Likewise, many middle peasants, who did not have a strong interest in obtaining land for themselves, opposed agrarian reform when it affected friends and neighbors and as a violation of traditional property rights. In terms of Quilalí's poor peasants who came to support the counterrevolution, land reform can best be described as a missed opportunity. By not effectively and rapidly responding to poor peasant demands for land, the FSLN failed to employ perhaps its most powerful policy instrument that could have potentially won over these peasants to the revolutionary cause. As it turned out, some landless peasants' frustrated desire for land became an important grievance against the FSLN. Similarly, the anti-Sandinista perception that agrarian reform was a particularly blatant example of patronage politics undermined the FSLN's credibility as a party in favor of the impoverished majority.

A final important issue remains to be addressed. Both anti- and pro-Sandinista poor peasants generally agree that the Somoza government offered little or nothing in the way of assistance or land to Quilalí's neediest residents. In contrast, the FSLN attempted to provide peasants with improved educational, health, and technical services, credit, and land. Yet paradoxically, in interviews poor contra collaborators and combatants offer little criticism of the Somoza regime that virtually abandoned them. Instead, their resentment is directed almost entirely at the FSLN and its "betrayal" of initial promises to provide individual parcels of land and other immediate benefits to poor peasants like themselves (CIPRES 1991, 30–31).

One possible explanation for this seeming contradiction lies in the fact that the dramatic overthrow of the Somoza dictatorship and the FSLN's revolutionary program encouraged the development of a series new demands on the part of a once quiescent peasantry.[18] Peasants who had expected—and received—little governmental assistance in prerevolutionary Quilalí now judged the FSLN by a higher standard. These poor peasants held the Sandinista government accountable for fulfilling its most fundamental promise, to better the lives of the poor. When the FSLN failed to meet these new expectations, some poor peasants—particularly those who had absorbed some of the Sandinista discourse and gained self-confidence through participation in the FSLN guerrillas or popular organizations—turned against the FSLN and became harsh critics of the revolutionary process. One such peasant, Carlos Sánchez, who fought briefly with the FSLN guerrillas and later took part in the failed landed invasion of the Guaná hacienda, states: "They [the Sandinistas] promised so many things. That everyone would be equal, that they would take land from the rich to give to the poor. But they didn't fulfill their promises."

In addition to resentment over the Sandinista failure to meet land demands, these "disillusioned Sandinistas" are also critical of the FSLN for favoring wealthy and urban interests over those of poor peasants. In terms of land distribution, for example, it can be argued that the FSLN's policy of national unity worked to the detriment of poor peasants by partially protecting the landowning class and blocking a more profound agrarian reform.[19] Other analysts identify a more generalized urban bias on the part of the FSLN in which "the majority of services, buying power, [and] subsidies accumulated in the cities, often to the detriment of the countryside" (CIPRES 1991, 303). As we have seen in Quilalí, most FSLN political posts, such as political secretary, were filled by young people from urban areas—privileged outsiders in the eyes of some Quilalí peasants. In interviews, several ex-contras also criticize "19th of July" opportunists, often from relatively well-off sectors, who assumed leadership roles in new Sandinista organizations and attempted to manipulate the revolutionary process to their personal benefit. In the words of Carlos Sánchez:

> We felt the scorn of the Sandinistas. The "19th of Julys" or the students sent us [ex-FSLN guerrillas] back to our houses, some missing a leg or arm, or with bullet wounds, to recover from our wounds

alone. Students have an easy life. They sit down to study in the shade, knowing that at mealtime their food will be waiting for them, while the campesino has to work for everything he has. He has to go into the fields at six in the morning, fill his stomach with the food there whether he likes it or not. . . . The rest of society depends on the labor and production of the campesino—the student, the government official, the worker.

It is interesting to note that some of these same poor peasants who criticize the FSLN for not fulfilling its promises to the poor also opposed the FSLN measures, expropriations in particular, that harmed elites who were friends and neighbors.[20] These contradictory attitudes serve to illustrate a fundamental dilemma faced by the Sandinistas that was never fully resolved: How could the FSLN develop a revolutionary program that did not alienate the still economically and politically influential wealthy minority in Quilalí and at the same time respond to the exploding demands of the poor for land and resources? Finally, it should be mentioned that most pro-Sandinista peasants also recognize that some revolutionary promises were not fulfilled in Quilalí. Unlike anti-Sandinistas, however, these peasants place responsibility on a series of events largely beyond the control of the FSLN, most importantly U.S. aggression and the escalating military conflict. These peasants believe that the FSLN was genuinely committed to bettering the lives of poor peasants and are convinced that under more favorable circumstances the Sandinista government would have aided Quilalí's poor majority even more than it did during its ten-year rule.

Economic Measures

A number of studies have identified Sandinista economic policies and market controls as a key source of tension between the FSLN and the rural population, in particular middle peasants (CIPRES 1991;

Kaimowitz 1988; Bendaña 1991; Colburn 1986). Under the Somoza regime, the government's role was largely limited to strategic interventions in the economy at key points with assistance from "a network of localized, multi-faceted agents who were well-informed of regional market conditions and had broad police powers" (Kaimowitz 1988, 127). In contrast, after 1979 the FSLN intervened in numerous areas of Nicaragua's rural economy, including the distribution of agricultural inputs and machinery, as well as the collection and storage, industrial processing, and distribution of crops to consumers (CIPRES 1991, 323). Spoor (1995, 67) characterizes these Sandinista attempts to administer a wide variety of economic activities as "well-intended," but poorly designed and managed, and hindered by fragmented and conflicting policies. Peasants were particularly harmed by the collapse of traditional transportation and distribution networks; shortages of labor and agricultural and consumer goods; as well as government controls that forced farmers to sell their crops to the state.

Contrary to expectation anti-Sandinista Quilalí peasants voiced few specific complaints about economic difficulties they had faced as agricultural producers or the prices the government paid for their crops, beyond the generalized grievance that the Sandinista government wanted to "control everything" and the FSLN "wouldn't let us work." Both anti-Sandinista men and women, however, expressed resentment about the government controls and shortages they faced as consumers. As of late 1982, the FSLN began to impose rationing measures nationwide that restricted the sale of such basic consumer and food products as sugar, soap, rice, cooking oil, clothing, and shoes (CIPRES 1991, 330). Simón Olivares, who oversaw Quilalí's rationing program as an official with the Ministry of Internal Commerce (Ministerio de Comercio Interior, MICOIN), remembers that MICOIN's goal was to ensure that all Quilalí residents had their basic food needs met and to prevent speculation and hoarding: "We thought we were doing something good for the people. We wanted everyone to have something, even if it was a little."

Under the program, Quilalí families were issued a ration card that allowed them to purchase limited quantities of rationed products twice a month at government-run or -regulated stores.[21] Anti-Sandinista peasants from all sectors—wealthy, middle, and poor—report in interviews that these controls violated the freedom they enjoyed under Somoza to buy goods when and where they chose. In the words of contra collaborator Juana Gómez: "Under the [Somoza] dictatorship you could buy a pair of shoes when you wanted, not when they told you. We're poor, but we're used to buying things when we have money."

In the case of sugar, Nicaraguan rural families when they can afford it will consume several pounds a week in baking and to sweeten coffee, milk, and fruit drinks. Each Quilalí family in theory was allotted four pounds of sugar per month (MIDINRA 1984d, 42). Yet in 1988 only 2.43 pounds of sugar per month per family were available for sale in stores outside the town of Quilalí, as compared to 5.75 pounds for town residents. Likewise, in 1988 a typical Quilalí family of six could purchase only half a liter of cooking oil and three small bars of laundry soap a month. Other consumer goods, such as rubber boots, kerosene for lamps, and toothpaste, were completely unavailable through official distribution networks (Spoor 1989).

Quilalí peasants, who purchased little to begin with, resented having to alter or reduce their traditional consumption habits. One peasant woman from the river valley lamented in an interview that during the war her young children often had to go without milk. As it turns out, the woman had several cows and plenty of milk. She refused, however, to give her children any milk when she did not have sugar to sweeten it. Likewise, peasants from Quilalí complain repeatedly that their ration of soap was insufficient to wash the family's dirty clothes. In addition, some anti-sandinista peasants believe that the rationing system was used by the FSLN as a means of political control. Contra collaborator Juana Gómez explains: "We had to carry coupons with us. Sometimes we walked all the way to the store for nothing. It was the beginning of the month, but no food or supplies ever arrived. And if you didn't associate with them [the Sandinistas], they denied you everything but basic food supplies."

During the war the FSLN in fact did limit the sale of some goods in Quilalí communities known to support the counterrevolution, apparently to control the siphoning off of sugar and other food to contra troops. Peasants from these communities instead had to travel to government-regulated stores in the town of Quilalí, or to one of four rural stores located in Quilalí's Sandinista cooperatives, to make purchases. Sandinista authorities also on occasion sent out inspectors to visit peasants and verify the number of family members. Peasants resented such government intrusions and felt themselves under investigation and suspicion.

In addition to shortages of consumer goods, the Sandinista government was also unable to always ensure the timely provision of agricultural inputs and machinery to farmers, thus hindering agricultural production and raising costs (Deere et al. 1985, 86). In prerevolutionary Quilalí, agricultural inputs were readily available from international distributors in Estelí and Managua. Many of these distributors closed in 1979 when their owners left the country and the government agency PROAGRO quickly became Quilalí's sole source of agricultural inputs. By the mid-1980s, however, Quilalí's PROAGRO office lacked adequate transportation and shortages of basic goods were common. A 1987 study found that farmers were sometimes unable to obtain sufficient fertilizer, barbed wire, veterinary medicines, sprayers, and milk buckets in the PROAGRO store (MIDINRA 1987, 50). Likewise, attempts by Sandinista officials to persuade peasants to sell their crops to the government often failed because the government lacked scarce goods like corn grinders that would serve as incentives. To give one example of the potentially devastating impact of such shortages on farmers, in the municipality of

Yalí a study found that in half a dozen communities coffee production by rich campesinos virtually collapsed because peasants were unable to obtain necessary inputs and transportation, and after 1982, labor.[22]

Another important source of tension between peasants and the FSLN in some zones of Nicaragua was government pressures until the mid-1980s that peasants sell their food crops to the state agency, the National Enterprise for Basic Foodstuffs (Empresa Nacional de Alimentos Básicos, ENABAS). Some peasants resented coercive measures that the FSLN employed to prevent contraband sale of basic grains in the cities, such as roadblocks (*tranques*) where a peasant's entire crop might be seized as punishment. Other peasants also were unhappy with the relatively low prices paid by ENABAS, which according to some studies did not allow poor peasants employing traditional technology to earn a profit.[23] In addition, peasants selling their harvest at official prices faced deteriorating terms of trade between many urban consumer goods they purchased and prices they received for their food crops. Between 1978 and 1984, for example, the price of a machete increased eighteen times and a shirt 140 times, while the official price of basic grains increased only seven times (Spoor 1995, 124).

In Quilalí, ENABAS purchased basic grains from peasants at several rural collection points (Centros de Acopio Intermedios, CAIs) in the countryside and stored the crops in six silos located on the outskirts of town. In addition, in the mid-1980s MICOIN established roadblocks on the major roads leading out of the town of Quilalí. Yet in contrast to other zones of Nicaragua, where complaints against the Sandinista roadblocks were common, none of the anti-Sandinista peasants interviewed for this study mentioned the roadblocks or the sale of crops to ENABAS as a complaint against the Sandinista government. When directly questioned about prices they received from ENABAS for their crops, anti-Sandinista peasants merely commented that government prices were "more or less all right."

Quilalí residents offer several possible explanations as to why controls over crops sales are not remembered as a major source of conflict in the municipality of Quilalí. First, former MICOIN authorities report that Quilalí's distance from major cities and the growing insecurity of roads limited opportunities for black market activity by Quilalí's peasants. Also, in some years peasants were able to take advantage of differences between subsidized consumer prices for grains and ENABAS producer prices. For the 1983–84 harvest, for example, Quilalí producers could sell their corn to ENABAS and receive 180 cordobas per quintal of corn and then purchase corn as consumers for only 100 cordobas per quintal (MIDINRA 1987, 59). ENABAS collected 83,500 quintales of corn that year because Quilalí peasants sold their entire crop, not holding back the usual 25 percent for family consumption. Elimination of the subsidy the following year, however, led to a drastic fall in the amount of corn sold to ENABAS.

A third factor that diminished tension over this issue was the FSLN policy shift in the mid-1980s that liberalized the sale of basic grains. Although this policy was not uniformly implemented across Nicaragua until as late as 1987, in Quilalí peasants were able to freely sell their corn in other regions as early as 1985. In the 1986–87 harvest many chose to sell their crops across the border in Jinotega, where even official prices were 20 percent higher (MIDINRA 1987, 59). A final important point is that the interviews took place during a severe postwar recession. In retrospect, Sandinista economic policies that did not please peasants at the time may not have seemed so harmful in comparison to the current economic crisis.

Outside versus Local Leadership

The FSLN was also hampered in winning the political support of Quilalí's peasantry by its primarily urban base, its relatively weak outreach to interior rural zones, and its perceived outsider status. As we have seen, from the outset the Sandinistas faced greater challenges in remote rural zones such as Quilalí than in urban centers. Many Quilalí peasants did not identify the intense, violent struggle against Somoza as their own, an important element that forged urban support for the FSLN. Most Quilalí peasants also had little opportunity for formal education, contact with outside ideas, or experience with organizations. The fact that little groundwork had been carried out to prepare peasants for the abrupt changes that occurred in their lives after 1979, the revolutionary programs and ideology that, in the words of one peasant, "turned everything upside down," made the FSLN's task more difficult.

Much of the FSLN's limited resources were also focused on national reconstruction and urban needs, leaving fewer resources for more remote rural areas like Quilalí. According to one study, in the months following the overthrow of Somoza the FSLN left virtually abandoned even traditional zones of support such as Yalí, Cerro Blanco, Quibuto, Pancasán, and Matiguás.[24] In addition, as we have seen, many of the early FSLN personnel assigned to the municipality of Quilalí were inexperienced young people from the cities, who were unfamiliar with the municipality and lacked the credibility of long-established community leaders.[25] In the early 1980s as well, the FSLN encouraged hundreds of families from the western Segovias to migrate to Quilalí. A number of these families, who tended to be FSLN supporters, received land in Quilalí's river valley, thus reinforcing the perception of Sandinistas as outsiders. In interviews a number of contra collaborators and combatants state that the FSLN wanted Nicaragua to "be like Cuba." Upon further questioning, it appears that "Cuba" in the minds of these informants is less representative of a particular type of political or economic system—most had little or no direct or indirect knowledge about life in Cuba—than of something foreign and negative, outside their experience.

In contrast, anti-Sandinista discourse, with its emphasis on a common peasant identity, was conveyed and reinforced by contra leaders, the majority of whom were from the northern mountains and familiar not only with the geography, but also with the social and cultural terrain of the municipality. Some of the former MILPA leaders who continued as field commanders with the contras after 1982 had developed a wide range of contacts among peasants throughout the northern mountains while fighting as FSLN guerrillas against Somoza. Others like the Meza brothers, Oscar Sobalvarro, and Israel Galeano came from large and influential families that provided the contras with an immediate base of support. As the FSLN guerrillas did a few years earlier, finqueros-turned-contra-commanders "buil[t] networks [of contra supporters] based on existing relationships of subordination and domination in the zones or communities" (Bendaña 1991, 39).

In addition to their personal and family networks, local finqueros who led recruitment incursions into Quilalí in the early 1980s were able to frame their struggle in language and concepts familiar to peasants. This study argues that the role of rural elites was more complex than simple manipulation or a top-down imposition of ideas and opinions.[26] Rather, these contra leaders developed an anti-Sandinista discourse that both responded to and intensified existing peasant fears and grievances discussed earlier. A study of zones under counterrevolutionary influence in the departments of Zelaya and Chontales also suggests that leaders of the Jorge Salazar contra forces "manage and manipulate the code of the cattle world better than the Sandinista revolution" (Escuela de Sociología-UCA 1987, 7). This leadership role of rural elites may also help explain why support for the contras was generally stronger in heterogeneous "multiclass" interior zones than in more homogenous zones.[27] As we have seen, in contrast to Sandinista efforts to mobilize the population along shared interests of the popular classes, the contra leadership appealed to an interior peasant identity that superseded class differences. Similarly, contra leaders deliberately downplayed the importance of their own powerful outside allies: the U.S. government and ex-National Guardsmen.

Militarization

Another factor in the growth of peasant political opposition to the revolutionary government in Quilalí was the perception of many anti-Sandinista peasants that the FSLN was responsible for the conflict that engulfed the municipality in the 1980s. One particularly dramatic manifestation of this violence was the 1983 attack on the El Coco cooperative. As we have seen, throughout the mountains of Nicaragua in late 1982 and 1983, contras targeted Sandinista self-defense agricultural cooperatives they considered to be "military barracks" (*cuarteles*) for harassment and attack. In response, Quilalí's three river valley cooperatives established twenty-four-hour-a-day lookout posts on the perimeters of their land. Members carried arms at all times, even while working the fields, and often patrolled the immediate zones around the cooperatives with EPS reserve battalions. By 1983, the contras for their part had organized civilian spy networks in a number of communities that provided them with information on the movements of Sandinista Army troops and the cooperative self-defense militias. As a rule, contras chose the moments when the EPS was far away and cooperative militias were out on patrol to launch assaults on cooperatives. Contras also generally attacked such "soft targets" with large quantities of men and arms as a further guarantee of military success.

In Quilalí, contras chose El Coco as the object of their first major assault on a cooperative in the municipality. The El Coco cooperative, eighteen kilometers southeast of the town of Quilalí, was established in 1982 by a dozen or so families from Quilalí and the dry zones of Telpaneca and Cusmapa of the western Segovias. Inés Delgado, originally from Telpaneca, was among the first to settle on El Coco. By the time the cooperative members were given formal title to 400 MZ of land in November 1983, they had built simple houses and a storage shed, and cleared 40 MZ of forested land to plant their first corn crop. Although about twenty more families joined the cooperative in 1983,

El Coco remained the most isolated of Quilalí's three valley cooperatives and was particularly vulnerable because neighboring communities such as La Vigía were already strong bases of contra support.

Inés Delgado remembers that on the morning of 18 December
1983 all but a few of the men of the cooperative were away on patrol
with the EPS when without warning the cooperative was surrounded: "Only old men and women were left to defend the cooperative. The attack began around nine in the morning. All the hillsides
were covered with clouds of olive green—contras. They had around
500 men. I told everyone to run to the bomb shelter behind the cooperative." From the surrounding hilltops, contras began to shell the cooperative with mortars as the women and children hid beneath their
beds or fled to nearby trenches which had been dug as a refuge. Only
twelve men and women militia members were left to face the contra
force, and although they were greatly outnumbered, the militia members held the contras off for close to two hours. When it became clear
that the contras were about to enter the cooperative, Inés Delgado led
twenty-three women and eighty-five children out of the cooperative
to hide in a nearby forest. The few surviving militia members covered
their retreat. The contras poured into the cooperative to loot and
burn the few houses that had not already been destroyed by the
shelling. Delgado remembers: "People were killed when they ran out
of ammunition and the contras slit their throats. They [the contras]
sprayed gunfire inside one house and killed the children hiding
under the bed. They cut out the eyes of a visiting doctor. About two
in the afternoon several trucks of EPS soldiers who were heading to
Wiwilí arrived and the real combat began."

After several hours of fighting, the dozens of Sandinista Army reinforcement troops were able to drive the contra force away. A total of
fourteen cooperative members were killed, including the twelve men
and women who had fought in their foxholes to defend the cooperative, and the two young children who were hit by gunfire in their
house. The cooperative itself was completely destroyed: "All the

houses were burned, as well as four electric saws, two tractors; all the farm implements stored in houses; 200 large sacks of corn stored in the warehouse. We had to abandon the crops we had in the field." The survivors of the attack fled to the neighboring cooperative in San Bartolo and were later given shelter in the Baptist church and school in the town of Quilalí. Some of the families would return to El Coco to rebuild a year later, while other families left the zone altogether. This was the single worst attack on a civilian cooperative in Quilalí and is still remembered in Quilalí as the El Coco massacre.

From 1983 onward contras carried out similar attacks on cooperatives throughout the northern and central mountains of Nicaragua. In two years alone, from 1983 through 1985, contras destroyed 182 cooperatives in Nicaragua's interior and on the Atlantic coast and killed 281 cooperative members (CIERA 1989, 6:316). The contras for their part portrayed the attack on the highly outnumbered El Coco cooperative members as a military victory. They claimed on their clandestine radio station, Fifteenth of September, that they had held the cooperative for ten hours and killed ninety Sandinista Army soldiers. In reality it appears that the contras' objective in attacking El Coco cooperative was as much political as military. The destruction of the El Coco cooperative was designed to send a clear message to Quilalí peasants: the Sandinistas were incapable of adequately protecting even their own followers. If peasants wished to receive land under the Sandinista land reform or participate in government programs, they understood they were putting their lives at risk. Ricardo Pérez, a middle peasant and contra collaborator who lived near El Coco in the community of La Vigía, heard firsthand accounts of the El Coco attack and drew his own conclusions:

> The Sandinistas will give you someone else's house or land, because it's not so easy to give away one's own possessions. Once they give you the house and land, you have to take up arms to defend it. Those in the cooperative had everything—houses, land, tractors—but they were deceived, because they had to pay with their lives. The Sandinistas

took someone who was a nobody and made him the head of a [cooperative] militia and left him to die. It's better to do without and survive than to accept things from the Sandinistas.

In this case, it was the nascent revolutionary state that was unable to provide sufficient protection to its supporters and so its legitimacy was weakened in the eyes of some peasants. In addition, to many anti-Sandinista peasants the attack on El Coco was a dramatic and frightening manifestation of the deepening militarization of the mountains, which they largely blamed on the FSLN. In interviews, these peasants hold the Sandinistas, and not the contras, responsible for bringing the violence that interrupted agricultural production, threatened the physical well-being of their families, and left them little safe, neutral ground. According to this anti-Sandinista narrative of the war, the FSLN was an external force that arrived to disrupt once peaceful communities with ideas and programs that turned everything upside down. In doing so, the argument goes, the Sandinistas provoked a defensive counterreaction on the part of those local sectors whose interests were threatened and pushed the municipality into polarization and war. These peasants did not necessarily idealize the Somoza government, but compared with the constant tension that families lived under in the 1980s, prerevolutionary days seemed idyllic. In the words of contra collaborator Virginia Moreno, "It's true it was a dictatorship for many years and maybe it wasn't so good for the poor, but [Somoza] never brought us this war that we've lived through."

One important aspect of this militarization that anti-Sandinistas mention frequently as a grievance in interviews is a loss of "freedom." To these Quilalí peasants freedom was not an abstract ideal, but rather concrete liberty to move about as they wished; to not take up arms; to express themselves without fear of persecution by Sandinista State Security; and to buy and sell goods and crops as they pleased. They desired in essence a continuation of the negative freedom to conduct their lives with minimal outside interference and autonomy that they had enjoyed during the Somoza era. By 1983, for example, many anti-Sandinista peasants remembered with nostalgia how in the 1970s they were able to travel without restriction on the paths and roads of the municipality any time day or night, something that became impossible once the MILPA bands became active in the municipality. In addition, as will be discussed in greater detail in the following chapter, many anti-Sandinista peasants viewed the Sandinista military draft implemented in late 1983 as a form of oppression that infringed upon their liberty.

Another frequently voiced complaint of contra collaborators and combatants is that with the rapid militarization of the municipality, they felt increasingly unable to openly express their opinions or criticize Sandinista policies. In fact, in March 1982 in response to increasing contra military attacks, the Sandinista government declared a state of emergency that suspended most constitutional guarantees, including freedom of the press, the right of assembly, and the right to strike (Gilbert 1988, 119). In Quilalí, however, local Sandinista authorities' tolerance for critical speech appears to have been linked less directly to national policies than to the state of military conflict in the municipality. Throughout the 1980s peasants who accepted the basic parameters of Sandinista political-ideological discourse and worked through pro-revolutionary structures such as the UNAG state that they felt very free to openly voice opposition to government policies. The FSLN for its part tolerated such criticism from within the boundaries of basic support for the revolutionary process and in fact on a number of occasions altered its policies in response to peasant concerns (see Luciak 1987b).

Once MILPA and contra groups became active in the municipality, however, the distinction between acceptable constructive critcism expressed by anti-Sandinista peasants and counterrevolutionary viewpoints and support for the contras tended to blur in conflictive zones and inhibit open expression of peasant complaints. In the words of an ex-contra and middle peasant from the northwestern community of Santa Ana:

The Sandinistas denied all citizens the right to express themselves freely. . . . If I began to talk to someone he might become suspicious. He might be a [Sandinista] informer listening to everything I said. Then later suddenly someone would appear from State Security and take me to jail. . . . The Sandinistas wanted Nicaragua to be a nation where everyone would have the same ideology. I don't believe that's possible in any country.

As Serra (1993, 29) suggests, the deepening militarization of much of Nicaragua's interior contributed to a disappearance of the conditions that would have allowed for political-ideological debate. For their part Sandinista authorities and supporters are adamant that the FSLN did not punish Quilalí peasants for simply expressing opinions against the FSLN, only for actively collaborating with the contras.

Finally, it should be noted that while Quilalí's pro-Sandinista peasants also recognize the negative impact of deepening militarization and polarization on the municipality, they do not hold the FSLN responsible. Cooperative leader Daniel López explains:

The war came because of politics. There was opposition, that's how wars begin. The rich make war against the poor. They have all the money and we're always on the bottom. A lot of rich people were resentful because the FSLN confiscated their farms to give them to the poor. . . . It was the very same Nicaraguans who screwed things up so much and caused the war. But without the support of the United States, there wouldn't have been supplies and weapons.

Chapter 6

Peasants in Arms

THE PREVIOUS chapter explored the factors that led a number of Quilalí peasants to oppose revolutionary ideology and programs from the outset or to withdraw their support and participation in the early 1980s. These factors include tensions between the FSLN ideology and prerevolutionary peasant values and beliefs, which were reinforced and amplified by contra leaders; violence by bands of contras targeted against perceived revolutionary projects in outlying zones of the municipality; and the perception that Sandinistas were outsiders responsible for the deepening militarization of the municipality. Given that by 1983 a significant number of Quilalí peasants were not pleased with the changes that had occurred since 1979, the question remains: What additional factors and dynamics pushed some 800 Quilalí peasants into active armed opposition to the revolution?

Scott's (1985, 1989, 1990) recent works on peasant resistance indicate that when faced with the "realities of power" peasants will express their discontent through acts of "everyday resistance." This observation holds true in Quilalí particularly among anti-Sandinista poor peasants, who, recognizing their own vulnerability, attempted to evade open confrontation with either of the two powerful political-military forces in the municipality. As will be discussed in greater detail in chapter 7, women, children, and older men in anti-Sandinista communities were generally able to avoid openly taking sides in the conflict and maintain at least the appearance of neutrality, although many covertly collaborated with the contras.

After 1983, however, in the municipality of Quilalí it was all but impossible for a young man between the ages of seventeen and twenty-five to avoid taking up arms with one side or the other. Whereas in nonconflictive zones of Nicaragua young men had a wider range of options to avoid fighting, in war zones like Quilalí a combination of the Sandinista military draft, State Security measures against contra collaborators, and contra intimidation and recruitment techniques pushed all but a few young men directly into combat with either the Sandinista Army or the contras. For young men who chose to remain in Quilalí the question was not so much whether they would take up arms, but rather which side they would take up arms with. In this latter decision young men were influenced by the ideological issues discussed in the previous chapter, as well as strong family and community pressures.

The Sandinista Draft

In the months before the December 1983 El Coco attack, contra forces had grown from several thousand men to as many as 8,500 troops and were now able to amass up to 1,000 combatants to attack border towns.[1] Inside Nicaraguan territory contras no longer patrolled in small groups of several dozen, but formed task forces, roughly equivalent to a company in a conventional army, of between 100 and 300 men. The new task forces included the Pedro Joaquín González, named after the leader of the 1980 attack on Quilalí; the Santiago Meza and the Salvador Pérez, which took their names from

Boy leading an oxcart (in the early morning mist). *Photo by the author*

Quilalí's ambulance, spray-painted by the recontras with their initials, "F.N.3.80" ("Frente Norte 3-80"). *Photo by the author*

Holy Week procession down Quilalí's main street. *Photo by the author*

Army soldier standing guard in the rain on a street corner of Quilalí. *Photo by the author*

Quilali's pool hall in the center of town. *Photo by the author*

Contras waiting to demobilize in 1990. *Photo by the author*

Contra soldier during the 1990 demobilization process. *Photo by the author*

Boys fishing in the Coco River. *Photo by the author*

Girls collecting water from a communal faucet. *Photo by the author*

MILPA leaders killed in combat; and the task force "Quilalí," which former MILPA leader Coral named after his home town. By 1983 these task forces were receiving a steady flow of U.S. military aid and ex-EPS soldiers remember that the contras were often better equipped and supplied than their Sandinista Army counterparts. The main contra FDN forces now ranged over 34,000 square kilometers of Nicaragua's interior and within this territory they disrupted agricultural production, road traffic, and services to the population (CIERA 1989, 6:281). They also established extensive networks of peasant collaborators in a number of mountain communities to provide them with food, shelter, and information.

This rapid expansion of the number of contra troops and their geographical range of military actions put the Sandinista Army on the defensive. According to the Sandinista Ministry of Interior, the number of armed encounters between army soldiers and contras increased from 61 combats in 1982 to almost 700 combats in 1983, with the bulk of the fighting taking place in military regions I and VI in the north of Nicaragua (MINT 1985). A general rule of military strategy holds that a conventional army must have at least ten times as many combatants as a guerrilla force to successfully put down a rebellion. In mid-1983, the EPS had some 24,000 men under arms, only triple the number of contra combatants (Walker 1991a, 86). In addition, thousands of the EPS's best troops were stationed not in the mountains where the contras waged war, but in Nicaragua's major cities as protection against a possible U.S. invasion.

EPS officers posted in Quilalí at the time remember that the military situation was in danger of slipping out of the Sandinista Army's control. Almost daily, groups of contras passed through the municipality heading south to Jinotega and Matagalpa or returning to Honduras for rest and resupplying. EPS informants report that at any given time they had a fairly good idea of the number and location of contras in Quilalí, but did not necessarily have the military capacity to hunt these groups down. In mid-1983 hundreds of Sandinista soldiers were stationed in the municipality of Quilalí at any given time. Quilalí's military brigade, the 311, eventually included a reserve battalion and a Permanent Territorial Company (Compañía Permanente Territorial, COPETE) as well as some Cuban military advisers who provided EPS soldiers with technical support and training.[2] Army soldiers, however, were often occupied with guarding roads, bridges, and other infrastructure in the zone, as well as cooperatives and state farms, and up to 40 percent of Quilalí's EPS troops were unavailable for search-and-destroy patrols against contras. On some occasions Sandinista Army patrols, far from having numerical superiority, were surprised and outnumbered by contra forces.

Confronted with the growing strength of the counterrevolution, national Sandinista leaders concluded that their volunteer army was insufficient to meet the contra threat. In late 1983 the FSLN decreed a military draft, known as the Patriotic Military Service (Servicio Militar Patriótico, SMP), under which every Nicaraguan male between the ages of seventeen and twenty-four was required to spend two years in the Sandinista Army. In the years following the draft, the EPS would become the largest armed force in Central America, with over 60,000 soldiers mobilized at any given time to confront and eventually contain the contra forces (Walker 1991a, 86).

In the municipality of Quilalí, the drafting of young men was coordinated for four years by Domingo Delgado. Originally from the city of Ocotal, Delgado joined the Sandinista Army in 1982 at age sixteen. After several years of combat in the mountains, Delgado was sent to Quilalí to take charge of military recruitment. Under the EPS's centralized draft process, regional military authorities in the city of Estelí required each zone such as Quilalí to supply a certain number of new recruits every three months. According to Delgado, a total of 576 young men from Quilalí officially completed military service in the Sandinista Army, roughly three-fourths the number of Quilalí peasants who joined the contras.

Under formal draft procedures, young men of draft age received notice to report to the local draft board in town and undergo a medical check-up. Delgado estimates that in the town of Quilalí almost half of draft-age boys either reported for military service on their own initiative or obeyed the formal summons they received. Other young men who failed to obey their summons, however, were recruited "by force." Delgado describes a forced recruitment in which the EPS entered a young man's house with a warrant: "They [the draftees] wanted to make fools out of the authorities here. . . . Sometimes the same young men would force us to make mistakes. We would forget to act as professionals and act in another way. A lot of people resisted when we took their son away and shouted insults and curses at us."

Young men from Quilalí attempted to evade the draft for a number of fairly obvious reasons. Nicaragua, unlike most Latin American nations, had no tradition of obligatory military service, and some peasants considered the Sandinista draft to be an infringement of their liberty. Many young men were also particularly reluctant to serve in the army under wartime conditions. By the time the draft came into effect, much of the earlier euphoria of the insurrection against Somoza had faded. While in the first few years of the revolution army officers remember that they sometimes had to turn away enthusiastic volunteers, by 1983 volunteers were the exception not the rule, particularly in interior areas like Quilalí. As the war deepened and the death toll mounted, many young men spoke openly of their fears of returning home in a body bag. In addition, in rural areas like Quilalí, the recruitment of young men often meant economic hardship for peasants, who depended heavily on family labor for agricultural production.

Political beliefs also led some families to oppose the draft. Some young men and their families disagreed with the revolutionary programs and ideology and were unwilling to serve in the openly political Sandinista armed forces. That is to say, in rural communities where the contras had already established a firm foothold, young men were reluctant to join an army fighting against their neighbors, friends, and even family. Also, some parents feared that FSLN military and political training would undermine patriarchal authority over children and that their sons would return from the EPS with revolutionary ideas.

Another factor that led to opposition to the draft in Quilalí was the inflexible manner by which some Sandinista authorities carried out recruitment. Conscientious objectors were not exempt from military service, for example, although some flexibility was shown toward evangelical Christians who did not wish to take up arms. Formal recruitment occurred only in the town of Quilalí itself, the four Sandinista cooperatives in Panalí, San Bartolo, El Coco, and La Reforma, and a few other rural communities to which FSLN authorities still had access and were able to monitor and locate draft-age men. The Sandinista Army's mobile recruiting team, however, simply could not enter more distant mountain communities or river valley zones where contra forces were present. According to Delgado: "The Military Service Delegation in Quilalí didn't have enough troops available— we were barely fifteen men—to enter the war zones. The [army] battalions took charge of that."

Military recruitment in Quilalí's conflictive rural communities was basically left in the hands of Sandinista Army units that passed through the zone on patrol or in pursuit of contras. According to ex–Sandinista Army officers, in some military units where conditions and commanding officers were particularly harsh, up to one-fifth of young SMP recruits deserted to go into hiding or join the contras. Patrols were left short of men and as they passed through mountain communities, officers' immediate military need for replacement troops at times took priority over the longer-term political costs of forced recruitment among peasants unsympathetic to the revolution.

Some peasant families in isolated rural communities with draft-age sons came to regard passing Sandinista Army patrols with fear and suspicion. An EPS patrol could arrive and without warning take their son away, allowing families little time to prepare emotionally or deal with practical concerns. Likewise, because military recruitment was left to the discretion of individual army officers and no formal draft procedure was followed in the countryside, there was opportunity for abuse. Underage boys might be recruited, for instance, if they were physically big enough. Delgado remembers a case in the northern mountains of Quilalí where an EPS lieutenant recruited at gunpoint a severely epileptic eighteen-year-old, much to the distress of the boy's family. Other EPS officials later protested that the young man was unfit for military service, and he was released and allowed to return home, but the political damage had already been done among the boy's family and community.

Special privileges and exemptions for wealthier Quilalí families also undermined the credibility of Sandinista military service. Within the town limits of Quilalí, well-off families employed a number of strategies to prevent their sons from completing military service. Some were able to send their sons abroad to Mexico, Honduras, Costa Rica, or the United States to study and thus avoid the draft. Other wealthy families were apparently able to bribe Sandinista authorities. Delgado states: "In the years that I was head of Military Service, I never knew a well-off young man who completed his military service. . . . The families paid to have their son called and then obtained a medical report, also paid for, which stated that their son was unfit for military service." Poor peasants who wished to evade the draft had fewer influential contacts and economic resources available to them and appear to have borne a disproportionate share of the sacrifice. One option they did have was to make the dangerous journey, usually on foot, to Honduras. From 1981 to 1987 approximately 1,000 Quilalí families went to Honduras and many ended up living near the border with almost 15,000 other peasants from the department of Nueva Segovia (CIAV-OEA, personal communication; FEDONG 1991, 79).

Once the draft took affect in Quilalí in late 1983, other young men decided to no longer visit the town of Quilalí and to hide on their family farms in the mountains. José Gómez, the son of Juana Gómez, the single mother and bread baker from Olingo, remembers: "When I went down to [the towns of] Murra or Quilalí they [army soldiers] made me offers. They said that I had to be a soldier for the FSLN. I stopped going into town. I looked for a way to escape. I hid myself." In Gómez's community, beyond the reach of formal recruitment procedures, young men took care to avoid EPS patrols which passed through their communities and established an informal lookout system: "When they [the neighbors] warned us that the [Sandinista] Army was approaching, all my brothers and I would leave by the back door and throw ourselves into the underbrush [*monte*]." As will be discussed later, a more drastic strategy young men employed, which in their minds was a way to avoid serving in the Sandinista Army, was to join the opposing contra forces. The year the Sandinista Patriotic Military Service went into effect, contra recruitment soared from 8,500 to 14,464 (Morales Carazo 1989, 57). In the words of several Quilalí ex-contras, "They called us National Guard when we were just a group of boys fleeing from the draft."

Surprisingly, approximately 20 percent of those former contras interviewed in Quilalí joined the contras when they were under draft age, a few as young as thirteen years old. These young boys were not directly recruited by the Sandinista Army when they decided to take up arms. They had, however, witnessed and heard of cases where friends and neighbors were drafted by force, and they state that they were fearful the same thing might happen to them. José Gómez, who joined the contras at age fourteen, explains: "They never grabbed me, but I saw it a lot with other young men who were working in the fields when an EPS patrol arrived. [The soldiers] would beat them and take them away."

State Security

In addition to fears of being drafted involuntarily into the Sandinista Army, other Quilalí peasants chose to take up arms when they became the target of Sandinista State Security investigations. Little public information is available about State Security operations during the war years, and former Ministry of Interior officials who served in Quilalí are wary of talking about their activities in part for fear of reprisals.[3] While the mission of the EPS was to confront the contra forces militarily, a key function of the Sandinista State Security apparatus, under the control of the Ministry of Interior, was to gather intelligence on the contras and antigovernment activities in general (CIPRES 1991, 270). In Quilalí in the early 1980s, State Security worked to uncover the networks of family, friends, and workers of finqueros who aided the original MILPA movement. Peasants who gave food, shelter, and information to the MILPA or later to bands of contras faced interrogation or even imprisonment by State Security, and some of these collaborators chose to become full-time contra combatants rather than risk going to jail.[4]

Of the twenty-seven ex-contras interviewed for this study, ten had either been jailed themselves or had an immediate family member jailed at some point by State Security. Carlos Sánchez from Jiquelite, for example, came under investigation by State Security after his brother, also a former FSLN guerrilla, joined the MILPAs. His mother explains: "My son went [into the contras] out of fear. He didn't want to, but he was afraid. [Sandinista State Security] came to ask for him by name. He left the next day." A few months later Sánchez's mother and the rest of the family traveled on foot to Honduras, where they remained as refugees for the rest of the war.

As can be seen, early on in Quilalí a dynamic developed in which peasants collaborated with MILPAs and later bands of contras and then were investigated and sometimes jailed by State Security. In response to this State Security "repression," more peasants took up arms in what they perceived as self-defense. Ex-FSLN Political Secretary Gilberto Santana explains: "Those first conflicts with Dimas and the MILPAs, that was the base of everything that followed. After the rise of the MILPAs came the [Sandinista] crackdown, a vicious circle: war, a [Sandinista] crackdown, peasant uprising, more crackdowns, more war." Finally, it should be emphasized that the actions of Quilalí State Security appear to have been largely a reaction to peasant support of and participation in armed anti-Sandinista bands in the municipality and were not necessarily a primary or initial cause of the conflict in the municipality. Almost all the anti-Sandinista peasants interviewed who were targeted by State Security acknowledged that they or close family members were already collaborating with the MILPAs-contras at the time they were investigated or arrested. Once the war was underway, however, as the above comment by Santana suggests, State Security crackdowns tended to further reinforce polarization and peasant resistance to the FSLN.

Contra Recruitment Tactics

Opposition to military service and draft evasion, of course, were not unique to Nicaragua's northern and central mountains. Unlike urban and Pacific coast residents, however, peasants in conflictive zones who did not wish to take up arms faced not only pressure from the Sandinista draft and State Security, but also intimidation and coercive recruitment by contras who were active in their communities. It is difficult to estimate accurately the number of peasants kidnapped or recruited against their will into the contra forces in isolated municipalities like Quilalí. Wartime conditions limited access to communities where forced recruitment took place. Also, some peasant families never reported the kidnappings, either because they feared reprisal by the contras or because of mistrust of Sandinista authorities. Adding to the uncertainty is the fact that contras carried out both long-term kidnappings to recruit combatants and short-term kidnappings. In the latter case, contras took local peasants at gunpoint and forced them to serve as trail guides, carry heavy loads and wounded soldiers, and walk lead as "human mine detectors" until they were released several days or weeks later. In recruitment kidnappings, however, peasants were taken all the way to the contras' Honduran base camps and held indefinitely until they agreed to serve as combatants or escaped.

According to statistics compiled by the Sandinista Ministry of Interior, nationwide a total of 6,984 peasants were kidnapped by the contras from 1980 to 1987 (MINT 1985, 1986, 1987b, 1988). Both Sandinista and anti-Sandinista Quilalí informants agree, however, that such kidnappings were relatively uncommon in the municipality. In zones like Quilalí, where the contras were able to develop a base of support among the peasant population, they did not always have to use such direct force to gain new recruits. The intimidating presence of well-armed contras in their community was often enough in itself to convince young men (a group recruited by both the Sandinista Army and the contras) to join the contras "voluntarily," rather than risk being kidnapped. An excellent example of contra use of intimidation to recruit combatants and control the civilian peasant population can be found in the testimony of a church worker who attended a meeting between contras and local peasants in the department of Matagalpa:

> At one point [the contra leader] called me out in front of the roughly sixty peasants and said . . . , "I have to respect our friend's life, just like I have to respect all of your lives. . . . Of course, if I find out that our friend is working with the Sandinistas, I have the right to execute him." . . . The [contra] commander asked the peasants if there was anyone who did not want to support and collaborate with the contras. . . . In a show of hands, all the peasants voted to collaborate. (personal communication, July 1989)

Many peasants also had firsthand knowledge of the harsh treatment—beatings and other physical abuse—that contra commanders doled out to reluctant recruits. A kidnapped peasant or new recruit who tried to desert the contras and was recaptured faced severe punishment or even summary execution. If this were not sufficient disincentive against desertion, contra leaders also warned their troops that Sandinista soldiers would torture and kill any contra deserters they found. Therefore, while it appears that direct forced recruitment accounted for only a small percentage of the over 800 contra combatants from the municipality of Quilalí, it is important to keep in mind that elements of intimidation were always present, either explicitly or implicitly, in contras' contacts with Quilalí peasants. In addition, as will be discussed in the following chapter, contras employed rumor and exaggeration to magnify peasant fears and resentment of the draft and State Security, and to present themselves as friends and protectors of peasants.

Contra leaders were also able to take advantage of polarization in the municipality to reinforce the dynamics of peasant collaboration and FSLN crackdowns described earlier and draw cautious peasants into deeper and deeper involvement with counterrevolution, essentially leaving peasants little alternative but to actively ally themselves with the contras. This process can be seen in the story of Mario Aguero from La Vigía, who became an organizer of a Sandinista adult education program in his community. He disagreed, however, with pro-revolutionary messages in the educational material the FSLN distributed, as well as Sandinista pressure on his community to farm cooperatively. In late 1980, Mario Aguero encountered by chance a small MILPA group in the forest:

> I was hunting wild pigs with some dogs. Then I passed by them [the MILPA guerrillas] and they spoke to me. They asked me questions: How did I see the country, if I was a soldier or militia member. . . . Then they told me that they were hungry, that they had gone three days without eating. . . . I left and told some friends to prepare a meal. We began to cook corn on the cob, tamales, *guirila, atol.* When I returned they took me to be someone important. I did it almost for charity. I made the decision because they were hungry.

Having successfully obtained a meal for themselves, the MILPA guerrillas were quick to press their advantage and establish a more long-term relationship with Aguero: "They called me a *correo* [collaborator]. . . . About a month later they sent me slips of paper. They sent 1,500 cordobas to secretly buy food, rice, and sugar for them. No one else knew about the work I was doing for them. I was afraid that people would that see I was involved in something."

Because of his precarious position as a poor peasant, Mario Aguero, like many Quilalí peasants, states that he did not wish to become "involved" (*metido*) in anything, although his ideological sympathies lay increasingly with the contras. Yet once this first step was taken, Aguero found it difficult to retreat into neutrality. He understood that if he attempted to end his collaboration with the counterrevolution he would have difficulties with the contras who recruited him. Likewise, if State Security authorities discovered he was a contra collaborator, Aguero would face interrogation and a possible jail term. Without ever having made a specific decision to collaborate with the contras, Aguero found himself in the role of contra correo. And two years later, in 1983, because of pressures from both State Security and the contras, Aguero became a full-fledged combatant with the contras.

Between Two Fires

By late 1983, given the pressures from both the Sandinista Army and the contras to recruit combatants for their cause, Quilalí young men who did not wish to take up arms with either side found themselves increasingly "caught between two fires," as the Quilalí countryside became the scene of daily battles and the space for neutrality grew smaller. In this climate of growing insecurity and violence, arming oneself was increasingly perceived as a measure of self-defense. Young men decided that they would be safer and better able to defend themselves as mobile, armed combatants, rather than as unarmed civilians awaiting a knock on their door in the middle of the night. The decision to be made was less whether they would take up arms than which armed force they would fight with. In those cases where overt force was not employed by either the EPS or the contras, a young man's choice was based on several factors, including his perception of the conflict and political sympathies, discussed in the previous chapter, and family and community pressures.

Israel Mena worked with his father and brothers growing coffee on a small piece of land they rented from a finquero in a northern community. He was twenty-two years old when the Sandinista draft took effect in late 1983. Mena wanted to stay on his family's farm with his wife and young child and continue working, but he feared that he would be drafted: "There were two paths. You went on their side [the Sandinistas] or you went into the Resistance or you were killed. The law [the draft] was hard and for that reason many people were obliged to defend their lives. . . . The Sandinistas never tried to recruit me because I knew they would try to draft me, so what I did was join the group fighting against them."

Anti-Sandinista peasants like Mena reasoned that if they were forced to take up arms, they would rather do so with the side that shared their opinions and values, the group with which many of their family and neighbors were fighting. In Mena's case, he joined a contra task force led by a friend of his, the son of a local finquero: "It's better to go with the Resistance of your own free will than to have them [the Sandinistas] grab you and put you in an IFA [military truck] and send you to the front lines. You don't even know why. In the Resistance it's voluntary. The [contra] commanders tell you you'll suffer hunger, thirst, exhaustion, long hikes." About the same time, several dozen of Mena's neighbors, mostly young men between the ages of fourteen and twenty-five, made the same decision to join the contras, and by 1984 only women, children and older men were left in the community.

In another case, Ramón Moreno, a poor landless peasant, served for a year as a volunteer member of the Sandinista Army. By 1981, however, he grew disillusioned with both army life and the FSLN. He reports that he was rarely paid on time, was assigned to remote posts, and was frustrated in his attempts to obtain a piece of land for his family in Quilalí's river valley. Moreno deserted the army and went to stay with friends near Quilalí. He remembers: "I wanted to forget all the acts of violence I committed with the FSLN. I wanted to forget it all and begin a new life, a religious life." One day, however, "a [neighbor] came and told me, 'Look, the army is searching for you and they're going to take you dead or alive.' . . . I felt so tired hearing that, but there was no way to turn back. I said, 'I don't want to fight with anyone. I want to work.' He said, 'But if you flee anybody could kill you. You don't know where you'll end up. It's better that we enter the war.'" That evening Moreno was able to convince fourteen neighbors to join him, and in a group they set off to make contact with a band of contras that had set up camp nearby.

Overall, eighty-nine percent of the former contras interviewed for this study expressed strong anti-Sandinista opinions. However, 44 percent of these ex-contras, mainly poor peasants, indicated that they felt some reluctance to take up arms and in some cases attempted to avoid doing so for as long as possible. A typical comment is: "We joined because of the repression, the recruiting [by the FSLN]. And if you went to Honduras a [contra] commander could easily grab you and force you take up arms [with the contras]." In contrast, the other 56 percent of ex-contras interviewed, generally those from more well-off families, report that they voluntarily joined the contras. Many indicated that they welcomed the opportunity that the contras, with their abundant U.S. weapons, equipment, and funds, offered them to resist the FSLN through arms.

Family Unity

Another key element that influenced peasants to take up arms with the contras, particularly from the mid-1980s onward, was family ties.

As we have seen, on Nicaragua's agricultural frontier extended families generally worked together as a unified body under male authority to ensure the family's economic well-being. For many young peasants the decision to take up arms with the contras was not an entirely individual decision, but rather was strongly influenced by their position in the family hierarchy—that is, the emotional and economic authority that older male relatives exercised over them. According to Quilalí anti-Sandinistas, once one member of the family—the father, an older son, or an uncle—became involved with the counterrevolution, he would serve as role model and often pull the rest of the family in as combatants and collaborators. As several ex-contras commented, "When the first one goes, all the rest follow."[5]

The oldest son of the García family, Santiago, for example, worked for the revolutionary government for two years until pressure from his father, who was anti-Sandinista, convinced him to quit his job and join the contras. In 1985, after García had achieved the rank of mid-level commander in the contras, he remembers: "Two brothers [of mine] were recruited for military service, but since I was with them [the contras] I sent word to my mother that we shouldn't fight against each other in the family; that they should come look for me because there was no way I could turn back. I believed it was a just cause. My brothers decided that it was better to follow me. They deserted the army and went with me into the mountains [with the contras]."

Eventually all of García's brothers joined the contras, with the exception of one who became an evangelical pastor. The former contra combatants interviewed in Quilalí had an average of five other close relatives in the contras. While boys and men made up the great majority of contra combatants, in a few cases Quilalí women also took up arms. In one instance, a woman combatant states that she felt "lonely" after her six brothers and father became contra combatants, and at age seventeen joined the same task force that her brothers served under. More commonly, however, once the sons of the family or husband had joined the contras, the women and older members of the family would remain behind in the community, often providing food, shelter, and information to passing contra troops, or they would move to Honduras. Peasants interviewed report that it was unusual for a poor peasant to take a political or military stance against his or her family. An ex-contra whose older brother was a contra commander explains: "If your family was against the Sandinistas, you couldn't be a Sandinista. You couldn't fire a gun against your own family." According to FSLN officials, if a contra combatant or collaborator was sought by the army or State Security, the family would also unite to shelter him or her from the authorities. In the words of one former State Security officer in Quilalí who frequently encountered this protective family shield: "They knew it was wrong, but it didn't matter because it was their family."

A son or daughter who challenged paternal authority and voluntarily joined the EPS or supported the revolution was often forced to break off contact with anti-Sandinista members of the family. FSLN activist and teacher Noris Pardo, for example, for years had no contact with his six brothers who fought for the contras. Even after the war ended the family remained divided, and in an interview an older Pardo brother stated emphatically, "There are no Sandinistas in our family."

Interestingly, Quilalí informants suggest that wealthy families were somewhat less politically unified than poor and middle peasant families. In one prominent family, the father was a deeply committed Sandinista, while one of his sons became a contra commander. Another son collaborated with the contras and ironically was killed when a vehicle he was in drove over a land mine planted by the contras, and a third son served as a Sandinista Army officer for ten years. One possible explanation for this may be that the greater range of educational and economic opportunities and outside contacts available to the sons and daughters of Quilalí elites gave some of these young people a stronger economic and ideological base from which to challenge family authority that poor peasants lacked.

Like the vicious circle of peasant collaboration with the contras and State Security crackdowns discussed earlier, family relationships were a crucial element in the dynamic of polarization and self-perpetuating conflict that took hold in the municipality of Quilalí by the mid-1980s. By the time they reached adolescence many Quilalí young men were already enmeshed through family ties in the struggle against the Sandinistas, and the original grievances that had led the family to take up arms against the FSLN were at times of only secondary importance to younger siblings.

Community Pressure

In addition to family loyalties, young men were also influenced to join the contras as combatants by community and peer pressure, as well as the potential status and power they would enjoy as contra combatants. In interviews, ex-contras report that typically up to a dozen young men from their community would gather and jointly make the decision to join the contras in what State Security officials termed mass uprisings. In the mountain community of El Porvenir, for example, a community member, apparently a contra collaborator, was killed under unclear circumstances by Sandinista soldiers as he left an evangelical church service. That evening some forty young men from the community gathered and, angered and frightened by the incident, they decided as a group to join the contras. It seems likely that at least a few of these peasants acting individually would not have chosen to take up arms, but were reluctant to remain behind alone without community support or feared being labeled cowards or even Sandinista sympathizers.

In some rural mountain communities, reflecting in part the municipality's culture of resistance, joining the contras appears to have become almost a rite of passage for a young man. By taking up arms, participating in combat, and enduring the harsh conditions of guerrilla life, a peasant demonstrated his courage and became recognized as a man in Quilalí's patriarchal society. In the postwar period in fact, young men at times have fabricated or exaggerated combat experience with the contras in an attempt to raise their status in the community. It is also important to keep in mind the youth of most contras. Of the over 22,000 men and women who took up arms with the contras, 36 percent were still under twenty years of age when they demobilized (CIAV-OEA 1990a). Among the ex-contras interviewed in the Quilalí zone, the average age of those joining the contras was eighteen. Overall, only 16 percent of contra recruits had more than a third grade education (CIAV-OEA 1990a). In Quilalí, many of these young men knew little of the world beyond their small mountain communities and their family farm, where they worked under their father's authority. As the war began to intensify, they were less likely to leave their communities, even to travel into the town of Quilalí. Some young men, bored or frustrated with the hard, monotonous work of farming, saw the respect and fear that passing contra troops commanded within their communities and report that they too wanted to enjoy such power and status.

U.S. military aid to the contras also played a critical role in some peasants' perception of contra military superiority. Contras arrived in rural communities well-equipped with the latest weapons and military equipment, wearing new durable, lightweight, and waterproof uniforms and boots issued by the U.S. army. In comparison, peasants remember that Sandinista Army soldiers wore clothing and boots of visibly poorer quality. Poor peasants, like other subordinate groups, are extremely sensitive to shifts in relationships of power (Scott 1989, 28–29). This tangible "proof" in the form of better uniforms and weapons of contra military strength and the visible support that the contras received from the United States, were sometimes sufficient to convince peasants to openly challenge the revolutionary regime.

Silvio Guerrero, son of a middle peasant family from La Vigía, explains why he ran off to join the contras when he was thirteen: "I went [into the contras] when I saw good friends with them. They were well-equipped and I wanted to walk around like that too." These young men, however, did not always find the adventure and status that they sought. In hindsight, Guerrero regrets his impulsive decision. At age thirteen he was too small to carry a heavy backpack over kilometers of mountainous terrain. One day on a long march he broke down sobbing and told his commander that he could walk no further. The commander yelled at him in front of the rest of the men and then sent him back alone in disgrace to Honduras. Guerrero states, "If I had been older maybe I would have thought differently."

The Contra Cause

As was discussed earlier, some peasants who opposed key aspects of the FSLN program and ideology, were frustrated in their expectations for land and benefits, or who blamed the Sandinistas more generally for the militarization of the municipality, welcomed the opportunity to join the contras as combatants and so actively resist the FSLN. Other Quilalí young men, likely the majority, took up arms more reluctantly. Some of these young men who joined the contras under pressure, however, report that once they became directly involved in the anti-Sandinista struggle the cause they were fighting for became clearer. According to one former contra: "When you enter the Resistance, when you go, you don't have a vision of what you're going to do. Maybe you join reluctantly [*resignado*]. But once inside the ranks, inside the movement, the sacrifice, the suffering, draw you into the cause, and you begin to understand why you're fighting, what the purpose is. This you get inside the ranks, because sometimes you're ignorant of things and only learn by experiencing them personally."

As was suggested earlier, the experiences of pro-Sandinista peasants in the Sandinista Army often served to broaden their worldview and deepen their sense of nationalism and class consciousness. Some anti-Sandinista peasants also report that during their time as contra combatants they came to see themselves part of a larger community and struggle. In their minds, they fought not simply for the individual and local concerns that drew them into the anti-Sandinista struggle in the first place, but also as part of a peasant army that would "liberate Nicaragua from Sandinista oppression" and in defense of the dignity and independence of Nicaragua's peasantry. One ex-contra explained: "We [peasants] are fighters. We don't like to kneel down before anyone."

In this manner elements of idealism, a sense of "right and wrong," were present among peasants on both side of Nicaragua's conflict.[6] Yet while most Quilalí contra combatants were clear as to what they were fighting against—the negative changes and militarization that they believed that the FSLN had brought to their communities— there was less clarity and agreement as to what the contras were fighting for; in other words, what type of economic and political system would replace the revolutionary regime? When questioned, 85 percent of Quilalí ex-contras interviewed responded that they took up arms to bring "democracy" to Nicaragua. Yet what exactly do these peasants mean by the term *democracy?* Quilalí's finqueros who led the MILPA rebellion, such as Mendoza, generally held a fairly standard understanding of democracy as contested elections and pluralist opposition linked to a neoliberal economic system with limited government market interventions that would implicitly provide opportunities for economic advancement of ambitious and entrepreneurial men like themselves.

In contrast, when Quilalí poor peasant ex-contras are questioned about the type of political and economic programs "democracy" would entail, many, rather than describing global or abstract characteristics of democracy, a topic that some find confusing, focus instead on concrete and local manifestations of democracy. That is, democracy would entail a series of negative freedoms: an end to the conflict and disruption to their lives, the draft, repression and vigilance by State Security, shortages and rationing, and above all, an end to the FSLN presence in Nicaragua's interior. Yet it would be an oversimplification to conclude then that the anti-Sandinista peasant struggle was simply a reactionary response to change that sought only to return to an idealized prerevolutionary past, because many poor ex-contras also saw in democracy the fulfillment of other individual aspirations. In contrast to the formal democracy and neoliberal economic system that most finquero and middle peasant contras supported, almost half of the poor ex-contra combatants and collaborators interviewed indicated that they were fighting for a "democratic" government that would favor poor peasants like themselves in a way that they believe the FSLN failed to do. These Quilalí poor peasants believed that in a "democratic" Nicaragua they would receive such things as parcels of land, credit, work opportunities, health care, and education, and that the well-being their families would be assured.[7] However, as will be discussed in greater detail in chapter 9, anti-Sandinistas tended to view these benefits as selective, clientelistic rewards for themselves and their families. In contrast, revolutionary discourse argued that such benefits were a right of all poor peasants.

Several analysts have cited the failure of the contra leadership to develop a single coherent ideology that would mobilize the population to support the counterrevolutionary cause as a serious weakness of the contra forces.[8] From another perspective, however, it may well have been an effective strategy for contra leaders to not present their economic and political objectives in great detail and instead encourage poor and middle peasants to believe in a "democratic" Nicaragua with peace, land, work, and prosperity for all while offering few concrete details on how this was to be achieved. By keeping the goals of the contra struggle—and the means by which such goals would be achieved—sufficiently vague, the contra leadership was able to effectively hold together a disparate, multiclass group of peasants into a single struggle. For the course of the war the contra leadership was able to direct peasant resentment outward against the "common enemy," the FSLN, and make the simple but powerful argument that everyone, wealthy and poor, was better off before the revolution (Escuela de Sociología-UCA 1987, 29). The potential contradictions and conflicts of interest between rural elites and poor peasants in terms of what was to come after a contra victory were largely submerged during the war years. Only after the 1990 elections did the "democratic" expectations created among peasants during the war years become a serious source of tension and instability.

With the Contras

Overall, of 18,225 combatants who gave their place of origin in a 1990 Organization of American States demobilization survey, 97 percent reported coming from Nicaragua's interior and Atlantic coast. In contrast only 627 (3 percent) former contras listed their place of origin as one of Nicaragua's Pacific coastal departments, where two-thirds of the nation's population is concentrated. The greatest absolute number of combatants came from the north-central departments of Jinotega and Matagalpa, while the greatest proportion of peasants who took up arms with the contras was in the department of Chontales. In addition, in twenty-seven municipalities more than 100 peasants joined the contras.

Because Quilalí is fairly close to the border, new recruits generally traveled with experienced contra troops directly to the base camps in Honduras. With millions of dollars in military and economic aid from the United States, and cooperation from Honduran military and political authorities, the contras' original primitive camps had been transformed into full-fledged military bases, which extended over hundreds of square kilometers. In Yamales, Honduras, new recruits from Quilalí and other interior zones underwent basic military

Table 6.1
Contra Demobilization Survey: Place of Origin
(departmental totals and municipalities
with over100 reported combatants)*

Departments and Municipalities	# of Contras	Departments and Municipalities	# of Contras
JINOTEGA	**3,946**	**ZELAYA****	**2,949**
Yalí	359	Siuna	140
Wiwilí	343	Waslala	132
Pantasma	274	Muelle de los Bueyes	119
San Rafael del Norte	168	**BOACO**	**1,363**
El Cuá	166	Camoapa	411
MATAGALPA	**3,418**	**NUEVA SEGOVIA**	**1,317**
Matiguás	331	Quilalí	467
Río Blanco	212	El Jícaro	165
Esquipulus	130	Jalapa	120
Muy Muy	125	**ESTELI**	**998**
CHONTALES	**3,049**	San Juan de Limay	119
Santo Domingo	380	Condega	118
Juigalpa	314	Pueblo Nuevo	105
Santo Tomás	209	**MADRIZ**	**558**
Acoyapa	168	San Juan del R.C.	158
San Pedro de Lóvago	138	**PACIFIC DEPTS.**	**627**
La Libertad	127		
		TOTAL:	**18,225**

*These figures are estimates only. It was not possible to clearly determine the place of origin of 4,206 respondents.

**This category includes the North Atlantic Autonomous Region, the South Atlantic Autonomous Region, and Zelaya Central.

Source: CIAV-OEA (1990b).

training as well as more limited political instruction. Contra foot soldiers from Quilalí remember most vividly political rallies led by Enrique Bermúdez, military commander of the contras, in addition to more informal political talks given by the commanders. Some Quilalí contras also attended speeches and training sessions given by North Americans. Overall, however, Quilalí peasants appear to have had very limited contact with their North American sponsors and little knowledge of the influence exercised by the CIA, and later U.S. State Department officials, over the contra leadership, the development of overall military strategy, intelligence gathering, and so forth. Similarly, while some Quilalí contra combatants would later come to criticize certain policy decisions of the U.S. government, most notably cut-offs of aid, few ever questioned the contra forces' overall dependence on the United States.

As the number of contra troops grew rapidly from late 1982 to 1984 the leadership had difficulty efficiently absorbing them all (Morales Carazo 1989, 57). By 1985, the contra forces were composed of four-teen regional commands, the equivalent of a battalion in a convention army, each with 800 to 1,000 men organized in two to four task forces (U.S. Department of State 1986, 8–9). As a rule, peasants from a par-ticular zone joined contra units that were either led by commanders from their region or operated in their region. Most Quilalí peasants were assigned to the Pedro Joaquín González, Quilalí, Santiago Meza, or Salvador Pérez regional commands, whose territory was the northern mountains of the Segovias and Jinotega. Quilalí peasants often knew their commanding officers from civilian life and served in the same units with friends and family. Once members of a task force, the new recruits no longer referred to themselves by their given names, adopting instead pseudonyms, often the names of animals.

The civilian hierarchy of Nicaragua's interior was generally repro-duced within contra military structures (CIERA 1989, 6:266–68; Es-cuela de Sociología-UCA 1987, 30). In other words, relatively well-educated finqueros generally headed regional commands or task forces. These upper-level field commanders recognized that their power and influence lay ultimately in the support and loyalty their troops gave them. With some notable exceptions, these commanders relied more on persuasion *(convocatorio)* than repression to maintain control of their troops and developed paternalistic ties, reflective of those found in civilian life, with troops from their zone (Dillon 1991,

353). Regional command and task force commanders in turn appointed group, platoon, and squad leaders who served beneath them. These lower-level field commanders were middle and sometimes poor peasants with good skills and experience on the battlefield or with leadership potential. And of course, the bulk of the troops were young poor peasants.

By the mid-1980s most contra foot soldiers received payments of approximately $1 per day (Kornbluh 1987, 31), roughly the going wage for agricultural field work, although few of Quilalí's contra foot soldiers appear to have accumulated any savings during the war. Task force commanders, on the other hand, received up to $400 to $600 a month (Dillon 1991, 109). It was the administrative staff in Honduras, many of them ex-National Guard officers, however, who profited most handsomely from the war. These officials earned from $1,000 to $2,000 a month and, more important, had ample opportunity to practice corruption and theft.[9] By the mid-1980s this widespread corruption in Honduras was a source of jealousies and tensions between the rearguard Honduran staff and field commanders. In the words of contra field commander Mendoza: "They [the commanders in Honduras] had perks: pickup trucks, air conditioning equipment, travel expenses, television, refrigerators, beds. Their housing was paid for. This led to social decay and corruption." Lower-ranking contra leaders and troops, on the other hand, appear to have had more limited knowledge of the corruption and wealth of many top contra leaders in Honduras. Many of the Quilalí contra foot soldiers interviewed did not begin to openly question the motives and honesty of their leadership until well after the war's end.[10]

The former contras interviewed for this study spent an average of seven years fighting with the contras, dividing their time between rest in the Honduran base camps and incursions into the Nicaraguan mountains. Conditions in the contra base camps were primitive, but poor peasants compare them favorably to the homes in which they were raised. Of the dozen contra task forces in 1984, the Jorge

Salazar groups—which operated in the departments of Matagalpa, Boaco, and Chontales deep inside Nicaraguan territory—most resembled a true guerrilla army and spent the longest periods of time in the field. Other contra task forces, such as the Pedro Joaquín González, the Quilalí, and the Salvador Pérez, where most Quilalí peasants served, were much more dependent on U.S.-funded food drops. Troops fled back across the border when their supplies failed to arrive and after congressional cutoffs of aid and spent many months inactive in Honduras.

When they describe daily life as guerrillas, contra foot soldiers and lower-level commanders report that they spent the most of their time hiking through the mountains seeking opportunities to threaten or attack Sandinista targets. Small contra bands operating in the Quilalí municipality might harass, kidnap, or kill suspected Sandinista sympathizers, mine roads, set ambushes, or attack soft targets such as poorly defended cooperatives. Contra overall military strategy was not always well-defined. According to their U.S. sponsors, the official purpose of the contras was originally to interdict arms shipments to El Salvador and later to pressure the FSLN into making democratic reforms. Contra field commanders and troops from Quilalí, on the other hand, report that they were fighting for nothing less than the overthrow of the Sandinista government, although they were not always clear as to the specific manner by which this was to be achieved.

Most former contras interviewed describe their time inside Nicaraguan territory in negative terms, as an experience of hardship and suffering that some would prefer simply to forget. While their aerial supply system, equipment, uniforms, and boots gave them an advantage over the Sandinista Army, the contras, like their EPS counterparts, still had to face the difficult conditions of the mountains and eastern rain forests. Contra troops walked up to twelve hours a day, hiking up and down steep, muddy hillsides, fording icy mountain rivers, and sleeping in hammocks in makeshift camps in the forest. In addition to the air drops of food and supplies contras received during much of the war, they also sought food and shelter from peasant collaborators, hunted, and scavenged wild fruits and plants. Mendoza remembers: "It was hard, a horrible experience. There were days when we could only sleep standing up. There were weeks when we only ate twice a week; days we had to spend in water up to our necks so that the enemy wouldn't detect us, days we had to fight for water . . . for a few jugs of water; zones where there was no cover, no security, and we had to turn into stones."

In another case, ex-contra combatant Santiago García remembers being wounded in the leg during combat. As he staggered through the forest, García saw a fellow contra lying on the ground, his face largely destroyed by shrapnel. The man grabbed him and tried to cling to him, but García, knowing EPS soldiers were close behind him, struggled to free himself. As he continued through the forests he heard his friend's incoherent screams echoing behind him. García was unfamiliar with that zone of the mountains and he wandered around lost for several days until he finally stumbled upon a farmhouse. The owner of the house was reluctant to take García in, but García forced the man and his wife to let him lie down on the floor and clean his badly infected wound. García rested for a week in the house until he was well enough to continue walking and find his way to another contra unit.

In addition to the violence they experienced, many ex-combatants, particularly those who joined the contras reluctantly or under coercion, suffered feelings of homesickness and longing to return to their families and communities. Mario Aguero, a poor peasant from La Vigía, remembers the first months after he joined the contras: "At that moment I didn't think about the FDN. I didn't think about fighting with anybody. I thought about my family, my mother and my children. I wasn't normal. I was conscientious, but something was missing. I felt like I was without a country, without a family, without hope, without anything."

Military Situation

When the military draft came into force by early 1984, the Sandinista Army was able to almost triple its forces from 24,000 men to at least 60,000 troops in roughly two years (Walker 1991a, 86). Thousands of other peasants, some fleeing the draft, joined the contras that same year, however, and the contra forces also grew rapidly. In the words of a former Quilalí EPS officer: "We created a company; the contras created a task force. They created a battalion; we created battalions." The military draft did, however, enable the Sandinista Army to launch large-scale counterinsurgency campaigns in the mountains that would halt the contra advance by the mid-1980s. By 1985 with the thousands of new draftees, the Sandinista Army had created a dozen Irregular Combat Battalions (Batallones de Lucha Irregular, BLIs), virtually self-sufficient mobile counterinsurgency battalions of 750 to 1,500 soldiers under the command of a regional military chief. The BLIs, along with newly formed Light Hunter Battalions (Batallones Ligero Cazador, BLCs) became the centerpiece of EPS counterinsurgency campaigns in the mountains, responding rapidly to contra attacks and carrying out search and destroy missions. By 1985 the Sandinista Army had also acquired a dozen or so Mi-24 HIND Soviet helicopter gunships, which gave the EPS a key advantage in the rapid transport of troops in the mountains and allowed the army to provide its troops with air cover.

The FSLN's new air power, the formation of the BLIs, and a series of counterinsurgency offensives by the EPS forced the contras to move much more cautiously. Contra leaders passing through Quilalí now divided their companies and task forces into smaller bands to avoid detection by more aggressive and numerous EPS patrols. Despite the EPS offensive and the suspension of military aid by the U.S. Congress from October 1984 until 1986, the contras were still able to organize several large-scale attacks against towns in northern

Nicaragua.[11] Dozens of contras from the Quilalí area, for example, participated in the 1985 attack on the northern town of La Trinidad, along the Pan-American Highway, and many Quilalí contras interviewed remember La Trinidad as the fiercest battle they experienced during the war. On 1 August hundreds of contra troops attacked La Trinidad at dawn. EPS helicopter gunships and planes quickly arrived and began a counterattack. Quilalí contras saw dozens of their fellow soldiers shot down by Sandinista helicopter gunfire and a few hours later the contras retreated in disarray. They suffered further heavy casualties over the next days as the Sandinistas pursued them through the countryside. By some accounts as many as 200 contras were killed and 400 wounded in the La Trinidad battle (Garvin 1992, 156–57; see also Dillon 1991, 161–62).

It was not until two years later, however, that contras launched their only major assault on the town of Quilalí. On 25 June 1987 three hundred contras, many of whom were local residents, attacked the town of Quilalí at dawn. They managed to enter Quilalí from the west and fought their way to within three blocks of the central park. The contra troops appear to have been poorly organized and disciplined, however, and they failed to burn either Quilalí's six grain silos or the gasoline storage tanks closer to the center of town, two key military targets. The contras did destroy the motor to Quilalí's water pump and blew up several electrical poles, but according to witnesses, in the heat of battle some entered bars along main street to drink liquor. Their subsequent inebriation may have made them easy targets for EPS reinforcement troops who arrived a few hours later and drove the contras out of town. A total of thirty-six contras were killed, as compared to only nine Sandinista soldiers and three civilians.

Nonetheless, in all these attacks, the contras demonstrated their ability to coordinate large-scale military assaults. They were met, however, with an equally massive Sandinista military response. Through its large numbers of men and resources dedicated to the war, the FSLN in the mid-1980s was able to effectively halt the advance of contra forces and prevent the contras from taking and holding any Nicaraguan territory. Although the contra forces would continue as a strong military force for several more years, the Sandinista Army kept roads open, and both small and large towns in the interior remained under EPS control and Sandinista political hegemony. However, the Sandinista government paid a heavy political and economic price for its military success. At the end of the decade an estimated 170,000 young Nicaraguans, out of a population of 3.5 million, had served in the Sandinista Army (Walker 1991a, 89). A total of 30,865 Nicaraguans were killed during the war, which caused over $9 billion worth of material and economic damage (Ministerio del Presidente, cited in Walker 1991c, 52–53). While the war was confined to Nicaragua's mountains and Atlantic coast, the draft meant that even urban Nicaraguan families were directly affected by the war, and in fact opposition to the military draft was an important element in the FSLN's 1990 electoral defeat (Oquist 1992; Castro 1992; CIPRES 1991).

In economic terms, the war not only disrupted agricultural production in Nicaragua's interior and destroyed infrastructure, but also led to labor shortages nationwide as working-age men were off fighting. In addition, from 1983 onward, 40 percent or more of the national budget was spent on defense (CIPRES 1991, 246). These huge military expenditures limited resources for programs in areas such as health and education, the cornerstones of the FSLN's commitment to benefit Nicaragua's poor majority, and were also a key factor in large government budget deficits and the inflationary expansion of the money supply. The true economic costs of the war would not become apparent until after 1988, when the FSLN finally enacted austerity measures to control budget deficits and hyperinflation, but in the long run the war effort seriously eroded not only the standard of living of Nicaragua's poorest citizens, but also popular support for the FSLN (see Conroy 1990).

Chapter 7

Life in the War Zone

As was shown in the previous chapter, from 1983 onward the deepening militarization of the municipality, recruitment pressures from both sides, and family and community dynamics made it extremely difficult for young men who remained in Quilalí to avoid taking up arms with either the EPS or the contras. This chapter will explore how women and older male civilian peasants in anti-Sandinista communities attempted to maintain an outward appearance of neutrality and minimize the danger to themselves and their families, while at the same time often carrying out everyday resistance to the FSLN through collaboration with the contras.[1] As will be seen, measures taken by the Sandinista government to control the contras' military presence in the municipality, in particular State Security investigations and the use of artillery fire, often served to reinforce this resistance to the FSLN. In contrast, the contras' strategy of selective repression was somewhat more successful in consolidating a civilian peasant base of support in outlying communities of Quilalí. Finally, the role of evangelical churches as a neutral haven for civilian peasants will be examined.

By late 1983 Quilalí was at war. From EPS military headquarters on a hillside at the edge of town, officers worked around the clock directing Sandinista Army soldiers on patrol throughout the municipality. Gunfire echoed in the mountains surrounding town and at night the sky above Quilalí was often lit with explosions. Quilalí residents would watch as artillery rockets flew across the sky and hear them land with explosions that shook the foundations of their houses. Helicopters passed overhead, and at times Sandinista Army antiaircraft guns opened fire on passing contra planes. Army trucks drove constantly up and down Quilalí's main street, transporting soldiers and supplies. School buildings were transformed into barracks for new recruits and Quilalí's main street became a "sea of olive green," crowded with men in uniform heading out into the mountains or returning from patrol. Quilalí's town population swelled to over 6,000 people, as peasants fled the conflict in the countryside (MID-INRA 1987, 14).

Outside the town limits, the roads were strewn with the burnt wreckage of army and civilian vehicles destroyed in contra ambushes. Convoys of army vehicles would leave the town of Quilalí suddenly without notice so that contra informants would not have time to pass word along to contra troops ready to prepare an ambush. By the mid-1980s, the contras had also acquired U.S.-made land mines, which they placed on Quilalí's roads. Civilian vehicles were often at as much as risk as military vehicles. On 22 September 1985, for example, a pickup truck traveling from Quilalí east to the town of Wiwilí struck an antitank mine contras had placed on the road and twelve of the truck's thirteen civilian passengers were killed. As contra land mines made travel increasingly perilous, often only one passenger truck a day made the eight-hour trip from the city of Estelí to Quilalí. At times roads were closed because of heavy combat and Quilalí residents were cut off from the outside world for days on end. Quilalí's only telephone, installed by the EPS, functioned only sporadically and contras at times blew up electrical towers leaving the town of Quilalí in darkness.

Peasants from outside Quilalí's town limits lived in a constant state of tension and insecurity during the war years. As several commented, "The war was horrible." During these years, peasant men in particular stayed as close to home as possible rather than risk running into an EPS or contra roadblock or being caught in a battle. Night was a particularly uncertain time. At any moment, under the cover of darkness, an armed group might knock on the door to demand food or shelter, or to question or take away a family member. One woman remembers: "We never ate peacefully. We never slept peacefully."

Export-oriented agricultural production in the municipality declined sharply by the mid-1980s. Little renovation or investment was undertaken in coffee production from 1979 onward and by the mid-1980s more than one-third of the municipality's coffee land, some 650 MZ, was abandoned because of the war (MIDINRA 1987, 26). Overall, coffee production in Quilalí fell from a prerevolutionary average of 17,000 quintales per year to 10,000 quintales in 1985 (26). Likewise, the number of cattle in the municipality dropped from a prerevolutionary high of 35,000 to less than 7,000 head by the mid-1980s (28, 30). In 1979, when the overthrow of Somoza appeared imminent, local Somoza supporters smuggled thousands of cattle into Honduras. Then in the months after the revolution cattle were often killed indiscriminately by peasants. The final blow to Quilalí's cattle herds came with the war, when soldiers and contras passing through Quilalí slaughtered thousands of animals. In contrast, the municipality's corn harvest remained fairly stable during the 1980s at just over 200,000 quintales, and during the war Quilalí played an important role on the regional and national level as a net exporter of corn.

By 1984 zones of political and military influence had emerged in Nicaragua's northern and central mountains. As a rule, the FSLN maintained military control and political influence over population centers, self-defense cooperatives, state farms, and the main roads. The contras in turn were able to consolidate a civilian base of support and a degree of military influence in many outlying rural areas.[2] In the

municipality of Quilalí, as a result of earlier contra targeting of Sandinista supporters, self-selection, and military dynamics, political allegiance and geography were clearly linked. The town of Quilalí
remained firmly in the hands of the Sandinista Army and was a relatively safe haven for both Sandinista supporters and peasants who
sought refuge from the violence there. Only on one occasion in 1987,
described earlier, were the contras able to penetrate Quilalí's town
limits. Quilalí's three cooperative river valley settlements—Panalí,
San Bartolo, and El Coco, as well as the La Reforma coffee cooperative, where over 400 peasant militia members carried out guard duty
around the clock—were also zones of Sandinista influence, although
they were continually harassed and threatened by contra troops
(MIDINRA 1987, 71). Half a dozen other nearby communities also remained largely under Sandinista control, with only occasional contra
incursions.

Civilian Collaborator Networks

In the mountains in the northern half of the municipality and in several river valley communities such as La Vigía, however, the community's active Sandinista supporters had long since departed. In these
rural communities, where the contras had a semipermanent presence, known Sandinistas were unable to enter the zone without a substantial military escort. According to ex-EPS lieutenant Rodrigo
Sosa: "If we went into those zones with fifteen men [the contras]
would kill us all. It was necessary to enter those zones with eighty or
a hundred men." The peasants who remained in these rural communities now lived "on top of " the contra forces, serving as both a reser-
voir of potential new recruits and a civilian base of support. As we
have seen, peasant families often made a unified decision to support
the contras. In turn an individual family member's role in the counterrevolution was determined largely by age and gender. Pressures

from the Sandinista draft and contra recruitment led a majority of young men under twenty-five years old in these communities to join the contras as combatants. Older men, women, and children remained behind because they were physically unable to endure the rigors of guerrilla life, were discouraged by traditional gender roles from engaging in combat, and because their presence was required at home to take care of children and maintain agricultural production. Although they did not join the contras, many of these peasants carried out everyday resistance to the revolution through such actions as feeding and sheltering contra troops, caring for wounded contra soldiers, and gathering information.[3] In some families, even very young children acted as lookouts and carried messages and food to the contras.

Years after the war officially ended, many such Quilalí peasant collaborators are still cautious about discussing the full range of clandestine activities they carried out to aid the contras. Some collaborators still seemed to fear punishment by the Sandinistas, although the FSLN was no longer in power and State Security was dismantled in 1990. Other peasants were concerned about possible reprisals by the families of victims if their role in certain ambushes and attacks during the war were revealed. In addition, some families were actively aiding armed recontra groups at the time of the interviews and were cautious about revealing these activities.

In a number of communities contras established formal collaborator networks. Such networks were generally headed by older middle-peasant or finquero males with some authority in the community, who also at times participated in ambushes or other armed actions near their homes. Anti-Sandinista peasants also resisted revolutionary authority in more informal, spontaneous interactions with contras and Sandinista military personnel. Virginia Moreno from La Vigía was left alone with her young children during the war when both her second husband and her oldest son, Ramón, went to fight with the contras. She remembers: "Thank God they [the Sandinistas] never found out we were involved with the Resistance, because we took care of those people and gave them food. We did it secretly. We would go out into the forest. My little boy was about five years old. We would put the food in a bucket and the boy would pretend that he was going to collect water. The boy left the food where he found their signs."

It appears that in communities under contra influence, peasants collaborated out of a sense of genuine conviction and support for the contras, and in other cases as a result of open and implicit contra intimidation. In the latter instance, these peasants tend to minimize the political and military implications of their activities to provide food to contra troops in interviews, commenting, "Those with arms give the orders." Under such circumstances peasant collaborators believe that Sandinista authorities were not justified in investigating or punishing them for their actions. In the words of Moreno: "I told the Sandinistas that I gave food [to the contras]. But I gave food to everyone who asked for food because how can you say no to someone who is hungry? It's not something to play around with. If the contras asked me for food I gave it. And the Sandinistas, too. Everyone here has done it. . . . Who were they going to throw in jail, everyone?"

Quilalí collaborators, however, commonly offered the contras more than an occasional meal. They also purchased supplies and medicines for contra troops, stored weapons, carried messages, sheltered contra combatants in or near their homes, nursed wounded contras until they were able to travel back to Honduras, and participated in occasional armed actions near their homes. In addition, Quilalí peasant collaborators served as guides (baquianos) to contra combatants unfamiliar with their communities, leading them through the mountains along secret trails concealed with underbrush, taking special precautions when crossing roads and open areas.

Another important task that contra collaborators carried out was spying and information gathering. On a local level, even ex-Sandinista military personnel agree that the contras' information network functioned well. A former contra intelligence agent explains: "My job consisted of organizing the people [Quilalí peasants] into intelligence cells to find out the location and capacity of [Sandinista Army] troops, the type of arms they carried, light or infantry . . . the volume of fire they could respond with if they were attacked by a [contra] patrol." Such peasant collaborators played a role in the 1983 attack on the El Coco cooperative and later attacks on the cooperatives of Panalí and La Reforma. Quilalí peasants who lived near the cooperatives sent word to contra patrols when the adult men of the cooperative and the Sandinista Army were away, allowing the contras to launch their attack when the cooperative was left relatively defenseless. Peasant collaborators also kept close track of the movements of Sandinista military and government vehicles and this information sometimes allowed contras to directly ambush vehicles or place mines in their path. According to a former State Security agent, "The contras' information system was so good that an army convoy could leave Quilalí at 12 o'clock and at 12:10 they would have an ambush set up on the hillside just outside town. They [contra collaborators] always knew where their family members were so as to get information to them."

The death toll was at times high in such ambushes. Ex-EPS officers remember that in 1986 in one such ambush in Las Palancas twenty-seven young army recruits were killed instantly. At other times, anti-Sandinista peasants acted as more informal lookouts. An informant explains: "They [Sandinista Army soldiers] could be five kilometers away and we would know where they came from and where they were going with the help of campesinos. In La Vigía we were united. If the army was headed toward La Vigía someone would jump on his horse and ride here to warn us. The men would head to the hills to hide. Or the contras would carry out some action to draw the army away."

As is typical of guerrilla struggles that take place in a confined space, at times the line between civilians and combatants blurred in Quilalí.[4] As a flexible response to the need of peasants to attend to their farms and continue to produce food for both their families and contra troops, and physical limitations that prevented some peasants from becoming full-time combatants, the position of armed correo was developed. An armed correo was a civilian peasant who lived and worked on his farm, concealed weapons, and occasionally participated in military actions in or near his community. According to ex-Sandinista Army officer Rodrigo Sosa: "Those 'part-time' contras planned ambushes. . . . The army would come later to search and wouldn't find anyone. They [the part-time contras] carried out the operation, hid their guns, and then pretended everything was normal. The contras used that style of combat quite a lot at certain times. The same man you questioned [about the ambush], he was the one who led the ambush."

Civilians and the Sandinista Army

Because their husbands and sons were often off fighting with the contras or in hiding, it was peasant women who had the most contact with armed groups.[5] In interviews, although anti-Sandinista peasants were distrustful of Sandinista soldiers and maintained important hidden transcripts, they express relatively few complaints about the treatment they received at the hands of the EPS. The most common grievance that anti-Sandinista peasant women interviewed had against Sandinista soldiers and the FSLN in general was, as was discussed earlier, that they tried to recruit family members. In the words of one woman from El Porvenir: "These people [the Sandinista Army] always showed up ready to make trouble. They always wanted to recruit my first husband."

According to other peasant women, the treatment they received at the hands of the Sandinista Army varied. They remember that at times soldiers arrived and there was "no problem," while at other times army soldiers arrived "angry" (*llegaron bravos*). It appears that

Sandinista Army soldiers took a more hostile attitude toward the civilian population, particularly after contra ambushes that killed fellow soldiers. In the view of EPS soldiers, civilian contra collaborators shared responsibility for such deaths. An ex-army officer explains: "What kills directly is the tongue, because if no one tells me that someone is waiting there armed, and I don't notice anything, then I die [in an ambush]. The [contra] correos knew all that information—where the [contra] troops were, how many there were."

While EPS soldiers were not always aware of the full extent of peasant collaboration with the contras, young soldiers often came to mistrust the peasant population in interior zones. This gulf between local Quilalí peasants and Sandinista soldiers was further widened by clashes between the urban culture of Sandinista Army soldiers, most of whom were from Nicaragua's Pacific coastal cities, and the mountain way of life. Just as urban FSLN political authorities had difficulty in effectively governing interior municipalities like Quilalí, so did some Sandinista soldiers find the ways of northern peasants, their unique expressions and customs, difficult to comprehend. In the words of ex-EPS Lieutenant Rodrigo Sosa, himself from Managua: "The majority [of EPS soldiers] were from the cities—Managua, León, Chinandega. . . . The people here in the north have a different mentality. The soldiers say this northern campesino is an Indian [*indio*]. These are true campesinos, who have never even been to a school. They've never even been to Managua!" Some Sandinista soldiers came to see Quilalí peasants as backward and ignorant, easily manipulated and deceived by contra lies. One former EPS officer in charge of community relations in the Quilalí zone expressed his frustration: "Because of their [Quilalí peasants'] [low] cultural level, their inability to understand, it's easier to trick [*engañar*] them than to convince them. We all speak the same Spanish, but not with the same meaning. You can tell them the truth a thousand times, but they'll always believe a lie."

For their part, urban Sandinista Army soldiers often had little understanding of the natural world and agricultural systems of peasants and sometimes unknowingly offended rural residents. Troops trampled through newly planted corn and bean fields, left gates open allowing animals to escape and destroy crops, and stripped valuable fruit trees bare in minutes. It was official EPS policy that soldiers pay for any food they consumed, but troops were chronically short of funds and this was not always possible. According to Sosa:

> People say it's easy to identify a [Sandinista Army] soldier by the hard look he has. A soldier has this look because of the fatigue, the exhaustion [he feels]. He's sweaty, hasn't washed for a week, and has no guidance [from superior officers]. . . . If he sees an orange he pulls it off the tree. If he sees a dog he gives it a kick. And the campesino gets mad. All this at certain moments has an impact. If the contras say, "the Sandinistas will pass by and eat your food," and then the EPS soldiers arrive saying, "give me that chicken," the campesino says, "Yes, it's true."

EPS officers and soldiers who served in Quilalí during the war strongly believe, however, that overall the Sandinista Army treated peasant civilians well. They saw themselves as part of a new revolutionary army that fought to defend the interests of poor peasants and that would never repeat the human rights abuses they saw carried out by Somoza's National Guard. Sandinista officials interviewed recognize that "anomalies" did occur in the field, but state that such abuses were the exception, not the rule, and were not condoned by higher officers.

State Security

In the municipality of Quilalí it is not the Sandinista Army but the State Security apparatus that anti-Sandinistas most remember with fear and hostility. As discussed earlier, the overall mission of Sandinista State Security was to gather intelligence on the contras and counterrevolutionary activities in general. In Quilalí and other conflictive zones, State Security employed double agents who joined the contra troops or collaborator networks, as well as a series of more casual informants who exchanged information for ideological reasons, money, or liquor (CIPRES 1991, 270). Once State Security had gathered sufficient information on a collaborator network, authorities in Quilalí and other zones generally carried out arrests of up to two dozen peasant suspects.[6]

From the viewpoint of Quilalí peasants who actively collaborated with the contras, arrest by State Security was a constant threat that hung over their daily lives. In the words of one anti-Sandinista peasant, "Our greatest fear was jail." Even years after the war ended and State Security was dissolved, peasants like Ricardo Pérez, whose sons fought with the contras, are still fearful: "If it came out in the newspaper today that I told you things against the Sandinistas, tomorrow they [State Security] would come take me away." Once arrested, suspected contra collaborators were usually sent to State Security jails, such as "La Chákara," near the city of Estelí. There, suspected peasants were held, often in isolation, from several weeks up to several months while their case was investigated by State Security.

Raúl Figueroa had worked secretly for several years as an armed correo when his network was uncovered by State Security. He remembers: "On 13 May 1985, twenty-five people were arrested. There was a correo deeply involved in the counterrevolution. They jailed him and he told everything; he gave all the names [of other collaborators]. I spent two months in the State Security jail while they carried out an investigation. They didn't mistreat me. The food was a problem. Sometimes all they gave us was powdered milk."

Peasants from Quilalí who were jailed by State Security agree that conditions were harsh. Prisoners were often locked in small, dark cells and given a poor diet. At times they suffered rough physical treatment, although none report physical torture. If sufficient evidence was compiled against a suspected collaborator, he or she would be brought before a three-person Anti-Somocista People's Tribunal (Tribunal

Popular Antisomocista, TPA), to be tried, and if found guilty, sentenced. Although defendants had a right to certain due process protections, the conviction rate at the trial stage of the TPAs was "extraordinarily high" (Americas Watch 1987, 91–97). Figueroa spent two months in La Chákara before he was brought before a TPA: "After two months in darkness, the brightness of the light hurt my eyes. They sentenced me to two years. Some people only received six months; others six years, up to thirteen years. People cried when they heard their sentence." Among the anti-Sandinista peasants interviewed for this study roughly one-third had either been jailed themselves or had one or more close relatives jailed at some point during the war.

In addition to State Security arrests, incidents also occurred in which suspected contra collaborators were summarily executed. According to human rights organizations such killings were isolated cases and not a deliberate policy or pattern sanctioned by higher Sandinista government authorities (Americas Watch 1990). In the municipality of Quilalí the killing of civilians by either the army or State Security appears to have been uncommon. One case that this study was able to document was the 1988 disappearance of a peasant from La Vigía, Catalino Galeano, in the hands of men whom the family recognized as State Security agents (see ANPDH 1991, 43). Galeano was a member of a large extended family and well known in his community, and his disappearance cost the Sandinistas a great deal of support among an already alienated peasant population. A neighbor recalls the agent that she believes was behind the disappearance: "There was one man called Chico Tiro. He was in State Security and he killed whoever he met. Everyone was afraid of him."[7]

By all accounts, Quilalí State Security was often successful in identifying and partially dismantling Quilalí collaborator networks, but at a heavy political cost. The FSLN did not commit the systematic human rights abuses commonly seen in other Latin American counterinsurgency campaigns that have sought to pacify peasants through terror. Yet paradoxically, the more moderate measures Sandinistas did take against rebellious peasants often seemed to have strengthened their resolve and resistance to the revolution.[8] Raúl Figueroa remembers a friend of his who was also arrested by Sandinista State Security: "They hit his feet with their gun butts. His toenails turned black and fell off. When he was released he told me, 'I'll hate the Sandinistas for the rest of my life.'"

It should be emphasized that Quilalí peasants who were sympathetic to the contras considered State Security arrests and imprisonment to be form of unjust Sandinista persecution and repression against them. In other words, these peasants did not judge the FSLN by an abstract, objective, or legalistic standard of human rights. Rather Sandinista "repression" was those actions that harmed their family and friends and restricted their personal liberty. Finally, virtually all those peasants interviewed who had been jailed by State Security admitted that they had at the time of arrest already been actively collaborating with the contras to a greater or lesser degree. This fact suggests that State Security crackdowns were in most cases not a root cause of peasant opposition to the FSLN, which had already emerged earlier, but rather that State Security actions at times served to reinforce and intensify peasant grievances and their sense of outrage.

Artillery Fire

In addition to contacts with Sandinista State Security and the EPS, another aspect of the war that reinforced civilian peasant resentment of the FSLN was Sandinista heavy artillery fire. For much of the war, the Sandinista Army stationed 122 mm Soviet mortar launchers on a hill outside the town of Quilalí and across the Río Coco in Pantasma, as well as Soviet multiple rocket launchers (BM21s) in Wiwilí, which could fire up to forty rockets more than twenty kilometers. When Sandinista army patrols located a large concentration of contras they would radio in the location coordinates to the Quilalí command post.

The artillery team would then fire the mortars at the contras in an attempt to soften them up before the EPS launched an offensive. According to ex-military personnel, at times contras positioned themselves close to populated areas of the mountains and artillery fire landed near civilian houses.

Peasant civilians would lie on the floor, under their beds, until the shelling stopped. For most it was a terrifying experience. Virginia Moreno recalls: "At first we thought we were going to die. Those fiery objects flying through the air, and then BOOM! The shock on landing would send us bouncing into the air. . . . We would go to my uncle's house, everyone trembling with fear. I told them to calm down, to remain there quiet and still because God knows what is just, and if God didn't want the bombs to fall on us, then nothing would harm us."

According to Quilalí anti-Sandinistas, EPS heavy artillery fire was a human rights violation that caused the death of a number of peasant civilians, particularly women and children, when their houses were destroyed by shells. This study, however, found little specific evidence to substantiate these claims of numerous civilians deaths. One case, which was verified in an interview with a family member, occurred in La Vigía in the mid-1980s when a mortar fired from Pantasma fell on a wooden house, killing a woman, Dora Moreno, and her three children. Almost every anti-Sandinista family interviewed in the surrounding community mentioned the deaths of Dora Moreno and her children as an example of Sandinista abuses against civilians. Clearly, when civilian deaths did occur at the hands of the Sandinista Army, even if accidental, they were a powerful propaganda tool for contra organizers.

Civilians and the Contras

Civilians living in the mountains of Quilalí in the mid-1980s had to contend not only with Sandinista artillery fire and military authorities, but also with groups of contras who traveled through and operated in the Quilalí zone. According to ex-contra combatants, Quilalí civilian peasants offered them spontaneous, overwhelming support, which they viewed as further legitimization of their struggle. These ex-contras tend to deny or minimize contra repression of the civilian population. Of twenty-seven Quilalí ex-contras interviewed, only four admitted witnessing or participating in any abuse or forced recruitment of peasant civilians. The national contra leadership as well attempted to conceal or downplay human rights abuses against peasants, although as an Americas Watch report summarizes, "The contras systematically assassinated civilians, killed and injured thousands of civilians in indiscriminate attacks, and mistreated and executed prisoners" (1990, 3).

The evidence from Quilalí suggests that human rights violations and selective repression against peasants by contra troops were not only condoned by many field commanders, but in fact were an important instrument by which the contras consolidated their control over rural communities.[9] The tacit rules of the game were well understood by peasants. Anyone suspected of collaborating or sympathizing with the Sandinista government would have, in the words of peasants, "problems" with the contras. A woman from El Súngano explains: "The comandos were well behaved. But if anyone smelled of Sandinismo they would get even [*pasarles la cuenta;* i.e., kill them]. Here in El Súngano there were no Sandinistas left when they evacuated [the mountains]."

Contra repression was generally "selective," directed primarily against suspected Sandinista sympathizers, but also broad in its definition of a "Sandinista" peasant. As suggested earlier, any peasant who participated in a government program or activity might fall under contra suspicion. In the case of Virginia Moreno, the fact that her husband had worked for several years on a state farm made the family a target of contra intimidation:

My husband was a night maintenance man on a state farm. When he came here [to Quilalí] they [the contras] wanted to kill him. They took him out into the forest, physically abusing him. They told him,

"We know you from when you worked in the [government-run] company. That's wrong." "Yes, sir," my husband said, "I've always worked, but I'm not anything. I'm not Sandinista because I don't have a gun." Politically we had to be evasive.

It was also widely understood in zones under contra influence that the punishment for being a suspected Sandinista supporter could be as severe as summary execution. Ex-contra Mario Aguero remembers an occasion when he and a small group of contras from the Quilalí Regional Command captured a peasant boy along a trail and ordered him to guide them across a nearby road. The boy refused. One of the contras called the boy a *piricuaco,* or rabid dog, a derogatory term for Sandinista, and pulled out his knife to slit the boy's throat. Aguero intervened, however, and convinced the rest of the group not to kill the boy: "The boy wasn't at fault. The fault lies with his father, who let him get involved with the ideologies of other people [Sandinistas]."

According to former Quilalí contra combatants, the "correct" procedure was not to kill a suspected Sandinista sympathizer, but rather to take him or her to the Honduran base camp for an "investigation." Investigation by the contras appears to have meant informal and sometimes abusive interrogation of the both the prisoner and other possible witnesses.[10] In some cases as well informants report that personal and political quarrels were not always clearly distinguished, and in these communities peasants who had disputes with their neighbors were in danger of being denounced as Sandinistas. According to Sandinista informants, the contras organized internal spy systems in the communities under their control. In the words of former FSLN Political Secretary Gilberto Santana:

We would come to a community. We would converse, talk. The people participated. Among those people there was an informer for the contras and he gathered information on everyone who was there. And among themselves they knew who he was, but they couldn't expose him. And when one of the participants wanted for one or another reason to express a concern, when we left that person would have a problem. They [the contras] would threaten him or maybe even kill him. There was a very strong system of terror and control organized by the contras.

While recognizing that contra repression did occur in the municipality, it should be emphasized that in many cases contras did not have to carry out overt violence to maintain control over the communities that formed their social base in the mountains. As we have seen in the discussion of contra recruitment, the presence of armed men and veiled warnings were often sufficient in themselves to ensure the cooperation of peasants adept at interpreting the realities of military power in their community. In fact, the majority Quilalí anti-Sandinista peasants interviewed describe the contras as "peaceful" and "well-behaved." A common response from anti-Sandinista women asked about their contacts with contras was, "I don't have any complaints about the Resistance."

Several points, however, need to be kept in mind in interpreting these peasants responses. First, some interviews took place in an insecure climate in which armed recontras were active and continued to exercise a degree of de facto authority in a number of outlying communities. For this reason, some peasants may have been cautious about openly criticizing the contras. It is also important to recognize that peasants who chose to remain in more remote communities after 1982 made the decision to adjust to life under contra influence rather than abandon their farms. As we have seen, these peasants often had family members and neighbors who served as contra combatants and kept a prudent distance from anything connected with the FSLN. To these peasants, the contras were not unknown outsiders with strange ideas and customs like Sandinista soldiers, but rather friends and family who fought for a cause with which many of them sympathized. In contrast to anti-Sandinista peasant outrage at key aspects of FSLN "repression"—the draft, State Security jailings, and artillery fire— peasants refer very matter-of-factly to contra actions against the civilian population. Implicitly, many of these peasants appear to have considered such contra selective repression to have been justified under wartime conditions.

Even taking this context into account, the fact that 55 percent of anti-Sandinista civilians interviewed volunteered positive comments about the contras' treatment of civilians suggests that selective repression was a partially successful contra strategy in consolidating peasant support in anti-Sandinista communities in Quilalí. In the words of Mario Aguero: "If you behaved well, you wouldn't have problems [with the contras]. If not, it was a mess. It was all according to the conduct of the person." To enhance the effectiveness of this selective repression, contras also encouraged the peasant population to view them as friends and protectors who defended the physical integrity of the rural family against Sandinista aggression. In the words of former contra Juan Chavarría: "We came to people's houses almost everyday. . . . To help people we carried medicines. We took care of them too, because some were being sought by the EPS. So in the zone where people were most persecuted by the EPS, we would patrol more closely so that the army couldn't penetrate the zone and bother the people who were there."

Contras, who were generally peasants themselves, also recognized the power of unsubstantiated rumors in rural culture and disseminated exaggerations and falsehoods about the FSLN to instill fear in peasants, draw them deeper into the counterrevolutionary cause, and to reinforce their image as the defenders of the peasantry. Peasant women remember, for example, "They [the MILPAs] told us that it was communism, that they [the Sandinistas] were going to send our children to Cuba to work and force us mothers to work here." Quilalí peasants also heard this type of anti-Sandinista propaganda on the contra radio station, Radio Fifteenth of September, throughout the war.

In another case, Marta Navas, a peasant woman whose son and husband were in the contras, explains why she decided to flee to Honduras after the EPS came looking for her:

[The EPS soldiers] yelled across the [Coco] river and asked for me by name. I told them, "She's not here. They took her to Pantasma." They were afraid to cross the river and come to my house because the comandos were nearby. I knew they would be back as soon as they found out I wasn't in Pantasma. They must have radioed from San Bartolo, because they returned the next day. They told me, "Come here, we only want to talk to you, not take you away." But I'd heard from a correo that they [the EPS soldiers] were going to kill me and my daughter, the one who was five months pregnant. They were going to cut her baby out of her stomach and eat it.

The true intentions of the EPS soldiers will never be known. They may have wanted to question Navas or even arrest her as contra collaborator, but they certainly were not going to eat her daughter's baby. Yet on the basis of this secondhand information from a contra collaborator, the woman fled her home with her children in the middle of the night and made a perilous overland crossing to Honduras.

Neutrality

In precarious wartime conditions many civilian anti-Sandinista peasants sought neutral ground whenever possible. Contra collaborators report that they attempted to conceal their involvement with the counterrevolution by presenting a "neutral face" to military and political Sandinista authorities.[11] When EPS soldiers entered known anti-Sandinista communities civilian peasants rarely expressed any overt opposition to their presence. In a few remote zones in fact, where the contras had apparently instilled a deep fear of the Sandinista Army, ex-EPS soldiers remember that peasant families literally shook with fear to see them approaching (see CIPRES 1991, 393–94). Ex-lieutenant Rodrigo Sosa remembers that he could always tell which communities were most deeply involved with the contras because residents would give his soldiers chickens, pigs, cattle, or anything else they wanted. In contrast, in pro-Sandinista rural communities, where residents had greater trust of the army and did not fear repercussions, "at most they would give us a day-old tortilla and a cup of coffee."

While anti-Sandinista peasants would generally provide food to Sandinista military personnel, they took care to reveal as little of their opinions and activities as possible. In the words of Virginia Moreno, peasant civilians "had to be politically evasive." She explains: "I told them [the Sandinista Army soldiers] that I had to give food to the Guardia [contras] because if I didn't they [the contras] would kill me, and it wasn't worth dying for a little bit of food. But it was a lie. I never had any complaints about the contras." Likewise, when Sandinista authorities attempted to converse with peasants and win them over to the revolutionary cause, anti-Sandinista peasants would typically listen politely, but rarely challenge the speaker. Former FSLN Political Secretary Gilberto Santana remembers such conversations: "These are people, you can talk politics to them one hour, two hours, and they won't offer any opinion of their own. And you can't tell if it's reaching them or not reaching them like a normal conversation. You have to have a lot more tact. In the first place, not to bore them. And second, to see what aspects might reach them. And third, to see the changes that occur over time." Overall, it seems that Quilalí anti-Sandinista peasants were relatively successful in presenting themselves, at times with a degree of truth, as "neutral victims" of the contras and concealing the full extent of their involvement with the counterrevolution. Some FSLN political and military authorities report that they did not realize until after the 1990 elections the depth of anti-Sandinista sentiments in some Quilalí communities.

Similarly, several peasants from anti-Sandinista communities suggest that because they lived in a rural community with an active contra presence they also were forced to maintain an appearance of conformity with the dominant military power, the contras, and hide their true feelings and opinions. According to one contra collaborator: "Here we lived very close to those people [the contras]. Maybe inside we felt something else, but we could never externalize it. The Frente Sandinista abandoned us." This collaborator implies that if the balance of power in his community had been different, and if the FSLN had maintained a greater military and political presence in the community, his political allegiance might have been different.

It is also important to note that poor and middle peasants had varying degrees of success in their attempts to occupy the delicate ground "between the two fires." Some families came through the war relatively unscathed while others, such as the Jiménez family, had difficulties with both the Sandinista government and the contras. State Security first arrested and mistreated Tomás Jiménez. After these incidents, according to a family friend,

> someone denounced the family, that they [the Jiménezes] were caring for a wounded Sandinista. [The contras] took him to Honduras. . . . They held him prisoner there in Honduras, but all the people in the Resistance knew the family and said, "Why did you kidnap this man who was working with us? [The family] gave food to the contras and cared for them when they were wounded." Then the contras brought him back to La Vigía.

After the contras released him, State Security arrested Jiménez again and interrogated him in a ditch full of mud. Jiménez never served time in jail, but was deeply traumatized by the "investigations" of both sides.

As can be seen, under such insecure conditions the main concern of anti-Sandinista families was often simply to keep the family alive and intact, and in the case of middle peasants in particular, to hold onto their land. Some peasant families report that they invested only the minimum labor and capital in their farms necessary to survive. In the words of a peasant woman from La Vigía: "Nobody wanted to work because nobody knew if they'd be here tomorrow . . . There was a lot of drinking and dice. But those who worked, like the [Pérez] family and the [Guerreros], are better off now. Those who sold their land are still here with no work or money."

A minority of finqueros and even some middle and poor peasants, however, were able to avoid open association with either Sandinista or anti-Sandinista forces in the municipality and use wartime conditions to their advantage to advance economically. The head of the UNAG in Quilalí describes what came to be known as patriotic producers: "The patriotic producer was one who thought like a Nicaraguan. His ideals were Nicaraguan, his piece of land. He didn't have to be Sandinista to be patriotic. . . . They weren't those producers who were involved in politics, shouting, 'Long live the FSLN! Death to Imperialism!' And sometimes they even had good instincts with the poor."

In contrast to the group of finqueros and their sons who provided the core leadership for the MILPA uprising and later served as field commanders for the contras, UNAG leaders estimate that roughly half of Quilalí finqueros fell into this category of patriotic producers who maintained at least the appearance of neutrality during the war years while taking pragmatic advantage of FSLN production incentives in the form of credit, subsidies, and technical assistance. In the 1986–87 agricultural cycle, forty-two such finqueros received 79 percent of government credit for cattle production (MIDINRA 1987, 55). A majority of these finqueros also joined the UNAG after 1984, when the membership of the organization was opened up to wealthy producers who in fact came to dominate the decision-making structures of the organization (Luciak 1995, 84).

A final important aspect of anti-Sandinista civilian wartime experience in Quilalí and other zones of conflict was the surge in membership in evangelical churches. Evangelical sects first began to penetrate the municipality in the early 1970s and by 1979 were well-established in the town of Quilalí and over a dozen outlying rural communities, often those where the Catholic church had limited outreach and Quilalí's priest was unable to visit more than a few times a year. The growth of evangelical sects appears to have accelerated in the early 1980s, particularly in anti-Sandinista communities and those that suffered the brunt of the conflict

Quilalí's most popular evangelical churches included the Jehovah's Witnesses and a number of pentecostal groups, such as the Assembly of God and the Church of God. Although members report a number of doctrinal differences between Quilalí evangelical sects—as to whether one should pray silently or out loud, for example—the pentecostal churches also share common practices and beliefs such as faith healing, speaking in tongues, and prophecy, and impose a strict code of conduct on their members. These churches also offer peasants a direct, intensely emotional spiritual experience while emphasizing the weakness and powerlessness of men and women in a world filled with constant danger and evil.

In the years following the revolution many Quilalí peasants did not feel empowered, but rather increasingly vulnerable as the war deepened and forces they did not always fully comprehend threatened their families and disrupted their lives. In interviews, several anti-Sandinista women describe seeking the spiritual and emotional support of an evangelical church at moments of crisis in their lives. Aura Guerrero occasionally attended mass in Quilalí's Catholic church before the war. Her oldest son became a contra commander in 1981 and one night just over a year later she heard a knock on the door. Several men entered carrying the bullet-ridden body of her son. Guerrero remembers: "I was blind. I fell to the ground. When I awoke I felt the presence of Jesus. Only God knows what I've suffered and I pray I won't suffer another calamity." Soon after her son's death, Aura Guerrero joined an evangelical church. Other Quilalí peasants also converted in moments of great stress, at the bedside of a gravely ill child or when a battle was taking place near their home. Dolores Jiménez, whose family was repeatedly threatened by both Sandinista State Security and the contras, describes the support she received from her religious faith: "We were pressured by both sides, humiliated by both sides, massacred by both sides. We were threatened and then tied up by one side and then the other. No one cared if it was women and children who died in this war. The only shelter we ever had was Jesus Christ."

At times, the chaos and violence in the secular world found its cathartic reflection in the spiritual world of evangelical churches. While the bombs and gunfire echoed around them outside, inside their church evangelicals saw themselves as engaged in a spiritual battle to defend themselves against temptation and the power of Satan. During prayer sessions Quilalí peasants often rise, and as the Holy Spirit overcomes them they begin to speak in tongues, their hands outstretched as they struggle to ward off the powers of darkness.[12] One evangelical Christian remembers that after she "received" Jesus Christ, she saw the devil's horns appear before her: "When you look for the power of God, the attacks come from all sides." Faith also provided a means by which peasants could make sense of violence as some churches suggested that the war was a fulfillment of biblical prophecy. Several anti-Sandinista peasants interviewed linked the FSLN to the role of the Antichrist. According to Guerrero: "They say the beast will come with a mark. They say it will be a political party."

It is interesting to note the strong differences between the evangelical doctrines, which dominated in areas of contra support, and Catholic liberation theology, which inspired a number Quilalí peasants to support the revolution. Both liberation theology and later revolutionary ideology promoted activism and empowerment, particularly of the poor. That is, peasants should not simply pray and wait for God to provide a solution to their problems, but rather they should take concrete action to put their Christian values into practice in the community, to transform unjust social and economic structures, and to create in their place "the kingdom of God on earth." In both liberation theology and among early supporters of the revolution there was a tremendous sense of voluntarism, a sense that Nicaragua and history itself could be radically transformed with sufficient faith and enthusiasm.

In contrast, evangelical Christians saw sin not in social structures but in the heart of man, whose only recourse in the face of the powerful forces of evil was to seek personal rebirth through the mysterious, almighty power of God (Stoll 1990, 137). As Quilalí evangelical Christians repeat often during services, "prayer is the most powerful weapon we have." Rather than confronting oppressive structures directly, evangelical Christians seek sanctuary and comfort in their faith.[13] A concrete example of the fundamentally different visions held by evangelical Christians and liberation theology can be seen in their response to high child mortality in the municipality. The activist liberation theology followers worked with the FSLN to organize immunization campaigns and programs to train community health promoters. Evangelical Christians, on the other hand, focused their efforts on offering families with seriously ill children moral and spiritual support with around-the-clock bedside prayer vigils.

In addition to providing spiritual refuge and support, such churches were one of the few remaining neutral spaces available to Quilalí's anti-Sandinista peasants. A number of evangelical churches took a pacifist stance and denounced the taking up of arms as a violation of God's will. One peasant explains: "I didn't subscribe to any political vision. I was an evangelical Christian according to the Bible. It's forbidden to express a political ideology; neither John nor Peter. We were neutral. That was our position." In practice, evangelical church leaders in some communities openly opposed the Sandinista military draft, but perhaps because of ideological sympathies or a recognition of the realities of power of their community, were more circumspect in confronting contras over their recruiting practices. As discussed earlier, although the FSLN did not officially recognize conscientious objectors, the Sandinista Army did show some flexibility and evangelical pacifists were sometimes assigned to noncombatant posts. Likewise, several peasants report that through church membership they were able to avoid active combat with the contras, who allowed them to remain at home and serve as collaborators.

Finally it should be noted that, despite their outward professions of neutrality, several evangelical sects in the municipality of Quilalí appear to have served as covert centers of resistance to the revolution. One such case, discussed in greater detail in the following chapter, occurred in the community of Santa Rita. In this strongly anti-Sandinista zone an evangelical sect, the Free Church, provided leadership and organizational resources that sustained and strengthened community opposition to FSLN efforts to integrate members into resettlement cooperatives.

Chapter 8

Sandinistas Regain Ground

SANDINISTA POLITICAL and military representatives interviewed report that they came to zones like Quilalí convinced that the revolution represented the best interests of the rural majority and that northern peasants, who had supported the liberation struggle of Sandino a generation earlier, would readily ally themselves with the Sandinista cause. These assumptions were challenged when, in the words of a former State Security official who oversaw operations in northern Nicaragua, "We woke up one day and found ourselves occupied [by the contras]." Other Sandinista authorities came to realize more gradually that the contras garnered important support from northern peasant collaborators and that Sandinista military strength alone was not sufficient to defeat the contra forces.

In response to this realization, FSLN officials undertook a series of coercive and persuasive measures designed to neutralize the contras' civilian support networks and eventually win peasants over to the revolutionary cause. As was discussed earlier, through State Security investigations the FSLN was able to partially dismantle contra collaborator networks. Many anti-Sandinista peasants, however, did not recognize the legitimacy of Sandinista punishment, and moral outrage at State Security may have deepened their support for the contras. Another measure undertaken by the Sandinista government, in part to weaken the contras' social base, was the evacuation of families from Quilalí mountain communities to valley resettlement projects in 1985. However, as will be seen, for a number of reasons—peasant resentment over the forced evacuation, internal tensions within the resettlement communities, the blurred civilian and military functions of cooperatives, and ongoing family links to the contras—the FSLN was only partially successful in this effort to gain peasant support.

The FSLN nationwide also carried out a series of pragmatic policy shifts in the mid-1980s to respond to peasant concerns. Specifically, the FSLN loosened government control over the sale of basic grains, distributed individual land titles, and in the municipality of Quilalí initiated material aid projects to meet peasant needs. As with the evacuations, these Sandinista policy reforms had limited success. In practice, the reforms did not reach important anti-Sandinista sectors of unorganized peasants and were generally overshadowed by the overall negative impact of wide-scale rural dislocation and violence.

Evacuation of the Mountains

In 1985 Sandinista authorities decided to evacuate a dozen communities in the municipality's northern mountains for several military and political reasons. First, although the Sandinista Army's mid-1980s offensive in northern Nicaragua was effective in halting the contras' military advance, the EPS's use of heavy artillery fire and helicopter gunships, as well as the intensified fighting, put civilians living in combat zones at great risk. Sandinista officials concluded that the only way to prevent further civilian deaths would be to evacuate civilian families and turn Quilalí's northern mountains into a free-fire zone.

Through these evacuations the FSLN was also employing a classic counterinsurgency strategy to weaken the contra forces by removing their source of food, shelter, and information: the civilian population. At the same time, Sandinista authorities viewed the evacuations as an opportunity to win the political support of these largely anti-Sandinista peasants. In the words of a State Security official: "It was a dramatic operation of dislodging people. We brought the campesinos from where the revolution didn't have impact to a place where we could influence them." Specifically, FSLN officials planned to resettle peasants in Quilalí's river valley, where they would receive land to farm, as well as access to services such as schools, health care, and child care that had not been available in the mountains.

FSLN authorities kept the evacuation plans a closely guarded secret, apparently because they feared that if peasants received advance warning they might move to Honduras or join the contras. The surprise evacuations began the third week of May 1985, when a convoy of Sandinista Army trucks set out from the town of Quilalí, headed north along a rutted dirt road into the mountains. The trucks halted in the community of El Súngano. Dozens of soldiers climbed out and went from house to house ordering peasants to pack their belongings and to leave their farms and houses. In some cases peasants who were reluctant to comply report that they were told by Sandinista authorities that if they did not leave, their houses would be burned.

Yet why were some of these peasants unwilling to leave the danger of the northern mountains for the relative safety of Quilalí's river valley? Part of the explanation lies in the fact that many of these peasants had family members in the contras and they wanted to stay in the mountains, where their sons or husbands would be able to visit or at least send messages with passing contra patrols. It is also noteworthy that almost half of the peasants evacuated owned farms of twenty five MZ or more (MIDINRA 1986, 38). As we have seen, this middle sector of peasants often acquired their farms through hard work and sacrifice and were unwilling to leave behind their houses, crops, animals, and fruit trees, and to risk losing the land itself. Although the FSLN gave these peasants new land in Quilalí's river valley and provided for their basic needs, many of the evacuated peasants had more land and a more varied diet, as well as a richer community life, in the mountains (MIDINRA 1986, 12).

In addition, many of these peasants had been exposed to anti-Sandinista propaganda from the contras and were fearful of being taken to the river valley "collectives" and "concentration camps." It is also important to keep in mind the very abrupt nature of the evacuations in which families were given little opportunity to prepare themselves to leave what was sometimes the only home they had ever known. One peasant woman states: "When they take you out of your home to go to another place, it's not the same as your own place. We weren't prepared to come here [to San Bartolo]."

Among those peasants who learned in advance of the evacuations, some chose to flee to Honduras rather than join settlement communities. Juan Chavarría and his family decided to hide when Sandinista troops came to avoid the evacuation:

> We spent about twenty days on the mountain of Chachagua. We were 180 families, around 500 people—children, young people, adults; people who had been forced to abandon everything. All these families had a son or cousin in the contras. Those contras didn't want to see their family restricted to a camp or settlement community and decided instead to take [their relatives] away. We were all headed along the same destiny. No one knew what to expect.

After spending several weeks hiding out in the forest, the families made contact with a passing group of contras who took Chavarría and the other young men with them to their base camp in Honduras, where they were trained as contra combatants. Another band of contras was sent a few weeks later to lead the remaining civilians to refugee camps in Honduras. As can be seen, the 1985 evacuations represented a further erosion of neutral space in the municipality.

Young men like Chavarría no longer had the option of evading military service and contra recruitment on their farms and now were forced to participate in one of the municipality's two dominant military forces.

While some families fled the evacuations, others such as Camilo Vargas, a poor peasant and evangelical pastor from El Súngano, resigned themselves to going to the resettlement communities: "The trucks pulled up to evacuate us the 18th, 19th, and 20th of May [1985]. As I was their pastor, I had to go with the majority. At that moment there was no crossing [with the contras] to Honduras. Without [contra] guides, women and children could die along the way. There were fierce battles taking place." The day of the evacuation Vargas and several hundred other families were given only a few hours to prepare for their departure to Quilalí's river valley. Those peasants who lived close to the road were able to take with them furniture, tools, cooking utensils, small farm animals, and other belongings to be loaded onto the army trucks. Families who had to walk long distances to the road, however, were only able to bring their clothing and the few small possessions they could carry. Many years later these peasants still remember with an intense feeling of loss the belongings they were forced to leave behind such as beds, sewing machines, tools, and prized animals.

A total of almost 20,000 MZ of municipality land was abandoned in the 1985 evacuations, and in a few communities the army burned peasants' houses to prevent contra troops from using them as shelter. The forest quickly reclaimed the abandoned fields and mountain paths. Farm animals left behind wandered loose, most to be eventually killed and eaten by passing soldiers and contras. In Region I, 84,000 peasants, or 29 percent of the population, were displaced by the war (FEDONG 1991, 77). Of those displaced, 18,300 went voluntarily or under duress to live in settlement communities; the other 65,700 dispersed (77).

The 300 peasant families evacuated from the northern mountains were taken by truck to Quilalí's three self-defense cooperatives in

Panalí, San Bartolo, and El Coco (MIDINRA 1987, 21). The FSLN had no housing immediately available for the evacuated families and for many peasants already upset by the sudden move, the over-crowded and poor conditions of the first months in the settlement communities worsened the situation. Camilo Vargas describes his family's first weeks in San Bartolo: "We spent twenty days in large [tobacco] sheds. Each family was given a space of four square meters, separated by black plastic. We suffered there. People screamed, cried, vomited, and had nervous attacks."

Several weeks later the evacuees were moved into better housing, but it was not until almost a year later that wood and cement houses were finally completed for the evacuated families. To provide the evacuees with sufficient land to farm, the FSLN turned 6,000 MZ of state farm land over to the displaced families (MIDINRA 1987, 21). Sandinista MIDINRA representatives also purchased or expropri-ated another 1,900 MZ from individual finqueros for the evacuated families. In addition, the Edwin Barahona cooperative in San Bartolo turned over 500 MZ of land to evacuated peasants. To farm this land, the resettled peasants were organized by community into almost a dozen production cooperatives. In addition to houses and land to farm, these families also received food subsidies for more than two years as well as access to schools, potable water, and health services. The creation of the settlement communities further transformed Quilalí's river valley. San Bartolo in particular grew from a commu-nity of several dozen families into a small town with over 300 families. In 1986 the population of Quilalí's three resettlement communities totaled approximately 3,500 people, or one-third of the municipal-ity's rural population and almost one-fifth of the municipality's total population (MIDINRA 1987, 14).

Evacuated peasants experienced a number of difficulties in adjust-ing to settlement life. Although the new settlements had ample agri-cultural land, for reasons of security and cost the new houses were built in rows only a few meters apart. Peasants from the mountains of Quilalí were used to having a large clearing around their houses, a *patio* where they could raise chickens, pigs, and other animals for food and income. Evacuated peasants report that they felt over-crowded in the settlement communities.[1] They longed for the free-dom and greater privacy of the mountains. In the words of Camilo Vargas: "I felt tied up. I was used to planting three or four MZ of land. I like to farm freely."

Another immediate difficulty that resettled peasants faced was their often tense relationship with the peasants who had originally es-tablished cooperatives in 1982 and 1983. As was discussed earlier, the founders of Quilalí's first three valley cooperatives were generally committed Sandinista supporters. These pro-Sandinista peasants suspected that evacuated peasants sympathized with the contras, par-ticularly after many of them refused to participate in self-defense mili-tias. For their part, newly arrived peasants were often resentful about the forced evacuation, and wary of the treatment they might receive. Some evacuated peasants, like Camilo Vargas, felt themselves trapped in the middle of Quilalí's conflict and viewed with hostility by both sides: "Here the Sandinistas said we civilians [resettled peasants] were Guardia [contras] because we didn't want to carry guns. And the other people [the contras] said we were Sandinista soldiers be-cause we lived here. We lived marginalized by all."

Military service was also a source of conflict. In Panalí, San Bar-tolo, and El Coco almost all the original cooperative members partic-ipated in self-defense militias and took turns serving in EPS Reserve Battalions from several months up to a year at a time. Many of the re-settled peasants, however, refused to take up arms. In the case of Panalí, former civilian defense coordinator Luis Zapata estimates that up to half the men in the community were unwilling to participate in the militia. Resistance to carrying arms in Panalí was particularly strong and well-organized among members of the evangelical Free Church from the community of Santa Rita, a strongly anti-Sandinista community known as a rest-and-recreation area for the contras. After their involuntary evacuation, the "free ones" argued that their reli-gious beliefs forbade them from taking up arms. In the words one evangelical Christian: "The Bible says you shall not kill, you shall not rob. . . . But if I pick up a gun, it's for killing someone and God wants us to love one another." Although the "free ones" did not express it openly to Sandinista authorities, it is also likely that they were reluctant to take up arms in favor of a government that they opposed ideologically, and to fight against contra groups to which family members, friends, and neighbors belonged.

Tensions grew in Quilalí's three settlement communities between the "soldiers"—peasants who participated in militias and felt they bore disproportionate burden of community defense—and the resettled "civilians," who refused to take up arms. As in other cases, the official Sandinista response was a mixture of coercion and concession. Some resettled peasants, such as Camilo Vargas, were jailed for short periods for refusing to serve in the Sandinista Army Reserve, as required of all Nicaraguan men ages twenty-five to forty. At other times, Sandinista authorities were more flexible and peasants who did not wish to serve in the militia were given the option of doing noncombatant "social works" such as digging trenches.

In addition to pressure to serve in militias, resettled peasants, many of whom as we have seen, preferred to farm individually, using family labor, were required to join cooperatives. In the words of a MIDINRA study: "[The evacuated families] were practically forced to join the CAS, which did not have the economic or organizational development to absorb the new members. At the same time, a type of social hierarchy formed in which the 'soldiers' [militia members] felt themselves very superior to the 'civilians'" (1986, 44).

All these problems led a large number of peasant families to desert the resettlement communities within weeks of being evacuated. Of the forty families who were brought to El Coco, for example, thirteen families deserted in the first two months (MIDINRA 1986, 46). When Quilalí Sandinista representatives realized how many families had deserted the resettlement communities, they launched an investigation to discover what lay behind this mass exodus. As a result of the investigation, in March 1986, several Sandinista party and government representatives were transferred and evacuated peasants were given the option of farming individually (40). While these actions by the FSLN did ameliorate some of the immediate discontent, for several more years evacuated peasants continued to resist full integration into resettlement projects and life. Rather than openly confront Sandinista representatives, peasants like the several dozen members of the Free Church of Santa Rita opted for a form of everyday resistance, a "crossed arms strike." The MIDINRA study characterizes this as a "lack of movement" in which "people were basically unwilling to mobilize around projects in their own objective interest" (1986, 47). According to the study: "A good deal of the resistance of the evacuees to taking the initiative to create a stable environment for themselves (completing their houses, planting fruit trees, improving their houses, etc.) is due to their wish to return to their home [*comarcas*] and native farms, their deep longing for campesino life" (11). It is also possible that some of these peasants wished to avoid participation in "Sandinista" projects, even those which would benefit them directly, because of ideological opposition to the revolution and to avoid problems with the contras.

Military versus Productive Functions

While the FSLN effectively responded to some of the immediate grievances of resettled peasants, a more long-term tension remained in the fact that the new resettlement communities served both military and productive functions. Specifically, the need to commit large amounts of human and material resources to defense activities undermined both agricultural production and FSLN political goals to win the support of resettled peasants. Cooperative militia members emphasize that that they were first and foremost civilian farmers who took up arms only out of necessity to defend their land and families against contra aggression. In contrast, contras considered the resettlement communities to have been legitimate military targets, arguing that peasants living in cooperatives abandoned their civilian status by closely supporting the Sandinista Army and participating in permanent militias. Also, as was discussed earlier, contra harassment and attacks not only diverted co-operative resources toward defense, but also undermined the legitimacy of the FSLN by demonstrating to both resettled families and neighboring communities that although the FSLN could offer them land to farm, it could not guarantee their physical security.

In Panalí, San Bartolo, and El Coco militia members guarded the communities' perimeters day and night, seven days a week. The president of the San Bartolo community governing board describes this defense system: "All around San Bartolo were guard posts. One man would sleep and the other would keep watch, taking turns every hour. Maybe they tried, but the contras were never able to penetrate San Bartolo. If we saw or heard the contras we would call for reinforcements on the radio. Together with the army we had an incredible structure. We had command posts, light artillery, tanks, long-range cannons." Every morning as well, militia patrols under army direction would sweep the roads leading in and out of the settlements searching for mines planted by the contras during the night. When the two patrols met the road was declared safe for vehicle traffic. At any given time, from one-fourth to one-half of the settlement members under forty who participated in settlement defense were on guard duty or away from the settlement on military missions with the army (MID-INRA 1987, 39). Quilalí's cooperative settlements also provided the FSLN with a strategic military foothold in the countryside and often served as a resting point for passing Sandinista Army soldiers. Pro-Sandinista settlement members report that they felt more secure when the EPS was close by, as the contras rarely attacked at such times.

Of Quilalí's three settlements, San Bartolo was the largest and the most well defended, and many of its founding cooperative members were experienced soldiers. The contras targeted instead the more weakly defended cooperatives in El Coco, Panalí, and La Reforma. Contras sent notes and started rumors that they were planning to attack, passed provocatively close to the community perimeters, and at times launched mortars into the resettlement communities. On 28 July 1986 approximately forty contras received word that the Sandinista Army was away on mission and attacked Panalí with M-79 mortars and rocket-propelled grenades. According to the civil defense coordinator at the time, Panalí's small militia was overwhelmed: "Some people instead of returning fire hid their weapons and acted like civilians. They weren't trained and had no chance against the Resistance [contras]. When there was an attack they went crazy."

Six Panalí residents were killed in the 1986 attack, including three children, and twenty-five people were wounded. A resident of Panalí whose brother was killed in a later 1987 attack stated: "I don't understand why [the contras] wish to burn and destroy here. Now we pass our nights in fear. We can't sleep peacefully in our homes. . . . My injured child cries often thinking that the contras will return, but we don't have anywhere else to go. . . . What we want is peace so that we can work and that there be no more children and old people injured" (quoted in Witness for Peace 1987, 2).

The defense priorities of these cooperatives also affected agricultural production and members' standard of living. On the one hand, the settlements were designed to provide peasants with land and the opportunity to improve their economic situation, as well as to boost the production of food and export crops and support Nicaragua's national economy. Local EPS officers, however, often saw the settlements as a close, convenient pool of reinforcement troops, and as Quilalí cooperative members were continually called away on military missions, farming output suffered.

In addition to conflicts between the productive, political, and military functions, Quilalí's cooperatives also confronted a series of challenges common to agricultural cooperatives throughout Nicaragua. One common problem was equal pay for unequal work. More hardworking and ambitious cooperative members report in interviews that they felt frustrated with other members who put little effort into collective work and practiced "turtle-paced work." Another challenge to Quilalí cooperative development was lack of education in the countryside. While as was discussed earlier, the FSLN offered a variety of educational programs for rural residents, not all were able or willing to take advantage of these opportunities. Even in the successful Edwin Barahona cooperative, leaders estimate that in the 1990s over half of the members were still functionally illiterate. Many cooperative members, therefore, lacked the knowledge and skills to make informed decisions or to administer Quilalí's large and complex cooperative structures. Low educational levels also meant that in practice that Quilalí cooperatives were effectively managed by a few relatively well educated peasants and government officials.

This situation offered opportunities for corruption and led to mistrust on the part of cooperative members who had little understanding or oversight of cooperative finances. According to the MIDINRA study of the Santos López cooperative: "The financial management of the cooperative is not clearly documented. It seems that the cooperative is heavily in debt and people openly voice suspicions not only of poor management, but also of embezzlement of collective funds by those in charge" (1986, 53). There was also little oversight of the use of cooperative machinery, and little administrative control over agricultural production. In El Coco, "seventy milk cows wander around loose, while you can't find a drop of milk in the settlement" (54).

In terms of transforming women's subordinate status, Quilalí's cooperatives were partially successful. Because so many men were off fighting, some women had the opportunity to engage in nontraditional agricultural work. The FSLN and international donors also sponsored several income-generating projects directed at women in the resettlement communities, including a collective garden and a baking cooperative, which are remembered very positively by women in these communities. On the other hand, Quilalí's twenty-seven production cooperatives had few female members, and peasant women had little voice in their management.[2]

Some local and regional Sandinista officials also unintentionally re-created new forms of dependent relationships with their peasant supporters in the cooperatives.[3] Cooperative members looked to the Sandinista government to provide them with tractors and other farm equipment at subsidized prices, forgive cooperative bank debts, and assist in administering the cooperatives. Until almost 1990, MID-INRA officials did much of the cooperatives' bookkeeping and managed the production of cooperative export crops such as tobacco (MIDINRA 1987, 40). Some FSLN leaders also adopted authoritarian "vertical" styles of leadership, which alienated potential peasant supporters, inhibited the development of leadership abilities among Quilalí's poorer peasants, and "led to unnecessary loss of resources and prestige by the FSLN and the government" (MIDINRA 1986, 5).

Cooperative Successes

Despite these many challenges, the FSLN was able to establish and consolidate in the municipality of Quilalí one of the most extensive cooperative blocks in the region. As of 1988 in the municipality, fourteen CASs, seven "work collectives" (Colectivos de Trabajo, CTs), and six "dead-furrow" cooperatives (Cooperativas de Surco Muerto, CSMs) had been established, along with twenty-four credit and service cooperatives.[4] In the 1980s more than 700 peasants received land in the municipality; 393 as members of CASs and work collectives, and 281 through participation in dead-furrow cooperatives (MID-INRA 1987). Another twenty or so peasants received individual land grants. Among those who received land, 613 peasants received access to at least ten MZ of land, an amount that in most cases would allow them to advance beyond subsistence farming into the status of middle peasants. Quilalí's broadly defined middle peasant sector grew from 34.7 percent of municipality farmers in 1979 to 61.5 percent of producers in 1987 (table 8.1).

Although, as will be seen, most Quilalí cooperatives dissolved in

Table 8.1
Rural Sectors in Quilalí, 1979 and 1987

Rural Sector	Farm Size (MZ)	# of Producers		% of Producers		Area (MZ)		% of Area	
		1979	1987	1979	1987	1979	1987	1979	1987
Large Landowners	1,000+ MZ	5	0	0.5%	0.0%	13,200	0	19.1%	0.0%
Finqueros	200 to 999	68*	68	6.8*	4.1	25,000	28,000	36.1	40.5
Middle Peasants	10 to 199	347*	1,025*	34.7*	61.5*	28,000	39,430*	40.5	56.9*
CAS/CT			393		23.6		9,294		13.4
CCS/CSM			539*		21.5*		14,136*		20.4*
Non-Organized			273		16.4		16,000*		23.1*
Poor Peasants	0 to 9	580	573*	58.0	34.4*	3,000	1,770*	4.3	2.6*
CCS/CSM			515*		30.9*		1,500*		2.2*
Non-Organized			58		3.5		270*		0.4*
TOTAL		1,000*	1,666	100%	100%	69,200	69,200	100%	100%

*Estimates.
Source: Calculated from MIDINRA (1987).

the early 1990s, in interviews pro-Sandinista peasants generally describe their cooperative experience in the 1980s in positive terms. These cooperative members agree that the problems described above weakened cooperatives, but blame many of their difficulties on the military conflict. They believe that if the war had not derailed so many plans, cooperatives would have truly flourished. According to Daniel López: "Where the revolution had influence, it did a lot—all these houses, land, the health center, the children's dining center. [Revolutionary] change has been worthwhile in San Bartolo."

Among Quilalí's twenty-seven production cooperatives, the three original cooperatives—Santos López, Edwin Barahona, and Augusto C. Sandino—established in 1983 enjoyed the most success and members appear to have achieved a higher standard of living than other peasants.in these communities. The greater success of Quilalí's original cooperatives may be attributed in part to the Sandinista government's generous distribution of resources such as land and farm equipment to cooperatives in the early years of the revolution. The sixty-seven-member Edwin Barahona cooperative originally received 1,958 MZ of land, almost 30 MZ per member, as well as eight tractors sold to the cooperative at highly subsidized prices (MIDINRA 1984d, 14). Members of Quilalí's original cooperatives also tended to share a strong ideological commitment to the revolutionary process and the success of their cooperatives. To those peasants who chose to remain in cooperatives throughout the war, harassment and attacks by contra forces often served to deepen their ties to the land. In contrast, the resettled peasants retained their primary loyalty to their original farms and were often simply waiting out the war to return to the mountains.

Although reliable data on the profits and losses of Quilalí cooperatives are not available, it is known that the cooperatives were able to maintain stable corn production throughout the 1980s. This production was concentrated in the river valley, where mechanized production techniques and chemical inputs led average corn yields to double in less than five years, from 16.5 quintales/MZ in the prerevolutionary period to 32 quintales/MZ by 1983 (MIDINRA 1984d, 45). Cooperatives typically sold up to 75 percent of their corn crop to EN-ABAS and distributed the rest to members, who used it both to help meet their food needs for the year, and for sale and barter (Spoor 1995, 187–88). Any profits the cooperatives earned were generally divided among members according to the number of days they had worked in the fields. The Edwin Barahona cooperative in San Bartolo and the Santos López cooperative of Panalí also grew tobacco as a cash crop. MIDINRA funded the construction of wooden curing houses and provided subsidized machinery, as well as technical assistance. In several years these cooperatives earned profits of thousands of dollars from the sale of their tobacco crop to the government for export (MIDINRA 1987, 40). In addition, cooperatives maintained small collective herds of cattle, and families owned livestock individually.

An additional positive aspect of cooperative life for peasants was their participation in the National Union of Ranchers and Farmers, the UNAG. Quilalí's UNAG representative estimates that at its height in the 1987, the organization had over 700 members in the municipality of Quilalí, approximately two-thirds of whom were cooperative members. The main purpose of the UNAG was to "unify Nicaragua's agricultural producers in an effort to revitalize and reform the rural sector" and ensure that the "transformation of the political economy benefited the previously marginalized peasant class" (Luciak 1995, 75). The UNAG's relative degree of autonomy from the FSLN allowed it to effectively pressure the government to implement policies in favor of the peasantry, such as the 1983 debt cancellation for basic grain producers and ensuring that cooperative association would be voluntary and not forced (114). As part of its national program to promote more effective distribution of agricultural inputs, the UNAG also opened a Tienda Campesina, a rural store to provide low-cost goods to farmers, in the town of Quilalí in 1987 (see 123–60).

Rural Policy Reforms

From 1984 onward the FSLN carried out an additional series of pragmatic policy reforms designed in part to respond to peasant needs
and grievances and so neutralize the contras' social base of support.
As discussed earlier, during the first three years of the revolution the
FSLN promoted a state-centered rural development model. In 1983
that policy was expanded to include the distribution of land directly
to peasants organized in production cooperatives, as well as a reduction in the amount of land held by the state. Several years later, FSLN
rural policy shifted again and for the first time the Sandinista government began to distribute land to individual farmers.

In the municipality of Quilalí in 1985, as was shown, Sandinista
authorities initially required resettled peasants to join production cooperatives to gain access to land. Local policy was modified in 1986,
however, to allow peasants to form six more loosely structured dead-
furrow cooperatives and seven work collectives. In addition to allowing more flexible forms of peasant producer associations, by 1988 the
FSLN distributed over 600 MZ to approximately twenty individual
peasants. The FSLN also passed a 1986 agrarian reform law that
eliminated the early lower size limit on expropriations of 500 MZ on
the Pacific coast and 1,000 MZ in Nicaragua's interior and legalized
land expropriation for public use or social interest.[5] An important
purpose of this law was to weaken the "internal front" of the counterrevolution, those farmers who intentionally left their land idle or
underused to harm the revolution (Luciak 1987a, 130). In the municipality of Quilalí, however, the new agrarian reform law appears to
have had only a limited impact because, as was discussed earlier, the
municipality's last major series of buyouts and expropriations occurred in 1985 before the law went into effect, when the FSLN
bought or confiscated 1,900 MZ of valley land to give to evacuated
peasants (MIDINRA 1987, 21). During this period as well, Sandinista
officials continued to reduce Quilalí's state farm sector, turning over

the final 6,000 MZ of state cattle and coffee land over to cooperatives in 1985 (MIDINRA 1987, 21).

Another important pragmatic FSLN policy shift in the mid-1980s was the liberalization of the sale of basic grains. In Quilalí, where this policy went into effect in 1985, peasants were no longer restricted in terms of where they could sell their corn and bean crops, a key source of peasant resentment in many parts of Nicaragua. In the 1986–87 harvest many Quilalí peasants took advantage of these new market opportunities to sell their crops in the neighboring department of Jinotega, where grain prices were 20 percent higher. In Nicaragua as a whole, there is some indication that from 1985 onward liberalized trade at least slowed the decline of basic grain producer income and real grain prices (Zalkin 1990, 54).

Several factors, however, limited the impact of these FSLN rural policy reforms. First, these new policies were not uniformly or completely implemented.[6] Despite the FSLN's new recognition of the political and economic importance of peasants, according to an IHCA study, 80 percent of rural state investment in 1986 was still directed toward capital-intensive, high-technology, long-term projects (cited in Martinez 1993, 481). Likewise, peasant sales of basic grains were still restricted in certain Nicaraguan departments as late as 1987 (Gilbert 1988, 102–3). In terms of the FSLN's more flexible land reform policies, it is important to emphasize the relatively limited amount of land and number of beneficiaries involved. In Quilalí only 600 MZ, or 3 percent of the total land distributed in the municipality, was given to 20 individual peasants, some of whom were reportedly already Sandinista supporters. Nationwide, 210,000 MZ of land were distributed to individual peasants, only 16 percent of the total 1.3 million MZ of land distributed by the FSLN (Wheelock 1990, 112, table 4). In terms of FSLN land titling, it is also not clear what degree of importance that peasants placed on receiving formal titles from the FSLN.[7] As we have seen, in zones like Quilalí on the agricultural frontier squatters' rights were generally respected in the prerevolutionary period. In the words of one peasant who received a land title from the FSLN, "It's true they [the Sandinistas] gave us land, but these were the same lands that we had bought years earlier through our sacrifice, through our individual efforts" (quoted in Bendaña 1991, 73). Another difficulty noted by several Quilalí peasants was that the Sandinista land titles did not permit them to sell their land. The FSLN included this provision as a protection for poor peasants, but in the eyes of some peasants this meant the titles were not real.

Development Projects and Political Outreach

Along with shifts in land reform, the FSLN developed programs such as the Plan General Único in the mid-1980s, under which regions I and VI, Nicaragua's conflictive northern and central interior regions, received direct attention from the National Directorate of the FSLN and priority in the distribution of material and human resources (CIPRES 1991, 414). In the municipality of Quilalí, ex-FSLN Political Secretary Santana explains the strategy behind these efforts: "We almost didn't talk about politics [with anti-Sandinista peasants] at all because it was useless. What we wanted to attack were the problems of campesinos; [among them] the problems of bank credit, transportation. [We wanted to] establish ties with them through concrete projects." As part of this policy, in the mid-1980s the FSLN promoted several development projects in Quilalí's river valley that benefited pro-Sandinista communities—Panalí, San Bartolo, and El Coco—as well as anti-Sandinista valley communities such as La Vigía. These projects included the purchase of irrigation equipment, tractors, and trucks and their purpose was both to increase agricultural production in the valley and to consolidate rural support for the revolution (MIDINRA 1987, 23).

In addition, in interviews both pro- and anti-Sandinista peasants mention the FSLN's generous rural credit policy as the single most important element of Sandinista material aid for peasants. As was seen earlier, nationwide rural credit exploded in 1980. Although amounts were cut back the following years, credit was widely available even to the poorest peasants throughout the decade. One anti-Sandinista peasant states: "[The Sandinistas] wanted to win over the people. They gave out money by the sack. Anybody who grabbed a piece of land could apply for credit." Quilalí peasants also report that when the Sandinista government was in power they had little fear that they would lose their land if they failed to repay loans. In fact, on several occasions, with pressure from the UNAG, the FSLN forgave all rural debt of basic grain producers. In addition, until the 1988 economic adjustment Nicaragua's accelerating inflation rates meant that peasants took out loans at negative real interest rates. Another Quilalí peasant remembers, "They [the Sandinistas] gave loans for a hundred calves and with ten cows you paid the loan back."

In Quilalí, FSLN political representatives also served as unofficial problem solvers and mediators between the local government and the civilian peasant population. A Quilalí peasant, who in the 1970s might have turned to his patron to resolve a problem, in the 1980s would often seek out the FSLN Political Secretary. Santana explains: "If there was a problem, we [FSLN party members] helped campesinos find a solution through a government agency. . . . If the bank put a thousand obstacles in the way of a loan, for example, we would visit and consult with the bank to see what the problem was and what we could do to cut through the bureaucracy."

FSLN political authorities also worked to resolve conflicts between the civilian population and the Sandinista Army and State Security, particularly when the narrower goals of Quilalí's military apparatus conflicted with the broader revolutionary interest in winning the political support of peasants. According to Santana:

We even dealt with the army in some cases, for example, to find out if someone was arrested, or where they were being held. People would arrive saying, "they took away my relative" or "we don't know where he is." We had access and we could say, "He's here. He's there. Don't worry." We also investigated possible abuses by the armed forces. They [peasants] couldn't go directly to the army, because the military leadership was very closed. They treated campesinos very brusquely. But we could go there to reason with them [military officers], to reach an agreement.

It is important to note several limitations of these Sandinista material aid projects in Quilalí. First, even after the policy reforms of the mid-1980s the FSLN continued to neglect individual peasants in more remote zones of the municipality. As late as 1987, MIDINRA continued to "intentionally marginalize" some 600 members of CCSs and channel technical assistance, training, and material resources to Quilalí's production cooperatives (MIDINRA 1987, 41). Also, the Sandinista government had virtually no contact with 305 of the municipality's "nonorganized peasants," who participated in neither CCSs or production cooperatives. This group represented almost one-fifth of the municipality's farmers but received only 11 percent of all bank credit. In contrast, Quilalí's production cooperatives and work collectives received 34 percent of all credit, and CCSs 55 percent (55).

Second, the exigencies and nature of the war itself undermined the effectiveness of these later Sandinista efforts to build a peasant base of support. That is to say, the corrections made because of the war were neutralized by that same war and the economic problems it brought (Bendaña 1991, 49). Most obviously, the war drained resources that under other circumstances could have been used for rural development projects, disrupted agricultural production, and led to large-scale dislocations of the peasant population. In the municipality of Quilalí the Sandinista government distributed more than 13,000 MZ of land to peasants, but an even greater amount, 20,000 MZ, was abandoned because of the war. In the Segovias as a whole, 6 percent of all land was expropriated for state farms; 8 percent of land went to production cooperatives; and by 1984, 21 percent was abandoned due to the war (Kaimowitz 1989, 404). In addition, as we have seen, military polarization made some peasants reluctant to participate in government programs, even those that would clearly benefit them. In the words of middle peasant Ricardo Pérez: "The Sandinistas held big meetings with us. Great battalions arrived, huge caravans of people. They talked about politics. They offered us big development projects, great things for La Vigía. But we didn't fall into the trap. Because once they gave us something the other people [the contras] would come and say that we were with them [the Sandinistas]."

Moreover, even where peasants benefited economically from FSLN policies, this did not necessarily translate into political support from peasants who were already bound to the contra struggle by a complex web of ideological sympathies, family ties, and fear. In fact, in some cases, such as La Vigía, a number of peasants appear to have accepted material aid from the Sandinistas and at the same time continued to collaborate closely with the counterrevolution, supplying contras with food grown with government assistance.[8] There is also evidence to suggest that some successful Sandinista development projects may have helped consolidate an economically prosperous peasant sector whose political and economic interests clashed with the long-term revolutionary goal of socialism.[9]

Partial FSLN Success

In assessing the impact of the FSLN's pragmatic policy shifts in the mid-1980s and political work with peasants, opinions of Quilalí informants are mixed. One ex-army officer concludes: "We gave them [anti-Sandinista peasants] vehicles. We went to the communities with basic grains and tools to give them, but it didn't change their attitude. They all had family members in arms [with the contras]. Even though they knew it was wrong, they wouldn't say anything because it was their family." Likewise, a former mayor believes in hindsight that during its decade in power the FSLN was never able to truly comprehend or win over Quilalí's population. He states, "Quilalí was always very rebellious for the FSLN, difficult to control."

Other Sandinista representatives from Quilalí, however, suggest that flexible Sandinista policies helped ease tensions in the municipality and build a better relationship between the FSLN and Quilalí peasants. According to Gilberto Santana:

> There are changes in silence, changes that are hidden, concealed
> . . . . You have to understand and know the campesinos, because
> they will never say, "I'm here to serve you. You can count on me," or
> "Give me the gun, I'm going to fight." You won't see a change like
> that. It's a smaller change. Maybe, "Would you like to come in have a
> glass of juice?" Maybe they won't say much, but they'll tell you a lot.

Santana remembers, for example, that in anti-Sandinista communities where the FSLN provided aid, peasants came to cooperate with Sandinista authorities in limited ways: "If a peasant in one of those [anti-Sandinista] communities tells you, 'don't take that path,' it's a small thing, but it's a very important thing." Indeed, a peasant who warned Sandinista officials about a potential ambush risked reprisal by the contras.

In terms of the peasants evacuated from Quilalí's mountain communities, the FSLN appears to have had partial success in winning their support. After the mid-1985 wave of desertions, settlement populations stabilized and remaining families adapted themselves to life in a Sandinista zone of influence. A number of resettled peasants, however, continued to resist participation in defense tasks, permanent incorporation into the community, as well as Sandinista attempts to influence their political views. In the words of evangelical pastor Camilo Vargas: "We had politics in the morning, politics in the afternoon, politics in the evening. I think you can raise the consciousness of a child, but an adult is very difficult."

For other resettled peasants, positive project experiences, Sandinista material aid, and ongoing exposure to the revolutionary ideology appear to have least softened their opposition to the FSLN. Several women who had been evacuated state, for example, "To me the FSLN wasn't so bad." Other resettled peasants in San Bartolo report that they enjoyed the companionship of living in the settlement, as well as such tangible benefits such as schools and easy access to health care. Another indication of the FSLN's moderate success in building a support base in the resettlement communities is found in the results of the 1990 election. In San Bartolo, El Coco, and La Reforma a strong majority of peasants voted for the FSLN, while in Panalí the vote was split roughly in half. Despite this, after the war ended and the contras officially demobilized, a majority of the resettled families left the resettlement communities, many returning to their farms in the mountains. In some cases husbands, fathers, and brothers who had been fighting with the contras came back to the municipality as civilians and took female relatives and children back to the mountains with them. Some women who had spent several years in the settlements may have felt some sympathy for the FSLN, but in this case their primary loyalties still lay with their families.

Cease-Fire

As the revolutionary state undertook a series of measures to win back the political support of Quilalí's peasantry, EPS offensives and the congressional cutoff of military aid to the contras from 1984 to 1986 combined to offer the municipality of Quilalí some respite from the military impact of the war. In 1986 bands of contras still passed through the municipality, harassed cooperatives, and skirmished with the Sandinista Army, but on a smaller scale. U.S. congressional approval of $100 million in aid renewed contra activities in 1987, but by that time the focus of conflict had shifted south to the five Jorge

Salazar Regional Commands operating in Region V, the departments of Boaco and Chontales.

During these years, within the contra forces former finqueros from the northern and central Nicaraguan mountains continued to play an important leadership role in recruitment and field operations. By the mid-1980s, almost a dozen of them had risen to the rank of Regional Commander, each with as many as 1,000 troops under his command. As suggested earlier, with a few notable exceptions the roots of their authority and influence within the contra forces lay in their combat and field skills and in their *convocatorio*, the ability to win and maintain the personal loyalty of peasant foot soldiers. Overall control of the contras in Honduras, however, still remained largely in the hands of Enrique Bermúdez and his circle of ex-National Guard officers. Relations between the Honduran administrative staff and largely rural contra field commanders remained tense throughout the 1980s. Conflicts centered on personal quarrels, corruption, and human rights violations on the part of ex-Guardsmen, as well as field commanders' desire for greater power within the contra forces (Morales Carazo 1989). One example of this was the ongoing conflict between Mendoza, by 1986 leader of a regional command, and ex-National Guardsmen, one of whom opened fire on Mendoza in the late 1980s, leaving him disabled and forcing him to give up his command. Like a number of former field commanders, Mendoza is critical of the contras' ex-National Guard leadership: "The [contra] administration [in Honduras] killed more comandos than the enemy. The administrators robbed the troops. They stole money, stole the aid. They hoarded it, making themselves rich. The administration also investigated [comandos], beat, killed, and raped."

Movements of dissident commanders against Bermúdez, who had important CIA backing, failed in 1984 and 1988, and it was not until the virtual end of the war in 1990 that Bermúdez formally resigned as head of the contra military wing and that field commanders Israel Galeano ("Franklyn") and Oscar Sobalvarro ("Rubén"), both former rural producers, took charge of the contras (see Dillon 1991, 218–26). Such internal conflicts were likely one factor in the inability of the contra forces to translate their vast U.S.-supplied material resources and large numbers of recruits into definitive military and political success that would topple the FSLN. With new funding in 1987, the contra troops infiltrated back into Nicaragua and coordinated several large-scale attacks on mining towns in the northern Atlantic coast region and against the Rama Road in southeastern Nicaragua. Despite this renewed military activity in the late 1980s, however, there was little sense of a cumulative drive to victory on the part of the contras or that the military or political collapse of the Sandinista government was imminent.

On a local level in Quilalí the contras did establish military and political hegemony in some outlying communities, but were never able to use this base of support to successfully penetrate the political and administrative heart of the municipality, the town itself. On the one occasion in 1987, when contra troops were to able breach Quilalí's town limits, their lack of discipline and the arrival of hundreds of EPS reinforcement troops forced the contras into retreat. On a national scale as well, the counterrevolution that was launched in the rural interior of Nicaragua was never able to extend itself either militarily or politically beyond the mountains to the Pacific coast, where the bulk of the country's population and productive economic activities are concentrated. With the exception of the 1984 sabotage missions against the port of Corinto, the contras carried out few significant military actions on the Pacific coast and were never able to build an effective urban base of support.

Some analysts point to the contras' weak, divided leadership and their lack of discipline and strategic planning as important factors in their failure to achieve a military victory.[10] Quilalí former contras and their supporters tend to look outward rather than inward in assigning blame for their lack of military success and cite in particular fickle U.S. policies and aid cutoffs at crucial moments. A former Quilalí contra combatant explains:

Our best successes were in 1987. After that they [the U.S. government] halted the aid. . . . They took away our shelter, we were trembling, we couldn't win the battle. We had it won. We won every encounter, captured prisoners, weapons; wherever we attacked it was victory. . . . Then we felt like they [the U.S. government] took our strength away. We couldn't achieve an armed liberation. It had to be a political victory.

While critical of specific U.S. policy decisions, Quilalí ex-contras and field commanders do not appear to have questioned the correctness of their overall political, military, and financial dependence on the United States. In contrast, several outside observers sympathetic to the contra cause argue that the contras' deep dependence on the United States prevented them from ever developing a strong, nationalist ideology of their own.[11] As suggested earlier, however, this lack of a well-defined, coherent contra ideology and political program may actually have been an advantage for the contras in sustaining a broad rural cross-class anti-Sandinista alliance and subsuming internal conflicts. Outside Nicaragua's mountainous interior contra field leaders were also unable to bring into play some of their strongest recruitment tools—personal ties with peasants and membership in extended family networks. Instead, the prominent role of ex-National Guardsmen in the contra leadership and contra human rights abuses led many urban and Pacific coast Nicaraguans to concur with the Sandinista argument that the contras were fighting for nothing more than a return to the unpopular Somocista past.

A tacit recognition on the part of the contras of their inability to move beyond a military stalemate with the Sandinista Army, combined with a subsequent U.S. military aid cutoff in early 1988 were two of the factors that led the contra leadership to enter into cease-fire negotiations with the Sandinista government from 1987 onward. For their part, as contra activity renewed in 1987, FSLN leaders came to recognize that a definitive military defeat of the contras would be difficult, if not impossible. The rugged and remote terrain of Nicaragua's interior as well as the contras' social base of support suggested that even without U.S. military aid, the contras might continue to operate indefinitely, albeit on a much smaller scale. In addition, direct and indirect military expenditures continued to drain the FSLN's economic and political resources, contributed to the deterioration of the living standards of Nicaragua's poorest sectors, and undermined the consolidation of revolutionary hegemony (Stahler-Sholk 1990, 55).

The Sandinista government financed the war through an expansive fiscal policy, and these budget deficits, combined with other macroeconomic imbalances, fueled hyperinflation that reached 33,657 percent in 1988 (Stahler-Sholk 1997, 81). For many years FSLN subsidies for basic goods and services had partially concealed the true economic costs of the war. In 1988, however, the FSLN was forced to adopt severe austerity measures that included government layoffs, a sharp devaluation of the cordoba, and the "dollarization" of credit. While the FSLN austerity measures eventually brought inflation under control, they also led to recession. In 1988 Nicaragua's per capita GDP fell 15 percent and urban dwellers in particular faced rising unemployment and further declines in real wages (81). Nicaragua's deepening economic crisis meant that many women and men in Quilalí and elsewhere who had devoted their time and energy to revolutionary projects now had to struggle simply to ensure their family's survival.

In addition, throughout Nicaragua the military draft continued to erode support for the revolution. Even committed pro-Sandinista Quilalí residents report that by the late 1980s what they most desired was an end to the conflict and the sacrifices it required of them. One ex-EPS officer, for example, remembers that he put aside his educational goals to serve in the army for six years in Quilalí, during which time he was only able to visit his wife and family a few times a year and missed seeing his children growing up. A sense of physical and emotional exhaustion was also taking hold in Quilalí's cooperatives by the late 1980s after years of continuous military duty and unremitting tension.

These military, economic, and political pressures were important elements that led the Sandinista government to join other Central American nations on 7 August 1987 in signing the Arías peace accord, which called for an end to outside aid to the contras in return for FSLN pledges for democratic reforms in Nicaragua. In early 1988, FSLN and contra leaders met for the first time in the Nicaraguan border town of Sapoá. After several tense rounds of talks, an agreement was signed on 21 March 1988, which called for a temporary cease-fire and the creation of three enclaves in the interior of Nicaragua where contras would gather until a definitive cease-fire agreement was reached.

The municipality of Quilalí fell within a cease-fire zone that stretched from the municipality of Murra through the community of El Súngano down to Caulatú and La Vigía. The Sandinista Army withdrew from this zone and in theory contra troops were to remain inside the security zone. In practice, the cease-fire was broken on a number of occasions, and minor skirmishes occurred. For the first time during the war in Quilalí, however, contra leaders and local Sandinista government and military officials came face-to-face to talk. In addition, local church and community leaders formed a Peace Commission to spread the word about the peace agreement and assist any contras who chose to disarm. During this period, however, only fifty-five Quilalí contras laid down their arms (MINT 1987a). The majority bided their time in Honduras and in the security zone waiting to hear the results of the peace negotiations.

Chapter 9

Rural Instability Continues

AS WILL be seen, the surprise UNO electoral victory on 25 February 1990 and the subsequent demobilization of the contras brought only limited peace and stability to Nicaragua's interior. In the following months neither the Sandinistas nor the newly coalesced opposition forces were able to establish a clear hegemony in Nicaragua, and intense conflicts ensued over issues of institutional and personal power, control of the army and police, and property rights. Postwar instability was further heightened by a weak and fragmented state that was unable to respond effectively to the new demands placed upon it, a postwar economic recession, and the demobilization of thousands of former contras, who now demanded a quota of power, land, services, and guarantees of physical security.

These national-level conflicts were in turn reflected and further reinforced by violent mobilizations at the local level. In Quilalí peasant discontent was expressed through the armed occupation of government buildings and the town itself; a series of land invasions; and, beginning in 1991, the emergence of armed recontra groups. Overall, violence became more complex in the 1990s as the sites, boundaries,

257

and nature of conflict shifted and fragmented between urban and rural, and the personal and political. During this postwar period the wartime Sandinista and anti-Sandinista cross-class coalitions also began to fray, opening up possibilities for the emergence of new horizontal links of solidarity among the poor around common needs and interests.

The Elections

The stage for the 1990 electoral confrontation between pro- and anti-Sandinista forces was set in August 1989, when Nicaragua's opposition parties formed the National Opposition Union (Unión Nacional Opositora, UNO) coalition, selecting as their candidate Violeta Barrios de Chamorro, widow of slain newspaper editor Pedro Joaquín Chamorro. In the following months, the UNO transformed "Doña Violeta"—serene, dignified, dressed completely in white—into a powerful symbol of the suffering and division of the Nicaraguan family and the hope for peace. The UNO political platform was less a positive program in and of itself than a reaction to the scope and nature of revolutionary change over the past decade. The UNO campaign focused on the war and economic hardship, two key areas of popular discontent, promising to end the military draft and inflation.

The FSLN's candidate, Daniel Ortega, on the other hand, led a boisterous, populist campaign that culminated in a massive rally in Managua attended by hundreds of thousands of supporters. The FSLN reaffirmed the legitimacy of key revolutionary transformations—land reform, credit, access to health care and education—while promising to build on these achievements. The FSLN's campaign slogan, "everything will be better," also implicitly recognized the daily hardships most Nicaraguans faced after a decade of conflict and several years of economic austerity.

In Quilalí it is generally agreed that campaign strategies and even specific political and economic issues were of secondary importance to voters. Rather, the elections came to embody the deep political and military cleavages of the municipality and represent a referendum on the revolution itself and the dramatic transformations and upheavals it had brought to the municipality. Both Sandinista and UNO candidates believe that much of municipality's polarized population had already decided the way they would vote before September 1989 and that national and local election campaigns had only a limited impact on the outcome.

When the campaign season officially opened in late 1989 military tensions in Quilalí had eased considerably, but perhaps because of the explosive issues involved and for fear of renewed violence, both the UNO and the FSLN ran relatively low-key election campaigns in Quilalí. As the election campaign drew to a close in mid-February 1990, departmental FSLN representatives visited Quilalí and both parties held rallies in the town of Quilalí. Outside the town limits, contras, officially inactive in the security zone, conducted campaigning of their own, visiting farms and telling families to vote against the FSLN. They also carried out several acts of intimidation and violence to disrupt the election campaign, and in October 1989 forty contras attacked a voter registration post in the community of Caulatú. These contra actions appear not to have had a major impact on the campaign process, however, and despite some security concerns, voting went forward as planned on 25 February in the town of Quilalí and several communities in the countryside. Preelection polls and the high turnout at FSLN election rallies had led many Nicaraguan and foreign observers to expect a comfortable victory for the FSLN. Instead, in the early morning hours of 26 February the news came over the radio that the UNO had won an upset victory with 55 percent of the national vote, compared to 41 percent for the FSLN.

In the municipality of Quilalí the UNO won a narrow victory— 2,595 votes (48%) to the FSLN's 2,524 (47%), with 275 votes (5%) going to other opposition parties—and the UNO gained three out of five positions on the municipal council. The close vote in Quilalí was a product of important voting differences within the municipality. In the town of Quilalí itself, the FSLN won 52 percent of the vote, as compared to 44 percent for the UNO and 4 percent to other opposition parties. Outside the town the UNO won 50 percent of the vote, the FSLN 45 percent, and other opposition parties 5 percent. The election results in Quilalí's rural areas tended to confirm earlier patterns of political polarization in the municipality. In the settlements of San Bartolo and El Coco and the cooperative La Reforma, informants report that the vote for the FSLN was extremely high. Quilalí's third settlement community, Panalí, however, was divided roughly equally between the UNO and the FSLN. Quilalí's twenty-nine other smaller rural communities, most of them bases of support for the contras, voted in high numbers for the UNO.[1]

Nationwide, support for the FSLN in urban areas was 44 percent, but reached only 36 percent in rural areas (Castro 1992, 131). In Nicaragua's interior, opposition to the FSLN was particularly strong in many of the same areas that had high abstention rates in the 1984 elections and those in which a relatively large number of young men joined the contras. In the departments of Boaco and Chontales, for example, which had a high number of reported contra combatants relative to their population, over 70 percent of the rural voting population supported the UNO. Overall, in twenty-seven of sixty-five interior municipalities, rural support for the UNO was at least 10 percent above the national rural UNO vote of 58 percent (CIPRES 1990b, 25–30). In contrast, in the municipality of Quilalí, despite its unusually high number of contra recruits, overall support for the FSLN was 6 percent above the national average.

This relatively strong support for the FSLN in the municipality can likely be explained by several political and military dynamics discussed in previous chapters. First, through its land reform policies the FSLN succeeded in consolidating a strong cooperative sector of hundreds of peasant families who, with the exception of some peas-

Table 9.1

Departmental Election Results by Urban and Rural Sectors, 1990

Department	% Urban Vote		% Rural Vote	
	FSLN	UNO	FSLN	UNO
PACIFIC COAST				
Chinandega	39.4%	57.2%	44.7%	50.7%
León	47.1	49.8	43.5	51.6
Managua	44.4	52.2	35.7	60.1
Masaya	42.8	54.3	40.8	55.5
Carazo	56.3	40.2	44.1	51.7
Granada	35.6	61.3	39.0	56.0
Rivas	45.8	51.1	44.3	52.5
Average Pacific Coast	**44.5%**	**52.3%**	**41.7%**	**54.0%**
INTERIOR				
Nueva Segovia	52.0%	44.6%	47.2%	48.1%
Madriz	51.2	45.0	35.2	60.0
Estelí	58.2	38.1	43.0	51.9
Jinotega	49.4	46.2	33.1	58.2
Matagalpa	39.4	56.9	33.3	60.5
Boaco	24.8	71.7	23.6	70.3
Chontales	39.4	57.6	17.5	78.5
Río San Juan	58.4	38.3	55.1	39.2
Average Interior	**46.6%**	**49.8%**	**36.0%**	**58.3%**
NATIONAL TOTAL	**44.2%**	**52.5%**	**36.3%**	**58.4%**

Source: Castro (1990b: 26, 29).

ants who had been forcibly evacuated in 1985, provided key support for the revolution. In addition, through the mid-1980s the municipality received a steady influx of peasant migrants from other zones in the departments of Nueva Segovia, Madriz, and Estelí—areas of generally high rural support for the FSLN. These peasants—together with landless Quilalí peasants without strong clientelistic ties to patrons, as well as education and health workers and artisans and small merchants from the town—formed a core of support for the FSLN in the municipality. The close vote in Quilalí may also have been in part a product of the remedial measures—more flexible land reform, development projects, and a prioritization of political responses over military goals—taken by the FSLN in the mid-1980s to gain peasant support. Finally, in examining voting results in Quilalí it is also important to keep in mind that within a year of the elections the population of the municipality increased by as much as one-fourth as hundreds of civilian peasants who had fled to Honduras during the war and as many as 500 contras and their families returned to Quilalí. By 1995 the municipality's population had grown to at least 20,000. These returned peasants were overwhelmingly anti-Sandinista and if they had been present during the elections the UNO likely would have won a greater percentage of the municipality's vote.

Nationwide, support for the UNO was strongest among the bourgeoisie, followed by rural residents, those employed in the informal sector, and homeworkers (Oquist 1992, 13–20). Among the rural population, one postelection survey found that support for the FSLN was weakest among medium-level peasants and workers on private farms (32% and 35% respectively), while 41 percent of poor peasants surveyed voted for the FSLN. The FSLN won an absolute majority of the support of sampled peasants in production cooperatives (51%), and of workers on state farms (55%) (Castro 1992, 137).

The experience of Quilalí offers some clues that may help to understand these national rural voting trends and patterns of political support and opposition to the FSLN. First, cooperative members and state farmworkers were a self-selected population who chose to enter these sectors of Sandinista influence because they were already sympathetic to a greater or lesser degree to the revolution, and for reasons of economic necessity. Once within a zone of Sandinista influence, as we have seen, peasants' support for the FSLN was strengthened by daily contact with revolutionary ideology, participation in collective organizations, and sacrifices made to defend the land against contra aggression.

In contrast, many Quilalí middle peasants, like finqueros, opposed fundamental economic and social aspects of the revolutionary model in favor of free markets, rural hierarchy, and respect for private property. After 1982 often the only contact that many of these peasants had with the revolution was military. Even after the policy reforms of the mid-1980s, several hundred of Quilalí's middle peasants received no attention from the FSLN. In fact, not only did the revolution fail to provide them with benefits, but the military conflict and later evacuations of the mid-1980s sharply reduced coffee and cattle production in the municipality, bringing to a halt for many middle peasants any process of economic advancement.

The low support of workers on private farms for the FSLN may in part be explained by their continued economic and ideological dependence on largely anti-Sandinista patrons. As we have seen, the failure of the FSLN to redistribute land on terms acceptable to these peasants, government programs that focused on the state farm sector, and growing shortages of transportation, services, and key agricultural inputs may actually have strengthened this dependence of poor peasants on local elites. In some cases elites made concessions to poor peasants to retain their loyalty in the face of wartime labor shortages and ideological competition by the FSLN. In addition to these broader, longer-term influences on levels of rural support for the FSLN, scholars have identified the economic crisis and the continued possibility of war under the FSLN as important more general factors in the FSLN's electoral defeat (Conroy 1990; Castro 1990b; Oquist 1992; Enriquez 1997).

Contra Demobilization

In the days following the elections a climate of shocked disbelief enveloped much of Nicaragua. Sandinista supporters were unprepared for their loss and even UNO supporters found it difficult to comprehend that they had truly defeated the revolutionary government that had so transformed and dominated Nicaraguan life for a decade. In Quilalí the day after the elections the streets of the town were virtually deserted. This uneasy calm was broken later that night when a group of angry Sandinista supporters gathered and stoned the houses of suspected contra supporters in town, before a Sandinista Army officer convinced them to disband. Paradoxically, one of the first opportunities that Quilalí residents had to express their differences by civic means under conditions of relative peace initially appeared to intensify the municipality's fundamental political schism. In the town of Quilalí, long a haven from the combat in countryside, civic political dissent on the part of anti-Sandinistas was muted during the war years. In the months following the elections, however, an anti-Sandinista backlash poured over Quilalí as many residents expressed grievances they had been unwilling or afraid to openly articulate in the 1980s. To Quilalí pro-Sandinistas, on the other hand, the months following the election was a period of demoralization. Many had put their educational and personal goals on hold for almost a decade to serve their revolutionary ideals. Some indicate that in the postelection period they felt betrayed by the same poor peasants for whom they had so long sacrificed, particularly as they came to realize the depth of support for the contras among certain rural sectors.

Nationwide, the eight-week transition period between the elections and the 25 April transfer of power was a time of great tension and uncertainty as Nicaraguans wondered whether the nation's first democratic transfer of power would occur peacefully. On the day of her inauguration President Violeta Chamorro announced that a Transition Accord had been reached with FSLN leaders under which Humberto Ortega, brother of ex-president Daniel Ortega, would remain as head of a new national, depoliticized army to ensure political and social stability. As will be seen, until Humberto Ortega resigned in February 1995, this continued Sandinista leadership role in Nicaragua's armed forces was vociferously opposed by ex-contras and right-wing political figures.

Several weeks before taking power, Chamorro also reached an agreement with contra leaders, the Toncontín Accord, under which the contras agreed to lay down their arms and integrate themselves into civilian society. In later agreements the government promised to turn over to the contras thousands of manzanas of land on the agricultural frontier to create "development poles," as well as to provide roads, housing, schools, and health centers. To implement this demobilization plan, nine disarmament zones were created, five in Nicaragua's interior and four in the Atlantic coast region.

Security zone number one, the Amparo security zone, extended from the municipal limits of Quilalí along the Río Coco southwest across the municipality of Yalí. The Sandinista Army pulled out of the area, and special United Nations (Organización de las Naciones Unidas para Centroamérica, ONUCA) peacekeeping forces took charge of the security zone, establishing checkpoints on the perimeters of the zone and a disarmament center near the town of Yalí to receive contras who wished to lay down their arms. The contras who entered the Amparo security zone in May 1990 were generally not a weary, demoralized army, but rather young men, well rested from their stay in the Honduran camps and well equipped with new uniforms and weapons, who considered the UNO victory to be their personal triumph. Many were proud of having, in their minds, defeated the FSLN, albeit indirectly, and of having brought democracy to Nicaragua.

Over the next month, the demobilization process moved at a slow pace. A few contras reported to the ONUCA camp near Yalí to turn in their arms, but the mass of troops remained armed and restless in the peacetime condition of camps. A number of Quilalí families traveled to the security zone to be reunited with relatives or receive news that family members had been killed in combat, sometimes years earlier. Within the security zones, internal contra discipline was weakly enforced and many contras passed the time drinking, gambling, fighting, harassing suspected Sandinista supporters, and at times firing off weapons at random.[2]

The most serious obstacles to contra demobilization in the weeks following the creation of the security zones were the contras' deep distrust of the FSLN and fears for their personal safety. Many of these contras had had no direct contact with the FSLN beyond combat since the early 1980s and had little of knowledge about Sandinista policies that was not filtered through the contra leadership structure. Contra fears were reinforced by the many rumors of Sandinista atrocities against demobilized contras that continually swept though the security zones. The fact that some of these rumors surfaced at key moments in the disarmament talks led some observers to suspect that the contra leadership played a role in disseminating rumors as a means to prevent troops from disarming of their own initiative.

Finally, after weeks of uncertainty, contra troops were given the signal by their commanders to begin to disarm in large numbers. On 30 May long lines of contras formed outside the UN demobilization tents near Yalí. The troops entered the camp one by one and handed over their weapons to UN officials who briefly interviewed them and took their pictures. After a medical checkup, former contras were handed an identity card, clothing, and boots and emerged to begin life as civilians. During May and June 1990, 2,894 contras disarmed in the Amparo security zone (CIAV-OEA 1990a). In Nicaragua as a whole, a total of 22,431 men and women disarmed (CIAV-OEA 1991). The official total of just over 22,000 demobilized includes a number of civilians who passed themselves off as combatants in the hopes of receiving land, food, and money. Although the total number of combatants is likely inflated, this still represents one of the largest military mobilizations of peasants in Latin America since the Mexican Revolution.

Postwar Quilalí

In the months following the contra demobilization, the aid projects and development poles the Chamorro government had promised the contras largely failed to materialize because of lack of funding and property conflicts (Armony 1997, 208). By 1991 many former contras had returned to their native communities in Nicaragua's interior, despite their fears of reprisals from Sandinista supporters (IHCA 1991, 14). Between May and September 1990 at least 500 former contra combatants returned to the municipality of Quilalí, often moving in with family and friends.[3] The agency assigned the task of facilitating the integration of these former combatants into civilian life, the International Support and Verification Commission and the Organization of American States (Comisión Internacional de Apoyo y Verificación–Organización de Estados Americanos, CIAV-OEA) opened a small office on Quilalí's main street. The CIAV-OEA provided ex-contras and their families with kitchen utensils, basic tools, and zinc for their roofs, as well as several cash payments equivalent to $50. The CIAV-OEA also regularly distributed food supplies to ex-contras from their warehouse in town. During this same period as many as 1,000 additional civilian families repatriated to Quilalí from Honduras and these repatriated families, together with the ex-contra combatants, increased Quilalí's population by as much as one-fourth in the space of a few months.[4]

Outwardly, the municipality of Quilalí was returning to normalcy after nearly a decade of war. One of Chamorro's first acts as president was to end to the military draft and begin a reduction of the Sandinista Army. Little by little olive green and camouflage fabric disappeared from Quilalí's streets. For the first time in years, one commonly saw young men in civilian clothing walking and riding horses down the main street, and in the stores, bars, and pool hall. Passengers trucks now traveled up to six times a day to Estelí and Ocotal, and the town of Quilalí was filled with consumer goods from

Costa Rica and Honduras, something unknown during the war years. In the mountains surrounding the town of Quilalí, families accelerated their return to the communities that had been evacuated during the war to rebuild their houses and clear the fields to begin to farm again.

In addition to the CIAV-OEA, another agency, the Development Program for the Displaced, Refugees, and the Repatriated (Programa de Desarrollo para Desplazados, Refugiados, y Repatriados, PRODERE), established an office in Quilalí and initiated a series of development projects designed to assist the demobilized and repatriated population of Quilalí, as well as to promote community reconciliation. Over the next three years, PRODERE projects included the construction of a bridge over the Río Jícaro, a new hospital, eleven rural schools, 160 houses, and 280 latrines, as well as the reparation of over twenty kilometers of penetration roads in the mountains surrounding the town of Quilalí (PRODERE 1992b). The presence of the CIAV-OEA and PRODERE meant that in comparison to other interior zones Quilalí was relatively well-off in terms of external assistance. Despite this fact, however, former contras and refugees who returned to the municipality of Quilalí in the early 1990s faced challenging socioeconomic conditions. Many of the earlier gains of the revolution in areas such as education and health had been wiped out by the war, infrastructure was deteriorated or destroyed, and as much as one-third of the municipality's land lay in a state of neglect. These economic and social problems in turn, which were further compounded by a postwar economic recession, played a role in the destabilization of the municipality in the early 1990s.

According to Quilalí's Social Security Institute, at least 300 Quilalí residents were killed as a direct result of the war, leaving behind roughly 900 widows and orphans in the municipality. Another 185 residents were left handicapped by the war, most commonly by loss of a limb (PRODERE 1991). Quilalí's Social Security representative estimated that in 1993 less than half of this group were receiving even minimal government assistance because they lacked proper documentation to apply for a pension. Twenty percent of Quilalí households were headed by women, generally because of death or abandonment by a spouse or companion.

Even families that did not suffer deaths or physical injury from the war continued to live in great poverty. According to a postwar PRODERE (1991) survey, one-third of Quilalí residents consumed less than 1,850 calories per day. Only 23 percent of Quilalí peasants drank milk regularly, while only 30 percent of households ate any kind of meat. In addition, 70 percent of Quilalí families lived in over-crowded housing, with anywhere between four to ten people sleeping in the same room. In terms of education, in 1991, 43 percent of Quilalí residents over ten years old were still illiterate. The figure was even higher (50%) for those peasants who spent the war in Honduras or with the contras. Unfortunately, the future educational outlook for children in Quilalí was not much better, as only about half of Quilalí children ages six to fourteen were attending elementary school. In sixteen mountain communities there were no schools within walking distance. In other cases, the postwar economic downturn meant that parents were unable to afford even such small expenses as the pencils and notebooks that were required for children to attend school. In terms of access to health services, the municipality fared somewhat better. PRODERE completed construction of a small hospital in the town of Quilalí staffed with half a dozen doctors and nurses, and a small health clinic continued to operate in the community of San Bartolo. In the 1990s medicines were more readily available in Quilalí than during the war years, but were relatively expensive, and some of the poorest families interviewed report that they were unable to afford even basic antibiotics.

Another difficulty Quilalí peasants faced in the 1990s, and a key source of postwar conflict, was lack of access to sufficient land to farm. After the war ended in 1990, almost all of Quilalí's 20,000 MZ of abandoned land was quickly reclaimed by its original owners, their

Table 9.2
Quilalí Land Survey, 1991: Farm Size

Farm Size[a]	# of Producers	% of Producers	Area (MZ)	% of Area
No Access to Land	555	22.0%	0	0.0%
0.1 to 5 MZ[a]	975	38.7	2,377	5.2
5 to 10 MZ	316	12.5	2,019	4.4
10 to 50 MZ	456	18.1	9,790	21.5
50 to 100 MZ	124	4.9	7,466	16.4
100+ MZ	94	3.7	23,862	52.4
TOTAL 99.9%[b]	2,520	99.9%[b]	45,514 MZ[c]	

[a]These data include landowners with and without formal title and those producers who rent, sharecrop, or borrow land.
[b]Rounding error.
[c]MIDINRA (1987) reports total land in the municipality as 69,200 MZ. The PRODERE data shown here do not include all farms in the municipality.

Source: PRODERE (1991).

Table 9.3
Quilalí Land Survey, 1991: Access to Land

Type of Access to Land[a]	# of Producers	% of Producers
Legal Title	488	22.2%
Rent/Borrow/Sharecrop	905	41.2
De facto Possession	350	15.9
Cooperative Member	407	18.5
Disputed Ownership	46	2.1
TOTAL	2,196	99.9%[b]

[a]Multiple responses were possible.
[b]Rounding error.

Source: PRODERE (1991).

family members, or speculators who had taken advantage of the war to acquire land at bargain prices. Although as we have seen in the 1980s the FSLN distributed over 13,000 MZ of land in the municipality of Quilalí, this was still insufficient to meet the postwar demand for land in the municipality.[5] In a 1991 PRODERE survey (summarized in tables 9.2 and 9.3), 22 percent of Quilalí peasants reported that they had no access to land at all, and 38.7 percent of families stated that they had access to 5 MZ of land or less, the bare minimum on which a peasant family could support itself. Among those with access to land, almost half rented, borrowed, or sharecropped the land. For those peasants without land, or with an insufficient amount of land, opportunities to work as wage laborers on cattle ranches or harvesting coffee were also limited in the early 1990s. Cattle and coffee production, which fell drastically in Quilalí during the war years, were slow to recover in postwar Quilalí, in part because of continued rural violence in the zone and the national economic recession discussed below.

The situation of poor Quilalí peasants was further worsened by shifts in national government economic policies in the 1990s. Unlike the Sandinista government, which gave out loans with few restrictions in the 1980s, the Chamorro government began in 1990 to apply market criteria to loans. Peasants or cooperatives with past debts to the bank or without clear title to their land, a common situation in postwar Quilalí and elsewhere, could no longer obtain bank loans. According to an official of the Quilalí branch of the National Bank, the number of Quilalí farmers who received loans declined dramatically from a high of 1,500 in 1988 to just under 300 loan recipients in 1990, and loans for export products (coffee and cattle) were prioritized to the detriment of basic grains. Nationwide, credit disbursed by the Central Bank of Nicaragua for corn and bean production fell over 75 percent between 1991 and 1993 (Jonakin 1997, 104).

Local economic conditions in Quilalí and other interior zones were further affected by the national economic downturn. Through postwar austerity measures, inflation which had accelerated again in the postelectoral period, was eventually brought under control, but the economy stagnated from 1990 to 1993 and unemployment and underemployment reached 53.5 percent (Stahler-Sholk 1995, 83). In rural areas like Quilalí the recession had a negative impact on those farmers who marketed export and food crops, as well as merchants in town. As will be seen, this economic situation also augmented tensions between highly mobilized postwar sectors—ex-contras, cooperative and union members, and former army officers—who saw themselves in competition for limited resources such as land, economic opportunities, and material aid.

Rural Instability

Another element in continued rural instability in Nicaragua was the failure of either anti-Sandinista or Sandinista forces to establish hegemony in the postwar period, as well as protracted struggles between these groups on the national and local level for control of a variety of public domains. Despite the FSLN's loss of formal power, in the early 1990s the Sandinistas retained control over the army and police and maintained strong influence in the judiciary, urban and rural unions, and student associations. The autonomy of unions in particular, vis-à-vis the FSLN leadership, increased in the months following the elections, and they soon began to independently confront the Chamorro government. In May 1990 the umbrella National Workers Front went on strike over government suspension of civil service laws passed under the Sandinistas and in reaction to the first UNO adjustment program (Stahler-Sholk 1995, 93). The May strike was settled peacefully, but in July another series of work stoppages quickly escalated into a general strike. Within a week the country was paralyzed by barricades on the streets of Managua and violent confrontations between pro-Sandinista strikers and anti-Sandinistas. Only with the active mediation of the FSLN centrist party leadership between the unions and the Chamorro government was the crisis resolved. As will be seen, anti-Sandinista groups in Quilalí closely followed these and subsequent national political struggles, were in contact with national right-wing leaders, and at times mobilized at least in part to support the demands of this sector.[6]

In interior zones like Quilalí, tensions quickly came to focus on the most visible manifestation of continued Sandinista influence—the armed forces, under the control of Humberto Ortega. Following the elections President Chamorro moved quickly to reduce the armed forces from over 60,000 troops in 1989 to 15,500 troops in 1993 and sharply reduce the military budget from $182 million in 1989 to $35 million in 1993 (Ejército de Nicaragua 1996, 197–98). The number of EPS soldiers stationed in Quilalí was also drastically cut from a wartime high of hundreds of troops to a small group of from twenty to sixty soldiers. Until recontra bands became active in 1991 these soldiers generally remained close to quarters and tried to avoid confrontations with Quilalí anti-Sandinistas. Yet to ex-contras in particular, any Sandinista Army presence, regardless of its nonconfrontational stance, was unacceptable. Former contra Ramón Moreno explains: "My youth was nothing but war and my body was mutilated by the war, but I still have the same point of view. . . . I don't have any quarrel with civilians, but with soldiers, yes. . . . A Sandinista party member is all right if he's working. He's my friend. But an armed 'brother,' I won't say a word to him."

Anti-Sandinista opposition in Quilalí to continued Sandinista activism and control of the armed forces can also be understood as the product of a civil war that reinforced the conflictive and exclusionary nature of Nicaraguan political culture, under which there are changes of regimes instead of changes of government. As discussed earlier, most Quilalí contras took up arms in favor of "democracy" but did not possess a uniform understanding of this term. Having spent years in the mountains among peasants who largely opposed the revolution, ex-contras came to see the Sandinistas as a repressive minority that ruled by force. Their understanding of democracy did not necessarily include coexistence with former FSLN foes or mean that Sandinistas should be allowed any voice in the governing of the municipality or the nation. Some Quilalí ex-contras interviewed report that they assumed that with the 1990 change in government all Sandinista supporters would go into exile as Somoza supporters did a decade earlier. They therefore perceived continued Sandinista influence over government policy and public institutions as an antidemocratic attempt to hold onto power. In the words of ex-contra Mario Aguero: "There is a dictatorship of the FSLN. They have power and we don't have power. . . . Without getting rid of the Sandinistas, Nicaragua is never going to advance because the Sandinistas don't believe in democracy."

Another key element in rural instability was a series of postwar expectations on the part of former contras and their willingness to employ violence to attempt to satisfy these demands. As we have seen, in prerevolutionary Quilalí poor and middle peasants were largely quiescent and expected little in the way of material aid or services from the Somoza regime. Rather than turning to the government in times of hardship, these peasants instead relied on extended family networks and clientelistic ties to elites as their principle safety net. Influenced by a decade-long experience of anti-Sandinista struggle and the demobilization process, former contras began to demand selective rewards and material benefits from the government in the 1990s. Equally important, military experience provided these peasants with the assertiveness and skills needed to mobilize in favor of these new demands. In contrast to anti-Sandinista peasants who remained in a vulnerable position as civilians in the 1980s, ex-contras interviewed generally express confidence in themselves and their abilities as guerrilla fighters. During the war they carried modern weapons, became skilled at warfare and survival in the mountains, and were received with fear and respect in rural communities. Many Quilalí ex-contras considered the 1990 UNO triumph as their own and expected to be rewarded for the role that they believed they had played in bringing democracy to Nicaragua. In addition, as we have seen, contra commanders encouraged their combatants to believe in a future "democratic" Nicaragua that, for poor peasants in particular, included access to land and economic well-being, without ever specifying how this was to be achieved. When benefits failed to materialize after 1990, ex-contras quickly came to blame both Sandinista groups and increasingly the Chamorro government, viewed as an FSLN puppet, for their postwar difficulties.

Contra postwar expectations for selective rewards were also further reinforced by the series of promises of land and services made by the Chamorro government during the demobilization process. Ex-contra Ramón Moreno states: "It's difficult when a father promises a child a piece of candy, and the child because he doesn't understand waits for the candy. If he doesn't get the candy, the child misbehaves and causes trouble. . . . Here it's the same thing. . . . The government promised land, work, tranquility, that everything was going to be different. . . . Today those men [the contras] are crying and furious because they're not being given what they want." Ex-contras and anti-Sandinistas in general also may have been indirectly influenced by the very revolutionary process they opposed. These peasants witnessed how in the 1980s the FSLN distributed over 13,000 MZ of prime farmland to peasants in the municipality. Although some anti-Sandinista poor peasants opposed the expropriation of well-known community members, the perceived politically partisan nature of Sandinista land reform, and the requirements for collective farming, the fact remains that the absolute nature of property rights had been challenged in Quilalí and elsewhere. A precedent of land redistribution had been set. During its time in power the FSLN also provided credit, health care, and schools to the population in general, as well as a series of material aid projects to the river valley cooperatives. Now that "their" government was in power, anti-Sandinista peasants demanded the same benefits for themselves that they had seen pro-Sandinista peasants receive from the FSLN in the 1980s.

Interviews with former Quilalí contras indicate three key sets of anti-Sandinista political and economic demands: (1) a political "clean sweep" that would eliminate or greatly limit Sandinista influence upon public policy and institutions, particularly the army, at both a local and national level; (2) land to farm, especially land with well-developed infrastructure and easy access to roads and markets; also access to credit, housing, water, health services, and education; and (3) guarantees of personal physical security in a context of growing political and personal violence (see CIPRES 1990b).

During the initial demobilization period ex-contras who returned to the municipality of Quilalí maintained a loosely structured organization that attempted by nonviolent means to pressure the national government for land and aid projects. According to one of the organizers of this group, government officials held several meetings with the hundred or so members of the group, but offered few positive concrete responses to contra concerns: "After a while [the ex-contras] didn't even want to bother to fill out the forms. They said it was a waste of time. When I saw none of the benefits were going to us, I quit." It is also likely that ex-contras' lack of formal education and minimal experience with formal organizations, as well as a lack of interest on the part of local finqueros to lead such civic efforts, contributed to the failure of this movement. Quickly frustrated with nonviolent strategies, ex-contras turned increasingly to confrontation and even violence to pressure the government to respond to their demands. Their experience in the contras likely influenced them to employ violence not as a strategy of last resort, but as a primary instrument to press their demands in an intensely competitive postwar environment.

One of the first postwar mobilizations by anti-Sandinistas in Quilalí occurred in November 1990 over the issue of continued Sandinista participation in the local government. More radical Quilalí

anti-Sandinistas believed that the UNO electoral victory should signify the exclusion of FSLN sympathizers from government posts and
pressured the mayor and municipal council to fire known Sandinista
supporters. In mid-1990, in a move apparently designed to ease
growing political tensions in the municipality, the Chamorro government ordered the EPS to pull out of Quilalí, leaving in place only a
small police force to maintain order. Taking advantage of the absence
of the army, a group of anti-Sandinista townspeople and ex-contras
occupied Quilalí's main government buildings in early November
and attempted to kidnap the UNO mayor, who opposed their demands. For over a month the anti-Sandinista group held the town of
Quilalí under virtual siege. The crisis was not resolved until a government commission from Managua and the rebel group negotiated a
settlement that included the resignation of the mayor and, apparently,
cash payments to the leaders of the uprising. After the siege was
ended, army soldiers were sent back to Quilalí and again became the
focus of anti-Sandinista ire.

The experience of the 1990 siege of the town of Quilalí illustrates
another key element in the continuation of rural violence in postwar
Nicaragua—the inability of the new government to exercise effective
political or military control of rural zones in Nicaragua. During the
1980s, more isolated interior zones were contested terrain, both militarily and politically, but the centralized FSLN political-military
structure maintained firm control over roads, interior towns and virtually all of Nicaragua's Pacific coastal region. Under the Chamorro
government, however, challenges to state authority were no longer as
geographically or politically circumscribed. Both left- and right-wing
forces mobilized across all of Nicaragua, their protests engulfing
urban centers, towns, and principle highways.

In meeting the challenge of governing a highly mobilized and polarized population, the Chamorro government faced several important
constraints on its power. Soon after the elections the original UNO
coalition fragmented. Right-wing UNO leaders, along with a majority

of Nicaragua's mayors, ex-contras, members of the Private Enterprise Council (Consejo Superior de la Empresa Privada, COSEP), and conservative church figures, promoted a more confrontational approach to the FSLN, a rollback of key revolutionary programs, and initiated a series of often violent mobilizations, such as the blockade of the Rama highway, protests in Nueva Guinea, and the four-day seizure of the town of Waslala in late 1990. The Chamorro group for its part formed by 1991 an informal alliance with FSLN centrists in the National Assembly to maintain a majority in the parliament, but politically remained weak and isolated. In addition, the Chamorro government's range of policy options were further constrained by the U.S. government and international financial institutions that pressured the government to impose austerity measures, remove Sandinistas from army and police leadership positions, and to either return expropriated properties of U.S. citizens or provide indemnification.[7]

Specific policies of the Chamorro government also served to reinforce postwar rural violence, as the government was unwilling or unable to deal systematically with underlying structural sources of rural violence (IHCA 1991, 14). A pattern emerged in the early 1990s across Nicaragua's rural interior in which tensions and demands would go unattended until some type of violent confrontation occurred. Only then would government officials arrive with a fire-fighting approach to resolve the immediate crisis. Typically, the government negotiated a limited clientelistic accord that provided concessions such as land and houses to a small number of participants active in the confrontation or rebel group. The government also commonly coopted rebel leaders with benefits such as cars, positions in the government, or direct cash payments (Saldomando and Cuadra 1994, 23).

It is easy to imagine how these policies might encourage both extremist political actions to gain the government's attention as well as the opportunistic use of violence as a means of personal economic gain. Also, the fact that the government generally employed only limited military force against rebel groups meant that the risks involved in participating in such actions were relatively low. In addition, poor follow-up by fragmented government institutions operating with contradictory goals meant that government agreements were often not fulfilled, leading to further cycles of uprising and rural violence (IHCA 1994a, 5).

Land Conflicts

In addition to competing claims for political and coercive power, another focal point of tension in many zones of Nicaragua's interior was a chaotic land situation characterized by multiple claims for properties, a contested legal framework, and a slow administrative process. In the postwar period, ex-contras, state farmworkers, cooperative members, former landowners, and the "historically landless" all competed to recover, hold on to, or obtain for the first time 71 percent of Nicaragua's land. As of 1995, 47 percent of the nation's total farmland was without legal title and former owners had filed 7,185 claims to over 2 million MZ of land, or 25 percent of total farmland (IHCA 1995, 19–20).

In the municipality of Quilalí, former landowners filed at least half a dozen claims with the government to recover their farms or receive compensation.[8] According to Quilalí cooperative members, one ex-owner of a valley cattle ranch planned a trip to the zone in 1992 to meet with peasants occupying his former hacienda, apparently to try and convince them to return the land in exchange for payment for improvements to the property. Cooperative members sent word to the ex-owner, however, that they planned to block the road and not allow him onto their land. Given this strong and organized peasant response, the ex-owner canceled his proposed visit and in the following years did not attempt again to contact cooperative members. As of the mid-1990s no expropriated land had been returned to the former terratenientes in Quilalí and the initial postwar fears of cooperative members that the land reform process would be immediately and violently reversed under the new government abated (IHCA 1994b, 22). Rather than attempting to dislodge land reform beneficiaries, the government instead generally compensated former owners with bonds that some used to purchase recently privatized state land and factories.

The end of the war in the municipality of Quilalí also accelerated the resettlement of land in the northern third of the municipality, which had been sold or abandoned during the previous decade. Although little information is available about these more isolated communities, it appears that through the purchase of land at low prices in the 1980s, certain local finqueros were able to expand their landholdings and the degree of land concentration in this zone. Another important component of the complex postwar land situation in Quilalí and elsewhere was the demands by ex-contras for land. In the national demobilization survey, 69 percent of contras reported that they owned no land (CIAV-OEA 1990a). This figure likely includes both contras from landless families and those who joined the contras at young age before they would have normally inherited or purchased land of their own. Although after demobilization some ex-contras settled on land provided by the government in such interior zones as El Almendro and Río Blanco, the majority of ex-contras instead returned to their place of origin and demanded the 50 MZ the government had originally promised them.[9]

As of April 1991, 80 percent of the approximately 6,900 ex-contras in southeastern Nicaragua had received land, largely former state cattle ranches, but only 25 percent of over 11,000 contras in Nicaragua's northern-central zone had received land (IHCA 1991, 13–14). In the municipality of Quilalí, where land pressures were less intense than other zones, local authorities estimate that approximately 100 ex-contras did not have access to sufficient land to support their families. In addition, hundreds of returned refugees and approximately 150 long-term landless peasants in the municipality were also demanding land. Frustrated by a lack of government response to their requests for land, at the beginning of the 1991 planting season groups of former contras took direct action and invaded five cooperatives in the municipality, as well as three individual farms they believed were owned by pro-Sandinista peasants.

Carlos Sánchez was a member of one such group of ex-contras that secretly organized an invasion of 315 MZ of land owned by a Panalí cooperative. Sánchez remembers: "February 18 we went at night to invade the land. We were twenty-five families. We raised the Nicaraguan flag here on the hill. We said we were taking all of Guaná [hacienda], so we could get a part of it." According to Sánchez, who had participated in an unsuccessful occupation of Guaná a decade earlier, ex-contras were rightfully claiming the 50 MZ of land that the government had promised them during demobilization. This group of ex-contras also alleged that their claim to the land was more legitimate than that of the Sandinistas, who, they argue, simply stole the land, because the former owner stated that a portion of his hacienda should be given to demobilized contras. These ex-contras also believed that their need to grow food crops and feed their families gave them an important moral right to the land, an argument similar to that used by pro-Sandinista peasants to justify FSLN land reform.

On the morning following the invasion, cooperative members from Panalí quickly gathered together a group of seventy or so peasants to march up the road to confront the land invaders. On top of the hill where the invaders had planted their flag, the two groups of peasants, machetes in hand, exchanged angry words. The situation threatened to turn violent when an ad hoc government commission arrived by truck from the town of Quilalí. The government representatives managed to convince the cooperative members to return home, promising to find a solution that would provide adequate land for both cooperative members and the ex-contras. According to Sánchez, shortly afterward a representative of the Nicaraguan Institute for Agrarian Reform

(Instituto Nicaragüense de Reforma Agraria, INRA) from Estelí visited them and told them they would be given title to the land. No land titles were forthcoming, however, and the former contras came to believe that the INRA official was secretly colluding with a wealthy cattle rancher from Quilalí who wished to acquire the land for himself.

Several years after the original invasion the conflict had still not been resolved. The ex-contra families continued to occupy more than 300 MZ of cooperative land. In fact, they were joined by about a dozen or more landless families who built small huts along the roadside and planted small plots of corn. Because none of the squatters had formal title to the land, however, they were unable to obtain bank loans. The former contras, deeply distrustful of government officials, express strong determination to hold onto the land. Carlos Sánchez states: "If they bring in the police or army to make us leave, we have a plan. We'll put our wives and children in front. They'll have to shoot us all down, but we'll never leave."

Nationwide, in the immediate postwar period, ex-contras occupied or attempted to occupy almost 200 Nicaraguan cooperatives.[10] While in the municipality of Quilalí cooperative lands were the main target of ex-contra land invasions, in other regions former contras also targeted state farms for invasion, at times with the encouragement of local landowners, who sometimes later purchased the land cheaply from the invaders.[11] From 1992 onward, pro-Sandinista peasant groups and politically mixed *(revuelto)* groups also carried out land invasions, sometimes targeting large private farms for occupation as a means of pressuring the government for land and to meet more urban-focused demands for jobs and housing.

For its part, the government at times removed land invaders by force, particularly in the case of private farms, but more commonly attempted to find alternative land for peasants, agreed to give the invaders title to the land, or took no effective action at all. Of the eight ex-contra land invasions in Quilalí in 1991 and 1992, in only two cases did the invaders receive formal title to the land. In the other six cases, the ex-contras maintained de facto control of the land, but three years after the original invasions, the legal question of land ownership had yet to be resolved. The cooperative members from Panalí who lost their land also had not received any assistance or compensation from the government.

In response to land invasions nationwide as well as pressure from recontra groups, the Chamorro government claims to have redistributed 1 million MZ of land from 1990 to 1995, or 12 percent of Nicaragua's total farmland and pasture (IHCA 1995, 15). Three-fourths of this was state farmland that was privatized and divided among former owners, ex-contras, former state farmworkers, and ex-EPS officers (15). By 1993, according to official government statistics, 16,834 ex-contras had received land (Saldomando and Cuadra 1994, 29). In the municipality of Quilalí, in large part as a response to the growth of recontra bands discussed below, INRA had purchased by 1994 eight private farms to hand over to former contras. Finally, in addition to land, ex-contras also demanded resources and services such as credit, housing, penetration roads, health services, and schools. In the mid-1990s, for example, Quilalí recontra groups, unhappy with what they viewed as the slow progress of certain development projects in their communities, threatened one organization's personnel and burned a project vehicle.

Personal Security

A final factor that perpetuated rural violence in the municipality of Quilalí and other interior zones was the postwar climate of physical insecurity and the fears of ex-contras that they were targeted by Sandinistas for persecution. In the words of one Quilalí ex-contra: "On the national level we're always threatened, watched by the army and State Security. Through the new armed movements [of former Sandinista soldiers] they track down the contra commanders. The

Sandinistas killed 3-80 [Enrique Bermúdez], [and Commander] Tiro al Blanco. The FSLN could kill us at anytime. We're nothing now."

As suggested earlier, these fears for physical safety, which also played a role in peasants taking up arms with the contras in the 1980s, were reinforced in the postwar period by a constant flow of stories from right-wing dominated media outlets about demobilized contras being killed by Sandinista military personnel and civilians. The most famous such case was the February 1991 murder of Enrique Bermúdez, the top contra military commander, who was idolized by many Quilalí contras. Many of these killings, including that of Bermúdez, were never adequately explained. With little reliable information available on the circumstances of these deaths or who the perpetrators were, it is difficult to establish how many ex-contra deaths were politically motivated and carried out by Sandinista supporters. In at least some cases, ex-contras were killed by other ex-contras in personal quarrels, or had taken up arms again for political reasons or to commit robberies. Nationwide from September 1991 to December 1992, for example, of 490 people killed in political violence in Nicaragua, 204 were ex-contras or recontras. Eighty-six of these ex-contras and recontras were killed by other recontras, 57 were killed in combat with the army, and 39 were killed in combat with recompas (CENIDH 1993, 1).

In the municipality of Quilalí there was no widespread persecution of civilian former contras and at most half a dozen unarmed ex-contras were killed in the early 1990s. One incident occurred in December 1990 when an off-duty Sandinista soldier threw a grenade at an ex-contra as he left Quilalí's discotheque. Alcohol and a personal quarrel were apparently factors in the killing, but Quilalí's anti-Sandinistas are convinced that it was an act of vengeance by the EPS soldier. Ex-contras' fears for personal security were exacerbated by Quilalí's ineffective police force, which allowed acts of violence to occur with virtual impunity. In the words of a Quilalí ex-contra whose house was burned by a renegade recontra band: "Here there's no security. There's anarchy in Nicaragua. The law doesn't exist. A criminal is as nonchalant as if he just came out of a sporting event. No one respects human life or property. The police are biased. The government has power only on paper." In Quilalí a shortage of funds, low pay, and the poor morale of police officers meant that murders of any type were almost never properly investigated and the guilty party was rarely punished. The Quilalí police in 1993 had only one vehicle to cover the entire municipality and at times were unable to afford gasoline to visit outlying rural communities. Furthermore, in Quilalí as elsewhere in the interior, the government began to incorporate ex-contras and some demobilized recontras into the local police force, often with little training or orientation.

Recontras

Fears for personal security, combined with frustrated demands for land and an end to Sandinista political and military influence, discussed earlier, led several hundred Quilalí ex-contras to take up arms again in the early 1990s as recontras. In the words of ex-contra Ramón Moreno: "There's no work, no aid. We'll have to go to the mountains again [join the recontras] to get what is rightfully ours." As during the war years, many of these peasants report that they felt safer, better able to defend themselves as armed guerrillas in the mountains. In addition, government response to earlier incidents of rural confrontation had convinced some ex-contras that violence was the most effective instrument by which to press their demands with the government. It is also likely that among some peasants, there was a degree of opportunism in their decision to take up arms again. Men who joined the contras when they were teenagers were unaccustomed to the hard work of farming, which often brought few immediate material rewards. The option of roaming the mountains with guns and receiving regular meals from the local peasant population was appealing, particularly when there was a relatively low probability of actually engaging in combat and it was a simple step to return to civilian life. Also, some of those who joined the recontras, were not ex-contras, but boys as young as fourteen who were children during the conflict of the 1980s. These young men may have sought economic benefits, adventure, and an opportunity to earn status and respect in a rural culture where going to war had become almost a rite of passage. In total, in the early 1990s an estimated 24,000 Nicaraguans participated in the rearmament cycle (Saldomando and Cuadra 1994, 21).

Unlike the contras of the 1980s, who had a clear, primary military and political mission, the armed groups of the 1990s were more complex. Some groups dedicated themselves almost entirely to banditry, the armed robbery of private and public vehicles, and kidnapping wealthy citizens. Other groups, such as the Frente Norte 3-80 (discussed below), were more directly linked to local and national political causes. Quilalí's recontras generally appear to have been led by former mid- and upper-level contra commanders, who relied, as they did in the 1980s, on networks of family members and friends to recruit followers. When recontra groups first formed in early 1991 they engaged in few militarily significant actions, although leaders were eager to seek national and even international publicity and they proved to be a serious embarrassment to the Chamorro government.[12] Not until mid-1991 did recontras led by "Indomable" (Indomitable) (José Angel Morán) and "Chele Rafael" (Rafael Herrera) launch a more serious assault against the town of Quilalí. On 27 June, from 40 to 200 recontras attacked Quilalí's police station and fought with the army for more than three hours before they were driven out of town.

After the June 1991 attack on Quilalí, the Chamorro government threatened on a number of occasions to launch military offensives against the recontra and bandit groups in the mountains north of

Quilalí, but in practice army military campaigns were small in scale and halfhearted. The government came to rely instead on the strategy, described earlier, of protracted disarmament negotiations and cooptation of leaders to disband recalcitrant recontra groups. In the second half of 1991, the Chamorro government and international commissions negotiated for several months with Indomable, Chele Rafael, and other recontra leaders. During these talks, Quilalí's municipal council members report that they used government funds to feed several hundred of these armed recontras in order to discourage them from assaulting vehicles to obtain money. In the final agreement reached in early 1992, recontras turned in their weapons for cash payments of up to $1,000. Local government officials claim that Indomable received a much larger payment in exchange for laying down his arms and moving to Miami.[13]

In September 1992, another Quilalí recontra group formed, the Frente Norte 3-80, named after slain contra military leader Enrique Bermúdez, "Commander 3-80." The Frente Norte was led by José Angel Talavera, or "Chacal" (Jackal), son of a prominent local family, and was the most well organized and clearly political armed mobilization in postwar Quilalí.[14] The Frente Norte 3-80 numbered several hundred peasants who had virtually free rein to move about as they pleased in the mountains of El Súngano to the north of Quilalí, where the army rarely entered. In addition to support from peasants in the mountains, the Frente Norte regularly sent "requests" for supplies and money to wealthy merchants in the town of Quilalí, who generally complied to avoid trouble.

The principle political demands of the Frente Norte 3-80 were the withdrawal of the EPS from Quilalí; a reduction of the army nationwide; the removal of Humberto Ortega from office; the integration of ex-contras in the rural police force; as well as land, credit, and development projects for ex-contras (IHCA 1993b, 7). While in public statements the Frente Norte reiterated its respect for the Nicaraguan government, in private Frente Norte leaders told Quilalí peasants that they sought to overthrow President Chamorro, seen as linked in "cogovernment" with the FSLN. Recontra groups in Nicaragua's northern interior also targeted Sandinista supporters and Sandinista cooperatives with threats and violence. The national head of the UNAG estimated that in the first three years of the UNO government over 300 peasant cooperative members were killed nationwide.[15]

In August 1993 the Frente Norte 3-80 in Quilalí provoked a national crisis by kidnapping a group of forty-one Sandinista parliamentary deputies, government officials, and Special Disarmament Brigade officers who had traveled to Quilalí to negotiate with Talavera. In retaliation, a pro-Sandinista Dignity and Sovereignty commando in Managua took several dozen opposition politicians hostage until this national crisis was resolved through negotiation. Following the release of the Quilalí hostages, the army launched a major offensive against the Frente Norte 3-80, and Talavera and his men were forced to flee to Honduras. In early 1994, however, the Frente Norte reached a disarmament agreement with the government. Talavera and 300 of his men surrendered their weapons in Quilalí in April 1994 in exchange for command of the Quilalí police force, land, and more teachers for schools in Quilalí and other zones.

While in the municipality of Quilalí recontra groups predominated, in other northern zones, such as Ocotal, it was armed *recompa* bands, made up of former members of the Sandinista Army and State Security that formed from 1991 onward. As a rule, recompa and politically mixed *revuelto* bands, who blocked highways and occupied farms from 1992 onward, had more links to urban sectors, and their demands centered on personal security, a resolution of property issues, and recontra disarmament, as well as land and services (Cordero and Pereira 1992, 28).

As the number of armed groups proliferated in the early and mid-1990s the boundaries of conflict further dissolved. Violence was no longer geographically confined to rural areas, but also took place in interior cities and on the Pacific coast and personal and political grudges often blended with outright criminality. In 1993 passenger vehicles traveling to Quilalí were robbed by armed gangs as often as once a week and armed groups also began kidnapping wealthy rural residents. Several Quilalí families paid thousands of dollars in ransom for the return of family members.[16] In such cases, it was not clear how much these funds were being used to further collective or political aims and how much was simply personal enrichment. Overall, the widespread and unpredictable nature of postwar rural violence led to a vicious circle in which violence reinforced Quilalí peasants' fears for physical security and led them to take up arms, leading to yet further violence. This insecure climate also hindered economic recovery in Quilalí and other interior zones, which fueled further instability and violence.

Sandinistas

Postwar insecurity affected not only anti-Sandinista peasants, but also pro-Sandinista peasants, some of whom indicate that ironically they had a greater sense of physical and economic security in the 1980s, in spite of the war. Cooperative leader Daniel López explains: "During the war, if someone knocked on my door in the middle of the night I would have my finger on the trigger of my gun. Now we've given up our arms and we're defenseless."

In the months following the 1990 UNO victory, many of Quilalí's former State Security agents and EPS officers left the municipality to settle in more secure urban areas such as Ocotal and Estelí, in large part out of fear for their personal safety. Some of them report that they would not even travel to Quilalí to visit family members because of the danger of being stopped by recontras along the road. Other known Sandinista activists who continued to live in Quilalí kept a low profile and avoided travel during periods of high tension, when recontras were active. In the words of one such ex-army officer: "We feel insecure. . . . [The recontras] know who is Sandinista and who isn't. There are places [in the municipality] where I don't go because I know I won't come out alive." In fact, despite the postwar instability, the presence of a relatively cohesive and militarily skilled pro-Sandinista sector in Quilalí capable of retaliation appears to have led to a rough balance of power in the municipality that limited targeted political killings. In the early 1990s, only a few unarmed pro-Sandinista peasants were killed by anti-Sandinistas or ex-contras and in some cases the motives were apparently personal as well as political.

In addition to continued concerns about physical safety, many pro-Sandinista peasants have also seen their economic security eroded in the postwar period. For former cooperative members, in the long term it may not be so much legal threats over land ownership as market mechanisms that could reverse the gains made in more equitable land distribution in the 1980s. One factor that will likely accelerate this process of restratification of landholdings in Quilalí is the rapid parcelization of land once held collectively by cooperatives. By 1992 all the municipality's cooperatives had voluntarily decided to divide their collective land into individual plots and distributed tractors, farm equipment, and other capital goods to individual members. Some peasants did not abandon the cooperative farming model completely, however, and maintained loosely structured groups of friends and family to collectively apply for credit and carry out certain agricultural tasks. Cooperatives formed by peasants evacuated in 1985, on the other hand, tended to dissolve completely as many families return to their native communities in the mountains. In all of Nicaragua, an estimated 90 percent of cooperative land had been converted into individual parcels by the mid-1990s, largely at the initiative of peasants themselves (IHCA 1994b, 18).

Quilalí's ex-cooperative members began to farm individually under difficult economic conditions and new government policies less favorable to poor peasants. Unlike the 1980s, peasants could no longer depend on the subsidized machinery and farming equipment, and the generous credit, provided by the Sandinista government. In the early 1990s the majority of former cooperative members had accumulated unpaid debts with the bank and were cut off from bank credit. To meet their needs for funds, ex-cooperative members appear to have accelerated decapitalization, selling off cattle, tractors, farm tools, and even the tobacco sheds they received during the revolution. One El Coco resident explains: "We fought here. My son and husband shed their blood for this land. Now everything is turning into a disaster. It's not fair. [Before], in spite of the war, we didn't suffer as much. We had money and food. Now everything is desperate."

Parcelization of cooperative land also appeared to be leading to growing wealth differences among peasants, once relatively equal in terms of land and income. Some peasants, who have invested wisely and have access to plentiful family labor and outside resources, report that their economic status is improving as individual farmers. Other peasants have not been as successful and have had to sell a portion or all of their land after 1990.[17]

The postwar economic recession and the dissolution of river valley cooperatives have weakened what was once a strong base of rural Sandinista support in the municipality. Also, as we have seen, in the 1980s the FSLN's multiclass support base was able to largely subsume potential internal conflicts and contradictions in the struggle against the common foe, the United States and the contra forces it sponsored. After 1990, however, as Stahler-Sholk points out, "The FSLN's electoral defeat forced the issue of internal democratization of the party and also exposed the diverging class and personal interests of some of the party's leaders" (1995, 88). One divisive issue was alleged abuses that occurred during the "piñata," the extensive distribution and titling of land, houses, and other goods by the government during the two-month transition period. Postwar charges of corruption by some party leaders undermined the FSLN's credibility and one of its most basic appeals to its followers, that Sandinistas were genuinely committed to bettering the lives of the poor. The FSLN was also hampered by a lack of clear policy alternatives to the economic crisis and structural adjustment programs carried out by the Chamorro government (Saldomando 1996). In fact, in the early 1990s the FSLN leadership and the Chamorro government made a series of "elite pacts," beginning with the Transition Accord, on key issues such as property and constitutional reform, and established an informal alliance in the National Assembly. This alliance, which was denounced by the opposition as "cogovernment," and viewed by FSLN leaders as a necessary step to maintain economic and political stability, constrained the FSLN from more effectively responding to the concerns of its grassroots supporters.

These issues, combined with a series of postwar urban crises, meant that the party was able to offer only limited support to rural areas like Quilalí. One Quilalí Sandinista supporter states: "Here after the elections the FSLN leaders from Nueva Segovia don't know what it is to go to a resettlement community. . . . These campesinos who gave their souls, their lives, to defend the revolution are suffering hunger. In spite of that, these campesinos are forgotten [by the FSLN]." Whereas wartime conditions and the common nationalist struggle against the contras and their U.S. sponsors promoted unity among Sandinistas, in the postwar period differences of class and privilege between the FSLN rank and file and its leadership emerged more sharply, particularly among former military personnel. In the words of an ex-lieutenant: "We retired army officers have been forgotten. [High-ranking EPS officers] don't even know if we have enough to eat, if we have houses, if we work, if we study. There is no help for us after we sacrificed so much for the nation and for them. Many of us would like to study abroad, learn technical skills, but nobody listens to us. To talk to a military officer you have to wait for hours. Now they don't even recognize us."

When the armed forces were reduced by over 45,000 men, the bulk of retirement benefits such as land went to only 6 percent of officials ranked captain and above (Cajina 1997, 304). Ex-Sandinista

Army officers who served in Quilalí generally had more education than former contras, but most were from urban centers where unemployment and underemployment was over 50 percent in the early 1990s. In Estelí, where many Quilalí ex-army officers relocated, some estimates put underemployment as high as 75 percent of the economically active population. Most of the ex-EPS officers interviewed for this study had been without steady work for a year or longer and were struggling to put food on the table even once a day.

As some former Sandinista supporters took a more critical attitude toward the FSLN leadership, some ex-contra foot soldiers also began to openly criticize their leaders of the 1980s. As a rule, well-off contra commanders returned to a much more advantageous situation in Quilalí than poor peasants. Unlike poor contra combatants, who had few economic or social resources to fall back on after the war, the families of most contra commanders generally managed to keep at least a portion of their wealth intact. Some of these men returned to their home communities and involved themselves again in agricultural production and community life, as well as local recontra movements. Other former commanders, however, began new farming or business ventures in other parts of Nicaragua or were able to obtain government posts where they received relatively high salaries and benefits such as houses, farms, and vehicles in exchange for their cooperation with the government.

Almost every poor ex-contra interviewed in this study listed as a major postwar complaint their perception that many of their former commanders had abandoned them and "sold out" and that politicians had failed to fulfill promises made during the demobilization process. In the words of a Quilalí ex-contra: "[Ex-contra commanders] have their cars and go to their meetings. It's betrayal. During the war . . . they promised us land and told us we were the only hope for liberty. Now they can't be bothered with us." Ex-National Guardsman and poor peasant Alfredo Aguero also recites with bitterness a series of disappointments in his life. In July 1979, Somoza fled

Nicaragua abandoning Aguero and his fellow National Guardsmen to their fate. Years later Aguero believes that contra leaders Israel Galeano and Oscar Sobalvarro betrayed him by negotiating an unfavorable disarmament agreement with President Chamorro, who later failed to fulfill her promises of assistance to ex-contras. In 1991, Aguero joined an armed band led by recontra chief Indomable. Indomable, however, eventually accepted a large cash settlement from the Chamorro government and left for the United States. Aguero remains as poor and frustrated as he was a decade ago, with no land or credit for farming.

Experiences like this have led some former contra combatants and collaborators like Aguero to criticize individuals who in their minds have broken the implicit norms of reciprocity of clientelistic relationships in the postwar period. It should be emphasized, however, that the majority of anti-Sandinista poor and middle peasants interviewed still did not necessarily question the key underlying assumptions of their worldview. In other words, they continued to look to elites to fulfill a traditional clientelistic role of leadership and assistance, rather than seeking to develop ties of solidarity with other poor peasants. In their minds the problem lies with a few "bad" individuals who have violated the norms of clientelism, and not necessarily in an intrinsic conflict of interests between well-off producers and the rural poor.

A few poor anti-Sandinista peasants interviewed, however, appear to conceptualize their difficulties in more class-based terms. Carlos Sánchez, a landless peasant who fought with the contras for seven years, complains that in postwar Quilalí: "The merchants pay us low prices for basic grains. There are no loans to plant with and no health centers. What use is it to go to Quilalí and have the doctor look at my child for a few seconds and prescribe four medicines that I can't afford? . . . The government only pays attention to those with money. . . . [Government leaders] are only interested in living well and doing business deals for dollars." In contrast to anti-Sandinistas,

almost all the pro-Sandinista peasants interviewed in Quilalí emphasize the common needs and interests shared by poor peasants regardless of whether they supported and opposed the revolution. A former
Sandinista mayor summarizes this point of view:

> The conflicts here in Quilalí are incomprehensible. How is it possible
> that we are all campesinos; that we are workers; that we are family
> members; that we are from the same place . . . and there is so much
> hate and resentment. We were manipulated by outside interests. We
> provided the dead. We gave our blood. It's sad that this [violence]
> continues because we fail to understand each other. The truth is that
> the politicians took advantage of the poor. . . . The rich now have
> all their possessions and we're still poor. The campesino is always
> going to be deceived by those who have economic power, political
> power. Here at the grassroots level we need to try and understand
> each other to build a better society. . . . We should work for recon-
> ciliation and focus on the problems of the poor, our common interests
> as poor campesinos.

Concretely, some pro-Sandinista community leaders have actively
promoted the new horizontal ties of class solidarity in the municipality of Quilalí at the individual level and through such organizations as
the UNAG. Anti- and pro-Sandinista peasants, for example, have carried out several small development projects together, made joint
efforts to lobby the government for more aid for disabled ex-combatants, and organized a baseball league. It appears, however, that as of
the mid-1990s only a minority of anti-Sandinista peasants were responding to such efforts at reconciliation. As during the 1980s, the
majority of former contra collaborators and combatants continued to
identify the municipality of Quilalí as fundamentally divided, not between the wealthy and the poor, but between pro- and anti-Sandinista peasants. This anti-Sandinista sector still considered other poor
peasants who supported the FSLN as rivals for political and military
power and limited material resources, rather than potential allies.
Armed mobilizations by anti-Sandinistas in the postwar period were

successful in drawing government attention to their grievances and led several international aid organizations to select Quilalí as a priority zone of attention. One possibility is that Quilalí's relatively privileged position in terms of external funds and projects will help ease conflicts over material resources and provide opportunities for greater cooperation among peasants. Quilalí peasant consciousness is dynamic and still evolving. It remains to be seen if in the future appeals for reconciliation directed at Quilalí's poor peasant majority will be able to successfully challenge the legacy of more than a decade of revolutionary and counterrevolutionary polarization and military conflict.

Chapter 10

Conclusion

THE EXPERIENCES of rural polarization and armed peasant movements in Quilalí suggest several more general conclusions about the nature of peasant response to revolutionary change and forms of resistance. First, to set the context of this peasant mobilization, it should be noted that despite its geographic isolation and the strength of local identities and loyalties, the development of the municipality Quilalí was the product of a complex interplay of international, national, and local forces that have at various points been embraced, adapted, and resisted by residents. Contemporary communities and peasant identity in the municipality did not emerge from a precapitalist communal culture or generations of shared tradition, the type of community identified by scholars as a key source of peasant resistance (Scott 1976; Wolf 1969). Rather Quilalí communities were the outcome of social and economic dislocations in the Segovias, in particular the expansion of cattle ranching, which pushed peasants toward periphery zones of the agricultural frontier in search of refuge from the harshest features of capitalist export expansion and opportunities for upward economic mobility.

By the 1970s, however, market forces had also penetrated the municipality of Quilalí. Many scholars have identified the expansion of capitalism into traditional rural zones as an important structural factor in generating discontent and peasant rebellion. The experience of Quilalí from the 1960s onward indicates that the dynamics of market integration, even within a single nation, may vary in important ways. As studies by Wheelock (1978), Williams (1986), and Gould (1990b) demonstrate, in certain regions of Nicaragua, such as the departments of León and Chinandega and specific zones of Matagalpa and Jinotega, the expansion of export crops led to a breakdown of paternalistic bonds between patrons and poor peasants, as well as to latent and overt conflicts over land. Yet in other zones of Nicaragua's mountainous interior such as Quilalí, partial market integration did not necessarily lead to either the complete breakdown of earlier relations of production or promote the formation of a large peasant sector receptive to revolutionary change.

In the municipality of Quilalí, the growth of cattle and coffee production for national and international markets, as well as commerce in general, led to structural changes that both favored and made more difficult radical rural transformation. On the one hand, increasing scarcity of land and insecurity of land tenure in the municipality likely increased the openness of some poor peasants to revolutionary appeals. On the other hand, the negative impact of partial market penetration in Quilalí was mitigated by the availability land on the nearby agricultural frontier, the continuation of traditional forms of access to land, and ongoing patron-client ties. Also, new market opportunities and the development of infrastructure not only attracted regional elites to Quilalí's river valley, but also allowed for the consolidation of a strong middle-peasant sector and a locally powerful group of finqueros. As we have seen, these sectors tended to view their interests as closely linked to the perpetuation of the previous neoliberal economic system and oppose revolutionary change.

It should be emphasized that although Quilalí poor peasants in particular were, as Colburn (1989a) indicates, concerned with securing their personal economic and physical well-being, they were not isolated actors. Rather they were members of broader communities with shared histories and values and enmeshed in often extensive and complex family and productive networks. Quilalí's patterns of migration and settlement, isolation, initial hardships, and the relative richness of the natural environment all served to strengthen a shared peasant identity. In the decades following World War II a local way of life took hold in Quilalí that encompassed patron-client ties and mutual aid, a strong work ethic, autonomy, patriarchy, and property rights.

The contemporary history of Quilalí lends support to the findings of scholars that such community and extended family networks may serve as powerful instruments of rural mobilization (Wolf 1969; Scott 1976; Gould 1990b; Wickham-Crowley 1992). In the 1970s FSLN guerrillas were able to tap into finquero-led networks to support their struggle to defeat the Somoza regime. Although Quilalí's terrateniente sector was largely dismantled after 1979, its finquero sector remained largely intact and continued to control almost half of agricultural production in the municipality throughout the 1980s.

As we have seen, some of these finqueros served as key intermediaries between the U.S. government, ex-National Guardsmen, and northern Nicaragua's poor and middle interior peasantry and helped to legitimize the contras as a "peasant army." Unlike their largely urban, more recently arrived pro-FSLN counterparts, MILPA leaders were able to draw on dense interpersonal networks to build a base of support for their anti-Sandinista struggle. It is important to emphasize that such networks were not composed solely of peasants of relatively equal economic status, such as subsistence smallholders. Rather, anti-Sandinista networks in Quilalí were multiclass in nature and led by finqueros who were not distinct outsiders separated from an autonomously acting poor majority, but were at the center of community life and activities.

Several scholars suggest that the transformation of old identities and the forging of new collective identities may be facilitated through ongoing political struggle (Gould 1990b; Kincaid 1987). In the 1980s the nature and boundaries of Quilalí collective peasant identities were influenced by the intense and violent struggle for peasant support between Sandinista forces and anti-Sandinista forces, which took place both in military combat and on an ideological level.

On the one hand, Sandinista revolutionary discourse mobilized peasants around a common identity first as Nicaraguans, defending the nation against the return of Somocismo and external aggression; and second, as the rural poor who had class interests that were, at least in part, distinct from those of the well-off minority. In contrast, the contras drew upon elements of the interior way of life described above and reinforced and reshaped in their discourse a multiclass relational identity, which stressed the common interests of interior residents in opposition to the "foreign" revolutionary ideology.

The experience of Quilalí suggests that framing their struggle as one of a united peasant community against the FSLN was an effective strategy that enabled the contras to at least temporarily subsume potential conflicts between the goals sought by the well-off leadership and those of poor-peasant foot soldiers. By arguing that all Quilalí peasants—wealthy, middle, and poor—were better off before the revolution, contras held together a stratified movement in which each peasant fought for his own version of a rather ambiguously defined "democratic" Nicaragua.

In addition to family and community networks, the present study provides confirmation of the important role that external agents and resources may play in peasant mobilization (Wickham-Crowley 1992). Priests and church layworkers active in liberation theology and FSLN guerrillas from outside the zone laid important groundwork, particularly in terms of transformation of peasant consciousness, for the development of a pro-Sandinista peasant base in Quilalí. Furthermore, to MILPA leaders the knowledge that ex-National Guardsmen were organizing across the border in Honduras, and by 1981 the availability of funding from the United States, were powerful inducements toward armed struggle against the revolutionary government. Until the definitive military aid cutoff in 1988, U.S.-supplied funding, weaponry, and organizational support for the contras served to deepen the tensions and contradictions between the FSLN and Nicaragua's interior peasantry, as well as to expand the scope and the intensity of the conflict. To some committed anti-Sandinista Quilalí peasants, the United States represented a powerful external ally who provided them with the means to openly confront the FSLN. At the same time, U.S. funding was a critical element in the militarization of Nicaragua's mountainous interior that made it all but impossible for young men, whatever their ideological sympathies, to avoid taking up arms with one side or the other.

If the experience of Quilalí demonstrates that local elites may wield political and economic power beyond their limited numbers, it also suggests that even revolutionary governments that come to power with the support of a broad multiclass coalition may have a difficult time maintaining the support of this sector (Paige 1997). In Quilalí, finqueros saw their own economic well-being and advancement as closely tied to a free market system. Even when measures such as land reform and market interventions did not directly harm them, many opposed Sandinista "communist" policies on principle. Also, as we have seen, elite opposition to the FSLN was more complex than simply calculated economic self-interest (Spalding 1994; Paige 1997). Attempts by Sandinistas to independently organize peasants and class-based revolutionary discourse created a sense of moral outrage among some finqueros and deepened their mistrust of the revolutionary regime. Given the intrinsic conflict of interest between those who in the past have prospered in a free-market system and a government promoting a transition to socialism, the best that a revolutionary regime such as the FSLN may be able to do is "neutralize" a portion of rural elites, who agree not to actively oppose the government in exchange for economic concessions that allow them to continue producing and generating profits. In Quilalí, as we have seen, roughly half of finqueros fell into this category of what came to be termed patriotic producers, and used Sandinista subsidies to advance their economic position and accumulate further land and capital in the 1980s.

The Sandinista strategy of economic concessions to elites was not without its costs, however. As Luciak (1995) indicates, during its time in power the FSLN faced a constant tension between its competing goals of popular hegemony and national unity. The complaints of Quilalí poor peasants about "19th of July Sandinistas" suggest, for example, that by directing limited resources toward local elites, the Sandinista government at least partially undermined its credibility as a government that gave high priority to the interests of the poor majority, a key underpinning of peasant support for the FSLN in the municipality. In addition, these Sandinista policies helped sustain inequalities in the municipality and unintentionally reinforced the dependence of the poor on locally powerful individuals.

The present study also tends to confirm the importance of a number of FSLN policies—including the state-focused and collective nature of agrarian reform, government market interventions, and neglect of nonorganized peasants—which scholars have identified as a key source of tension between the FSLN and the peasantry (CIPRES 1991; Bendaña 1991; Zalkin 1990; Martinez 1993; Kaimowitz 1988; Baumeister 1991). While these policies were implemented throughout rural Nicaragua, they represented a particularly intense challenge to the interior values and social structures discussed above. In fact, this study suggests that certain Sandinista policies can be better conceptualized not as "errors" subject to easy rectification, but rather as a reflection of more intractable tensions between two distinct pro-Sandinista and anti-Sandinista worldviews with conflicting perspectives on the nature of society, distribution of resources, and core values.

On the one hand, Sandinista ideology identified conflicts of interest between the wealthy and poor, introduced the concept of exploitation to Quilalí, and called for a more egalitarian rural society. The dominant prerevolutionary rural culture, however, viewed the wealthy and poor as mutually dependent and sharing common interests and tacitly accepted the existing social and economic hierarchy. Likewise, in the anti-Sandinista worldview market freedoms were highly valued and private property was considered an absolute right. The FSLN, however, justified land reform and market interventions on the grounds of social justice and the right of the poor to basic subsistence. Other areas of ideological tension include nationalism over local family and community loyalties; an urban-versus-rural orientation; and collective over individual farming.

The degree to which these competing discourses were adopted or rejected by Quilalí peasants was a complex process that was influenced by selective and collective benefits offered by the FSLN and the contras, the dynamics of military power in local communities, and peasants' economic status. In Quilalí the majority of wealthy producers and middle peasants, most of whom had opposed the Somoza regime on political grounds but otherwise had been doing relatively well economically as Quilalí modernized, opposed major aspects of Sandinista programs and ideology. Sandinista calls for greater rural equality and land reform had little appeal to these sectors. Middle peasants already owned sufficient land and had little interest in becoming land reform beneficiaries. On the contrary, although land reform in the municipality was relatively moderate in scope, affecting only five terratenientes and a dozen or so finqueros, it was still viewed as unjust and a potential threat to their landholdings by many finqueros and middle peasants.

A number of analysts have also cited evidence that middle peasants in particular were resentful of Sandinista market interventions, such as limitations on the buying and selling of crops and consumer goods, and suffered from generalized FSLN neglect (CIPRES 1991; Bendaña 1991; Zalkin 1990). In the case of Quilalí the most vociferous complaints about Sandinista economic policies from peasants of all classes referred to rationing and shortages of basic consumer goods. It should also be emphasized that Quilalí middle peasants and others who received few positive benefits from the revolution did not blame the Sandinista government for merely "neglecting" them. Rather in their perception of events, the FSLN was directly or indirectly responsible for bringing to their communities a war that threatened the physical integrity of their families, disrupted agricultural production, and in some cases forced them to abandon their farms altogether.

While well-off producers and middle peasants tended to support the anti-Sandinista worldview, the political consciousness of Quilalí's poor peasants was more divided and contested, offering confirmation that the rural poor, in particular those who have insufficient access to land and who are not bound by patron-client ties, are the most likely potential supporters of revolutionary change (Enriquez 1997). In the case of Quilalí, peasants who had participated in liberation theology movements or had family histories of support for Sandino or FSLN guerrillas were most likely to view revolutionary change favorably. This base of pro-Sandinista peasantry was further reinforced during the 1980s by educational opportunities, exposure to revolutionary discourse, cooperative organizational experiences, and peasants' struggle to defend militarily the land they received under the agrarian reform.

Other poor peasants reflect a more divided political consciousness. On the one hand, they were attracted to certain aspects of the Sandinista program—most important, the possibility of receiving land; but also credit, educational and health services, and calls for greater social and economic equality. At the same time, however, these peasants were pulled toward the anti-Sandinista cause by continued ideological and economic dependence on local elites; doubts about the viability of the FSLN program; and a recognition of the growing strength of contra forces in the municipality and the potential costs of supporting the revolution.

The initial FSLN land reform policy that turned over 11,000 MZ of high-quality Quilalí agricultural land into state farms in 1979 can clearly be seen as a missed opportunity to have won the support of the dozens of peasants who participated in land invasions in the first months of the revolution and other poor peasants who wavered between revolutionary and anti-Sandinista sympathies. Although the FSLN modified its policies several years later, in 1983, and began to distribute land to peasants who were willing to join production cooperatives, the terms of land distribution, collective farming and participation in self-defense militias, as well as the growing military polarization of the municipality made this option unacceptable to many poor peasants. By initially placing national economic concerns and the development of the state sector above the needs and desires of poor peasants, the FSLN failed to use one of its best potential instruments to win peasant support. In fact, frustration over the failure of the Sandinistas to provide them with individual parcels of land influenced some of these landless peasants to support the contras.

Furthermore, the great majority of peasants interviewed who collaborated or fought with the contras shared, with varying degrees of coherency and conviction, the basic assumptions of the anti-Sandinista worldview. Yet this ideological orientation did not prevent some Quilalí residents from taking advantage of revolutionary programs and wartime conditions in a pragmatic manner to earn economic benefits for themselves. Poor and middle peasants in the river valley community of La Vigía, for example, accepted Sandinista credit and subsidies while at the same time secretly collaborating with the contras. Likewise, a small group of finqueros who did not openly affiliate themselves with either the FSLN or the contras were able to substantially improve their economic standing during the 1980s.

Another lesson suggested by the contemporary history of Quilalí is that governments like the FSLN that wish to implement major transformations of society will have only a short time available to them in which to attempt to build revolutionary hegemony before national and international opposition to revolutionary change mobilizes. In the case of Quilalí, this period was unusually short, less than a year before the MILPAs began organizing in the municipality. The rapidly emerging MILPA-contra challenge to Sandinista military hegemony in the early 1980s in turn seriously undermined the FSLN's struggle to establish political hegemony. As the armed conflict spread, revolutionary advances in areas such as health, education, and other services were halted, and government interaction with the peasant population was greatly limited by security concerns. In fact, after 1982 in the municipality virtually the only contact the FSLN had with certain outlying communities was military. In such zones the frightening realities of armed conflict soon overwhelmed all other aspects of life and many anti-Sandinista poor peasants in particular came to equate the period of FSLN rule with war, death, and destruction.

The pressure on the FSLN to quickly consolidate revolutionary political hegemony was further complicated by the fact that revolutions by their very nature tend to generate high demands and expectations on the part of the population. In Quilalí, many peasants who were largely quiescent under the Somoza government held the FSLN, with its explicit promises to assist the poor, to a higher standard. In many cases they expected immediate benefits of land, goods, and services. At the same time, revolutionary governments like the FSLN face numerous competing priorities—reconstruction and economic reactivation; the demands of an urban population that provided the revolution's core support; a policy of national unity with economic elites; and international pressures. Under these circumstances some degree of neglect of rural areas by the FSLN seems almost unavoidable, leaving such zones as a potential weak flank of revolutionary regimes.

Another important lesson to be drawn from the present study is that once a dynamic of political and military polarization takes hold, it often takes on a life of its own that is difficult to reverse. In Quilalí it appears that while some peasants were not especially pleased with changes that occurred in the municipality after 1979, the poor in particular preferred as their first option everyday resistance rather than open confrontation with either of the two military forces in the municipality (Scott 1985, 1989, 1990). The goal of many poor peasants in conflictive zones was simply to keep their families intact, hold on to their land, and maintain at least the appearance of neutrality to avoid difficulties with either Sandinista or contra military personnel. As we have seen, in anti-Sandinista communities gender norms and age considerations largely limited the role of women and older men to that of civilian collaborators.

Many anti-Sandinista young men, however, when faced with obligatory Sandinista military service and recruitment pressures from the contras, concluded that their only option was to take up arms with the contras as a measure of "self-defense." This dynamic of armed mobilization was further reinforced by family and community pressures, as well as State Security crackdowns against networks of contra collaborators. A subsequent series of FSLN policy reforms in the mid-1980s, which included the evacuation of the northeastern mountain communities, distribution of land to individuals, and the liberalization of the sale of basic grains, was only partially successfully in winning peasant support because many of these potential benefits to peasants were overwhelmed by the ongoing negative impact of the war.

A final conclusion suggested by this case study of Quilalí is that peasant consciousness cannot be understood in the abstract, as static and unchanging. Rather, as studies by Enriquez (1997) and Gould (1990b) suggest, Nicaraguan peasant consciousness is dynamic, and in the case of Quilalí has been molded by a variety of life experiences, and cultural, political, and structural influences. Over the course of the decade the FSLN was able to build an important base of active support among Quilalí peasants. A key element in this post-1979 consolidation of a pro-Sandinista peasant base outside the town limits was the FSLN's development of an extensive subsidized cooperative sector that assured members both economic subsistence and a relative degree of physical security. At the same time, as suggested earlier, through such experiences as cooperative and UNAG membership, combat with the Sandinista Army, defense of their land against contra attacks, and ongoing exposure to FSLN discourse, pro-Sandinista peasants came to share FSLN revolutionary and nationalist ideals. By the end of the decade, many of these Quilalí peasants came to view themselves as active participants in a larger ideological cause and a number of them made important personal sacrifices for what they believed was the defense of the rights of poor peasants and workers and national sovereignty.

Many anti-Sandinista peasants also originally took up arms with the contras largely over a series of concrete local grievances such as fear of the draft, opposition to Sandinista land reform, and the desire to buy and sell goods and move about freely. Once integrated into the contra forces, however, some of these peasants report that they began to see their struggle in broader terms as a means to liberate all of Nicaragua from perceived Sandinista tyranny and allow the interior peasantry to live in peace and dignity.

In addition, a further shift in anti-Sandinista peasant consciousness emerged in the postwar period. Many anti-Sandinista young men gained a sense of their own strength and importance while fighting with the contras in the 1980s and were also indirectly influenced by the examples of the revolution they opposed. When they returned to Quilalí in the early 1990s they were no longer the largely quiescent peasantry of an earlier era, but instead brought with them a series of new demands and expectations of the government, and a willingness to employ violence if necessary to achieve these goals. It is important to emphasize, however, that anti-Sandinistas who mobilized in the postwar period generally did not seek collective benefits for the poor peasantry as a whole. Unlike pro-Sandinistas peasants, who emphasize in interviews the common needs of poor peasants of all political viewpoints, anti-Sandinistas mobilized to pressure the state for selective rewards for themselves and their families consistent with a clientelistic worldview. This highly mobilized peasant sector as well as economic recession, weak government authority, and intense national political disputes were key elements in the continued postwar violence in Quilalí and other zones of Nicaragua's interior.

The failure of some ex-contra leaders to resume their paternalistic role in civilian life, and their preoccupation with reestablishing their personal economic well-being in the postwar period, contributed to the fragmentation of the anti-Sandinista cross-class alliance. Conflicts of interest between the contras' well-off leadership and its poor combatants, which had been largely subsumed in the 1980s, began to emerge more openly in the 1990s. It should be emphasized, however, that most Quilalí poor peasants who express these feelings of disillusionment with particular former leaders who they believe have "sold out" and abandoned them do not necessarily take their critique a step further. In general, they still do not question the effectiveness of their ties to the well-off as a strategy for advancing their interests as poor peasants.

A similar postwar dynamic was taking place in the pro-Sandinista alliance. It can be argued that the FSLN put on hold for many years potential divisions between its grassroots supporters and its national leaders, many of whom came from relatively privileged backgrounds, in the face of the common threat—the contras and their U.S. sponsors. After 1990, issues such as the scandal surrounding the "piñata" and the generous retirement benefits received by the highest ranking army officers led some Quilalí pro-Sandinistas to begin to openly criticize the FSLN political and military leadership.

Finally, the dynamic nature of peasant consciousness should also serve as a caution against concluding too quickly that the Nicaragua's interior peasants were a revolutionary lost cause, a traditional and conservative sector that resisted all types of progressive change and was easily recruited by counterrevolution. Rather it appears that under certain circumstances interior poor peasants in particular represent a potential base of support that could mobilize in favor of revolutionary change. The experience of Quilalí suggests that the construction of such a rural support for radical change is facilitated by longer-term preparatory consciousness raising work with peasants in peacetime conditions; local rather than outside leadership; good knowledge of and respect for local customs and norms; flexible policies and programs that respond to the felt needs of peasants; and the ability of guerrillas or revolutionary states to ensure the basic physical and economic security of peasant supporters.

It is also likely that the process of transformation of peasant consciousness in the municipality of Quilalí and other zones will continue in the future. One possibility may be that as vertical ties and the intensity of earlier political loyalties weaken pro- and anti-Sandinista poor peasants, who share many of the same problems—notably the need for access to land, credit, and services—instead of viewing each other as competitors for scarce resources will identify common interests and begin to construct horizontal linkages. A majority of pro-Sandinista Quilalí residents already favor such efforts at reconciliation and are actively seeking to establish new ties and alliances with those poor peasants they once fought against in the past decade. Many anti-Sandinista peasants, however, continue view the fundamental division in the municipality as one between pro- and anti-Sandinistas and it remains uncertain whether such efforts at reshaping peasant collective identities will achieve success.

Appendix A

Methodology

WITHIN THE voluminous literature on the Nicaraguan revolution and the war between the Sandinista government and U.S.-sponsored contra rebels, a great deal of analysis and debate has focused on policy decisions at the top levels of government both in Nicaragua and the United States. Yet the voice of peasants from the rural communities where the war was fought has been largely absent. To begin to address this void, this study of the municipality of Quilalí takes a bottom-up approach to analyzing Nicaragua's conflict and makes extensive use of the firsthand testimony of Quilalí residents. It attempts to explore the contemporary history of the municipality as experienced and articulated by the peasants who were both direct protagonists and victims of the conflict. The interviews that form the basis of this study were carried out from November 1992 through May 1993, during which time a total of 105 peasants were formally interviewed. I also conducted less formal follow-up interviews with key informants during a visit to Quilalí in September 1994.

Only since the official end of the war in 1990 has it been possible to visit rural interior areas like Quilalí and speak in depth with peasants who fought and collaborated with both the Sandinistas and the contras about their experiences. During the 1980s in the municipality of Quilalí, outside civilians were able to move freely about the town of Quilalí and most of the river valley. The danger of mines, ambushes, and frequent military clashes, however, limited access to the municipality's outlying mountain zones, where most of Quilalí's anti-Sandinista communities were concentrated. And even when visits were possible, anti-Sandinista peasants were understandably reluctant at the time to speak openly of their ongoing activities in support of the counterrevolution.

Although Nicaragua's conflict officially ended 1990, a number of serious limitations to gathering information in Quilalí still remained when I first arrived to conduct interviews in 1992. Armed groups of bandits and recontras were active in the municipality and surrounding zones after the war, creating a climate of insecurity and violence. Robberies and assaults on vehicles traveling to and from Quilalí were a common occurrence, and while I was living in Quilalí at least one or two residents were killed each week in some type of violent clash.

The insecure conditions in the municipality at the time of my research limited my access to outlying zones of the municipality and meant that a random survey sample of the municipality was simply not possible. Drawing upon my background knowledge of the municipality and advice from community leaders, I instead interviewed a purposive sample of Quilalí residents selected to reflect as much as possible the diversity of viewpoints and experiences in the municipality.

The following criteria were used to choose interview subjects: (1) political orientation: pro- or anti-Sandinista; (2) role in supporting the contras: civilian collaborator or combatant; (3) class origin: poor peasant, middle peasant, or finquero; and (4) zone of origin: the town of Quilalí, the river valley, or an outlying mountain community. In addition, I interviewed a number of community leaders who had special knowledge of important events in the municipality's history, as well as former Sandinista Army and State Security personnel. Table A.1 provides a description of the peasants interviewed for this study.

Table A.1
Description of Interview Sample

	Economic Status			Place of Origin			Sex		TOTAL
	Finquero	Middle	Poor	Town	Valley	Mountains	Male	Female	
Pro-Sandinistas	3	9	11	5	14	4	18	5	**23**
Anti-Sandinistas									
Ex-Combatants	10	6	11	2	11	14	26	1	27
Collaborators	5	7	19	3	13	15	15	16	31
Community Leaders/ Military Personnel									**21**
TOTAL	**18**	**22**	**41**	**10**	**38**	**33**	**59**	**22**	

n = 102

Before coming to Quilalí, I was able to obtain a list of key community leaders, and from these initial contacts I received further suggestions of people to interview. While living and working in Quilalí, I also met a number of potential interview subjects through day-to-day informal encounters. In addition, I conducted random house-to-house interviews in three communities in the municipality: El Pimiento, a small settlement of ex-contras and their families on the outskirts of town; San Bartolo, a largely pro-Sandinista cooperative settlement community in Quilalí's river valley; and La Vigía, a strongly anti-Sandinista community also located in the river valley.

I had originally planned to conduct an additional series of house-to-house interviews in the northern mountain community of El Súngano, but was unable to visit more than a few families there because of the ongoing military activity in the zone. In order to include the perspective of more remote mountain communities, I relied instead on peasants from these communities who had recently settled in town or the river valley. Along with my research in Quilalí, I also traveled to the northern cities of Estelí and Ocotal to interview former Sandinista Army officers and FSLN party members who had served in Quilalí during the war years.

In all these interviews my primary concern was to create an atmosphere of trust in which peasants felt secure and free to express their opinions as honestly as possible. As suggested by the experience of the 1990 elections, in which the majority of surveys inaccurately predicted an FSLN victory, Nicaraguans may be reluctant to reveal to interviewers their views on sensitive political topics (Bischoping and Schuman 1992, 1994; Barnes 1992; Anderson 1994a). In addition, many Quilalí peasants have faced hostile interrogations over the course of the war, and because their very survival has at times depended on it, they have mastered the art of evasion and silence. Some poor peasants are also unused to speaking with foreigners or outsiders, and women in particular are often initially shy and quiet with strangers.

For these reasons, and because of the high levels of illiteracy in the municipality, a quantifiable questionnaire was discarded as unworkable for Quilalí and for the sensitive topics being covered. I chose instead to conduct semistructured interviews composed of open questions that covered key points of the peasant experience in Quilalí and at the same time allowed peasants to bring up any other information and opinions they felt were important. Appendix B presents an outline of interview topics.

I tape-recorded these semistructured interviews whenever possible. As a rule, this was possible during interviews conducted in the town of Quilalí itself. In the countryside, however, many peasants were reluctant to have their conversation taped, and I relied instead on handwritten notes. In other more informal conversations where taking notes would have been inappropriate, I wrote down a summary of the conversation as soon as possible afterward.

While in the 1990s new opportunities for research opened up in formerly conflictive zones, collecting peasant testimonies in the municipality of Quilalí still presented a number of unique challenges. One important difficulty in conducting research in Nicaragua's rural interior in the early 1990s was the deep postwar polarization of peasant communities. Typical of conflictive research sites in which "no neutrals are allowed" (Sluka 1990), Quilalí was deeply divided into Sandinista and anti-Sandinista camps, and many residents attempted to quickly assess the political sympathies of outsiders to the municipality. This assessment in turn might influence a subject's responses during the interview process.

During my stay in Quilalí I was often asked if I was staying at the home of a well-known Quilalí Sandinista activist. Implicit in the question was a query as to whether or not I myself was sympathetic to the FSLN. Later, when word spread that the family with whom I was staying had relatives who had fought with the contras, several Sandinista military officials questioned whether I might be working for the CIA. In view of this situation, I took great care during my stay in

Quilalí to maintain as neutral an appearance as possible. I frequently explained that the purpose of the interviews was to allow Quilalí residents from both sides of the conflict to share their experiences and opinions, and that as an outsider to the zone it was not my role to judge or take sides. I also always attempted to balance the time I spent with pro-Sandinistas and anti-Sandinistas.

During interviews I was careful as well to employ neutral language and avoid politically charged terms. I referred to the contras, for example, as "the Resistance" *(la Resistencia)* or the "comandos," terms that anti-Sandinistas prefer. As an indication of the importance of language in Quilalí and other mountain zones, it is interesting to note that peasants developed their own code words for the two armed groups. Rather than refer to them directly by name, Sandinista Army soldiers are "these people" *(esta gente),* and the contras "those people" *(esa gente).* Contras are also commonly referred to as the "people of the underbrush" *(la gente del monte)* or the "cousins" *(los primos).* Some Quilalí residents were not entirely comfortable with my neutral stance and pressed me to more clearly define my own political views. Most peasants, however, appeared to accept my outsider status, and in some cases it may have even been an advantage in allowing peasants a cathartic expression of their grievances and fears to an outside listener.

The continued violence and presence of armed recontra bands in the municipality also meant that some peasants remained cautious about expressing their opinions or speaking openly on certain sensitive topics. A community leader in one settlement community who was an active Sandinista supporter, for example, became uncomfortable and changed the subject when I asked how long he had supported the FSLN. Later that same evening, recontras visited the settlement community, attempted to kidnap several people, and threatened the man I had spoken to earlier.

Furthermore, fear of retribution by recontras may have prevented some anti-Sandinista civilians from speaking openly of contra and recontra abuses against the peasant population. To underscore this point, in one interview I was given a not so veiled warning by a recontra supporter: "If you go into the mountains and speak badly of the Resistance [contras], you won't come out again." Many anti-Sandinista civilian peasants also expressed fear of Sandinista State Security (which in fact was dissolved in 1990), and some were reluctant to discuss their full range of activities with the contras in the 1980s or with the recontras in the 1990s.

To broach the sensitive topic of human rights with ex-contras, rather than asking former contras directly if they themselves had committed human rights abuses, a question almost certain to lead to an automatic denial and to mistrust, I asked instead, "Did you ever see or hear of abuses committed against civilians by the Resistance?" From peasants' response to this question, I was able to gauge their openness to further discussing the issue.

In general a Quilalí peasant will rarely state directly, "I don't want to talk to you," or "I don't want to answer that question." Instead he or she will offer an ambiguous answer or change the subject. In such cases, I would rephrase the question and ask it again later. If the respondent still gave no clear answer or seemed uncomfortable, I dropped the topic altogether. For this reason, not all the topics in the semistructured questionnaire were addressed in every interview, as would have been ideal.

As a rule, pro-Sandinista peasants in the town and the river valley settlement communities were the most willing to talk and share their opinions and experiences. This may be in part because of the positive experiences these peasants had with foreign visitors during the war years, and their greater familiarity with meetings and interviews. In the postwar period many Quilalí Sandinista supporters, particularly former Sandinista Army officers, also speak very openly with outsiders about FSLN internal divisions and Sandinista policy errors, something that may not have been as common during the war. Among Quilalí's ex-contras, there was also a fair degree of openness to be interviewed, and all agreed to allow the conversation to be taped. Many ex-contras, while unwilling to discuss certain aspects of their wartime experience, in fact used these interviews as an opportunity to vent their frustration and anger over the postwar situation.

The most difficult interviews to conduct were those with civilian contra collaborators. In general, these peasants were more fearful than ex-contra combatants, perhaps as a by-product of their vulnerable situation as civilians in a war zone and their lack of previous contact with either foreigners or journalists. I therefore carried out interviews with anti-Sandinista peasants more informally, and in most cases taping was not possible.

In a number of cases I found it helpful to sit with the family for a little while, often while women were busy with household chores, and talk about day-to-day matters—the children, the weather, the crops. Only when I sensed that the family felt comfortable with my presence would I broach more serious matters. In some cases, multiple visits were necessary to gain the confidence of the family. At other times I was clearly unsuccessful in winning the trust of peasants. I attempted, for example, to interview peasant members of the evangelical Free Church who carried out a campaign of passive resistance against Sandinista authorities. The families were openly reluctant to speak with me and instead directed me to the houses of several well-known Sandinista supporters in the community.

In addition to these challenges of interviewing peasants in a polarized and conflictive context, several points should be made about the accuracy and veracity of the testimony gathered. First, as a rule Quilalí peasants have a poor memory for dates and numerical data. Wherever possible, I attempted to independently verify such information through other sources such as government reports and the few written studies that exist on the municipality.

Another challenge that arose was the tendency of some interviewees to distort or exaggerate the facts. This can be seen in part as a product of a deeply polarized society in which defending and sustaining one's point of view or particular worldview takes precedence over factual accuracy. In Quilalí's rural culture little importance is placed on verifying the facts, and unsubstantiated rumors and accounts of events play a powerful role in the municipality's oral tradition.

In cases where I questioned the accuracy of the portrayal of an event, I made an effort to confirm the information by consulting with other knowledgeable Quilalí residents. To give an example, one anti-Sandinista informant told me that soon after the FSLN took power hundreds of Cubans were brought to Quilalí to take over all government functions. After discussing the issue with several other Quilalí residents, I was able to conclude that this was an exaggeration, although dozens of Cuban doctors and military personnel did serve in Quilalí during the war. As a rule, the testimony that is directly cited in this study is drawn from those respondents whom I judged to be the most credible. Given the ultimately subjective nature of the testimonies on which this study is based, however, and because little written documentation exists on the contemporary history of Quilalí, it is likely that despite my best efforts to independently confirm events and information, there are still some inaccuracies.

Finally, I would like to emphasize that the overwhelming majority of Quilalí residents, both pro-Sandinista and anti-Sandinista supporters, warmly welcomed me into their homes. They showed great patience in sharing their life experiences and taking the time to answer the many questions of a curious gringa. In this study, I have attempted to represent as accurately as possible the experiences of Quilalí peasants and to integrate often conflicting points of view into a common local history as coherently as possible. I also recognize that much work remains to be done on this fascinating and tragic period of Nicaragua's rural history.

Appendix B

Interview Guide

Demographic Data

- Date of birth
- Brothers and sisters/spouse/children
- Educational level
- Community of origin
- Amount of land owned, sharecropped, borrowed, or rented by you/your family
- Number of animals owned by you/your family
- Crops raised
- Assessment of living conditions to determine economic status

Prerevolutionary Background

- Where is your family from?
- When did they come to Quilalí and why?

- What was life like in Quilalí at that time?
- What were your aspirations at that time?
- What difficulties did peasants face at that time?
- What political parties, other organizations, or religions did you/ your family belong to?
- What were relations like between the colonos and the patrons?
- Description of the land situation in Quilalí before the revolution
- Was it easy to obtain land?
- Who owned the land at that time?
- Were families more or less equal or did some families have more than others? Why?
- Describe colono (sharecropping) arrangements.

FSLN Guerrillas and the Revolution

- Did you have any contact with the FSLN guerrillas?
- Who were they? What were they fighting for? Did you support their cause?
- What did you think when you heard that the Sandinistas had defeated Somoza?
- What program did the FSLN have for Nicaragua?
- Did you agree with this? What did you like about the revolution? Dislike?
- Did you participate in any new organizations or activities during the revolution? Describe your experience.
- How did the FSLN carry out land reform here in Quilalí? Did you agree or disagree? Were you or family/friends directly affected?
- Would you support land reform? What type of land reform?
- How would you describe the relationship between Nicaragua and the United States?
- How would you describe wealthy residents of Quilalí?

- Did the revolution benefit or hurt Quilalí? Who benefited? Who was hurt?
- Why was there war in Quilalí?

Counterrevolution

- Who were the first people to rise up against the Sandinistas? Why did they do it?
- Did you agree or disagree with them?
- How did the FSLN respond to the first MILPA bands?
- What were the contras fighting for? What type of political/economic program?
- What do you mean by democracy/communism (if these terms were used by respondent)?
For Anti-Sandinistas:
- When did you first come in contact with the contras?
- When did you begin to collaborate with them? Why?
- What did you do for them?
- When did you take up arms with the contras? Why?
- Were other family members/friends also in the contras?
- Description of time spent with contras, including leadership/military aspects/training role of United States

Civilian Population/Human Rights

- Describe day-to-day life during the war.
- How were things economically during the war?
- Was farming (corn, cattle, coffee, tobacco) profitable?
- Did you agree or disagree with selling your crops to ENABAS?
- Did you participate in any religious activities?
- How did the Sandinista Army treat you/other civilians?

- How did Sandinista State Security treat you/other civilians?
- How did the contras treat you/other civilians?

Postwar Quilalí

- Describe the postwar situation
- Is Nicaragua now a democracy?
- What is your opinion of the Chamorro government?
- Why does violence continue in Quilalí?
- What is necessary for peace?
- Do you support the actions of the recontras?
- What are the greatest needs/problems you/other peasants face now?

Notes

Preface

1. In this study the terms *interior* or *the mountains* encompass the following northern and central departments: Estelí, Madriz, Nueva Segovia, Jinotega, Matagalpa, Boaco, Chontales, and Zelaya Central.

2. In this study the term *peasant* refers broadly to those individuals who work in agriculture and occupy a subordinate position in a hierarchical economic and political order (Colburn 1989b, ix) and is roughly equivalent to the Spanish term *campesino* as used in Nicaragua.

3. It is highly likely that the actual number of contra combatants is somewhat less than this figure indicates. Apparently in the weeks before the contra demobilization, weapons were distributed to civilians who wished pass themselves off as contra combatants in order qualify for land and other potential postwar benefits.

4. In 1987 the contras officially changed their name from the Nicaraguan Democratic Force (FDN) to the Nicaraguan Army of Resistance (Ejército Nicaragüense de la Resistencia).

5. See for example, Michael Klare and Peter Kornbluh, eds., *Low Intensity Warfare: Counterinsurgency, Proinsurgency and Anti-Terrorism in the Eighties* (New York: Pantheon Books, 1988); Peter Kornbluh, *The Price of Intervention: Reagan's War against the Sandinistas* (Washington, D.C.: Institute for Policy Studies, 1987); William I. Robinson and Kent Norsworthy, *David and Goliath: The U.S. War against Nicaragua* (New York: Monthly Review Press, 1987); and Roy Gutman, *Banana Diplomacy: The Making of American Policy in Nicaragua, 1981–87* (New York: Simon and Schuster, 1988).

6. One exception to this is Bendaña's (1991) collection of testimonies of former contras.

7. For further discussion of the methodological issues and challenges involved in carrying out these interviews, see appendix A.

Chapter 1

1. In contrast, Paige (1975), who focuses on the role of social relations of production in shaping rural rebellion rather than specific rural sectors, views peasant revolutionary mobilization as coming from within already established capitalist sectors in the countryside.

2. Wickham-Crowley (1992) also addresses the broader structural context of peasant rebellion and links the FSLN's success in overthrowing the Somoza government both to sustained rural support and multiclass opposition to a "sultanistic" regime.

3. Starn (1995) also warns against dualistic analysis that labels peasant movements as either resistant or hegemonic, subversive or coopted. He argues that counterinsurgency rondas campesinas in Peru, while subject to army control and abuses and coercive in nature, have also provided protection and violence-free space, and perhaps even a sense of empowerment to peasant participants. In Quilalí, the experience of peasants as contra combatants fostered new demands on the state, many of which extended beyond the original aims of the contras as defined by its leadership, and gave peasants the self-confidence and military skills to pursue those demands thorugh violence.

4. See, for example, Deere et al. (1985); Baumeister and Neira Cuadra (1986); Kaimowitz (1986, 1988, 1989); Luciak (1987a, 1987b, 1990, 1995); Zalkin (1987, 1988, 1990); and Enriquez (1991, 1997).

5. Vandon and Prevost (1993); Oquist (1990); Castro (1992); Bendaña (1991); and CIPRES (1991) offer a sympathetic yet not uncritical analysis of FSLN policies. Radu (1990); Miranda and Ratliff (1993); and Morales Carazo (1989) are strongly critical of the FSLN and sympathetic to the contras. For example, according to Morales Carazo the contras emerged as a "desperate armed response to the abuses, imposition of dogmatic schemes, and errors of perception and implementation of the Sandinistas" (1989: 28).

Chapter 2

1. These municipalities are Condega, Pueblo Nuevo, Limay, Estelí, La Trinidad, and San Nicolas in Estelí; Totogalpa, Somoto, San Lucas, Las Sabanas, Cusmapa, Yalaguina, and Palacaguina in Madriz; and Macuelizo, Ocotal, and Santa María in Nueva Segovia (CIPRES 1990b, 39).

2. One *manzana* (MZ) equals 1.7 acres.

3. All Quilalí names used in this study are pseudonyms, with the exception of several nationally recognized contra and recontra leaders. All translations are the author's.

4. Houses were burned in the hamlets of Jabalí, Plan Grande, El Barro, Ventillas, and Buena Vista (Selser 1979, 115). See also Schroeder (1993, 448–49).

5. "Pedrón," as he was popularly known, was Sandino's general most accused of human rights violations. See Schroeder (1993, 507) for discussion of Sandino's tactics of knife cuts *(cortes)*, summary executions, and extortion.

6. FSLN guerrilla leader Omar Cabezas writes, for example, that northern peasants had a "Sandinista history, a history of rebellion against exploitation, against North American domination" (quoted in Wickham-Crowley 1992, 246).

7. One quintal equals 100 lbs.

8. In the western Segovian municipalities of Estelí and Condega, 44 percent and 34 percent of peasants, respectively, participated in sharecropping arrangements (CIERA 1984, 64).

9. According to a peasant from Matagalpa: "We didn't go to the judge or to the lawyer. We did what we call a promise of sale *(promesa de venta)* . . . with two witnesses from the same community" (quoted in Bendaña 1991, 72).

10. The largest such IAN project, the Rigoberto Cabezas Project, brought approximately 5,000 families to live in the Nueva Guinea zone of southeastern Nicaragua. Each family was given perpetual rights to between 25 and 70 MZ of national land (Aznar et al. 1989, 117).

11. One arroba equals 25 lbs.

12. Estimate of a Quilalí UNAG representative.

13. Basic data about these sectors are taken from MIDINRA (1987), the only detailed study of the municipality's pre-1990 class structure available. Because of this limited information on class structures in Quilalí, I have confined my discussion and analysis to the four broad economic sectors described below. While ideally I would have liked to have been able to further break down, for example, the class that is broadly termed here middle peasants, those who own from 10 to 199 MZ of land, reliable data are not available. In the literature a variety of different definitions and terms are used, not always consistently, to describe Nicaragua's rural classes (Spalding 1994, 263). The size of landholdings has most commonly been used to categorize Nicaragua's rural population (226). The use of the size of landholdings as

the only measure of rural class is not entirely satisfactory, however, as it fails to take into account such important variables as land quality, crops grown, the purchase and sale of labor, and forms of access to land. I have tried to indicate wherever possible how the terms I use here correspond to those found in other studies.

14. Large landowners are also referred to as the large bourgeoisie *(la gran burguesía)* and in most studies are clearly distinguished from the finquero sector described below.

15. Spalding (1994, 93–94), drawing on Núñez, characterizes these elites as those who run who their farms from afar, are closely tied to international markets and the U.S., and are involved in profitable processing and marketing.

16. The extensive cattle ranches of the Segovias were characterized by low productivity and little creation of work (Kaimowitz 1989, 402).

17. By 1944 the Somoza family owned fifty-one cattle ranches and forty-six coffee plantations throughout Nicaragua (Booth 1985, 67).

18. This roughly defined finquero sector is referred to by a variety of terms: the *chapiollos,* middle bourgeoisie *(mediana burguesía),* strong farmers *(agricultores fuertes),* and middle cattlemen *(medianos ganaderos).* (See CIERA 1981a, 1982; MIDINRA 1983, 1987.) The group that this study labels finqueros also falls within Zalkin's (1989) classification of "upper rich peasant" and Kaimowitz's (1986, 1988) "peasant capitalists" and "medium commercial producers."

19. Other general characteristics of this "peasant capitalist" sector are that they: (1) participate directly in production and also hire labor; (2) are socially part of the peasant milieu; (3) are commercial producers highly sensitive to prices and economic incentives and seek to maximize profits; (4) emerged on the agricultural frontier or are small merchants and professionals who have purchased land; and (5) politically received few benefits from Somoza (Kaimowitz 1986, 103–4). Luciak also characterizes these chapiollos as rooted in domestic culture with a "deep emotional attachment to their land" (1995, 84).

20. In the department of Jinotega these *agricultores fuertes,* who owned from 50 to 100 MZ of coffee, were often members of prominent Jinotega families who went into the mountains as young men. They were either given land by their father or paid for mejoras on national lands and began farming food crops, later expanding into coffee (CIERA 1981a, 12).

21. These merchants and farmers were part of a widespread "complex network of rural intermediaries who, although exploitative, made available

the necessary capital goods and manufactured personal consumption items in exchange for agricultural products" (Kaimowitz 1988, 117).

22. Zalkin (1989, 578) defines middle peasants as those who neither purchase nor sell labor on a regular basis. Bendaña (1991, 41) characterizes middle and rich peasants as that 25 percent of rural population that participates directly in agricultural production, owns oxen or a vehicle, and occasionally hires outside labor. Unlike Bendaña, I would argue that while this sector provided strong support for the counterrevolution, the initial internal leadership for the contra movement did not come from this stratum, but a distinct, wealthier, and numerically smaller finquero sector.

23. For a description of this process in the Nueva Guinea zone, see Aznar et al. (1989, 118).

24. Kaimowitz (1988, 118). See also Serra (1993, 22–23) and CIERA (1981a, 17) for a description of the role of the *agricultores fuertes* (strong farmers) in controlling both internal relations in rural hamlets and as intermediaries to the exterior world. In Wiwilí, poor peasants saw their patron as an "economic model . . . lender to the poor, source of work, the *compadre,* a person with power, even if he was arrogant, abusive, and exploitative. . . . The poor know they had nothing to gain and much to lose, rebelling against their patron" (Mendoza 1990, 33).

25. Bendaña (1991, 17) describes wealthy peasants as "transmission belts of values, perceptions, and examples that profoundly impacted the rest of peasants" and a link between the bourgeoisie and the poor. I had the opportunity to witness such relationships firsthand during a stay at the house of a finquero in the town of Yalí. The man's house was located on a road leading out of town and throughout the day peasants would pass by on foot and horseback and stop to share news, ask favors, and seek advice.

26. Among Quilalí residents there is a tendency to present the prerevolutionary period as completely *tranquilo* and trouble-free, particularly in comparison to the war that followed, and this may lead informants to minimize earlier conflicts and tensions between extended families or social classes. In this case, however, there was almost unanimous agreement among informants that harmony prevailed between the wealthy and poor in prerevolutionary Quilalí.

27. By 1964, 10,000 residents of the department of Chinandega had participated in peasant movements (Gould 1990a, 72).

28. Between 1962 and 1969, villages in the department of Matagalpa with assistance from the Nicaraguan Socialist Party organized at least twenty-one peasant unions to resist encroaching cattle haciendas (Gould 1990a, 79; see

also Williams 1986, 129–34). Williams (1986), Booth (1985), and Wickham-Crowley (1992) cite such insecurity of landholdings and abuses against the rural poor as an important factor in peasant support for FSLN guerrillas in Nicaragua's northern mountains. In contrast, studies of other zones such as the municipality of Yalí report that, as in Quilalí, there was no local history of "violent and large-scale dislodgings" (MIDINRA 1985b). (See also Escuela de Sociología UCA 1987.)

Chapter 3

1. The Quilalí residents identified to me by other community members as former Somoza supporters or National Guard spies were very reluctant to discuss their prerevolutionary political views or activities on behalf of the Somoza regime.

2. See Wickham-Crowley (1992, 138–40) on the importance of existing social networks in the successful development of peasant support for guerrilla groups.

3. Spalding (1994, 49). Paige (1997, 279) interviewed Nicaraguan large growers, who reported that they deeply resented the corruption, intrusiveness, and backwardness of the Somocista state. The great majority of these growers, however, were not directly economically harmed by the Somoza regime and their opposition to Somoza's economic policies was global and not specific (280).

4. See also the testimony of well-off producer, merchant, and contra leader Luis Fley ("Jhonson") from the department of Matagalpa. According to Dillon, who interviewed Fley extensively: "Like the vast majority of rural men who joined the contras, he [Fley] was fighting for a simple vision of good government" (1991, xiii). In an interview with Castillo Rivas (1993, 151), MILPA leader Tirzo Moreno "Rigoberto" also stated that his "democratic convictions" led him to take up arms against the FSLN. Paige (1997, 295) reports that large growers he interviewed listed the Sandinistas' commitment to political pluralism and democracy, understood as contested elections and oppositional rights, as an important factor in their support for the FSLN.

5. Wickham-Crowley (1992, 231) links relatively strong support for the FSLN guerrillas in Quilalí and other interior zones to four key factors: (1) a high rate of sharecropping or squatting; (2) recent or long-term histories of assault on land security; (3) a history of resistance to central authorities; and

(4) social and cultural structures that provide access to the peasant population. The analysis presented here places greater emphasis on the latter two factors. While Quilalí, like other agricultural frontier zones, had a large number of squatters, none of the peasants interviewed for this study identified assaults on land security as a prerevolutionary source of conflict.

6. In the western Segovian communities studied by CIPRES (1990a, 107), prerevolutionary community leaders, who tended to be from more well off sectors, often assumed new roles after 1979 as the heads of credit cooperatives and CDSs.

7. Hale (1994, 132) describes a similar process on Nicaragua's Atlantic coast in which the defeat of Somoza released a "floodgate of aspirations."

8. In 1980, INRA merged with the Ministry of Agriculture to become the Ministry of Agricultural Development and Agrarian Reform (Ministerio de Desarrollo Agropecuario y Reforma Agraria, MIDINRA).

9. In the department of Nueva Segovia as a whole the amount of land held by the largest farms (500 MZ or more) fell from 71 percent in 1978 to 57 percent in 1984 (Kaimowitz 1989, 404).

10. For further discussion of mass organizations and their relationship to the FSLN, including tensions generated by the FSLN tendency toward top-down, vertical control of organizations and the development of grassroots democracy, see Ruchwarger (1987, 1989), Serra (1991, 1993), Vandon and Prevost (1993), and Luciak (1995).

11. It is important to keep mind that the description of revolutionary ideology presented here is taken from the point of view of Quilalí peasants themselves. I would argue that certain aspects of the Sandinista program, in particular the FSLN's attitude toward the wealthy, were more ambivalent and complex than the version given here.

Chapter 4

1. The Quilalí-Yalí MILPAs described here should not be confused with the MILPAs that were associated with the ultra-left Movimiento de Acción Popular-Marxist Leninista (MAP-ML) during the insurrection and that carried out activities of sabotage.

2. Half of those who participated in the original MILPA uprising were "large or small bourgeoisie" and their sons (CIERA 1989, 6:253).

3. Bendaña (1991, 47). See also the FSLN's El Crucero document (IHCA 1990, 38), which cites early indiscriminate expropriations of large, middle, and some small producers as one factor in the 1990 Sandinista electoral defeat.

4. The reasons behind this law were: (1) to bring idle land back into production and increase basic grain output; (2) to meet peasant demand for secure access to land; and (3) to quiet the fears of the bourgeoisie by resolving the land issue (Deere et al. 1985, 91).

5. Unfortunately, little documentation exists that would allow us to accurately judge the extent, timing, or political impact of such expropriations in interior zones where the contras were active. Politically motivated expropriations were also reported in the municipality of San Juan del Río Coco, where members of the "local bourgeoisie" organized an association of coffee growers (CORCASANJ). In mid-1982, Sandinista State Security found out that the leaders of this group had joined the contras and confiscated their possessions (MIDINRA 1983, 7).

6. One Sandinista official estimated that nationwide 80 percent of forced buyouts occurred in 1984–85, when the war was already well under way (Spalding 1994, 84).

7. Evidence that fear of future expropriations rather than actual land confiscations were the impetus for the MILPA uprising comes from the municipality of Yalí. In the communities of La Rica and Constancia, where the MILPAs were strongest, no expropriations of land had taken place as of 1980 (CIERA 1989, 6:255).

8. In her survey of Nicaraguan elites Spalding (1994, 146) found, not surprisingly, that 88 percent who underwent full-scale expropriation had a strongly or moderately negative view of the Sandinista regime. Yet even among those elites who had never been expropriated, 65 percent moderately or strongly opposed the FSLN. Spalding concludes that the fact that elites had not yet undergone this experience gave them little sense of permanent security or protection. Large growers interviewed by Paige (1997, 283–84, 286), who had either been directly affected by expropriation or knew of friends or family who had, also gave universal and bitter complaints about land confiscations, which they viewed as arbitrary, illegal, and politically motivated.

9. A similar process occurred on the Atlantic coast in which FSLN efforts at controlled mobilization and empowerment of formerly quiescent communities were eventually turned against the Sandinistas. As Hale (1994,

162) notes, by removing the constraining effects of historical Anglo affinity on the Atlantic coast, "the revolution paradoxically engendered an ethic militancy of unprecedented depth and intensity" that rapidly led to armed conflict between the FSLN and coastal antigovernment groups.

10. Similarly, the bourgeoisie had little incentive to participate under Sandinista hegemony "as long as it considered the overthrow of the regime a viable option" (Luciak 1995, 41).

11. Unfortunately, I was unable to determine the exact nature of these demands.

12. It is possible, of course, that former MILPA leaders wish to conceal the fact that they received external aid as early as 1980 in order to enhance the image of their own initiative and sacrifice. Peasants report, however, that in 1980 and 1981 the MILPAs appeared to be very ragtag bands possessing only a few old weapons. Only after about mid-1982, when most MILPA combatants were formally integrated with ex-National Guardsmen into the FDN, do Quilalí residents remember seeing uniformed, well-armed counterrevolutionary groups in the municipality.

13. Further details about the organization and participants in the July 1980 attack on Quilalí can be found in Dillon (1991, 49).

14. CIERA 1989, 6:244–45. A government study based on interviews with captured participants characterizes the ideology of the MILPA bands as "bourgeois," with a strong emphasis on the defense of private property. Participants reported, "they [the MILPA leaders] told us that they [the Sandinistas] were going to expropriate everything, that communism was coming."

15. While Bendaña (1991, 29) correctly points out the military insignificance of the MILPAs, I would argue that it is also important not to overlook the ideological importance of these groups.

16. The participation of finqueros in the MILPA bands above all else, "legitimated to the majority of the population of the *comarca,* counterrevolutionary activity" (CIERA 1981a, 19). Morales Carazo (1989, 35) also argues that without the MILPA leaders, ex-National Guardsmen would never have obtained a popular base or credibility.

17. As part of this study I interviewed two ex-National Guardsmen from the Quilalí zone, neither of whom was willing to discuss his experiences in the National Guard.

18. Morales Carazo (1989, 35) argues that with this bargain of necessity *(trueque de necesidades)* the MILPAs paid the high price of losing their autonomy and leadership with their new guardsmen partners.

19. According to U.S. Department of State (1987, 2) estimates, which may be inflated, in 1982 Nicaragua received approximately $160 million in military assistance from the Soviet bloc and Cuba, an amount that increased to $590 million in 1986.

Chapter 5

1. These zones include Río Blanco (MIDINRA 1984b, 11) and Siuna (MIDINRA 1985a, 25).

2. Biondi-Morra (1992, 25–27). Biondi-Morra blames the failure of state farms on incoherent government food pricing policies, which led to shortages and inefficiencies in storage and processing; an overvalued exchange rate, which reduced the profitability of exports; low salaries, which reduced productivity; and subsidized credit, which led state farms to take on massive debts.

3. This pattern in Quilalí followed a national trend in which paternalistic services were replaced with "standardized bureaucratic norms which provided little flexibility for interacting with local labor and commodity markets. Often they [state farms] became 'islands' of socialism, connected more closely to Managua than the surrounding communities" (Kaimowitz 1988, 124).

4. According to Wickham-Crowley (1991, 235), a guerrilla force, as a counterstate in formation, is obliged to protect the peasantry from retaliatory violence if it wishes to continue to maintain their support. The same argument can be applied here, that a revolutionary state attempting to consolidate its military and political hegemony must provide physical and economic security to its supporters.

5. Castro (1992, 137). It is likely, however, that these voting results are also in part a reflection of self-selection, that is peasants who were to some degree already sympathetic to the FSLN joined and remained in cooperatives.

6. In the municipality of Paiwás, in the department of Matagalpa, progressive Catholic church programs were instrumental in creating a strong base of peasant support for revolutionary change. In 1983, however, local church leaders report that as contra groups began to target church leaders and community activists, thousands of peasants fled the mountains and sought refuge inside the town of Paiwás (personal communication with church workers).

7. CIPRES (1990b, 82–83). During my travels in Nicaragua's interior, I was told of a process of geographical polarization of peasants in such diverse areas of Nicaragua as the departments of Estelí and Chontales. See also the MIDINRA (1984b, 11) Río Blanco study.

8. The term *exploitation*, which was spontaneously mentioned by a number of both Sandinista and anti-Sandinista respondents, was a very emotionally charged issue. To give one example, returning from a conversation with known Sandinista supporters, I was approached by a former contra on Quilalí's main street who asked me in an agitated manner: "They [the Sandinistas] told you it was exploitation didn't they? They always talk about exploitation."

9. It is important to remember that while this section focuses on the explicit and implicit ways in which the FSLN challenged paternalistic ties, overall Sandinista policy toward the wealthy was more ambiguous than the somewhat simplified perspective presented here. FSLN programs economically benefited a number of finqueros, and politically the FSLN made a number of efforts to coopt what came to be known as Quilalí's patriotic producers. For a different interpretation of FSLN policy in the neighboring municipality of Wiwilí, see Mendoza (1990), who argues that national revolutionary discourse created artificial class barriers in once harmonious communities. The present study holds that, based on economic criteria, class divisions already existed in Quilalí before the arrival of the revolution and that what the FSLN did was for the first time explicitly question their fairness and legitimacy.

10. See Hale's (1994, 163) argument that the support of Nicaragua's poor for their patrons is not simply "confusion" or "false consciousness," but rather has a material base.

11. In the western Segovias, paternalistic networks gained strength in the 1980s with the scarcity of labor and agricultural inputs (CIPRES 1990a, 78). Well-off producers maintained their leadership roles in the western Segovias by either blocking revolutionary organizations or using them to respond their particular interests. A study of the municipality of San Juan del Río Coco also found that the influence of the local bourgeoisie increased after 1979 and that by the mid-1980s this group was the only one with functioning trucks (MIDINRA 1983, 29).

12. In her study of several Nicaraguan villages, Anderson describes relationships of "ecological interdependence" in which peasants are "constantly aware of their own vulnerability and of the extent to which they depend on community support for survival" (1994, 3). I would argue that it is also im-

portant to examine carefully the role that wealth and power differences may play in shaping the terms of interdependence as well as actual and potential conflicts of interest between community members.

13. These views are not necessarily unique to Quilalí peasants. In a 1990 postelection poll, 71 percent of rural respondents agreed that "the poor need the rich in order to live" (Castro 1992, 135).

14. In his informal survey of contra combatants Morales Carazo found that an important objective that these peasants fought for was to be able to "believe freely in God and practice their religion, whatever it may be, respecting their spiritual guides, customs, and traditions" (1989, 69).

15. According to Kaimowitz (1988, 125–26), Sandinista rural policies "offer little to the poorest peasants" and the FSLN policy of support for state farms and large private producers' land rights left poor peasants with little hope of gaining more access to land.

16. A study of rural social classes in Chontales reports that poor peasants were more favorably inclined toward the revolution but tended to resent the "discipline" of mass organizations, particularly attempts to control consumption of alcohol (CIERA 1982, 237).

17. A post-1990 election survey of peasants provides additional evidence that the FSLN's agrarian reform was viewed as a politicized process by anti-Sandinista peasants. A majority of those who voted for the UNO opposition believed that the FSLN benefited Sandinistas or "others." In contrast, 73.7 percent of those peasants who believed that the FSLN benefited the poor voted for the FSLN in 1990 (Castro 1990a, 13).

18. A similar process took place on the Atlantic coast, where the arrival of the FSLN created new expectations among the population. Hale (1994, 79) states "I sensed the collective excitement of this period only through brief excerpts in accounts burdened by all that followed"—the "troubles" that began in February 1981.

19. Luciak (1987a, 139) argues that the slow pace of land redistribution from 1981 to 1985 was primarily a product of the FSLN's desire for national unity and a response to a very negative reaction by the bourgeoisie to expropriations from 1981–82.

20. For example, in the department of Wiwilí, "a poor peasant felt the blow when they [the FSLN] confiscated his patron, and at the same time he felt threatened and abandoned when [the FSLN] coddled [favored and protected] his patron. Both feelings at once" (Mendoza 1990, 34).

21. In 1987 there were sixteen officially recognized stores run by private individuals and CASs in the municipality. Six were located in the town of

Quilalí, seven in the river valley, two in the western section of the municipality, and one in the northern sector (MIDINRA 1987, 62).

22. MIDINRA (1985b). A study of the municipality of Pantasma also reported that small coffee growers in three communities that were among the first to take up arms with the contras were economically harmed by lack of adequate infrastructure and services, and credit delays (MIDINRA 1984c, 85).

23. Peter Utting found that in the 1983–84 harvest, for highly mechanized corn producers, production costs were only 57 percent of the producer price paid by the government. For peasant producers using traditional technology, however, production costs surpassed producer prices by 18 percent leading to net losses (cited in Spalding 1994, 92).

24. CIERA (1989, 6:53). In some interior rural zones, such as Río Blanco, no effective FSLN party structure had been established as late as 1984 (MIDINRA 1984b, 2).

25. A post-1990 election survey by Castro (1992, 143–44) indicates that the FSLN was most successful in those communities where the Sandinista leadership had roots in the community and responded to local demands. In such cases the FSLN gained "credibility" and "real power."

26. A number of Sandinista supporters in Quilalí, for example, argue that poor peasants in particular supported the contras because they were "deceived" and manipulated by contra propaganda.

27. Escuela de Sociología-UCA (1987, 17). The contras' Jorge Salazar Regional Command, which operated in the twenty-eight comarcas of Villa Sandino and Santo Domingo under study, was able to unite workers, colonos, middle, and rich peasants in a common defense against Sandinista aggression toward their economic world. In Matiguás, Matagalpa peasants from a variety of different social classes also participated in the counterrevolution (CIERA 1989, 6:262).

Chapter 6

1. Estimates of the number of contra combatants throughout the 1980s vary considerably. This figure is taken from Morales Carazo (1989, 57).

2. According to ex-army officers in Quilalí, they learned useful technical and organizational skills from the Cubans, but their trainers seemed more knowledgeable about conventional combat of fixed positions than the guerrilla warfare being waged in Quilalí's mountains.

3. In 1992, for example, a former Sandinista State Security agent who had worked in Quilalí was killed by an ex-contra.

4. Hale (1994, 147) also reports a sharp increase in recruits to the counterrevolutionary forces after 1983 when the FSLN initiated a direct military presence in the community of Sandy Bay and strict security measures. The subsequent investigations and arrests of friends and relatives convinced many young men to take up arms.

5. Mendoza's (1990, 40) study of Wiwilí also reports that once one family member joined the contras he dragged others in.

6. As Anderson's study of Nicaraguan and Costa Rica villages suggests, peasants may act not only out of rational, calculated economic concerns, but also because of "moral concerns with right and wrong and the need for self-respect and dignity" (1990, 107).

7. Morales Carazo (1989, 69–72) conducted informal surveys of contra combatants and found that contras desired such things as freedom of religion; an end to foreign intervention and the draft; peace and a united family; respect for human rights and private property; and democracy. In terms of positive programs, contras requested credit and technical assistance; transportation; practical education; health; services for orphans, widows, and the disabled; and "that no one would be hungry." In this latter list paradoxically, appear many of the declared aims of the FSLN.

8. Morales Carazo (1989, 14). A CIPRES (1991, 45) study argues that the contra leadership never had a coherent vision of what they were fighting for or a popular program, and that the objectives the leadership did have differed from those of their poor- and middle-peasant base.

9. Dillon (1991, 109). He also reports that Bermúdez's field staff regularly stole half the FDN's food budget, leading to hunger among the troops (127).

10. Many Quilalí lower-ranking contras in particular seem to have regarded Colonel Enrique Bermúdez, "Comandante 3-80," with awe and few questioned his judgment in giving free rein to a circle of corrupt and abusive ex-National Guard officers in Honduras.

11. During this period, when U.S. aid was officially suspended, the contras received at least $32 million channeled through the National Security Council (Dillon 1991, 140).

Chapter 7

1. Everyday resistance is not formally organized and does not draw attention to the individual. It does, however, require tacit cooperation among resisters as well as networks of understanding and shared practices (Scott 1989, 6–7).

2. A study of the Jinotega and Matagalpa departments, Region VI, confirms this general trend. The agricultural frontier (the zone north of Kilambé, Bocay, Waslala, Río Blanco, and Paiwás) and the zones beyond the population centers of Yalí and Pantasma were zones of contra influence, where the only revolutionary presence was military. In contrast, the major towns—such as Jinotega, Matagalpa, Waslala, and Matiguás—were under FSLN control, with constant incursions by contra forces. The third zone of the region, which includes the dry areas such as San Dionisio, Sébaco, and Darío, was firmly under Sandinista control (CIPRES 1990b, 83).

3. Peasant support for guerrilla movements can be measured by (1) how many peasants are willing to commit resources to the guerrillas; (2) what kinds of resources they provide; and (3) under what circumstances (Wickham-Crowley 1992, 52). In the case of Quilalí, in at least twenty rural communities the contras appear to have received a wide variety of forms of support from the majority of the population.

4. "Terror is particularly common in guerrilla warfare because there is an aggregation and mixture of combatant, noncombatant, and support system into a very small social and geographical space" (Wickham-Crowley 1991, 255).

5. It seems likely that peasant women in Quilalí's conflictive zones were at particular risk of rape and other types of sexual abuse. Given the very sensitive and hidden nature of this topic in some rural communities, however, I did not feel it was appropriate in interviews to directly question women about it, and none of the women included in this study voluntarily mentioned sexual violence.

6. An Americas Watch (1987, 57) investigation found that mass arrests such as those carried out in the Quilalí area were common practice by Sandinista State Security in rural areas where the contras were active. It estimated that in the mid-1980s at any given time 300 such prisoners were held in State Security prisons.

7. "Chico Tiro," Francisco González Siles, was head of State Security in Pantasma. He was arrested and sentenced by Sandinista authorities to thirty years in prison for killing a civilian in 1988 (Americas Watch 1989, 27).

8. According to then vice minister of the MINT Luis Carrión, in the early years of the revolution the state carried out "many indiscriminate arrests." This policy changed by the mid-1980s, however, and the MINT varied its treatment of suspected peasant collaborators depending on their degree of involvement with the contras. Those who were "ideologically convinced" were repressed, and the poor were handled with techniques of persuasion

(cited in CIPRES 1991, 270). The Quilalí anti-Sandinista peasants interviewed, however, perceived no shift in State Security policy. In their minds, the repression continued unabated throughout the 1980s.

9. In response to reports of human rights abuses by contras, the U.S. Congress included in its 1986, $100-million aid package to the contra forces $3 million to promote contra programs and activities for the observance and advancement of human rights. As a result, some former contras from Quilalí received training in human rights and report being taught such things as "not to steal" and "to respect peasant women." Until the end of the war it appears that contra leaders could violate human rights with virtual impunity, however, and there are few documented cases in which contra commanders were punished, even for gross human rights violations (see Dillon 1991). For a different point of view see Radu (1990, 272), who argues that the U.S. government imposed "unrealistic" human rights standards on the contra forces that were incompatible with effective guerrilla warfare.

10. Dillon (1991) also provides details of a series of such abuses that took place in the Quilalí Regional Command in the late 1980s.

11. See Scott (1990) on such "hidden transcripts." Such an attitude is also found in the traditional Nicaraguan folktale of the Güegüense, who misleads or mocks authority from behind a mask of conformity (Barnes 1992, 89).

12. I observed several such church services in anti-Sandinista communities.

13. Stoll (1990, 313) argues that the open defiance of authority encouraged by liberation theology is in many cases "suicidal" and that the evangelical approach is much more in harmony with the instincts of the poor to avoid confrontation.

Chapter 8

1. Peasants from the zone of Nueva Guinea, who also were evacuated involuntarily, expressed similar complaints and remembered their earlier life in the mountains as "an idyllic world where man and nature lived in harmony and where family labor resulted in an improved well-being" (Aznar et al. 1989, 127).

2. Nationwide in 1989 only 33 percent of cooperatives had female members and 7 percent of individual land reform titles were held by women, generally the wives and mothers of soldiers killed in the war (Luciak 1995, 173).

3. Serra (1993, 40) argues that the FSLN essentially re-created patron-client relationships between the leaders of organizations, who had the power to distribute material and symbolic goods, and members who joined.

4. Data from Quilalí UNAG representatives. Work collectives were smaller than cooperatives and generally consisted of an extended family group that farmed collectively. In "dead furrow" cooperatives, individual members worked plots of land separated by an uncultivated furrow.

5. Whereas earlier expropriations were evenly divided between the Pacific coastal region and Nicaragua's interior, 76 percent of properties confiscated under the 1986 law were in Nicaragua's interior (Baumeister 1991, 239).

6. Kaimowitz (1986, 113). See also Spoor (1995) and Martinez (1993, 480) who argues that in the mid-1980s the FSLN simply incorporated new political and military goals into an existing policy framework with no reappraisal of the framework, and that these new policies still faced antipeasant bias in implementation.

7. Martinez notes, "legalizing tenure to small producers in and of itself, does nothing to alter agrarian social relations . . . in some instances it can even serve to tie peasants to highly exploitative relations" (1993, 482).

8. A study in the neighboring municipality of Wiwilí also found that certain communities that had benefited from FSLN agricultural assistance and had high levels of corn, coffee, and cattle production were strongly pro-contra (Mendoza 1990, 41).

9. See Enriquez's (1997) study of a government-sponsored development project in the Carazo plateau region, which finds that while individual landowners received economic benefits from the project, this did not necessarily translate into greater levels of political support for the FSLN.

10. Morales Carazo (1989). Miranda and Ratliff (1993, 249–50) blame the contras' military failure on: (1) lack of a legitimate nationalist program; (2) lack of strong political leadership; (3) the National Guard stigma; (4) lack of an urban presence; and (5) U.S. vacillation.

11. See Morales Carazo (1989), Radu (1990, 270). Leaders of indigenous anti-Sandinista forces on the Atlantic coast also never questioned their fundamental dependence on the United States, only specific requests and conditions that the CIA sought to impose (Hale 1994, 151).

Chapter 9

1. Estimates by Quilalí election officials.

2. In the disarmament zone, where I stayed in the department of Chon-

tales, inebriated contras shot off rounds of gunfire day and night, exploded grenades, and at times even fired into the UN camp.

3. Estimates of the number of contras who returned to Quilalí in the early 1990s vary widely from a low of 428 (CIPRES 1990b, 35) to a high of 1,000 (CIAV-OEA Estelí, personal communication).

4. Estimates of refugees who returned to the municipality also vary widely, from 1,000 individuals to as many as 5,000 returnees.

5. The 1991 PRODERE land survey shows a significantly greater number of landless and poor peasants than the data from MIDINRA (1987) would suggest. Part of the explanation for this discrepancy may lie in the hundreds of refugees and former contras who returned to the municipality in 1990 and lacked land. In addition, the PRODERE survey may have oversampled poor and landless peasants and some peasants may have understated their access to land in hopes of bolstering their claims to land being distributed by the government and international agencies at that time.

6. Many anti-Sandinista civilians and ex-contras in Quilalí regularly listened to Managua-based anti-Sandinista right-wing radio stations. Such programs tended to reinforce local fears that, for example, the Sandinista-controlled army and police force continued to persecute and kill former contras, although in fact such postwar abuses were uncommon in Quilalí.

7. At the urging of Senator Jesse Helms, U.S. government assistance to Nicaragua was suspended from May 1992 until April 1993 over these issues.

8. See IHCA (1992b) for a summary of the complex legal procedures and institutions involved in resolving property claims.

9. As of 1991, 1,900 ex-contras were in Region I (Nueva Segovia, Madriz, Estelí); 9,300 in Region VI (Jinotega, Matagalpa); 6,900 in Region V (Boaco, Chontales, Zelaya Central); and 4,800 were "dispersed" (IHCA 1991, 14).

10. UNAG statement, 18 March 1991.

11. I investigated several cases of this type in Region V of Nicaragua in 1991.

12. In 1991 recontra bands operated in the zones of Quilalí, Wiwilí, El Jícaro, Murra, Yalí, Pantasma, San Rafael del Norte, Abisinia, El Cuá, and Bocay (Cordero and Pereira 1992, 27).

13. CENIDH (1992, 17) reports that Indomable and another recontra leader, Dimas, may have received as much as $100,000. From 1990 to 1993 the government spent almost $102 million on purchasing weapons and carrying out disarmament agreements (Saldomando and Cuadra 1994, 34).

14. Talavera was reported to have a larger network of contacts in Managua

and Miami that provided him with financing and weapons (Morales 1995, 107). Morales (105) also argues that recontra groups like the Frente Norte 3–80, which emerged in 1992, were more unified than earlier groups and directly linked to efforts by extreme right-wing national political figures to force President Chamorro out of power and effectively destroy the FSLN as a political and social force in Nicaragua.

15. Reported in *Barricada,* 16 February 1993.

16. An ironic footnote to this was the call by several well-off Quilalí anti-Sandinistas for the army to return and protect them from the excessive monetary demands and kidnappings of the recontras.

17. Such economic pressures and the tendency of poor peasants to sell their land were not limited to former cooperative members. In Region V, for example, by 1994 ex-contras had sold one-third of the land they received under the Chamorro government at low prices ranging from $75 to $150 per MZ. Those who bought the land include 300 owners of large cattle ranches, both Sandinistas and anti-Sandinistas, who often used government credit to purchase the land (IHCA 1994b, 17–18).

Bibliography

Abbreviations in the Bibliography

ANPDH   Asociación Nicaragüense Pro-Derechos Humanos (Nicaraguan Human Rights Association)

CENIDH   Centro Nicaragüense de Derechos Humanos (Nicaraguan Human Rights Center)

CEPAL   Comisión Económica para América Latina (Economic Commission for Latin America)

CIAV-OEA   Comisión Internacional de Apoyo y Verificación–Organización de Estados Americanos (International Support and Verification Commission–Organization of American States)

CIERA   Centro de Investigaciones y Estudios sobre la Reforma Agraria (Center for Research and Study of Agrarian Reform)

CIPRES   Centro para la Promoción, la Investigación, y el Desarollo Rural y Social (Center for Promotion, Research, and Rural and Social Development)

CRIES   Coordinadora Regional de Investigaciones Económicas y Sociales (Regional Coordinator of Economic Research)

DEA   Departamento de Economía Agrícola (Department of Agricultural Economics)

DGEC   Dirección General de Estadística y Censos (General Board of Statistics and Census)

EDUCA   Editorial Universitaria Centroamericana (Central American University Press)

ESECA   Escuela de Economía Agrícola (School of Agricultural Economics)

FEDONG	Federación de Organismos No Gubernamentales de Nicaragua (Nicaraguan Federation of Nongovernmental Organizations)
FLASCO	Faculdad Latinoamericana de Ciencias Sociales (Latin American Faculty for the Social Sciences)
IEP	Instituto de Estudios Peruanos (Institute of Peruvian Studies)
IES	Instituto de Estudio del Sandinismo (Institute for Sandinista Studies)
IHCA	Instituto Histórico Centroamericano (Central American Historical Institute)
INATEC	Instituto Nacional Tecnológico (National Technological Institute)
INEC	Instituto Nacional de Estadísticas y Censos (National Institute of Statistics and Census)
IPADE	Instituto para el Desarrollo de la Democracia (Institute for the Development of Democracy)
MIDINRA	Ministerio de Desarrollo Agropecuario y Reforma Agraria (Ministry of Agricultural Development and Agrarian Reform)
MINT	Ministerio del Interior (Ministry of the Interior)
PRODERE	Programa de Desarrollo para Desplazados, Refugiados, y Repatriados (Development Program for the Displaced, Refugees, and the Repatriated)
UCA	Universidad Centroamericana (Central American University)
UNAN	Universidad Autonoma de Nicaragua (Autonomous University of Nicaragua)

Organizations are alphabetized by their acronyms.

Akram-Lodhi, A. Haroon. 1992. "Peasants and Hegemony in the Work of James C. Scott." *Journal of Peasant Studies* 19.3,4: 181–201.

Amador A., Freddy, Rosario Ambrogi R., and Gerardo Ribbink. 1991. *La reforma agraria en Nicaragua: De Rojinegro a Violeta.* Managua: DEA.

Amador A., Freddy, and Gerardo Ribbink. 1992. *Nicaragua: Reforma agraria, propiedad y mercado de tierra.* Managua: CIES/ESECA.

Americas Watch. 1986. *Human Rights in Nicaragua: 1985–1986.* New York: Americas Watch.

———. 1987. *Human Rights in Nicaragua: 1986.* New York: Americas Watch.

———. 1988. *Human Rights in Nicaragua: August 1987 to August 1988.* New York: Americas Watch.

———. 1989. *The Killings in Northern Nicaragua.* New York: Americas Watch.

———. 1990. *Nicaragua: A Human Rights Chronology, July 1979–July 1989.* New York: Americas Watch.

Anderson, Leslie E. 1990. "Post-Materialism from a Peasant Perspective: Political Motivation in Costa Rica and Nicaragua." *Comparative Political Studies* 23.1: 80–113.

———. 1992. "Surprises and Secrets: Lessons from the 1990 Nicaraguan Election." *Studies in Comparative International Development* 27.3: 93–119.

———. 1994a. "Neutrality and Bias in the 1990 Nicaraguan Preelection Polls: A Comment on Bischoping and Schuman." *American Journal of Political Science* 38.2: 486–94.

———. 1994b. *The Political Ecology of the Modern Peasant: Calculation and Community.* Baltimore: Johns Hopkins University Press.

ANPDH (Asociación Nicaragüense Pro-Derechos Humanos). 1991. *Problemática del Norte.* Managua: ANPDH.

Armony, Ariel C. 1997. "The Former Contras." In *Nicaragua without Illusions: Regime Transition and Structural Adjustment in the 1990s,* edited by Thomas W. Walker. Wilmington, Del.: SR Books.

Aznar, Pablo, Oscar Salamanca, Jazmin Solís, and Sandra Zúniga. 1989. "Ideología campesina: Los desplazados de guerra de Nueva Guinea." *Encuentro* 37/38 (July–December): 115–36.

Banco Central de Nicaragua. 1975. *Compendio estadístico 1965–1974.* Managua: Ministerio de Economía, Industria y Comercio.

Barnes, William A. 1992. "Rereading the Nicaraguan Pre-Election Polls." In *The 1990 Elections in Nicaragua and Their Aftermath,* edited by Vanessa Castro and Gary Prevost. Lanham, Md.: Rowman and Littlefield.

Barry, Deborah, and Luis H. Serra. 1989. *Diagnóstico nacional de Nicaragua sobre refugiados, repatriados y población desplazada, 1988.* Managua: CRIES.

Bates, Robert H. 1984. "Some Conventional Orthodoxies in the Study of Agrarian Change." *World Politics* 36 (January): 234–54.

Baumeister, Eduardo. 1985. "The Structure of Nicaraguan Agriculture and the Sandinista Agrarian Reform." In *Nicaragua: A Revolution under Siege,* edited by Richard L. Harris and Carlos Vilas. London: Zed Books.

———. 1991. "Agrarian Reform." In *Revolution and Counterrevolution in Nicaragua,* edited by Thomas W. Walker. Boulder, Colo.: Westview Press.

Baumeister, Eduardo, and Oscar Neira Cuadra. 1986. "The Making of a Mixed Economy: Class Struggle and State Policy in the Nicaragua Transition." In *Transition and Development: Problems of Third World Socialism,* edited by Richard R. Fagen et al. New York: Monthly Review Press.

Bendaña, Alejandro, ed. 1991. *Una tragedia campesina: Testimonios de la resistencia.* Managua: Editora de Arte.

Biderman, Jaime M. 1982. "Class Structure, the State and Capitalist Development in Nicaraguan Agriculture." Ph.D. dissertation, University of California, Berkeley.

Bilbao, Jon, A. Belli, and E. Rivas. 1989. "Reforma Agraria, Migraciones y Guerra: Asentamientos en Nicaragua." *Encuentro* 37/38 (July–December): 97–113.

Biondi-Morra, Brizio N. 1992. *Revolución y política alimentaria: Un análisis crítico de Nicaragua.* Managua: Fondo Editorial, Banco Central de Nicaragua.

Bischoping, Katherine, and Howard Schuman. 1992. "Pens and Polls in Nicaragua: An Analysis of the 1990 Preelection Surveys." *American Journal of Political Science* 36.2: 331–50.

———. 1994. "Pens, Polls and Theories, The 1990 Nicaraguan Elections Revisited: A Reply to Anderson." *American Journal of Political Science* 38.2: 495–99.

Booth, John A. 1985. *The End and the Beginning: The Nicaraguan Revolution.* 2d ed. Boulder, Colo.: Westview Press.

———. 1990. "Socioeconomic and Political Roots of National Revolts in Central America." *Latin American Research Review* 26.1: 33–73.

———. 1991. "Theories of Religion and Rebellion: The Central American Experience." *Journal of Third World Studies* 8 (Fall): 50–74.

———. 1994. "Assessing Candidate Preference Polling and Other Survey Research in Nicaragua, 1989–90: Comments on Anderson, and Bischoping and Schuman." *American Journal of Political Science* 38.2: 500–13.

Brass, Tom. 1991. "Moral Economists, Subalterns, New Social Movements, and the (Re-)Emergence of a (Post-)Modernised (Middle) Peasant." *Journal of Peasant Studies* 18.2: 173–205.

Brockett, Charles D. 1988. *Land, Power, and Poverty: Agrarian Transformation and Political Conflict in Central America.* Boston: Unwin Hyman.

———. 1991. "The Structure of Political Opportunities and Peasant Mobilization in Central America." *Comparative Politics* 23.3: 253–74.

Cajina, Roberto J. 1997. *Transición política y reconversión militar en Nicaragua, 1990–1995.* Managua: CRIES.

Castillo Rivas, Donald. 1993. *Gringos, contras y sandinistas: Testimonios de la guerra civil en Nicaragua.* Santafé de Bogotá, Colombia: Tercer Mundo Editores.

Castro, Vanessa. 1990a. *Análisis sobre el campesinado: Resultados sectoral sobre las pérdidas de las elecciones por el FSLN.* Managua: IPADE.

———. 1990b. "El papel de la conciencia en la derrota electoral del FSLN." *Avispa* 1 (October-November): 24–30.

———. 1992. "Electoral Results in the Rural Sector." In *The 1990 Elections in Nicaragua and Their Aftermath,* edited by Vanessa Castro and Gary Prevost. Lanham, Md.: Rowman and Littlefield.

Castro, Vanessa, and Gary Prevost, eds. 1992. *The 1990 Elections in Nicaragua and Their Aftermath.* Lanham, Md.: Rowman and Littlefield.

CENIDH (Centro Nicaragüense de Derechos Humanos). 1992. *Derechos humanos en Nicaragua informe anual, abril 1991–abril 1992*. Managua: CENIDH.

———. 1993. *Derechos humanos en Nicaragua informe anual, abril 1992–abril 1993*. Managua: CENIDH.

CEPAL (Comisión Económica para América Latina). 1981. *Nicaragua: El impacto de la mutación política*. Santiago, Chile: United Nations.

CIAV-OEA (Comité Internacional de Apoyo y Verificación–Organización de Estados Americanos). 1990a. *Cuadros estadísticos del proceso de desmovilización en Nicaragua*. Managua: CIAV-OEA Nicaragua.

———. 1990b. *Unpublished Demobilization Survey Data*. Managua: CIAV-OEA Nicaragua.

———. 1991. *Total personas atendidas*. Managua: CIAV-OEA Nicaragua.

CIERA (Centro de Investigaciones y Estudios sobre la Reforma Agraria). 1980. *Diagnóstico socioeconómico del sector agropecuario: Nueva Segovia*. Vol 9. Managua: MIDINRA.

———. 1981a. *Las clases sociales en el campo de Jinotega*. Managua: MIDINRA.

———. 1981b. *Diagnóstico general de la región Matagalpa-Jinotega*. Managua: MIDINRA.

———. 1982. *Apuntes sobre las clases sociales en Chontales*. Managua: MIDINRA.

———. 1984. *Y por eso defendemos la frontera: Historia agraria de las Segovias occidentales*. Managua: MIDINRA.

———. 1989. *La reforma agraria en Nicaragua, 1979–1989*. 9 vols. Managua: CIERA.

CIPRES (Centro para la Promoción, la Investigación y el Desarrollo Rural y Social). 1990a. *Cooperación y subordinación en las familias campesinas*. Managua: CIPRES.

1990b. *La inestabilidad política y su impacto socioeconómico en el campo*. Managua: CIPRES.

———. 1991. *La guerra en Nicaragua*. Managua: CIPRES.

Colburn, Forrest D. 1986. *Post-Revolutionary Nicaragua: State, Class, and the Dilemmas of Agrarian Policy.* Berkeley: University of California Press.

———. 1989a. "Foot Dragging and Other Peasant Responses to the Nicaraguan Revolution." In *Everyday Forms of Peasant Resistance,* edited by Forrest D. Colburn. Armonk, N.Y.: M. E. Sharpe.

———. 1989b. Introduction to *Everyday Forms of Peasant Resistance,* edited by Forrest D. Colburn. Armonk, N.Y.: M. E. Sharpe.

Conroy, Michael. 1990. "The Political Economy of the 1990 Nicaraguan Elections." *International Journal of Political Economy.* 20.3: 5–33.

Cordero, Virginia, and Ricardo Pereira. 1992. "Recompas y recontras ponen fin a la guerra." *Avispa* 8 (January-February): 23–31.

Coronel, José. 1996. "Violencia política y respuestas campesinas en Huanta." In *Las rondas campesinas y la derrota de Sendero Luminoso,* edited by Carlos Ivan Degregori et al. Lima: IEP Ediciones.

DEA-UNAN (Departamento de Economía Agrícola). 1985. *Diagnóstico socio-económico de la producción agropecuaria en la región I (las Segovias).* Managua: DEA-UNAN.

Deere, Carmen Diana, and Peter Marchetti. 1981. "The Worker-Peasant Alliance in the First Year of the Nicaraguan Agrarian Reform." *Latin American Perspectives* 29.2: 40–73.

Deere, Carmen Diana, Peter Marchetti, and Nola Reinhardt. 1985. "The Peasantry and the Development of Sandinista Agrarian Policy, 1979–1984." *Latin American Research Review* 20.3: 75–109.

Degregori, Carlos Ivan. 1996. "Ayacucho, después de la violencia." In *Las rondas campesinas y la derrota de Sendero Luminoso,* edited by Carlos Ivan Degregori et al. Lima: IEP Ediciones.

Del Pino, Pociano. 1996. "Tiempos de guerra y de dioses: Ronderos, evangélicos y senderistas en el valle del Río Apurímac." In *Las rondas campesinas y la derrota de Sendero Luminoso,* edited by Carlos Ivan Degregori et al. Lima: IEP Ediciones.

DGEC (Dirección General de Estadística y Censos). 1954. *Censo general de población de la república de Nicaragua, 1950.* Managua: DGEC.

———. 1964a. *Censos nacionales 1963: Población.* Vol 2. Managua: DGEC.

————. 1964b. *Población y viviendas por municipios y comarcas resumen.* Managua: DGEC.

————. 1966. *Censos nacionales 1963: Agropecuario.* Managua: DGEC.

Dillon, Sam. 1991. *Comandos: The CIA and Nicaragua's Contra Rebels.* New York: Holt.

Eckstein, Susan, ed. 1989. *Power and Popular Protest: Latin American Social Movements.* Berkeley: University of California Press.

Ejército de Nicaragua. 1996. "Naturaleza, funciones, organización, estructura y despliegue operativo del ejército de Nicaragua." In *Nicaragua: Gobernabilidad democrática y reconversión militar,* edited by Oscar-René Vargas. Managua: Centro de Estudios Estratégicos de Nicaragua.

Enriquez, Laura J. 1991. *Harvesting Change: Labor and Agrarian Reform in Nicaragua, 1979-1990.* Chapel Hill: University of North Carolina Press.

————. 1997. *Agrarian Reform and Class Consciousness in Nicaragua.* Gainesville: University Press of Florida.

Enriquez, Laura J., and Marlen L. Llanes. 1993. "Back to the Land: The Political Dilemmas of Agrarian Reform in Nicaragua." *Social Problems* 40.2: 250–65.

Escuela de Sociología-UCA. 1987. *Elementos para la caracterización político-ideológica de la base social contrarevolucionaria en la V region: Estudio de zonas de guerra en Chontales y Zelaya.* Managua: mimeographed.

FEDONG (Federación de Organismos No Gubernamentales de Nicaragua). 1991. *Diagnóstico de la población desplazada, repatriada, refugiada y desmobilizada y plan de acción.* Managua: FEDONG.

Foroohar, Manzar. 1989. *The Catholic Church and Social Change in Nicaragua.* Albany: SUNY Press.

Garvin Glenn. 1992. *Everybody Had His Own Gringo: The CIA and the Contras.* Washington, D.C.: Brassey's (US).

Gilbert, Dennis. 1988. *Sandinistas: The Party and the Revolution.* New York: Basil Blackwell.

Gorman, Stephen M., and Thomas W. Walker. 1985. "The Armed Forces." In *Nicaragua the First Five Years,* edited by Thomas W. Walker. New York: Praeger.

Gould, Jeffrey L. 1990a. "Notes on Peasant Consciousness and Revolutionary Politics in Nicaragua, 1955–1990." *Radical History Review* 48 (Fall): 65–87.

———. 1990b. *To Lead as Equals: Rural Protest and Political Consciousness in Chinandega, Nicaragua, 1912–1979.* Chapel Hill: University of North Carolina Press.

———. 1993. "¡Vana Ilusión!' The Highlands Indians and the Myth of Nicaraguan Mestiza, 1880–1925." *Hispanic American Historical Review* 73.3: 393–429.

———. 1997. *El mito de "la Nicaragua mestiza" y la resistencia indígena, 1880–1980.* San José, Costa Rica: EDUCA.

Guerrero Castillo, Julian N., and Lola Soriano de Guerrero. 1969. *Nueva Segovia.* Managua: Artes Gráficas.

Gutman, Roy. 1988. *Banana Diplomacy: The Making of American Policy in Nicaragua, 1981-1987.* New York: Simon and Schuster.

Haggis, Jane, Stephanie Jarrett, Dave Taylor, and Peter Mayer. 1986. "By the Teeth: A Critical Examination of James Scott's *The Moral Economy of the Peasant.*" *World Development* 14.12: 1435–55.

Hale, Charles R. 1994. *Resistance and Contradiction: Miskitu Indians and the Nicaraguan State, 1894–1987.* Stanford: Stanford University Press.

Hawley, Susan. 1997. "Protestantism and Indigenous Mobilisation: The Moravian Church Among the Miskitu Indians of Nicaragua." *Journal of Latin American Studies* 29: 111–29.

IES (Instituto de Estudio del Sandinismo). 1986. *Ahora sé que Sandino manda.* Managua: Editorial Nueva Nicaragua.

IHCA (Instituto Histórico Centroamericano). 1985a. "Los campesinos nicaragüenses dan un giro a la reforma agraria." *Envío* 4 (September): 1c-19c.

———. 1985b. "Las elecciones que Reagan quiere enterrar: Un análisis del voto popular el 4 de Noviembre." *Envío* 4 (April): 1b-30b.

———. 1990. "Qué hacer: Hacia el congreso FSLN." *Envío* 105 (July): 36–48.

———. 1991. "Los recontras: Campesinos armados con amplia base social." *Envío* 119 (September): 11–20.

———. 1992a. "Los revueltos: ¿Estallido social o chantaje político?" *Envío* 126 (May): 11–24.

———. 1992b. "El rompecabezas de la propiedad." *Envío* 133 (December): 11–24.

———. 1993a. "Polarización al rojo vivo." *Envío* 141 (September): 3–15.

———. 1993b. "Los rearmados del norte." *Envío* 135 (March): 3–10.

———. 1994a. "¿La calma antes de la tempestad?" *Envío* 149 (June): 3–13.

———. 1994b. "Descolectivización: Reforma agraria 'desde abajo.'" *Envío* 154 (November): 17–23.

———. 1995. "La propiedad agraria y la estabilidad." *Envío* 165 (November): 15–23.

INEC (Instituto Nacional de Estadísticas y Censos). 1996. *Censos nacionales 1995: Cifras oficiales finales.* Managua: INEC.

Isbell, Billie Jean. 1992. "Shining Path and Peasant Responses in Rural Ayacucho." In *The Shining Path of Peru,* edited by David Scott Palmer. New York: St. Martin's Press.

Jenkins, Craig J. 1982. "Why Do Peasants Rebel? Structural and Historical Theories of Modern Peasant Rebellions." *American Journal of Sociology* 88.3: 487–514.

Jonakin, Jon. 1996. "The Impact of Structural Adjustment and Property Rights Conflicts on Nicaraguan Agrarian Reform Beneficiaries." *World Development* 24.7: 1179–91.

———. 1997. "Agrarian Policy." In *Nicaragua without Illusions: Regime Transition and Structural Adjustment in the 1990s,* edited by Thomas W. Walker. Wilmington, Del.: SR Books.

Kagan, Robert. 1996. *A Twilight Struggle: American Power and Nicaragua, 1977–1990.* New York: Free Press.

Kaimowitz, David. 1986. "Nicaraguan Debates on Agrarian Structure and Their Implications for Agricultural Policy and the Rural Poor." *Journal of Peasant Studies* 14.1: 100–17.

———. 1988. "Nicaragua's Experience with Agricultural Planning: From State-Centered Accumulation to the Strategic Alliance with the Peasantry." *Journal of Development Studies* 24.4: 115–35.

————. 1989. "The Role of Decentralization in the Recent Nicaraguan Agrarian Reform." In *Searching for Agrarian Reform in Latin America,* edited by William C. Thiesenhusen. Boston: Unwin Hyman.

Keller, Frank. 1986. *Wiwilí 1980: Monografía de un municipio nicaragüense en cambio.* Frankfurt am Main: Vervuert.

Kincaid, Douglas. 1987. "Peasants into Rebels: Community and Class in Rural El Salvador." *Comparative Studies in Society and History* 29.3: 466–94.

Kornbluh, Peter. 1987. *The Price of Intervention: Reagan's War against the Sandinistas.* Washington, D.C.: Institute for Policy Studies.

Lechner, Norbert. 1992. "Some People Die of Fear: Fear as a Political Problem." In *Fear at the Edge: State Terror and Resistance in Latin America,* edited by Juan E. Corradi, Patricia Weiss Fagen, and Manuel Antonio Garretón Merino. Berkeley: University of California Press.

Lichbach, Mark I. 1994. "What Makes Rational Peasants Revolutionary? Dilemma, Paradox, and Irony in Peasant Collective Action." *World Politics* 46.3: 383–418.

Luciak, Ilja A. 1987a. "National Unity and Popular Hegemony: The Dialectics of Sandinista Agrarian Reform Policies, 1979–1986." *Journal of Latin American Studies* 19.1: 113–40.

————. 1987b. "Popular Democracy in the New Nicaragua: The Case of a Rural Mass Organization." *Comparative Politics* 20.1: 35–55.

————. 1990. "Democracy in the Nicaraguan Countryside: A Comparative Analysis of Sandinista Grassroots Movements." *Latin American Perspectives* 17.3: 55–75.

————. 1995. *The Sandinista Legacy: Lessons from a Political Economy in Transition.* Gainesville: University Press of Florida.

Macaulay, Neill. 1967. *The Sandino Affair.* Chicago: Quadrangle Books.

Magagna, Victor V. 1991. *Communities of Grain: Rural Rebellion in Comparative Perspective.* Ithaca, N.Y.: Cornell University Press.

Martinez, Philip R. 1993. "Peasant Policy within the Nicaraguan Agrarian Reform, 1979–89." *World Development* 21.3: 475–87.

Mendoza, René. 1990. "Los costos del verticalismo: Un FSLN sin rostro campesino." *Envío* 107 (September): 19–50.

Messing, F. Andy, Jr., and Allen B. Hazelwood. 1989. "A Farewell to Alms." *Policy Review* (Fall): 14–19.

MIDINRA (Ministerio de Desarrollo Agropecuario y Reforma Agraria). 1983. *Café, clases sociales y estrategia de la reforma agraria en San Juan del Río Coco.* Managua: MIDINRA.

———. 1984a. *Informe sobre la situación actual del campesinado en la VI region.* Managua: MIDINRA.

———. 1984b. *Propuesta de plan de desarrollo: Río Blanco.* Managua: MIDINRA.

———. 1984c. *Propuesta de plan de desarrollo cooperativo: Pantasma.* Managua: MIDINRA.

———. 1984d. *Proyecto de desarrollo agropecuario "La Vigía."* Estelí: MIDINRA.

———. 1985a. *Diagnóstico y propuesta: Zona de reforma agraria Siuna.* Managua: MIDINRA.

———. 1985b. *Movimiento campesino y formas organizativas tradicionales en Yalí.* Managua: MIDINRA.

———. 1986. *La transición de asentamientos de guerra a pueblos rurales: Los casos de Panalí y El Coco.* Managua: MIDINRA.

———. 1987. *Quilalí: Diagnóstico y propuesta para la Organización Territorial de la Producción e Intercambio.* Estelí: MIDINRA.

Migdal, Joel S. 1974. *Peasants, Politics, and Revolution: Pressures toward Political and Social Change in the Third World.* Princeton, N.J.: Princeton University Press.

Miller, Peter V. 1991. "Which Side Are You On? The 1990 Nicaraguan Poll Debacle." *Public Opinion Quarterly* 55: 281–302.

Millett, Richard. 1979. *Guardianes de la dinastia: Historia de la Guardia Nacional de Nicaragua, creada por Estados Unidos, y de la familia Somoza.* San José, Costa Rica: EDUCA.

MINT (Ministerio del Interior). 1985. *El MINT en Cifras 1984.* Managua: MINT.

————. 1986. *El MINT en Cifras 1985*. Managua: MINT.

————. 1987a. *Acogidos al decreto de amnestía diciembre 1983-julio 1987*. Managua: MINT.

————. 1987b. *El MINT en Cifras 1986*. Managua: MINT.

————. 1988. *El MINT en Cifras 1987*. Managua: MINT.

————. 1990. *El MINT en Cifras 1979-89*. Managua: MINT.

Miranda, Roger, and William Ratliff. 1993. *The Civil War in Nicaragua: Inside the Sandinistas*. New Brunswick, N.J.: Transaction Publishers.

Moore, Barrington. 1966. *Social Origins of Dictatorship and Democracy: Lord and Peasant in the Making of the Modern World*. Boston: Beacon Press.

Morales, Abelardo. 1995. *Oficios de paz y posguerra en Centroamerica*. San José, Costa Rica: FLASCO.

Morales Carazo, Jaime. 1989. *La contra*. Mexico City: Fascículas Planeta.

Núñez Soto, Orlando. 1990. "La derrota electoral del FSLN y las dos caras del poder." *Avispa* 1 (October-November): 3–7.

Oquist, Paul. 1990. *Investigación dinámica socio-política de las elecciones nicaragüenses, 1990*. 2d ed. Managua: Friedrich Ebert Foundation.

————. 1992. "Sociopolitical Dynamics of the 1990 Nicaraguan Elections." In *The 1990 Elections in Nicaragua and Their Aftermath*, edited by Vanessa Castro and Gary Prevost. Lanham, Md.: Rowman and Littlefield.

Ortega, Marvin. 1989. "Las cooperativas sandinistas: Entre la democracia y el verticalismo." In *El debate sobre la reforma agraria en Nicaragua*, edited by Raul Ruben and Jan P. de Groot. Managua: Editorial Ciencias Sociales.

————. 1990. "The State, the Peasantry and the Sandinista Revolution." *Journal of Development Studies* 26.4: 122–42.

Paige, Jeffery M. 1975. *Agrarian Revolution: Social Movements and Export Agriculture in the Underdeveloped World*. New York: Free Press.

————. 1989. "Revolution and the Agrarian Bourgeoisie in Nicaragua." In *Revolution in the World-System*, edited by Terry Boswell. New York: Greenwood Press.

———. 1997. *Coffee and Power: Revolution and the Rise of Democracy in Central America.* Cambridge, Mass.: Harvard University Press.

Palmer, David Scott. 1992. Introduction to *The Shining Path of Peru,* edited by David Scott Palmer. New York: St. Martin's Press.

Pastor, Robert A. 1987. *Condemned to Repetition: The United States and Nicaragua.* Princeton, N.J.: Princeton University Press.

Popkin, Samuel L. 1979. *The Rational Peasant: The Political Economy of Rural Society in Vietnam.* Berkeley: University of California Press.

Prevost, Gary. 1992. "The FSLN in Opposition." In *The 1990 Elections in Nicaragua and Their Aftermath,* edited by Vanessa Castro and Gary Prevost. Lanham, Md.: Rowman and Littlefield.

Prevost, Gary, and Harry E. Vanden, eds. 1997. *The Undermining of the Sandinista Revolution.* New York: St. Martin's Press.

PRODERE (Programa de Desarrollo para Desplazados, Refugiados y Repatriados). 1991. *Breve descripción de la características generales de la población establecida y reinsertada del municipio de Quilalí.* Estelí: PRODERE.

———. 1992a. "Las cooperativas agropecuarias en Quilali y San Juan del Río Coco: Un proyecto frustrado o una alternativa para el campesinado." *Comunidad y Desarrollo* (February): 13–17.

———. 1992b. "Entrevista al Señor Carlos Altamirano, Alcalde Municipal de Quilalí." *Comunidad y Desarrollo* (September): 5–7.

Radu, Michael, ed. 1990. *The New Insurgencies: Anticommunist Guerrillas in the Third World.* New Brunswick, N.J.: Transaction Publishers.

Rivera Quintero, Francisco. 1989. *La marca del Zorro: Hazañas del Comandante Francisco Rivera Quintero.* Edited by Sergio Ramírez. Managua: Editorial Nueva Nicaragua.

Robinson, William I. 1992. *A Faustian Bargain: U.S. Intervention in the Nicaraguan Elections and American Foreign Policy in the Post–Cold War Era.* Boulder, Colo.: Westview Press.

Robinson, William I., and Kent Norsworthy. 1987. *David and Goliath: The U.S. War against Nicaragua.* New York: Monthly Review Press.

Ruben, Raul, and Jan P. de Groot, eds. 1989. *El debate sobre la reforma agraria en Nicaragua.* Managua: Editorial Ciencias Sociales.

Ruchwarger, Gary. 1987. *People in Power: Forging a Grassroots Democracy in Nicaragua.* South Hadley, Mass.: Bergin and Garvey.

———. 1989. *Struggling for Survival: Workers, Women and Class on a Nicaraguan State Farm.* Boulder Colo.: Westview Press.

Saldomando, Angel. 1996. *Nicaragua con el futuro en juego.* Managua: CRIES.

Saldomando, Angel, and Elvira Cuadra L. 1994. *Los problemas de la pacificación en Nicaragua: Recomposición de grupos armados y conflictos sociales.* Working Paper no. 94/2. Managua: CRIES.

Schroeder, Michael J. 1993. "To Defend Our Nation's Honor: Toward a Social and Cultural History of the Sandino Rebellion in Nicaragua, 1927–1934." Ph.D. dissertation, University of Michigan.

———. 1996. "Horse Thieves to Rebel Dogs: Political Gang Violence and the State in the Western Segovias, Nicaragua, in the Time of Sandino, 1926–1934." *Journal of Latin American Studies* 28: 383–434.

Scott, James C. 1976. *The Moral Economy of the Peasant: Rebellion and Subsistence in Southeast Asia.* New Haven: Yale University Press.

———. 1985. *Weapons of the Weak: Everyday Forms of Peasant Resistance.* New Haven: Yale University Press.

———. 1989. "Everyday Forms of Resistance." In *Everyday Forms of Peasant Resistance,* edited by Forrest D. Colburn. Armonk, N.Y.: M. E. Sharpe.

———. 1990. *Domination and the Arts of Resistance: Hidden Transcripts.* New Haven: Yale University Press.

Selbin, Eric. 1993. *Modern Latin American Revolutions.* Boulder, Colo.: Westview Press.

Selser, Gregorio. 1979. *Sandino, general de hombres libres.* 2d ed. San José, Costa Rica: EDUCA.

Serra, Luis H. 1991. *Movimiento cooperativo campesino: Su participación política durante la revolución sandinista, 1979–1989.* Managua: UCA.

———. 1993. "Democracy in Times of War and Socialist Crisis: Reflections Stemming from the Sandinista Revolution." *Latin American Perspectives* 20.2: 21–44.

Shanin, Teodor. 1972. *The Awkward Class: Political Sociology of Peasantry in a Developing Society: Russia 1910–1925.* London: Oxford University Press.

Sklar, Holly. 1988. *Washington's War on Nicaragua.* Boston: South End Press.

Skocpol, Theda. 1982. "What Makes Peasants Revolutionary?" *Comparative Politics* 14.3: 351–75.

Sluka, Jeffrey A. 1990. "Participant Observation in Violent Social Contexts." *Human Organization* 49.2: 114–26.

Sobel, Richard. 1995. "Contra Aid Fundamentals: Exploring the Intricacies and the Issues." *Political Science Quarterly* 110.2: 287–306.

Spalding, Rose J. 1994. *Capitalists and Revolution in Nicaragua: Opposition and Accommodation, 1979–1993.* Chapel Hill: University of North Carolina Press.

Spoor, Max. 1989. *Mercados rurales en la región I.* Managua: DEA-UNAN.

———. 1990. "Rural Employment and Agrarian Markets in Transition: Nicaragua (1979–89)." *Journal of Peasant Studies* 17.4: 520–45.

———. 1995. *The State and Domestic Agricultural Markets in Nicaragua: From Interventionism to Neo-Liberalism.* New York: St. Martin's Press.

Stahler-Sholk, Richard, ed. 1989. *La política económica en Nicaragua, 1979–88.* Managua: CRIES.

———. 1990. "Stabilization, Destabilization, and the Popular Classes in Nicaragua, 1979–1988." *Latin American Research Review* 25.3: 55–88.

———. 1995. "The Dog That Didn't Bark: Labor Autonomy and Economic Adjustment in Nicaragua under the Sandinista and UNO Governments." *Comparative Politics* 28.1: 77–102.

———. 1997. "Structural Adjustment and Resistance: The Political Economy of Nicaragua under Chamorro." In *The Undermining of the Sandinista Revolution,* edited by Gary Prevost and Harry E. Vanden. New York: St. Martin's Press.

Starn, Orin. 1995. "To Revolt against the Revolution: War and Resistance in Peru's Andes." *Cultural Anthropology* 10.4: 547–80.

Stoll, David. 1990. *Is Latin America Turning Protestant? The Politics of Evangelical Growth.* Berkeley: University of California Press.

———. 1993. *Between Two Armies in the Ixil Towns of Guatemala.* New York: Columbia University Press.

Taylor, James R. 1969. *Agricultural Settlement and Development in Eastern Nicaragua.* Research paper no. 33. Madison, Wis.: Land Tenure Center.

Towell, Larry. 1990. *Somoza's Last Stand: Testimonies from Nicaragua.* Trenton, N.J.: Red Sea Press.

U.S. Department of State. 1986. *Documents on the Nicaraguan Resistance: Leaders, Military Personnel, and Program.* Special Report no. 142. Washington, D.C.: U.S. Department of State.

———. 1987. *Soviet Bloc Assistance to Cuba and Nicaragua versus U.S. Assistance to Central America.* Washington, D.C.: U.S. Department of State.

———. 1988. *Nicaraguan Biographies: A Resource Book.* Special Report no. 174. Rev. ed. Washington, D.C.: U.S. Department of State.

Vanden, Harry E., and Gary Prevost. 1993. *Democracy and Socialism in Sandinista Nicaragua.* Boulder, Colo.: Lynne Rienner Publishers.

Vargas, Oscar-René, ed. 1996. *Nicaragua: Gobernabilidad democrática y reconversión militar.* Managua: Centro de Estudios Estratégicos de Nicaragua.

Vilas, Carlos M. 1989. *State, Class, and Ethnicity in Nicaragua: Capitalist Modernization and Revolutionary Change on the Atlantic Coast.* Boulder, Colo.: Lynne Rienner Publishers.

Walker, Thomas W. 1991a. "The Armed Forces." In *Revolution and Counterrevolution in Nicaragua,* edited by Thomas W. Walker. Boulder, Colo.: Westview Press.

———. 1991b. *Nicaragua: The Land of Sandino.* 3d ed. Boulder, Colo.: Westview Press.

———, ed. 1991c. *Revolution and Counterrevolution in Nicaragua.* Boulder, Colo.: Westview Press.

———, ed. 1997. *Nicaragua without Illusions: Regime Transition and Structural Adjustment in the 1990s.* Wilmington, Del.: SR Books.

Walter, Knut. 1993. *The Regime of Anastasio Somoza, 1936–1956.* Chapel Hill: University of North Carolina Press.

Walton, John. 1984. *Reluctant Rebels: Comparative Studies of Revolution and Underdevelopment.* New York: Columbia University Press.

Werner, Patrick S. 1996. *Los reales de minas de la Nicaragua colonial y la ciudad perdida de Nueva Segovia.* Managua: Instituto Nicaragüense de Cultura.

WFP (Witness for Peace). 1987. *Large Resettlement Community Escapes Destruction but One Killed.* Managua: Witness for Peace.

Wheelock, Jaime. 1978. *Imperialismo y dictadura: Crisis de una formación social.* 5th ed. Mexico City: Siglo Veintiuno Editores.

———. 1990. *La reforma agraria sandinista: Diez años de revolución en el campo.* Managua: Editorial Vanguardia.

White, Christine Pelzer. "Everyday Resistance, Socialist Revolution and Rural Development: The Vietnamese Case." *Journal of Peasant Studies* 13.2: 49–63.

Wickham-Crowley, Timothy P. 1990. "Terror and Guerrilla Warfare in Latin America, 1956–1970." *Comparative Studies in Society and History* 32.2: 201–37.

———. 1991. *Exploring Revolution: Essays on Latin American Insurgency and Revolutionary Theory.* Armonk, N.Y.: M. E. Sharpe.

———. 1992. *Guerrillas and Revolution in Latin America: A Comparative Study of Insurgents and Regimes since 1956.* Princeton: Princeton University Press.

Williams, Robert G. 1986. *Export Agriculture and the Crisis in Central America.* Chapel Hill: University of North Carolina Press.

Wilson, Richard. 1991. "Machine Guns and Mountain Spirits: The Cultural Effects of State Repression among the Q'eqchi of Guatemala." *Critique of Anthropology* 11.1: 33–61.

Wolf, Eric R. 1969. *Peasant Wars of the Twentieth Century.* New York: Harper and Row.

Zalkin, Michael. 1987. "Food Policy and Class Transformation in Revolutionary Nicaragua, 1979–86." *World Development* 15.7: 961–84.

———. 1988. "Nicaragua: The Peasantry, Grain Policy, and the State." *Latin American Perspectives* 15.4: 71–91.

———. 1989. "Agrarian Class Structure in Nicaragua in 1980: A New Interpretation and Some Implications." *Journal of Peasant Studies* 16.4: 575–605.

———. 1990. "The Sandinista Agrarian Reform: 1979–1990?" *International Journal of Political Economy* 20.3: 46–68.

Index

Monographs in International Studies

Titles Available from Ohio University Press

Southeast Asia Series

No. 56   **Duiker, William J.** Vietnam Since the Fall of Saigon. 1989. Updated ed. 401 pp. Paper 0-89680-162-4 $20.00.

No. 64   **Dardjowidjojo, Soenjono.** Vocabulary Building in Indonesian: An Advanced Reader. 1984. 664 pp. Paper 0-89680-118-7 $30.00.

No. 65   **Errington, J. Joseph.** Language and Social Change in Java: Linguistic Reflexes of Modernization in a Traditional Royal Polity. 1985. 210 pp. Paper 0-89680-120-9 $25.00.

No. 66   **Binh, Tran Tu.** The Red Earth: A Vietnamese Memoir of Life on a Colonial Rubber Plantation. Tr. by John Spragens. 1984. 102 pp. (SEAT*, V. 5) Paper 0-89680-119-5 $11.00.

No. 68   **Syukri, Ibrahim.** History of the Malay Kingdom of Patani. 1985. 135 pp. Paper 0-89680-123-3 $15.00.

No. 69   **Keeler, Ward.** Javanese: A Cultural Approach. 1984. 559 pp. Paper 0-89680-121-7 $25.00.

No. 70   **Wilson, Constance M. and Lucien M. Hanks.** Burma-Thailand Frontier Over Sixteen Decades: Three Descriptive Documents. 1985. 128 pp. Paper 0-89680-124-1 $11.00.

No. 71   **Thomas, Lynn L. and Franz von Benda-Beckmann,** eds. Change and Continuity in Minangkabau: Local, Regional, and Historical Perspectives on West Sumatra. 1985. 353 pp. Paper 0-89680-127-6 $16.00.

No. 72   **Reid, Anthony and Oki Akira,** eds. The Japanese Experience in Indonesia: Selected Memoirs of 1942–1945. 1986. 424 pp., 20 illus. (SEAT, V. 6) Paper 0-89680-132-2 $20.00.

No. 74   **McArthur M. S. H.** Report on Brunei in 1904. Introduced and Annotated by A. V. M. Horton. 1987. 297 pp. Paper 0-89680-135-7 $15.00.

No. 75   **Lockard, Craig A.** From Kampung to City: A Social History of Kuching, Malaysia, 1820–1970. 1987. 325 pp. Paper 0-89680-136-5 $20.00.

No. 76   **McGinn, Richard,** ed. Studies in Austronesian Linguistics. 1986. 516 pp. Paper 0-89680-137-3 $20.00.

No. 77   **Muego, Benjamin N.** Spectator Society: The Philippines Under Martial Rule. 1986. 232 pp. Paper 0-89680-138-1 $17.00.

No 79   **Walton, Susan Pratt.** Mode in Javanese Music. 1987. 278 pp. Paper 0-89680-144-6 $15.00.

No. 80   **Nguyen Anh Tuan.** South Vietnam: Trial and Experience. 1987. 477 pp., tables. Paper 0-89680-141-1 $18.00.

No. 82   **Spores, John C.** Running Amok: An Historical Inquiry. 1988. 190 pp. Paper 0-89680-140-3 $13.00.

No. 83   **Malaka, Tan.** From Jail to Jail. Tr. by Helen Jarvis. 1911. 1209 pp., three volumes. (SEAT V. 8) Paper 0-89680-150-0 $55.00.

No. 84   **Devas, Nick, with Brian Binder, Anne Booth, Kenneth Davey, and Roy Kelly.** Financing Local Government in Indonesia. 1989. 360 pp. Paper 0-89680-153-5 $20.00.

No. 85   **Suryadinata, Leo.** Military Ascendancy and Political Culture: A Study of Indonesia's Golkar. 1989. 235 pp., illus., glossary, append., index, bibliog. Paper 0-89680-154-3 $18.00.

No. 86   **Williams, Michael.** Communism, Religion, and Revolt in Banten in the Early Twentieth Century. 1990. 390 pp. Paper 0-89680-155-1 $14.00.

No. 87   **Hudak, Thomas.** The Indigenization of Pali Meters in Thai Poetry. 1990. 247 pp. Paper 0-89680-159-4 $15.00.

No. 88   **Lay, Ma Ma.** Not Out of Hate: A Novel of Burma. Tr. by Margaret Aung-Thwin. Ed. by William Frederick. 1991. 260 pp. (SEAT V. 9) Paper 0-89680-167-5 $20.00.

No. 89   **Anwar, Chairil.** The Voice of the Night: Complete Poetry and Prose of Chairil Anwar. 1992. Revised Edition. Tr. by Burton Raffel. 196 pp. Paper 0-89680-170-5 $20.00.

No. 90   **Hudak, Thomas John,** tr., The Tale of Prince Samuttakote: A Buddhist Epic from Thailand. 1993. 230 pp. Paper 0-89680-174-8 $20.00.

No. 91   **Roskies, D. M.,** ed. Text/Politics in Island Southeast Asia: Essays in Interpretation. 1993. 330 pp. Paper 0-89680-175-6 $25.00.

No. 92   **Schenkhuizen, Marguérite, translated by Lizelot Stout van Balgooy.** Memoirs of an Indo Woman: Twentieth-Century Life in the East Indies and Abroad. 1993. 312 pp. Paper 0-89680-178-0 $25.00.

No. 93   **Salleh, Muhammad Haji.** Beyond the Archipelago: Selected Poems. 1995. 247 pp. Paper 0-89680-181-0 $20.00.

No. 94   **Federspiel, Howard M.** A Dictionary of Indonesian Islam. 1995. 327 pp. Bibliog. Paper 0-89680-182-9 $25.00.

No. 95   **Leary, John.** Violence and the Dream People: The Orang Asli in the Malayan Emergency 1948–1960. 1995. 275 pp. Maps, illus., tables, appendices, bibliog., index. Paper 0-89680-186-1 $22.00.

No. 96   **Lewis, Dianne.** *Jan Compagnie* in the Straits of Malacca 1641–1795.

1995. 176 pp. Map, appendices, bibliog., index. Paper 0-89680-187-x. $18.00.

No. 97 **Schiller, Jim and Martin-Schiller, Barbara.** Imagining Indonesia: Cultural Politics and Political Culture. 1996. 384 pp., notes, glossary, bibliog. Paper 0-89680-190-x. $30.00.

No. 98 **Bonga, Dieuwke Wendelaar.** Eight Prison Camps: A Dutch Family in Japanese Java. 1996. 233 pp., illus., map, glossary. Paper 0-89680-191-8. $18.00.

No. 99 **Gunn, Geoffrey C.** Language, Ideology, and Power in Brunei Darussalam. 1996. 328 pp., glossary, notes, bibliog., index. Paper 0-89680-192-6. $24.00.

No. 100 **Martin, Peter W., Conrad Ozog, and Gloria R. Poedjosoedarmo, eds.** Language Use and Language Change in Brunei Darussalam. 1996. 390 pp., maps, notes, bibliog. Paper 0-89680-193-x. $26.00.

No. 101 **Ooi, Keat Gin.** Japanese Empire in the Tropics: Selected Documents and Reports of the Japanese Period in Sarawak, Northwest Borneo, 1941–1945. 1998. 740 pp., two volumes. Illus., maps, notes, index. Paper 0-89680-199-3. $50.00.

No. 102 **Aung-Thwin, Michael A.** Myth and History in the Historiography of Early Burma: Paradigms, Primary Sources, and Prejudices. 1998. 210 pp., maps, notes, bibliography, index. Paper 0-89680-201-9 $21.00.

No. 103 **Pauka, Kirstin.** Theater and Martial Arts in West Sumatra: Randai and Silek of the Minang Kabou. 1999. 288 pp., illus., map, appendices, notes, bibliography, index. Paper 0-89680-205-1 $26.00.

Africa Series

No. 46 **Burness, Don,** ed. Wanasema: Conversations with African Writers. 1985. 103 pp. Paper 0-89680-129-2 $11.00.

No. 47 **Switzer, Les.** Media and Dependency in South Africa: A Case Study of the Press and the Ciskei "Homeland." 1985. 97 pp. Paper 0-89680-130-6 $10.00.

No. 51 **Clayton, Anthony and David Killingray.** Khaki and Blue: Military and Police in British Colonial Africa. 1989. 347 pp. Paper 0-89680-147-0 $20.00.

No. 53 **Makinde, M. Akin.** African Philosophy, Culture, and Traditional Medicine. 1988. 172 pp. Paper 0-89680-152-7 $16.00.

No. 54 **Parson, Jack,** ed. Succession to High Office in Botswana: Three Case Studies. 1990. 455 pp. Paper 0-89680-157-8 $20.00.

No. 56   **Staudinger, Paul.** In the Heart of the Hausa States. Tr. by Johanna E. Moody. Foreword by Paul Lovejoy. 1990. In two volumes., 469 + 224 pp., maps, apps. Paper 0-89680-160-8 (2 vols.) $35.00.

No. 57   **Sikainga, Ahmad Alawad.** The Western Bahr Al-Ghazal under British Rule, 1898–1956. 1991. 195 pp. Paper 0-89680-161-6 $15.00.

No. 58   **Wilson, Louis E.** The Krobo People of Ghana to 1892: A Political and Social History. 1991. 285 pp. Paper 0-89680-164-0 $20.00.

No. 59   **du Toit, Brian M.** Cannabis, Alcohol, and the South African Student: Adolescent Drug Use, 1974–1985. 1991. 176 pp., notes, tables. Paper 0-89680-166-7 $17.00.

No. 60   **Falola, Toyin and Dennis Itavyar**, eds. The Political Economy of Health in Africa. 1992. 258 pp., notes, tables. Paper 0-89680-168-3 $20.00.

No. 61   **Kiros, Tedros.** Moral Philosophy and Development: The Human Condition in Africa. 1992. 199 pp., notes. Paper 0-89680-171-3 $20.00.

No. 62   **Burness, Don.** Echoes of the Sunbird: An Anthology of Contem-po-rary African Poetry. 1993. 198 pp. Paper 0-89680-173-x $17.00.

No. 64   **Nelson, Samuel H.** Colonialism in the Congo Basin 1880–1940. 1994. 290 pp. Index. Paper 0-89680-180-2 $23.00.

No. 66   **Ilesanmi, Simeon Olusegon.** Religious Pluralism and the Nigerian State. 1996. 336 pp., maps, notes, bibliog., index. Paper 0-89680-194-2 $26.00.

No. 67   **Steeves, H. Leslie.** Gender Violence and the Press: The St. Kizito Story. 1997. 176 pp., illus., notes, bibliog., index. Paper 0-89680-195-0 $17.95.

No. 68   **Munro, William A.** The Moral Economy of the State: Conservation, Community Development, and State-Making in Zimbabwe. 1998. 510 pp., maps, notes, bibliog., index. Paper 0-89680-202-7 $26.00.

No. 69   **Rubert, Steven C.** A Most Promising Weed: A History of Tobacco Farming and Labor in Colonial Zimbabwe, 1890–1945. 1998. 264 pp., illus., maps, notes, bibliog., index. Paper 0-89680-203-5 $26.00.

Latin America Series

No. 9   **Tata, Robert J.** Structural Changes in Puerto Rico's Economy: 1947–1976. 1981. 118 pp. Paper 0-89680-107-1 $12.00.

No. 13   **Henderson, James D.** Conservative Thought in Latin America: The Ideas of Laureano Gomez. 1988. 229 pp. Paper 0-89680-148-9 $16.00.

No. 17 **Mijeski, Kenneth J.,** ed. The Nicaraguan Constitution of 1987: English Translation and Commentary. 1991. 355 pp. Paper 0-89680-165-9 $25.00.

No. 18 **Finnegan, Pamela.** The Tension of Paradox: José Donoso's *The Obscene Bird of Night* as Spiritual Exercises. 1992. 204 pp. Paper 0-89680-169-1 $15.00.

No. 19 **Kim, Sung Ho and Thomas W. Walker,** eds. Perspectives on War and Peace in Central America. 1992. 155 pp., notes, bibliog. Paper 0-89680-172-1 $17.00.

No. 20 **Becker, Marc.** Mariátegui and Latin American Marxist Theory. 1993. 239 pp. Paper 0-89680-177-2 $20.00.

No. 21 **Boschetto-Sandoval, Sandra M. and Marcia Phillips McGowan,** eds. Claribel Alegría and Central American Literature. 1994. 233 pp., illus. Paper 0-89680-179-9 $20.00.

No. 22 **Zimmerman, Marc.** Literature and Resistance in Guatemala: Textual Modes and Cultural Politics from El Señor Presidente to Rigoberta Menchú. 1995. 2 volume set 320 + 370 pp., notes, bibliog. Paper 0-89680-183-7 $50.00.

No. 23 **Hey, Jeanne A. K.** Theories of Dependent Foreign Policy: The Case of Ecuador in the 1980s. 1995. 280 pp., map, tables, notes, bibliog., index. Paper 0-89680-184-5 $22.00.

No. 24 **Wright, Bruce E.** Theory in the Practice of the Nicaraguan Revolution. 1995. 320 pp., notes, illus., bibliog., index. Paper 0-89680-185-3. $23.00.

No. 25 **Mann, Carlos Guevara.** Panamanian Militarism: A Historical Interpretation. 1996. 243 pp., illus., map, notes, bibliog., index. Paper 0-89680-189-6. $23.00.

No. 26 **Armony, Ariel.** Argentina, the United States, and the Anti-Communist Crusade in Central America, 1977–1984. 1997. 312 pp., illus., maps, notes, bibliog., index. Paper 0-89680-196-9. $26.00.

No. 27 **Hoyt, Katherine.** The Many Faces of Sandinista Democracy. 1977. 204 pp., notes, bibliography, index. Paper 0-89680-197-7. $23.00.

No. 28 **Sandoval, Cira A. and Boschetto-Sandoval, Sandra M. eds.** José María Arguedas: Reconsideration for Latin American Studies. 1998. 352 pp., notes, bibliog. Paper 0-89680-200-0. $23.00.

Ordering Information

Individuals are encouraged to patronize local bookstores wherever possible. Orders for titles in the Monographs in International Studies may be placed directly through the Ohio University Press, Scott Quadrangle, Athens, Ohio 45701-2979. Individuals should remit payment by check, VISA, or MasterCard.* Those ordering from the United Kingdom, Continental Europe, the Middle East,. and Africa should order through Academic and University Publishers Group, 1 Gower Street, London WC1E, England. Orders from the Pacific Region, Asia, Australia, and New Zealand should be sent to East-West Export Books, c/o the University of Hawaii Press, 2840 Kolowalu Street, Honolulu, Hawaii 96822, USA.

Individuals ordering from outside of the U.S. should remit in U.S. funds to Ohio University Press either by International Money Order or by a check drawn on a U.S. bank.** Most out-of-print titles may be ordered from University Microfilms, Inc., 300 North Zeeb Road, Ann Arbor, Michigan 48106, USA.

Prices are subject to change.

* Please add $3.50 for the first book and $.75 for each additional book for shipping and handling.

** Outside the U.S. please add $4.50 for the first book and $.75 for each additional book.

Ohio University
Monographs in International Studies

The Ohio University Center for International Studies was established to help create within the university and local communities a greater awareness of the world beyond the United States. Comprising programs in African, Latin American, Southeast Asian, Development and Administrative studies, the Center supports scholarly research, sponsors lectures and colloquia, encourages course development within the university curriculum, and publishes the Monographs in International Studies series with the Ohio University Press. The Center and its programs also offer an interdisciplinary Master of Arts degree in which students may focus on one of the regional or topical concentrations, and may also combine academics with training in career fields such as journalism, business, and language teaching. For undergraduates, major and certificate programs are also available.

For more information, contact the Vice Provost for International Studies, Burson House, Ohio University, Athens, Ohio 45701.